The Tarot Café

By
Sang-Sun Park
Jung-Su Kim
Volume 3

TOKYOPOP®

HAMBURG // LONDON // LOS ANGELES // TOKYO

The Tarot Cafe Vol. 3
created by Sang-Sun Park
written by Jung-Su Kim

Translation - Sukhee Ryu
English Adaptation - Kristin Bailey Murphy
Retouch and Lettering - Gloria Wu
Production Artist - Lucas Rivera
Cover Design - Kyle Plummer

Editor - Julie Taylor
Digital Imaging Manager - Chris Buford
Production Managers - Jennifer Miller and Mutsumi Miyazaki
Managing Editor - Jill Freshney
VP of Production - Ron Klamert
Publisher and Editor-in-Chief - Mike Kiley
President and C.O.O. - John Parker
Publisher and C.E.O. - Stuart Levy

A  Manga

TOKYOPOP Inc.
5900 Wilshire Blvd. Suite 2000
Los Angeles, CA 90036

E-mail: info@TOKYOPOP.com
Come visit us online at www.TOKYOPOP.com

ISBN: 1-59532-557-3
First TOKYOPOP printing: September 2005
10 9 8 7 6 5 4 3 2 1
Printed in the USA

Story so far...

Meet Aaron, an accidental werewolf with a painful past of abuse and abandonment. He seeks an answer to his problem, and decides to take a position at the Tarot Café while he searches for a solution. A glimpse into Pamela's life before the Tarot Café is laden with prejudice and persecution. 700 years ago, Pamela's mother made the ultimate sacrifice for her daughter...but even now, is the fear that doomed her mother really gone?

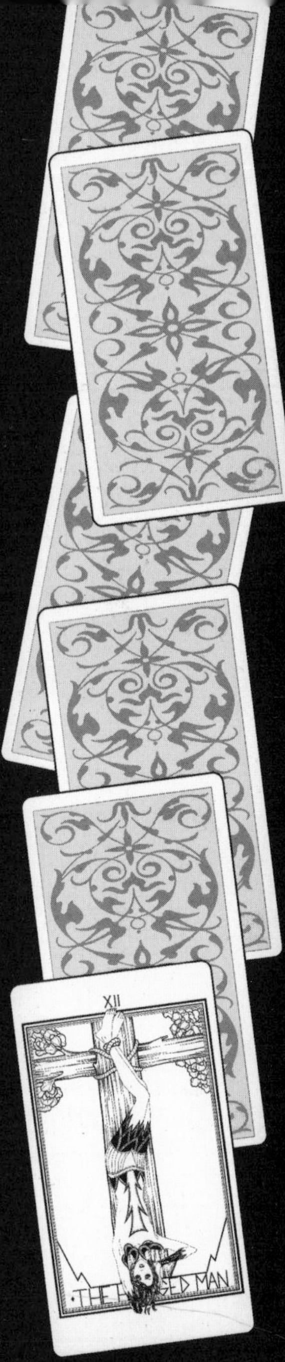
XII

Table of Contents

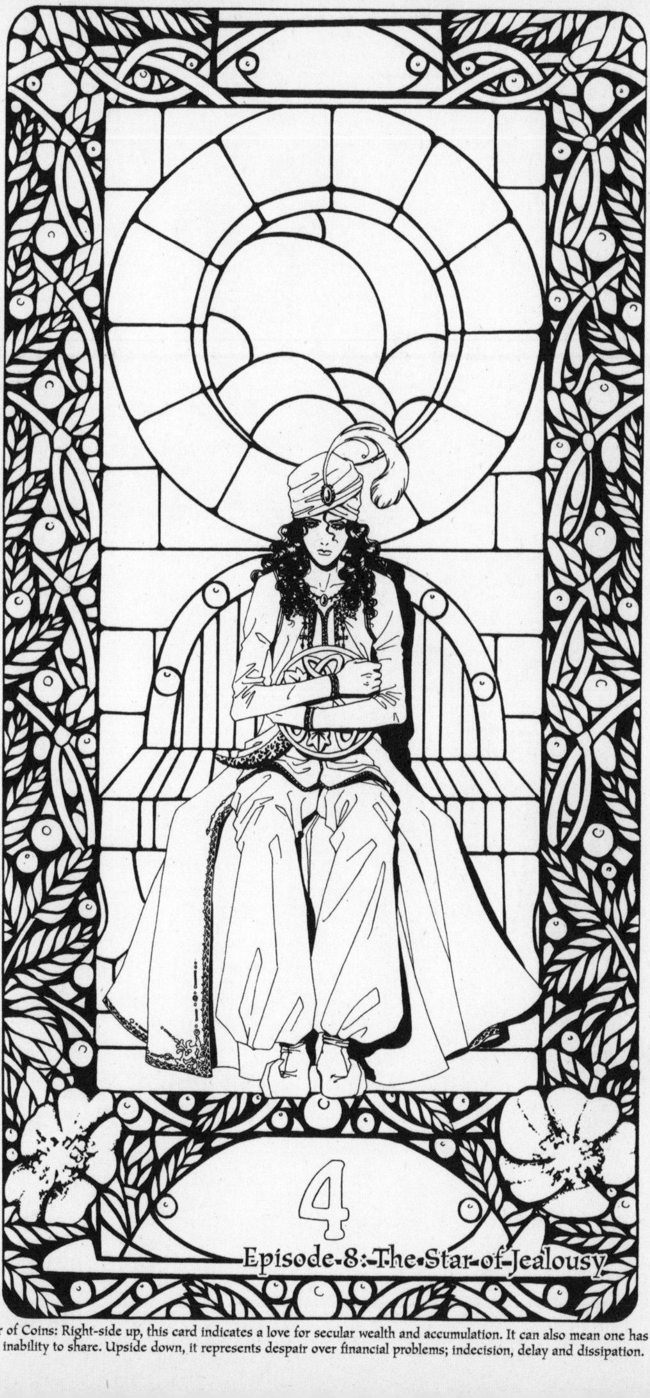
4
Episode 8: The Star of Jealousy

Four of Coins: Right-side up, this card indicates a love for secular wealth and accumulation. It can also mean one has the inability to share. Upside down, it represents despair over financial problems; indecision, delay and dissipation.

ILLUSTRATION FROM ART NOUVEAU TAROT DECK

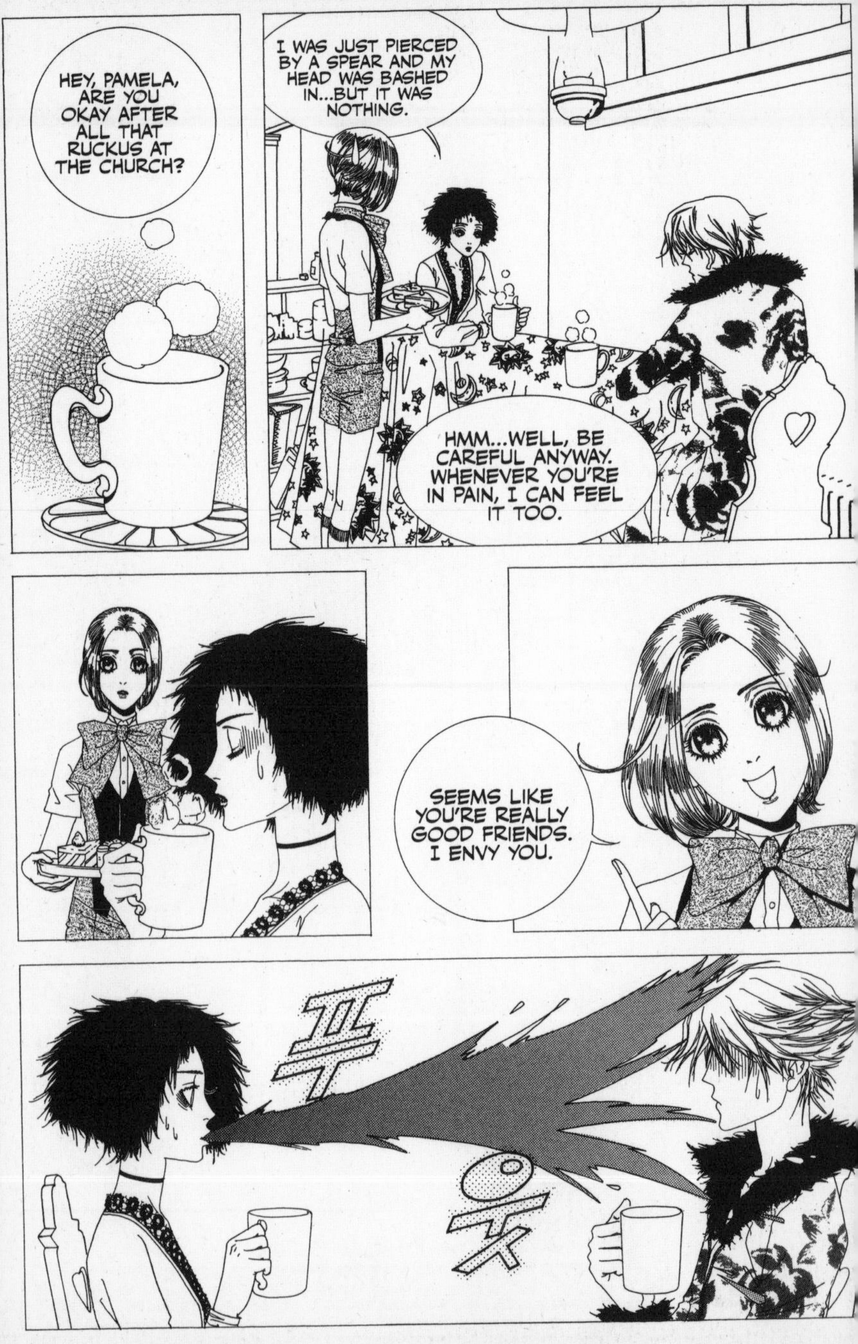
HEY, PAMELA, ARE YOU OKAY AFTER ALL THAT RUCKUS AT THE CHURCH?
I WAS JUST PIERCED BY A SPEAR AND MY HEAD WAS BASHED IN...BUT IT WAS NOTHING.
HMM...WELL, BE CAREFUL ANYWAY. WHENEVER YOU'RE IN PAIN, I CAN FEEL IT TOO.
SEEMS LIKE YOU'RE REALLY GOOD FRIENDS. I ENVY YOU.

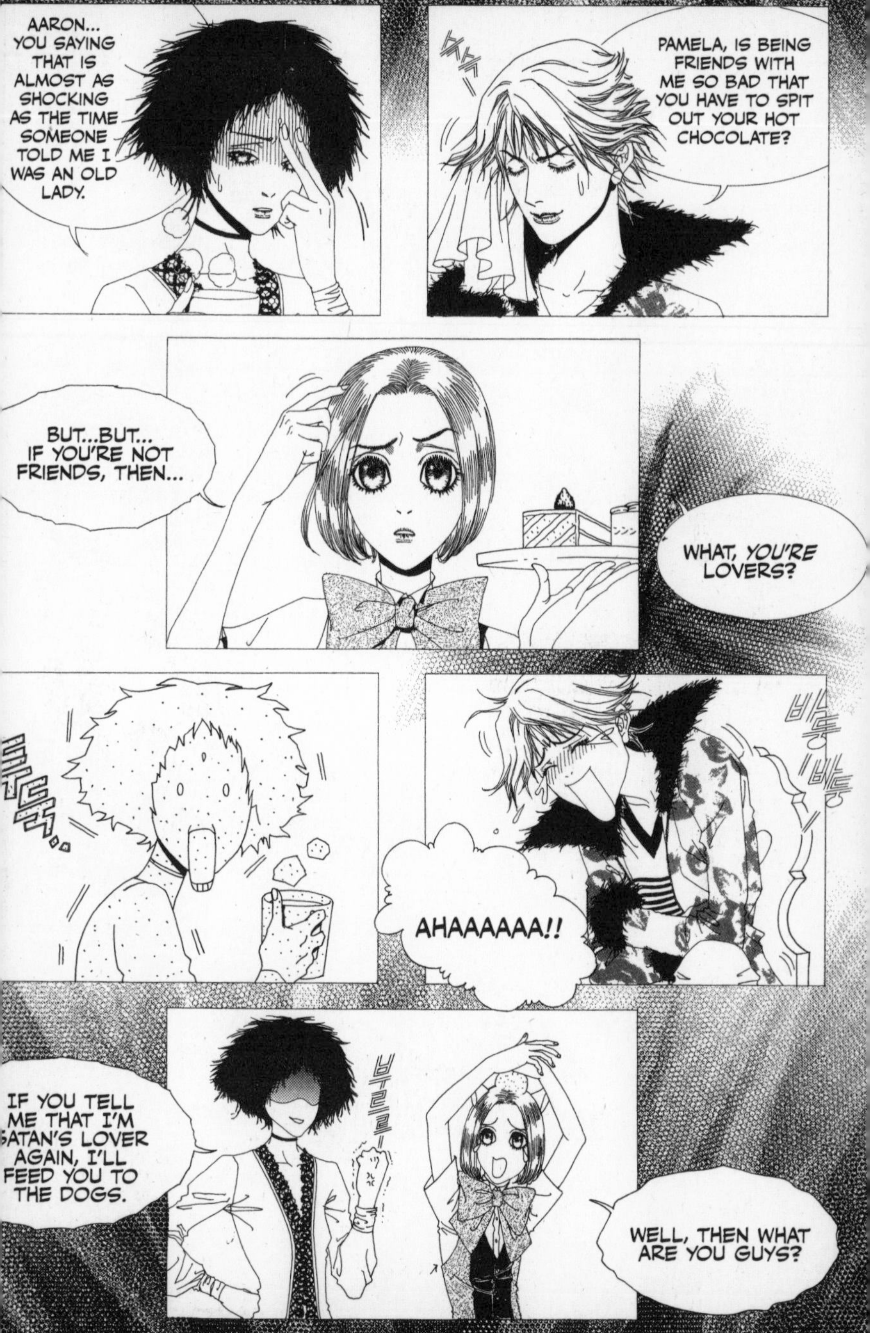
AARON... YOU SAYING THAT IS ALMOST AS SHOCKING AS THE TIME SOMEONE TOLD ME I WAS AN OLD LADY.
PAMELA, IS BEING FRIENDS WITH ME SO BAD THAT YOU HAVE TO SPIT OUT YOUR HOT CHOCOLATE?
BUT...BUT... IF YOU'RE NOT FRIENDS, THEN...
WHAT, *YOU'RE* LOVERS?
AHAAAAAA!!
IF YOU TELL ME THAT I'M SATAN'S LOVER AGAIN, I'LL FEED YOU TO THE DOGS.
WELL, THEN WHAT ARE YOU GUYS?

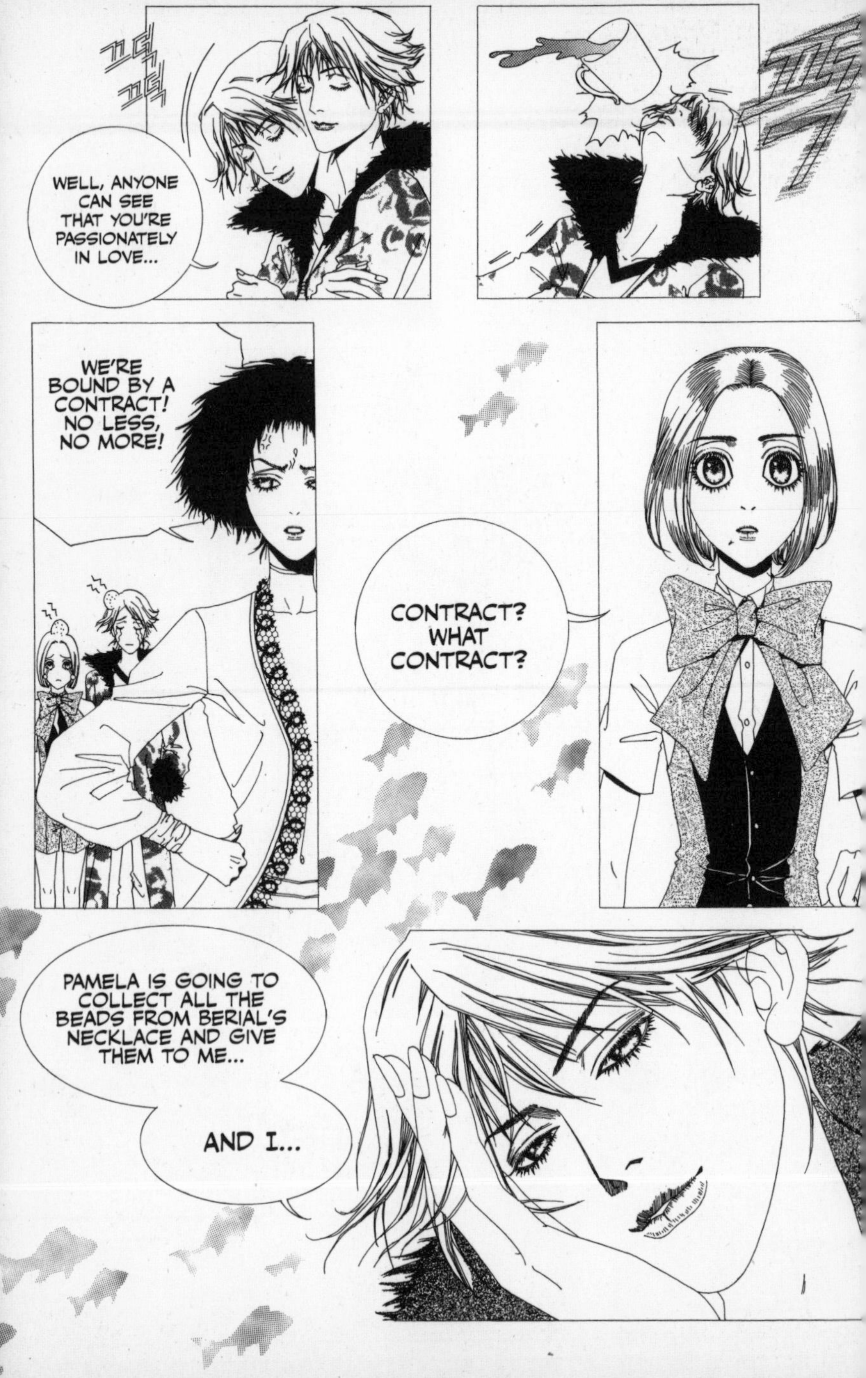
끄덕 끄덕
WELL, ANYONE CAN SEE THAT YOU'RE PASSIONATELY IN LOVE...
WE'RE BOUND BY A CONTRACT! NO LESS, NO MORE!
CONTRACT? WHAT CONTRACT?
PAMELA IS GOING TO COLLECT ALL THE BEADS FROM BERIAL'S NECKLACE AND GIVE THEM TO ME...
AND I...

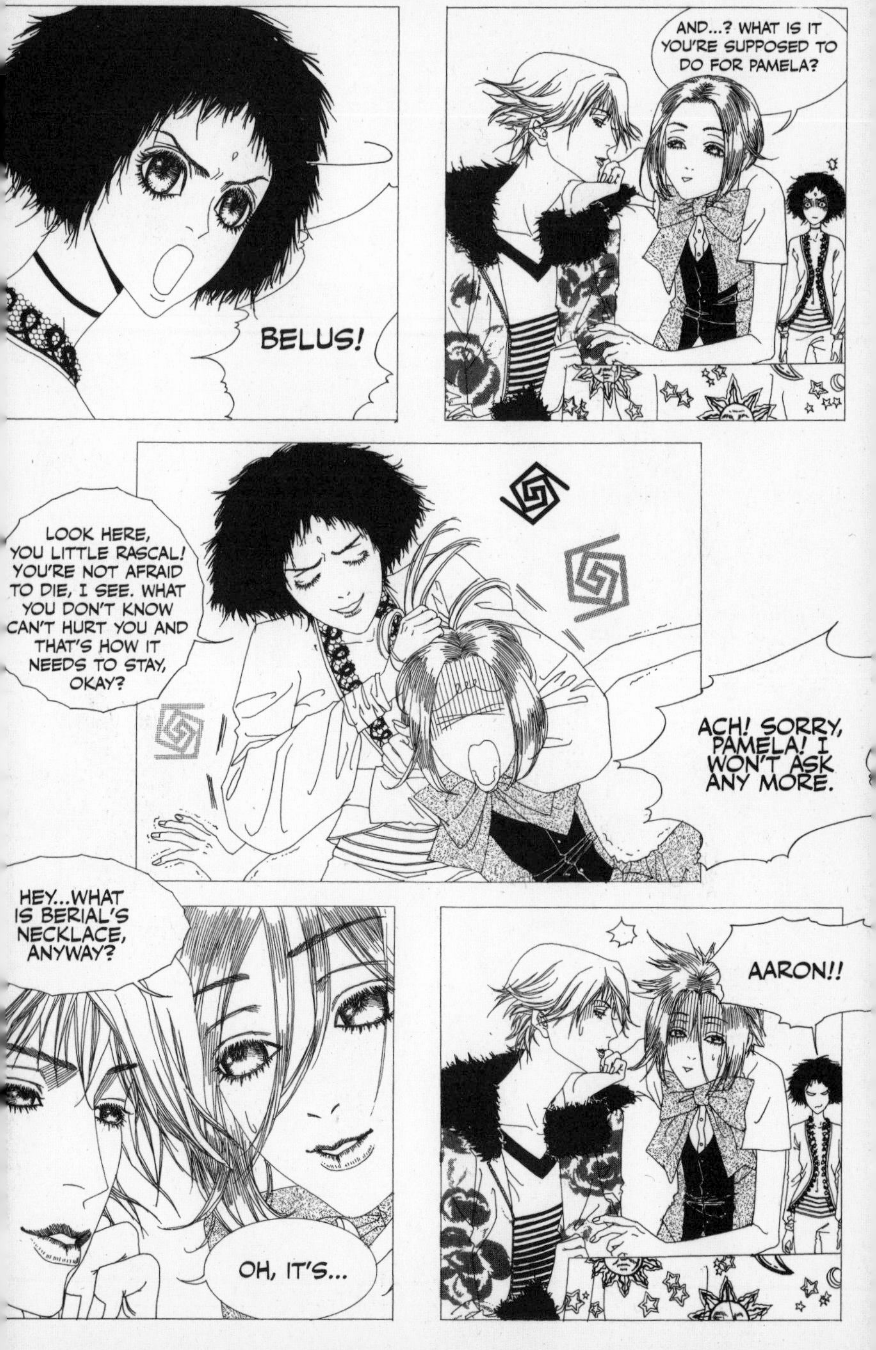
BELUS!
AND...? WHAT IS IT YOU'RE SUPPOSED TO DO FOR PAMELA?
LOOK HERE, YOU LITTLE RASCAL! YOU'RE NOT AFRAID TO DIE, I SEE. WHAT YOU DON'T KNOW CAN'T HURT YOU AND THAT'S HOW IT NEEDS TO STAY, OKAY?
ACH! SORRY, PAMELA! I WON'T ASK ANY MORE.
HEY...WHAT IS BERIAL'S NECKLACE, ANYWAY?
OH, IT'S...
AARON!!

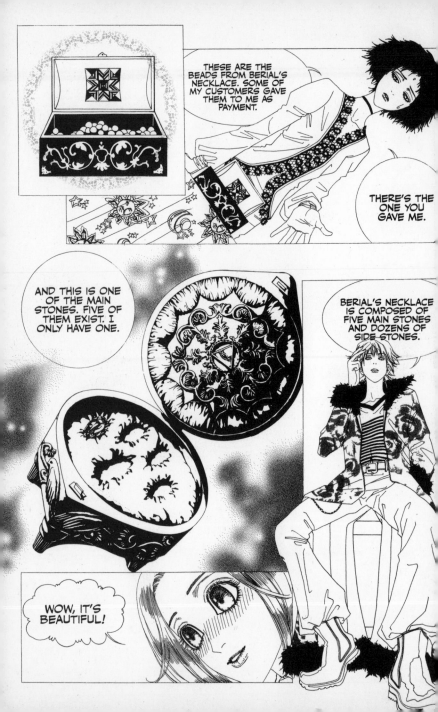

THESE ARE THE BEADS FROM BERIAL'S NECKLACE. SOME OF MY CUSTOMERS GAVE THEM TO ME AS PAYMENT.

THERE'S THE ONE YOU GAVE ME.

AND THIS IS ONE OF THE MAIN STONES. FIVE OF THEM EXIST. I ONLY HAVE ONE.

BERIAL'S NECKLACE IS COMPOSED OF FIVE MAIN STONES AND DOZENS OF SIDE STONES.

WOW, IT'S BEAUTIFUL!

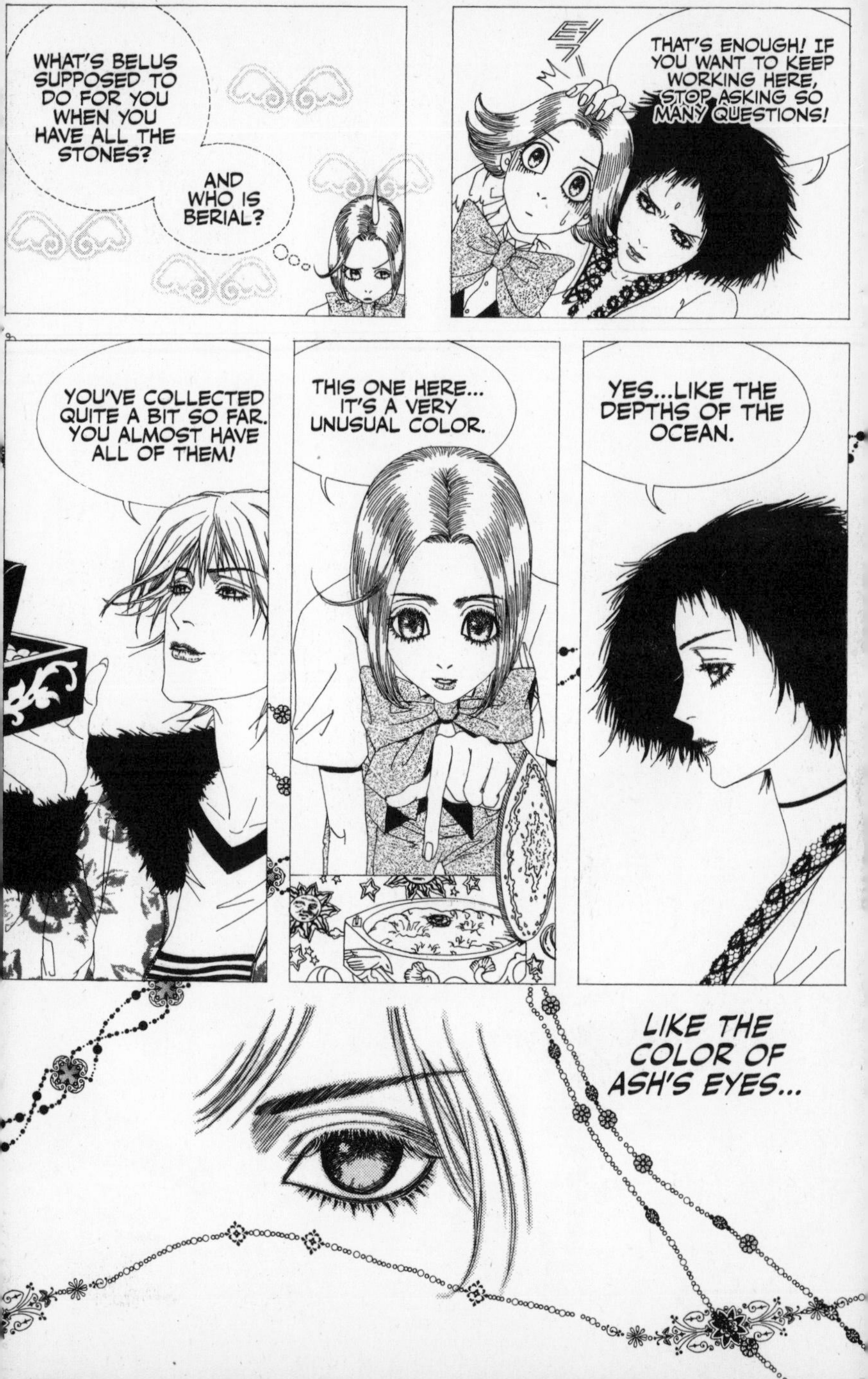
WHAT'S BELUS SUPPOSED TO DO FOR YOU WHEN YOU HAVE ALL THE STONES?
AND WHO IS BERIAL?
THAT'S ENOUGH! IF YOU WANT TO KEEP WORKING HERE, STOP ASKING SO MANY QUESTIONS!
YOU'VE COLLECTED QUITE A BIT SO FAR. YOU ALMOST HAVE ALL OF THEM!
THIS ONE HERE... IT'S A VERY UNUSUAL COLOR.
YES...LIKE THE DEPTHS OF THE OCEAN.
LIKE THE COLOR OF ASH'S EYES...

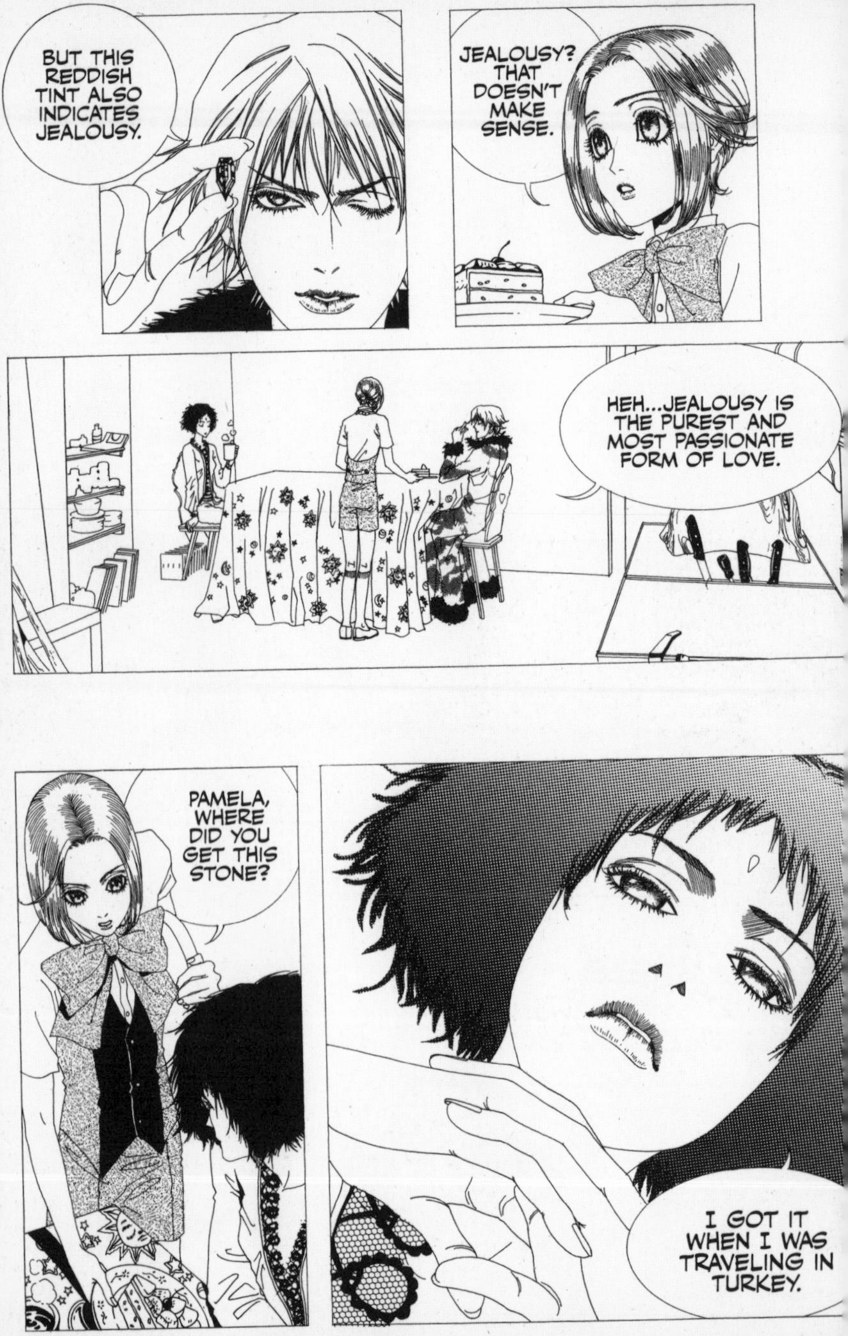
BUT THIS REDDISH TINT ALSO INDICATES JEALOUSY.
JEALOUSY? THAT DOESN'T MAKE SENSE.
HEH...JEALOUSY IS THE PUREST AND MOST PASSIONATE FORM OF LOVE.
PAMELA, WHERE DID YOU GET THIS STONE?
I GOT IT WHEN I WAS TRAVELING IN TURKEY.

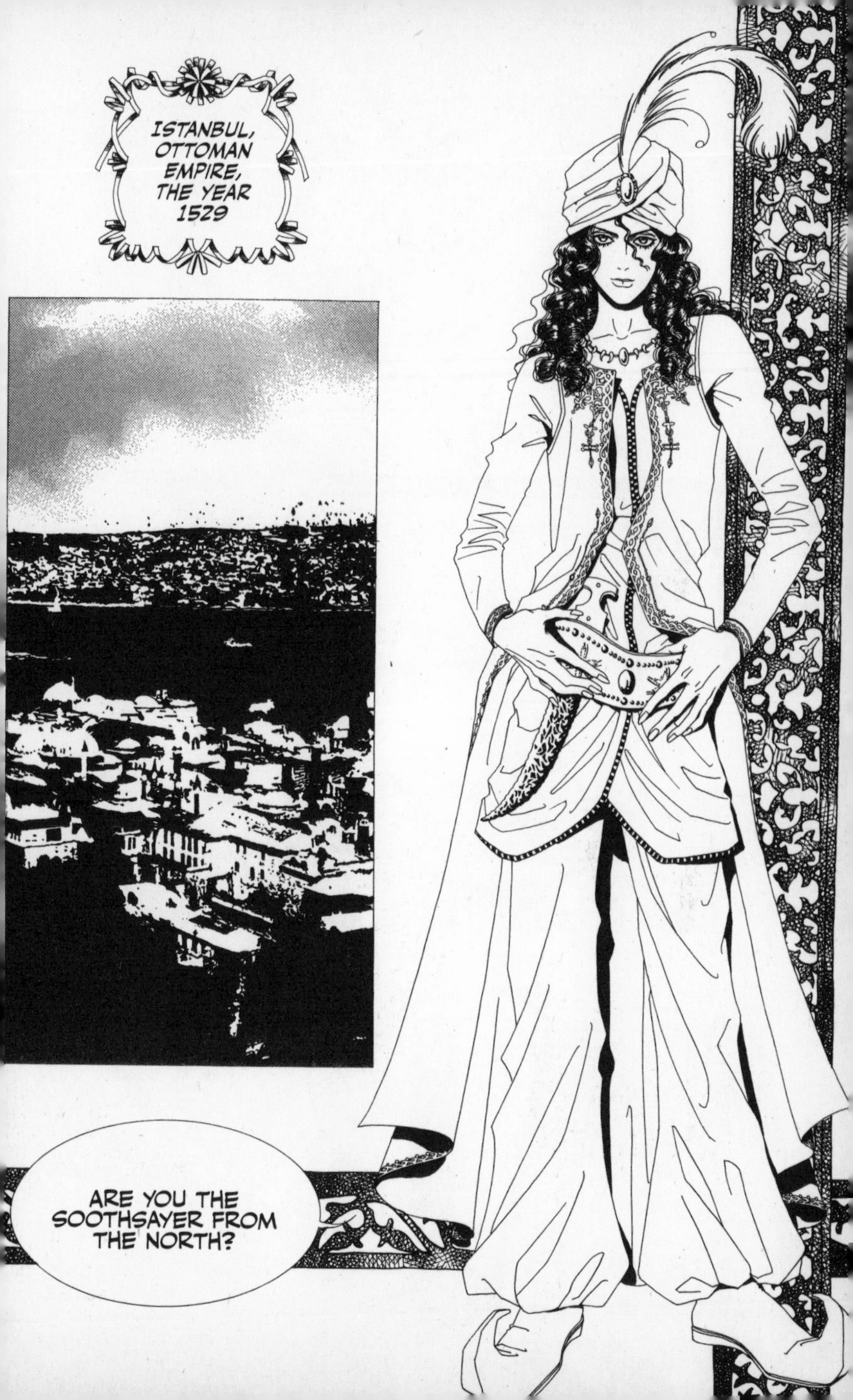
ISTANBUL, OTTOMAN EMPIRE, THE YEAR 1529
ARE YOU THE SOOTHSAYER FROM THE NORTH?

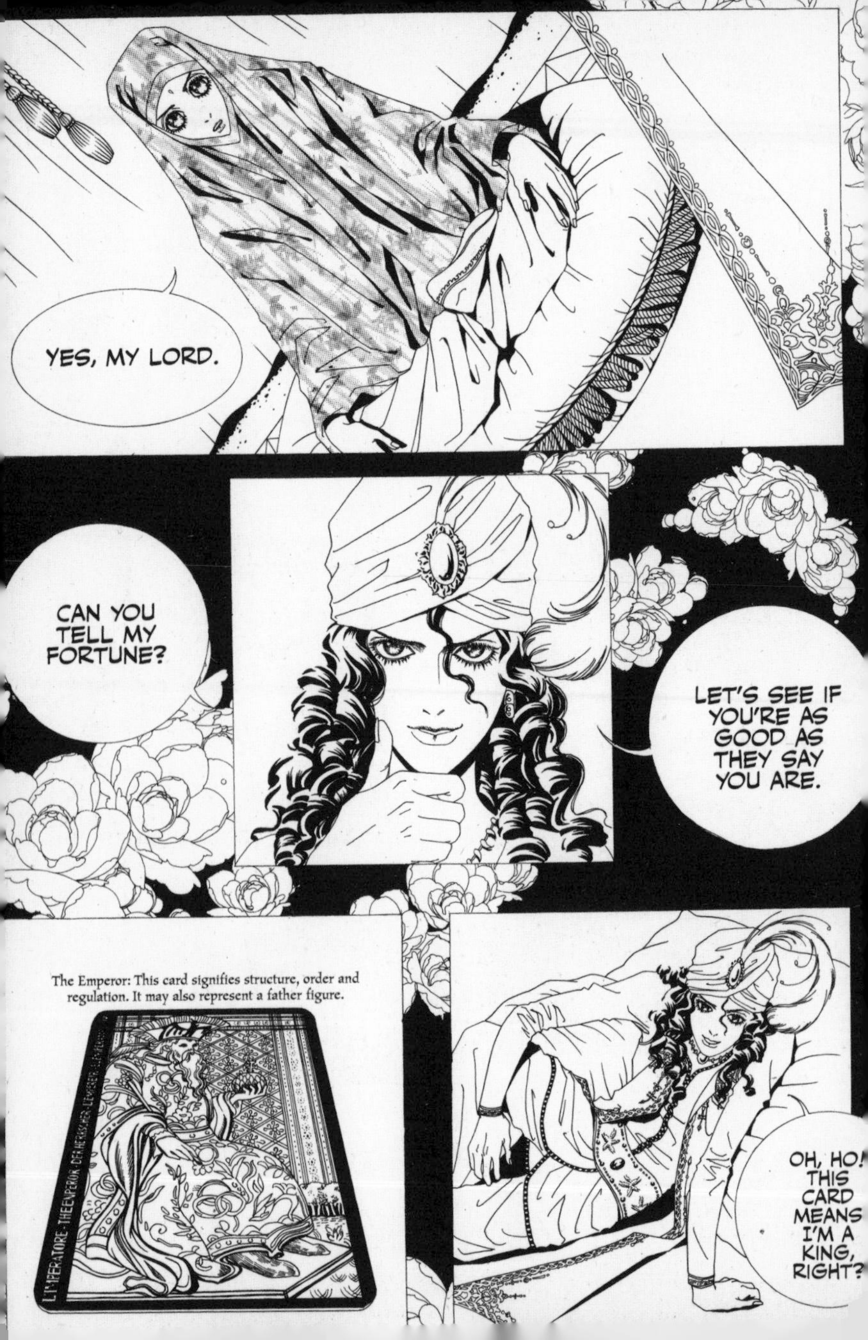
YES, MY LORD.
CAN YOU TELL MY FORTUNE?
LET'S SEE IF YOU'RE AS GOOD AS THEY SAY YOU ARE.
The Emperor: This card signifies structure, order and regulation. It may also represent a father figure.
OH, HO! THIS CARD MEANS I'M A KING, RIGHT?

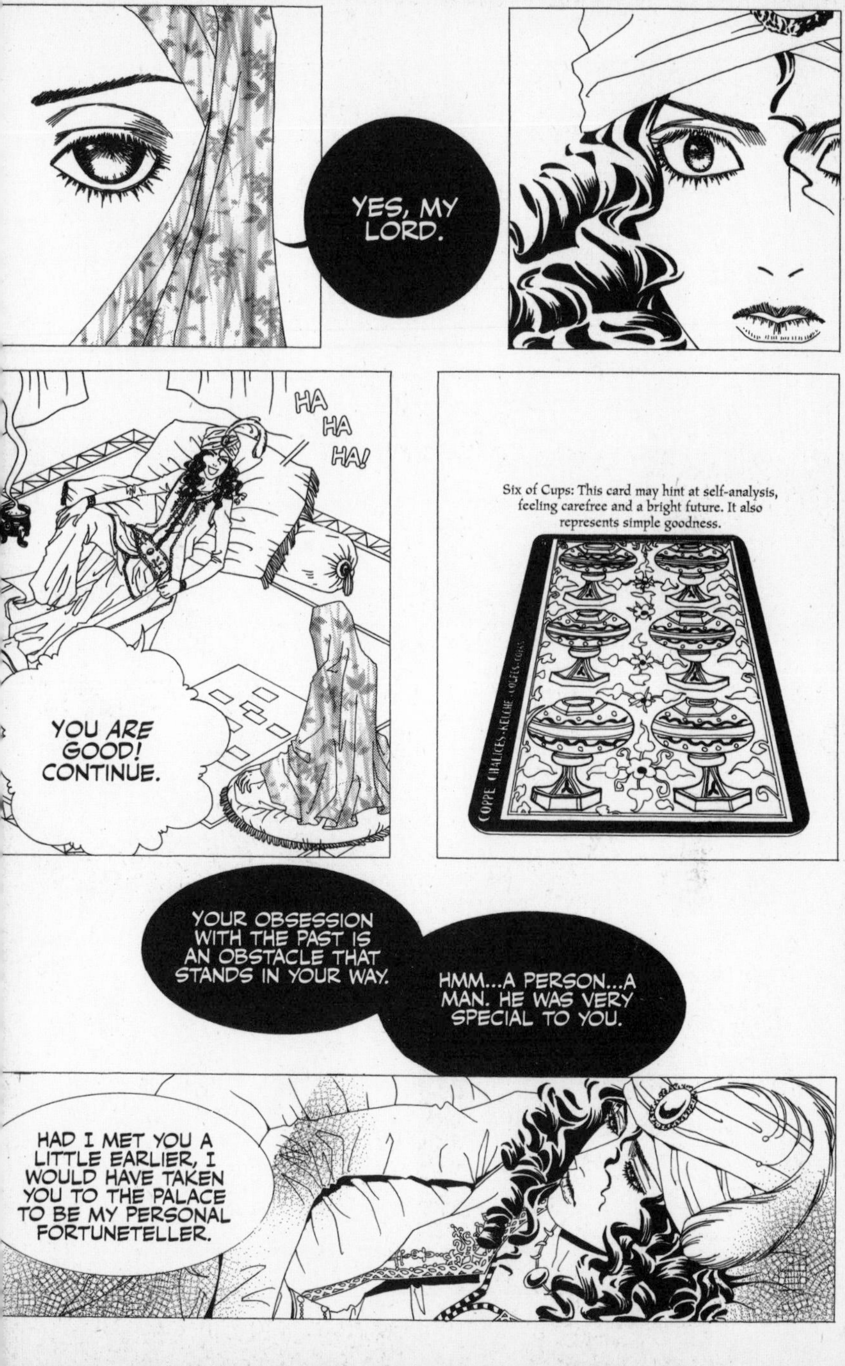
YES, MY LORD.
HA HA HA!
YOU ARE GOOD! CONTINUE.
Six of Cups: This card may hint at self-analysis, feeling carefree and a bright future. It also represents simple goodness.
YOUR OBSESSION WITH THE PAST IS AN OBSTACLE THAT STANDS IN YOUR WAY.
HMM...A PERSON...A MAN. HE WAS VERY SPECIAL TO YOU.
HAD I MET YOU A LITTLE EARLIER, I WOULD HAVE TAKEN YOU TO THE PALACE TO BE MY PERSONAL FORTUNETELLER.

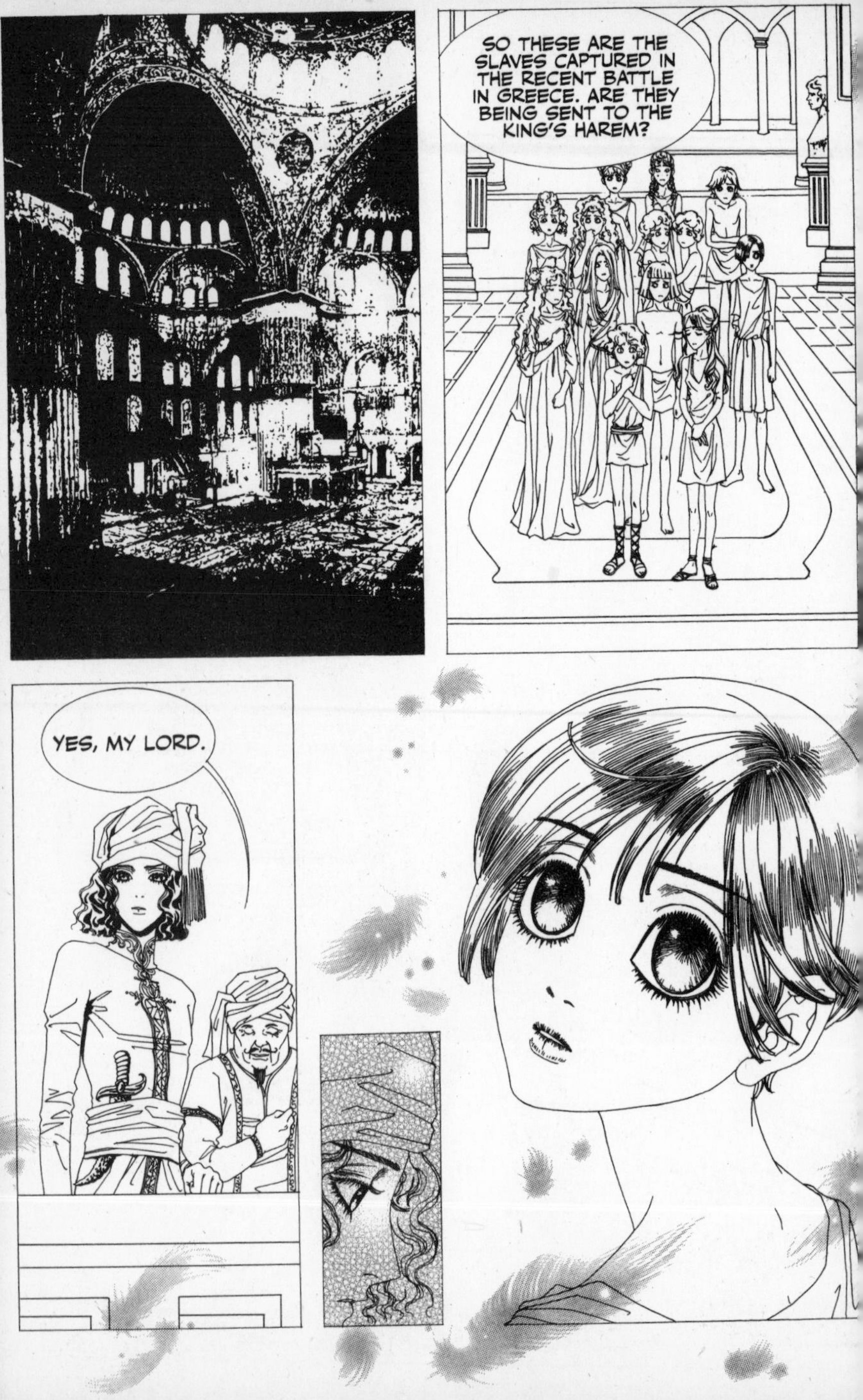
SO THESE ARE THE SLAVES CAPTURED IN THE RECENT BATTLE IN GREECE. ARE THEY BEING SENT TO THE KING'S HAREM?
YES, MY LORD.

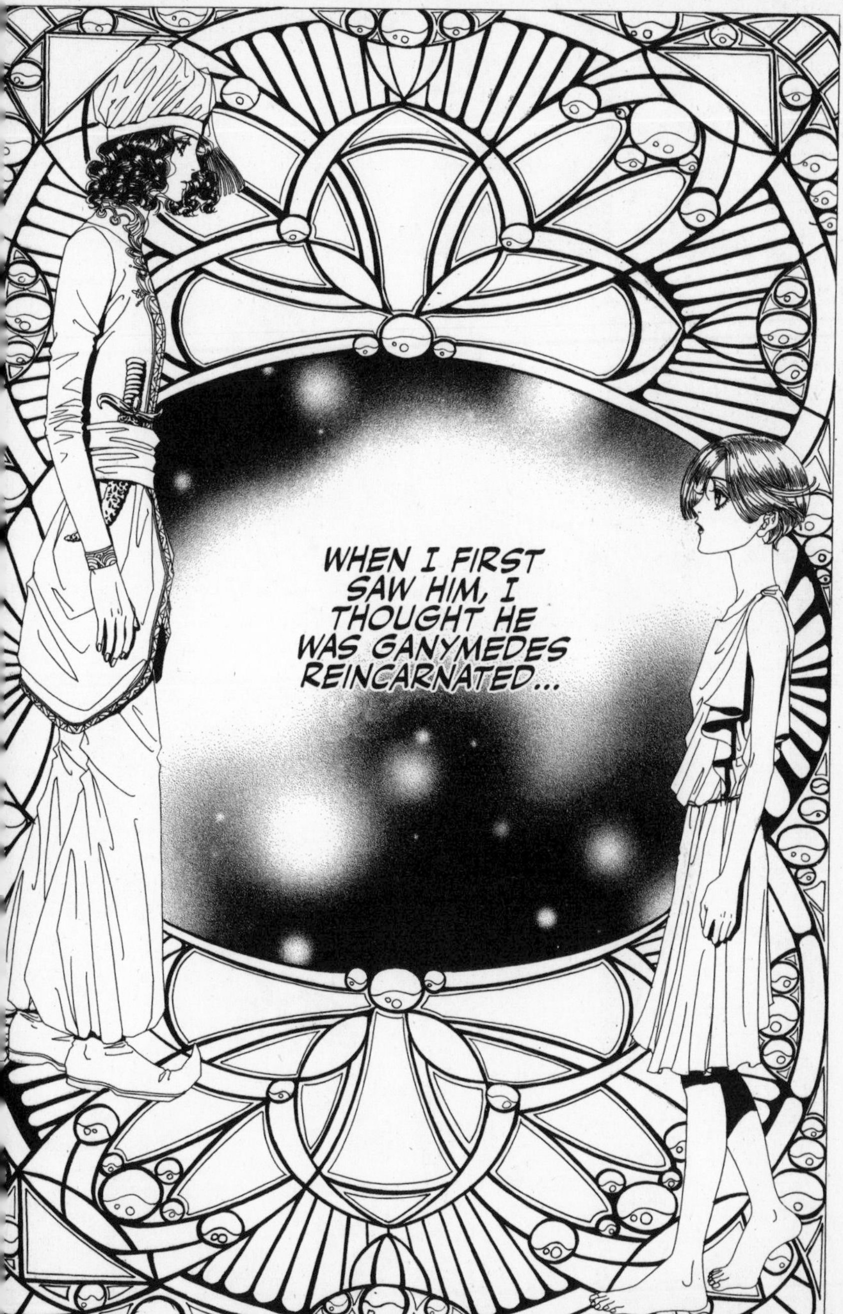
WHEN I FIRST SAW HIM, I THOUGHT HE WAS GANYMEDES REINCARNATED...

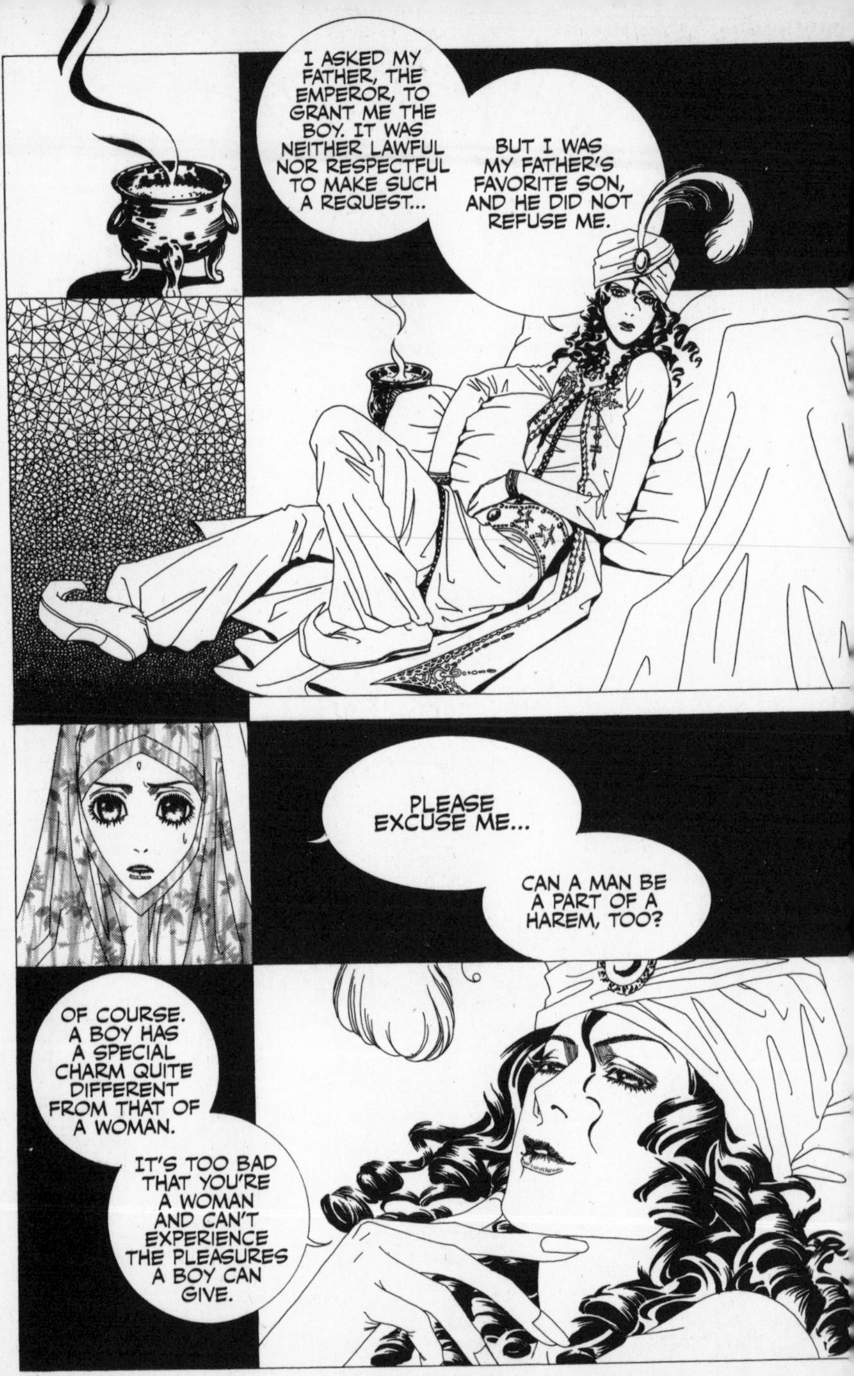
I ASKED MY FATHER, THE EMPEROR, TO GRANT ME THE BOY. IT WAS NEITHER LAWFUL NOR RESPECTFUL TO MAKE SUCH A REQUEST...
BUT I WAS MY FATHER'S FAVORITE SON, AND HE DID NOT REFUSE ME.
PLEASE EXCUSE ME...
CAN A MAN BE A PART OF A HAREM, TOO?
OF COURSE. A BOY HAS A SPECIAL CHARM QUITE DIFFERENT FROM THAT OF A WOMAN.
IT'S TOO BAD THAT YOU'RE A WOMAN AND CAN'T EXPERIENCE THE PLEASURES A BOY CAN GIVE.

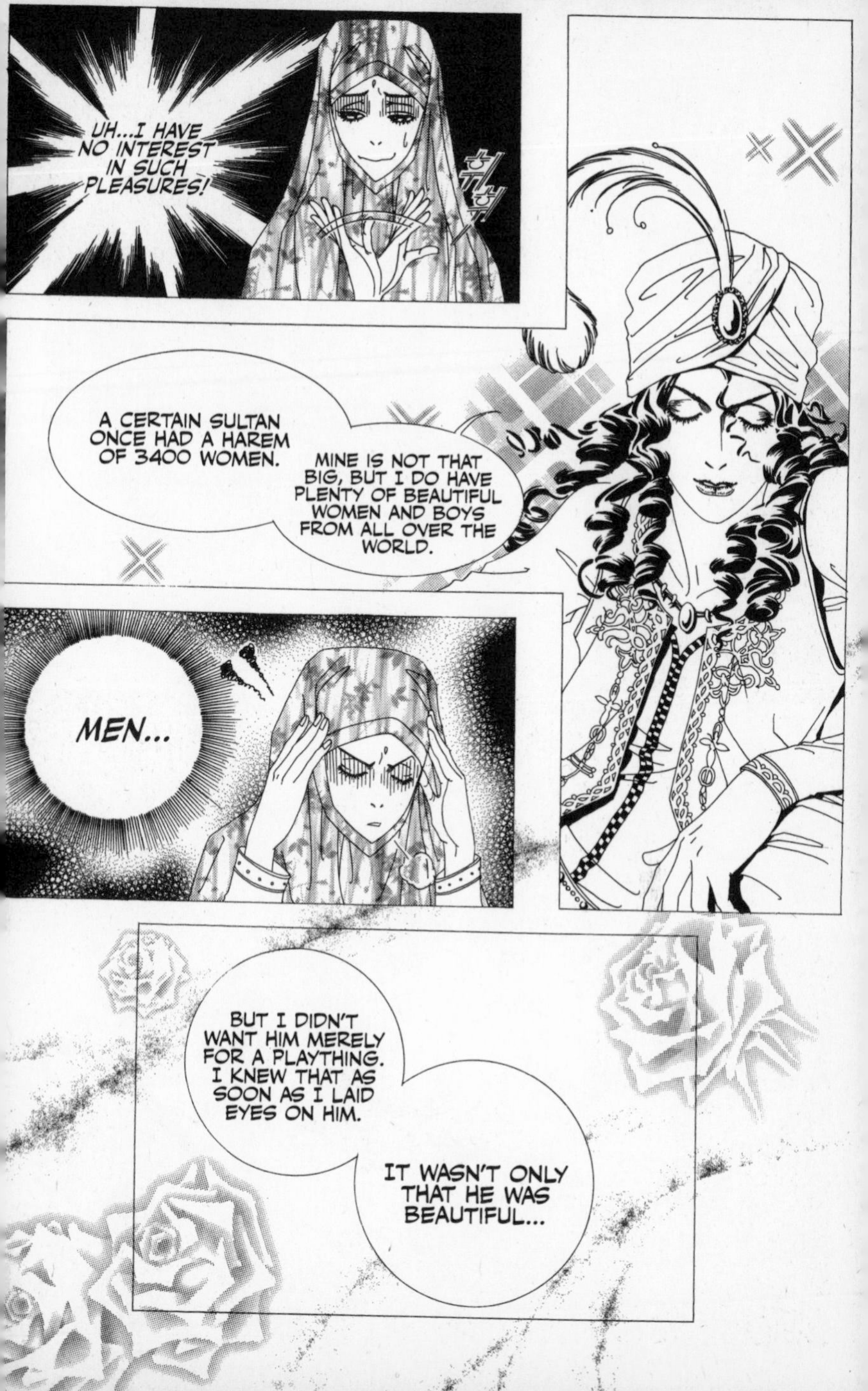
UH...I HAVE NO INTEREST IN SUCH PLEASURES!
A CERTAIN SULTAN ONCE HAD A HAREM OF 3400 WOMEN.
MINE IS NOT THAT BIG, BUT I DO HAVE PLENTY OF BEAUTIFUL WOMEN AND BOYS FROM ALL OVER THE WORLD.
MEN...
BUT I DIDN'T WANT HIM MERELY FOR A PLAYTHING. I KNEW THAT AS SOON AS I LAID EYES ON HIM.
IT WASN'T ONLY THAT HE WAS BEAUTIFUL...

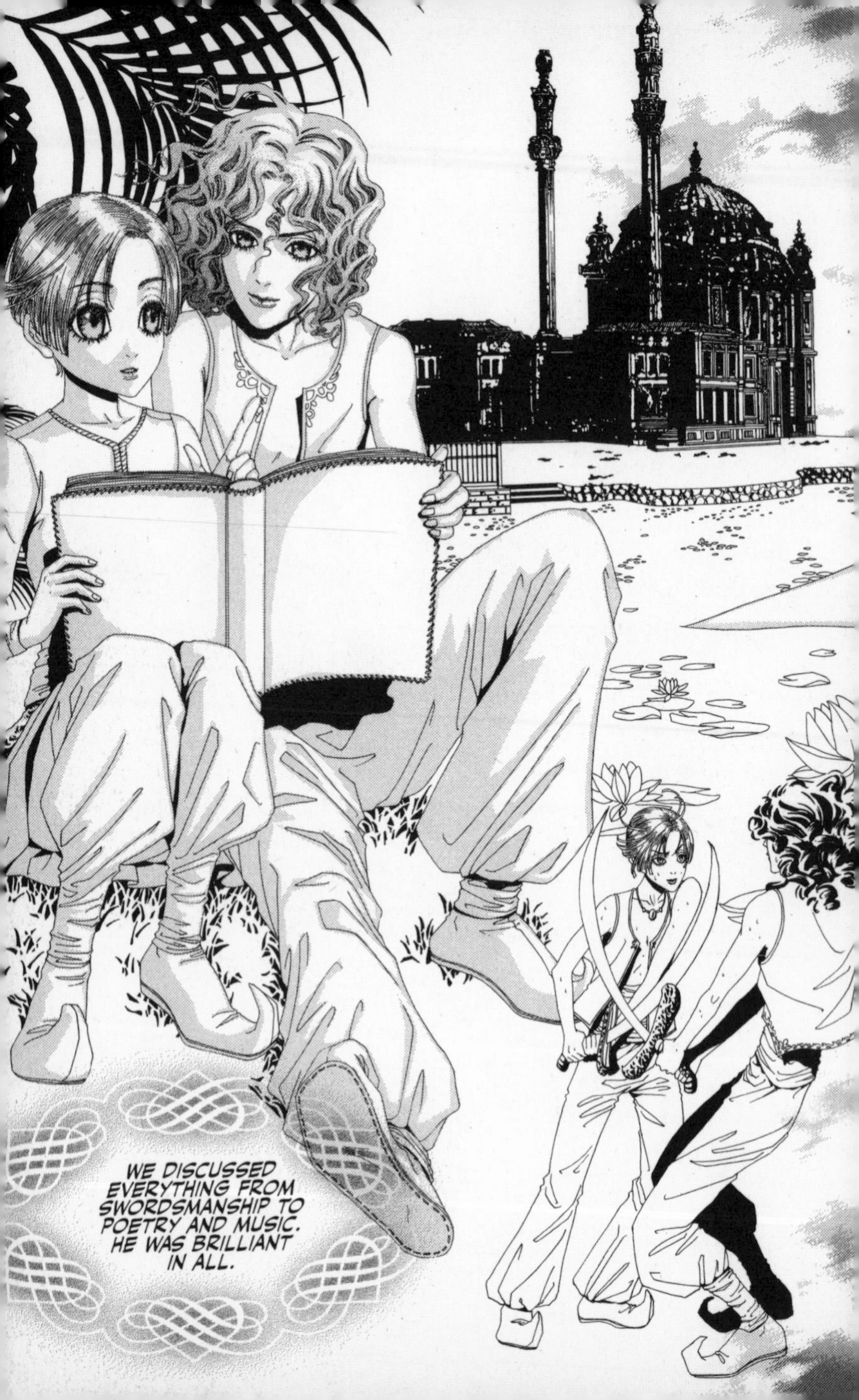
WE DISCUSSED EVERYTHING FROM SWORDSMANSHIP TO POETRY AND MUSIC. HE WAS BRILLIANT IN ALL.

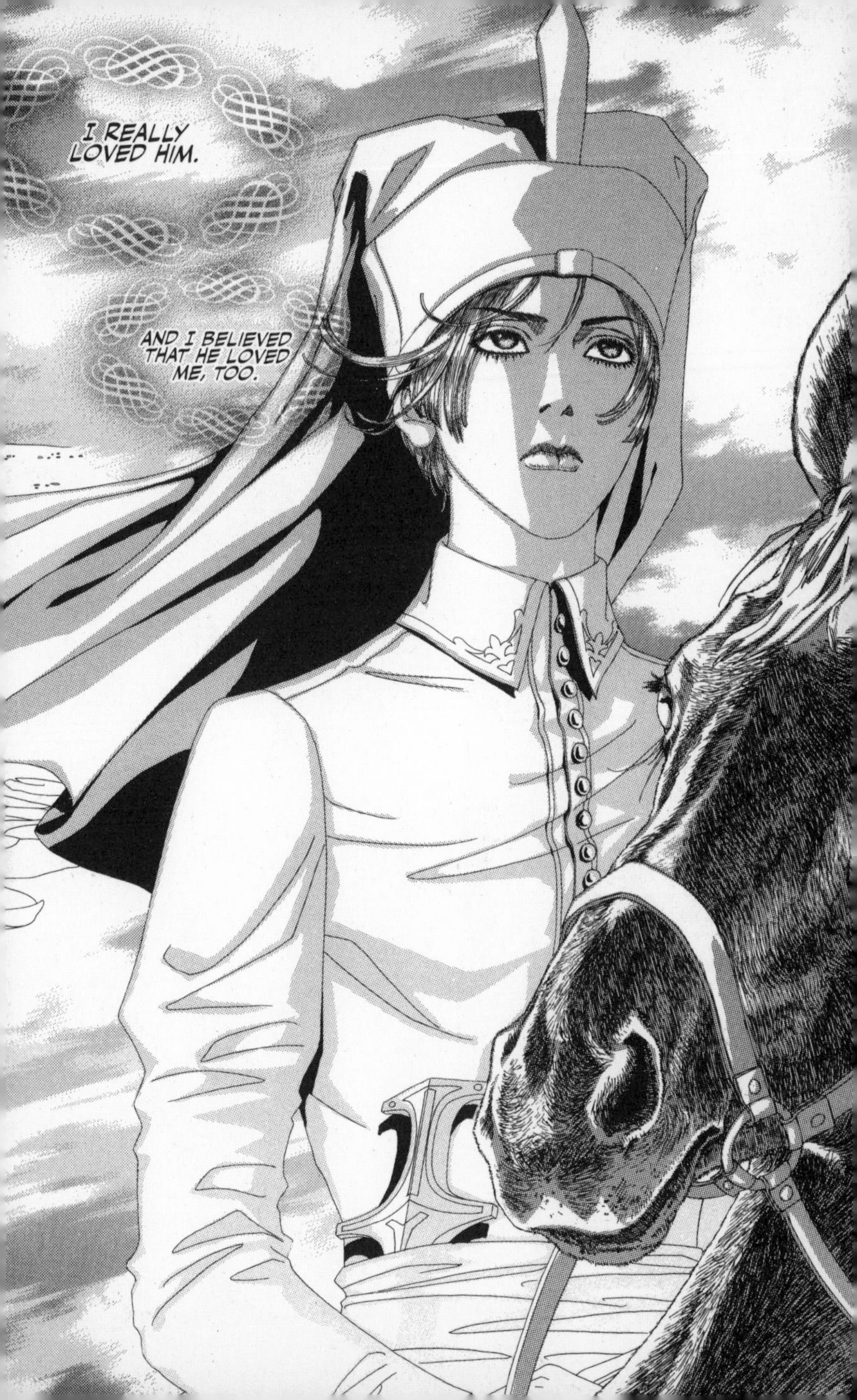
I REALLY LOVED HIM.
AND I BELIEVED THAT HE LOVED ME, TOO.

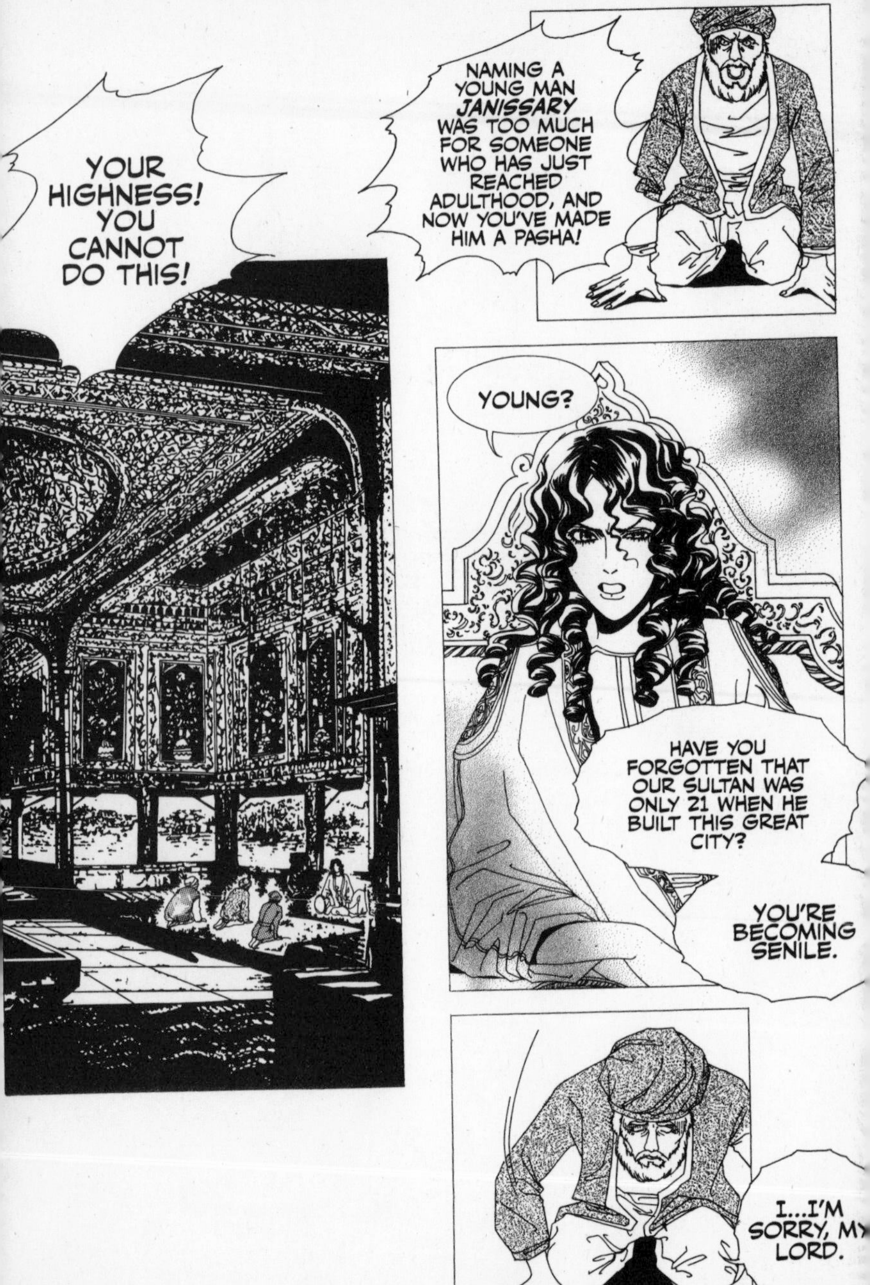
YOUR HIGHNESS! YOU CANNOT DO THIS!
NAMING A YOUNG MAN *JANISSARY* WAS TOO MUCH FOR SOMEONE WHO HAS JUST REACHED ADULTHOOD, AND NOW YOU'VE MADE HIM A PASHA!
YOUNG?
HAVE YOU FORGOTTEN THAT OUR SULTAN WAS ONLY 21 WHEN HE BUILT THIS GREAT CITY?
YOU'RE BECOMING SENILE.
I...I'M SORRY, MY LORD.

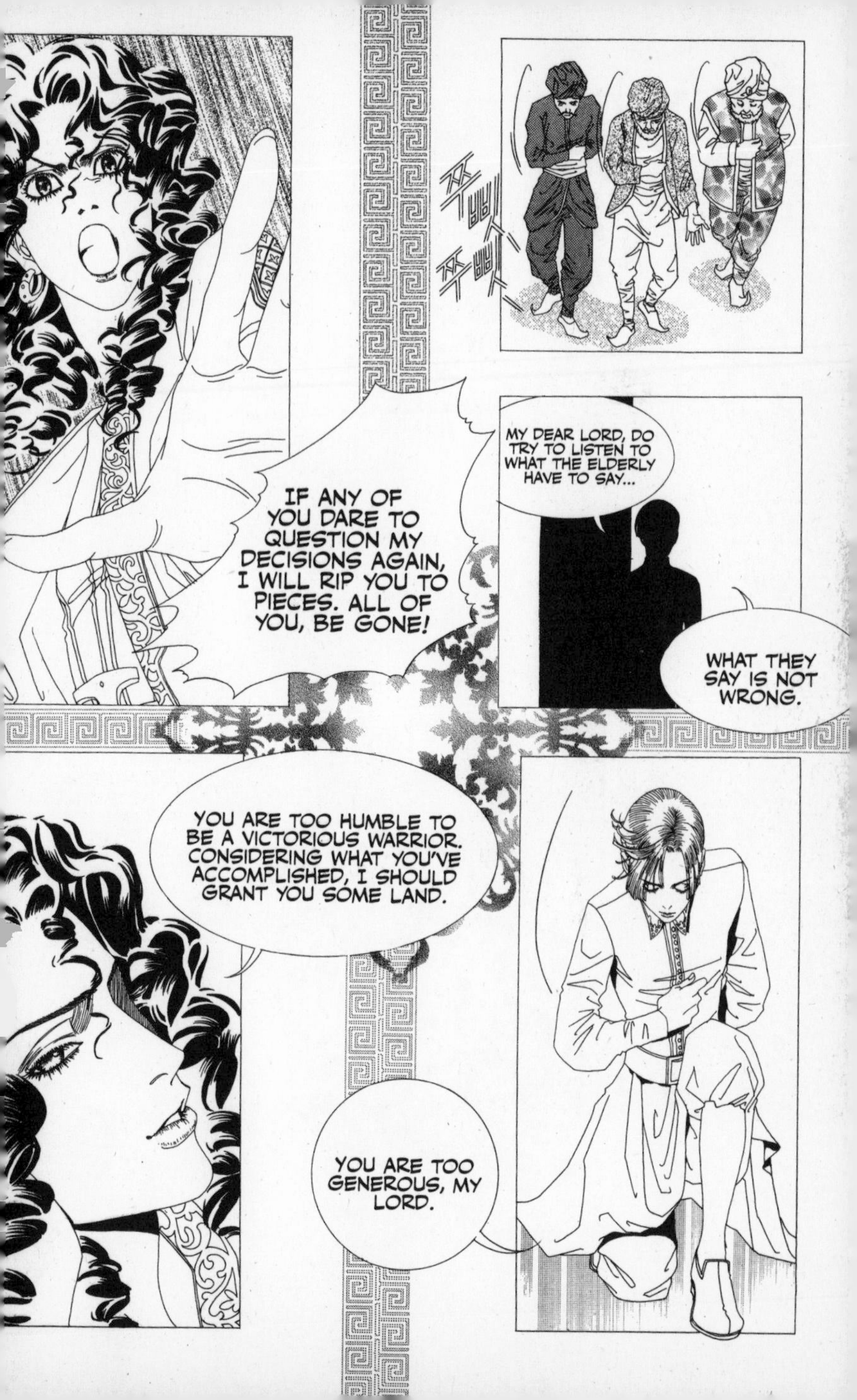
IF ANY OF YOU DARE TO QUESTION MY DECISIONS AGAIN, I WILL RIP YOU TO PIECES. ALL OF YOU, BE GONE!
쭈삣 쭈삣
MY DEAR LORD, DO TRY TO LISTEN TO WHAT THE ELDERLY HAVE TO SAY...
WHAT THEY SAY IS NOT WRONG.
YOU ARE TOO HUMBLE TO BE A VICTORIOUS WARRIOR. CONSIDERING WHAT YOU'VE ACCOMPLISHED, I SHOULD GRANT YOU SOME LAND.
YOU ARE TOO GENEROUS, MY LORD.

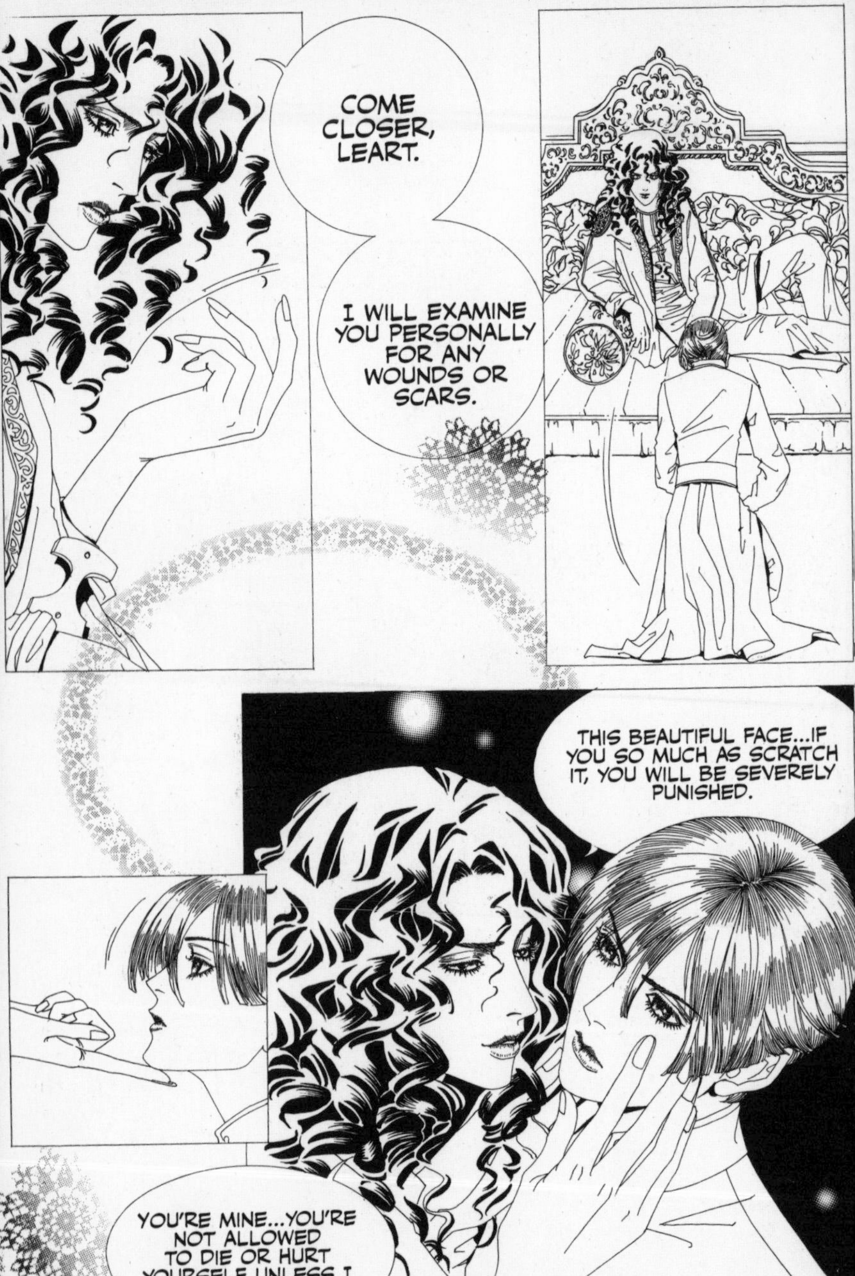
COME CLOSER, LEART.
I WILL EXAMINE YOU PERSONALLY FOR ANY WOUNDS OR SCARS.
THIS BEAUTIFUL FACE...IF YOU SO MUCH AS SCRATCH IT, YOU WILL BE SEVERELY PUNISHED.
YOU'RE MINE...YOU'RE NOT ALLOWED TO DIE OR HURT YOURSELF UNLESS I ORDER IT MYSELF.

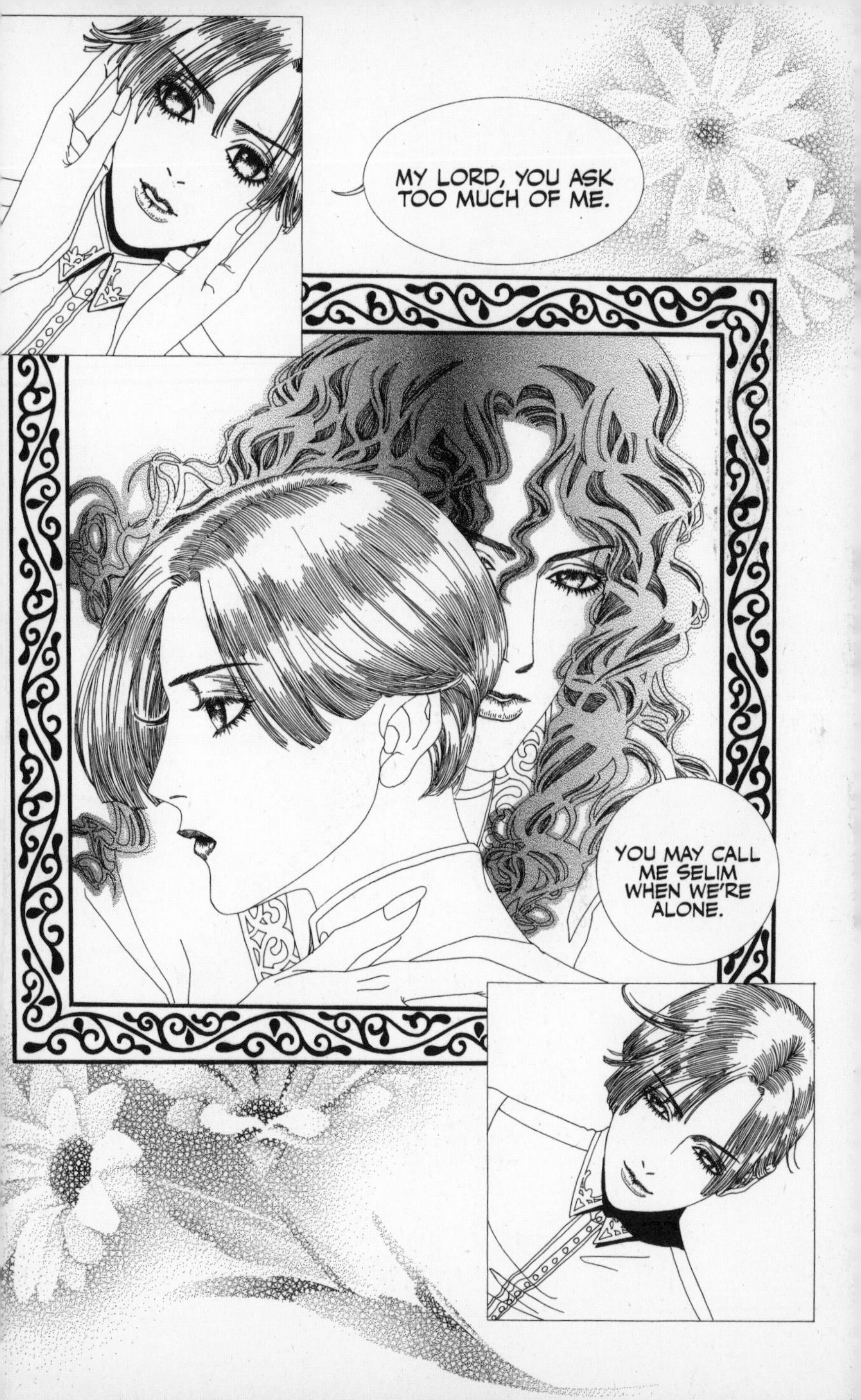
MY LORD, YOU ASK TOO MUCH OF ME.
YOU MAY CALL ME SELIM WHEN WE'RE ALONE.

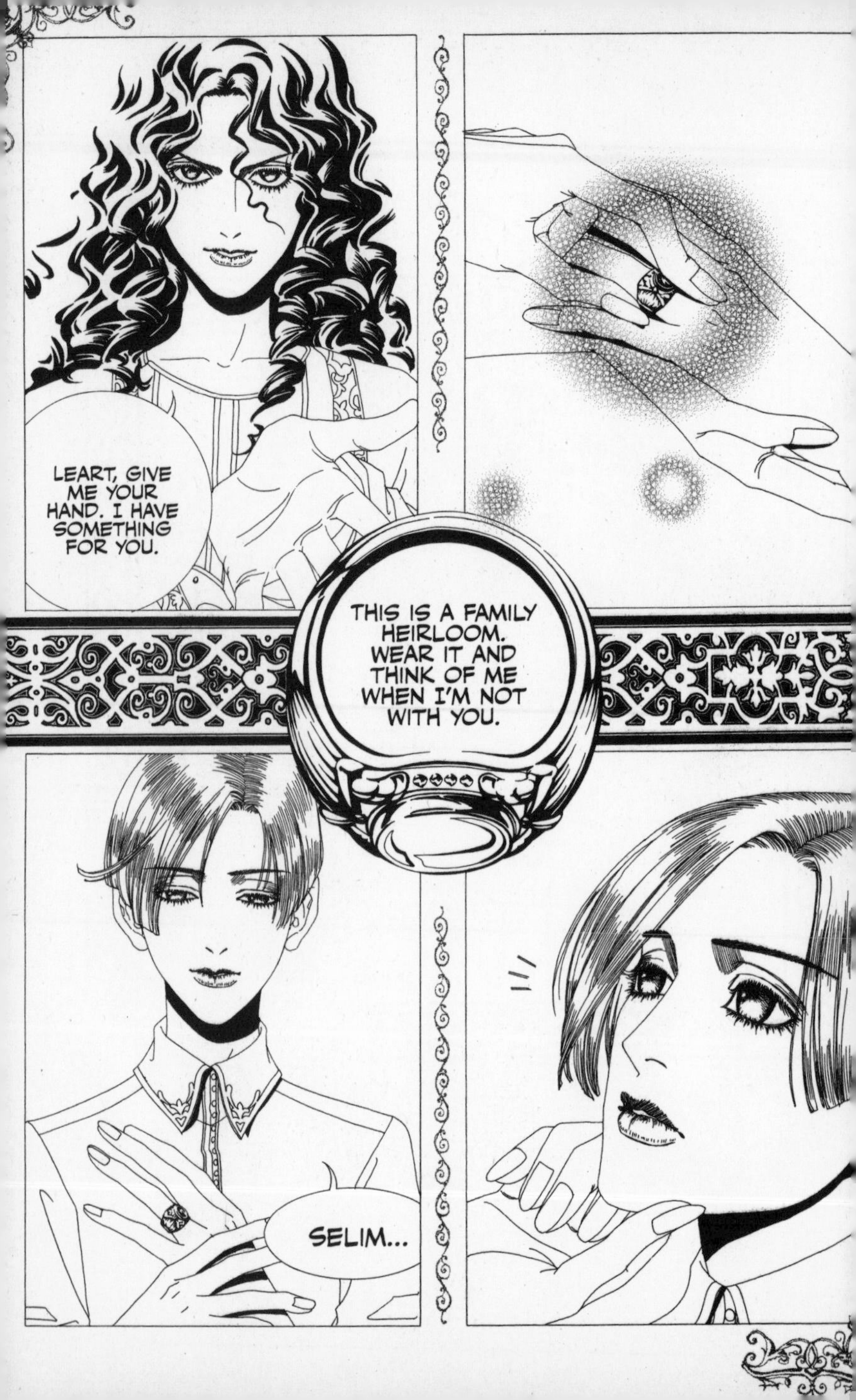
LEART, GIVE ME YOUR HAND. I HAVE SOMETHING FOR YOU.
THIS IS A FAMILY HEIRLOOM. WEAR IT AND THINK OF ME WHEN I'M NOT WITH YOU.
SELIM...

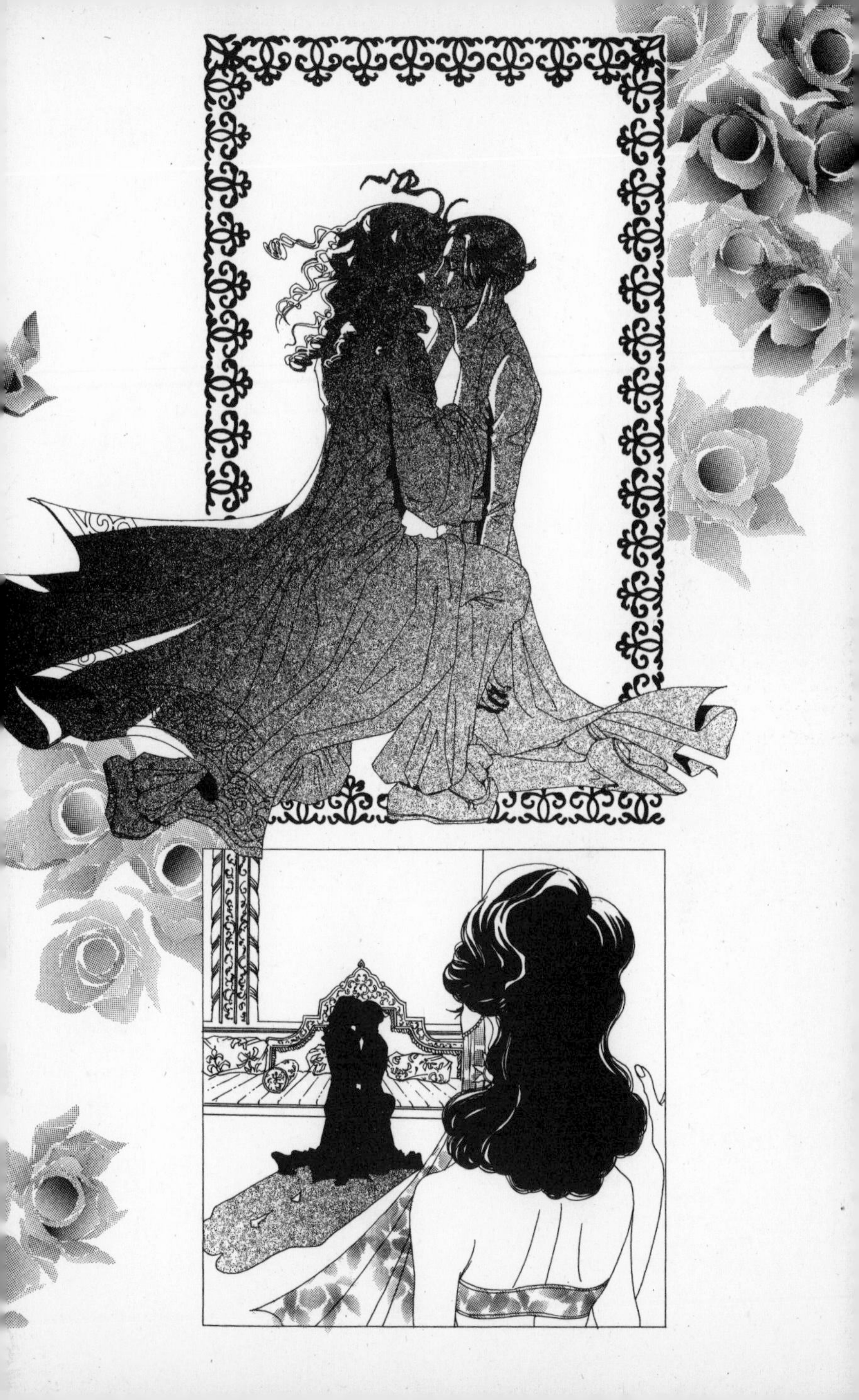

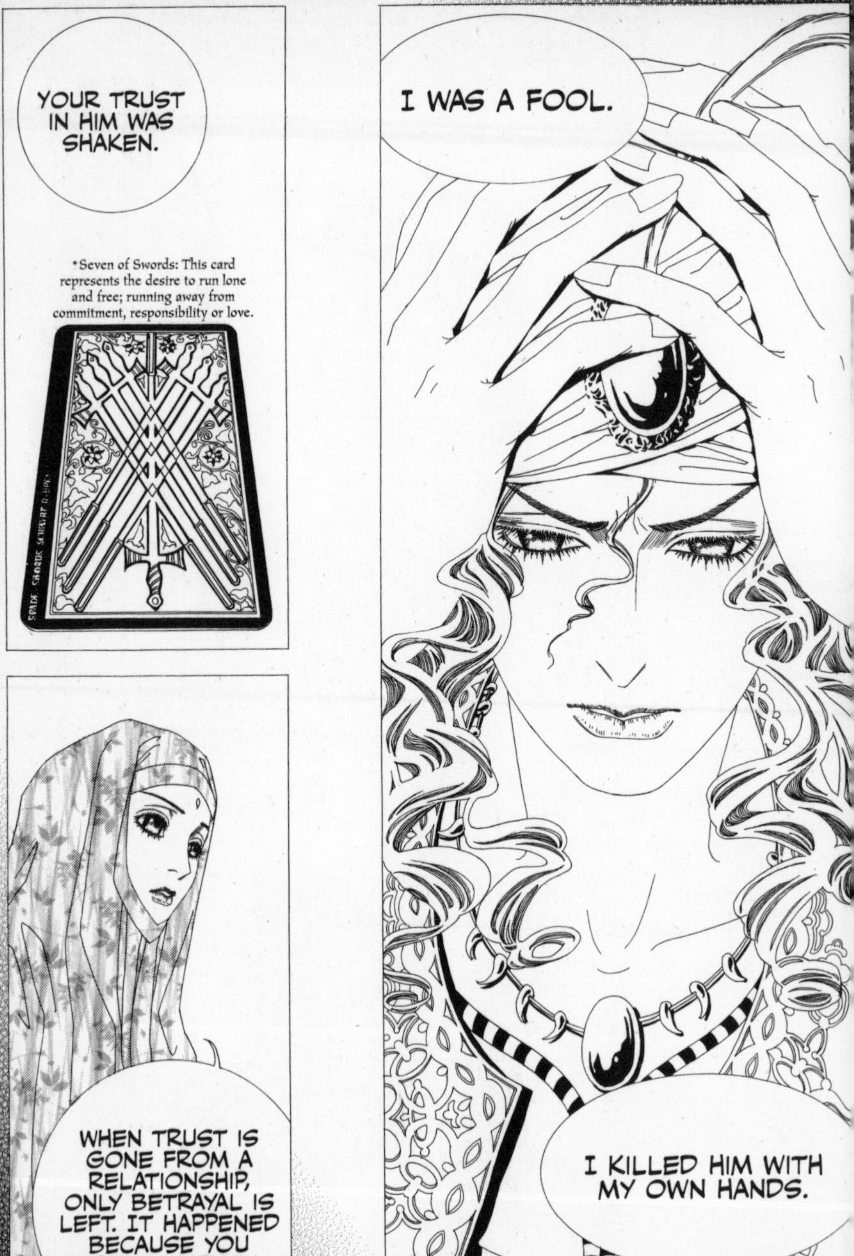
YOUR TRUST IN HIM WAS SHAKEN.
*Seven of Swords: This card represents the desire to run lone and free; running away from commitment, responsibility or love.
WHEN TRUST IS GONE FROM A RELATIONSHIP, ONLY BETRAYAL IS LEFT. IT HAPPENED BECAUSE YOU WEREN'T CAREFUL.
I WAS A FOOL.
I KILLED HIM WITH MY OWN HANDS.

ILLUSTRATION FROM ART NOUVEAU TAROT DECK

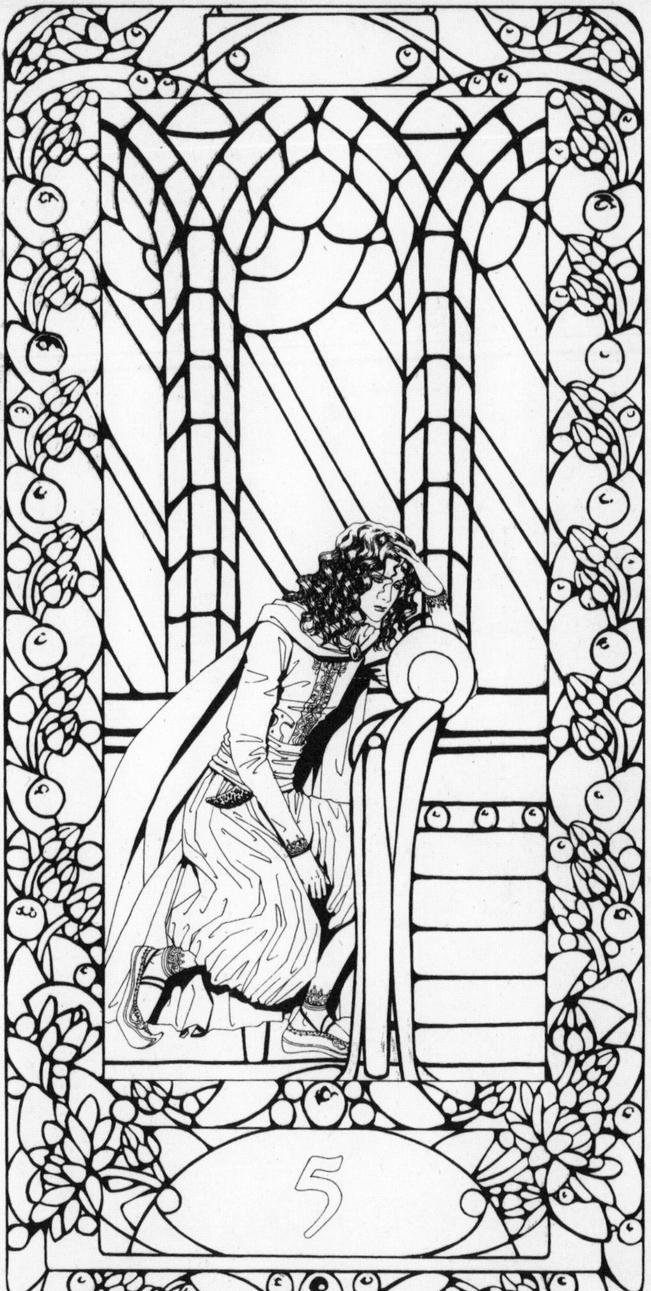
5

*Five of Cups: Right-side up, this card represents regret, loss of love and bereavement. Upside down, it means bright prospects, new alliances and reunion.

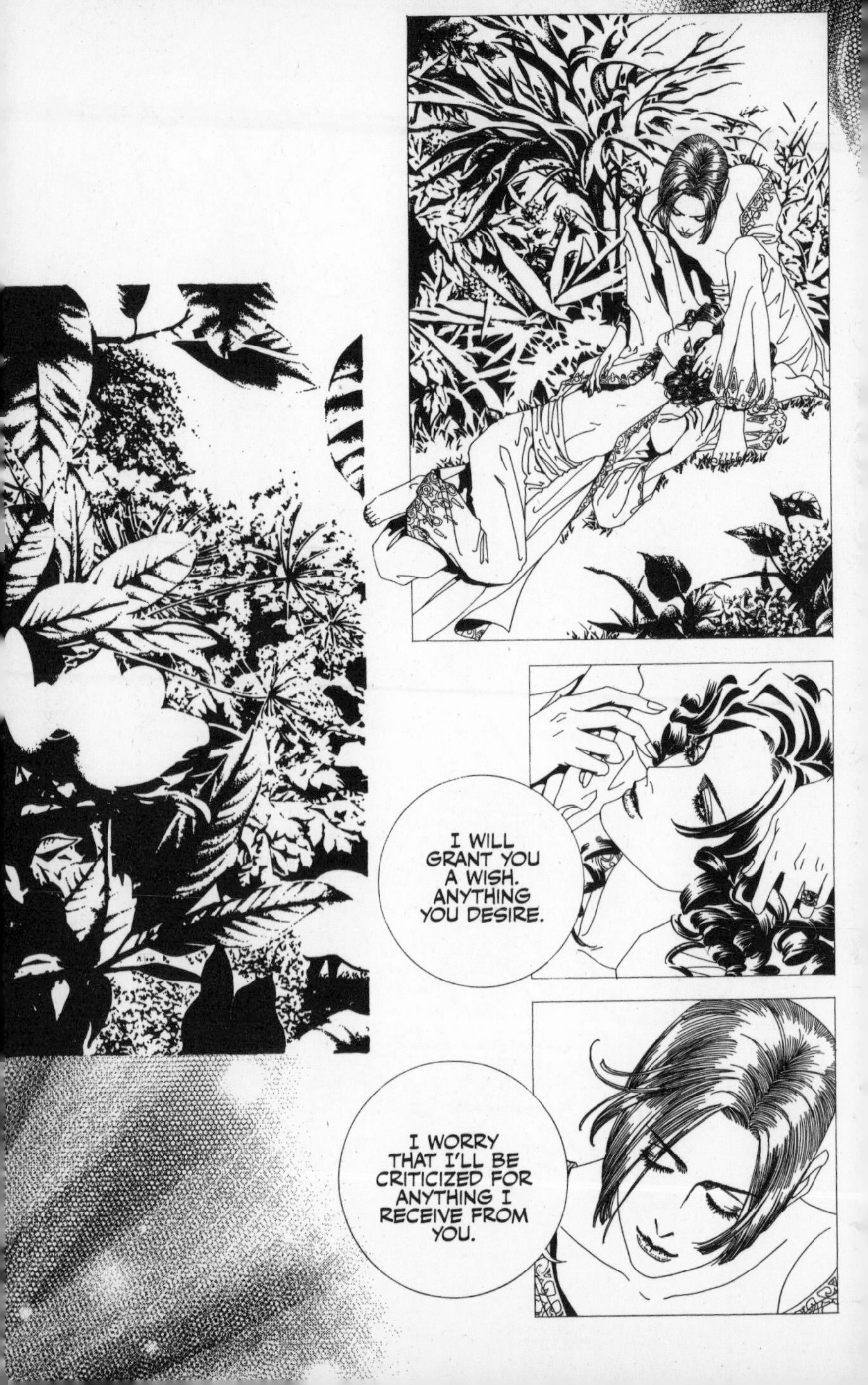
I WILL GRANT YOU A WISH. ANYTHING YOU DESIRE.
I WORRY THAT I'LL BE CRITICIZED FOR ANYTHING I RECEIVE FROM YOU.

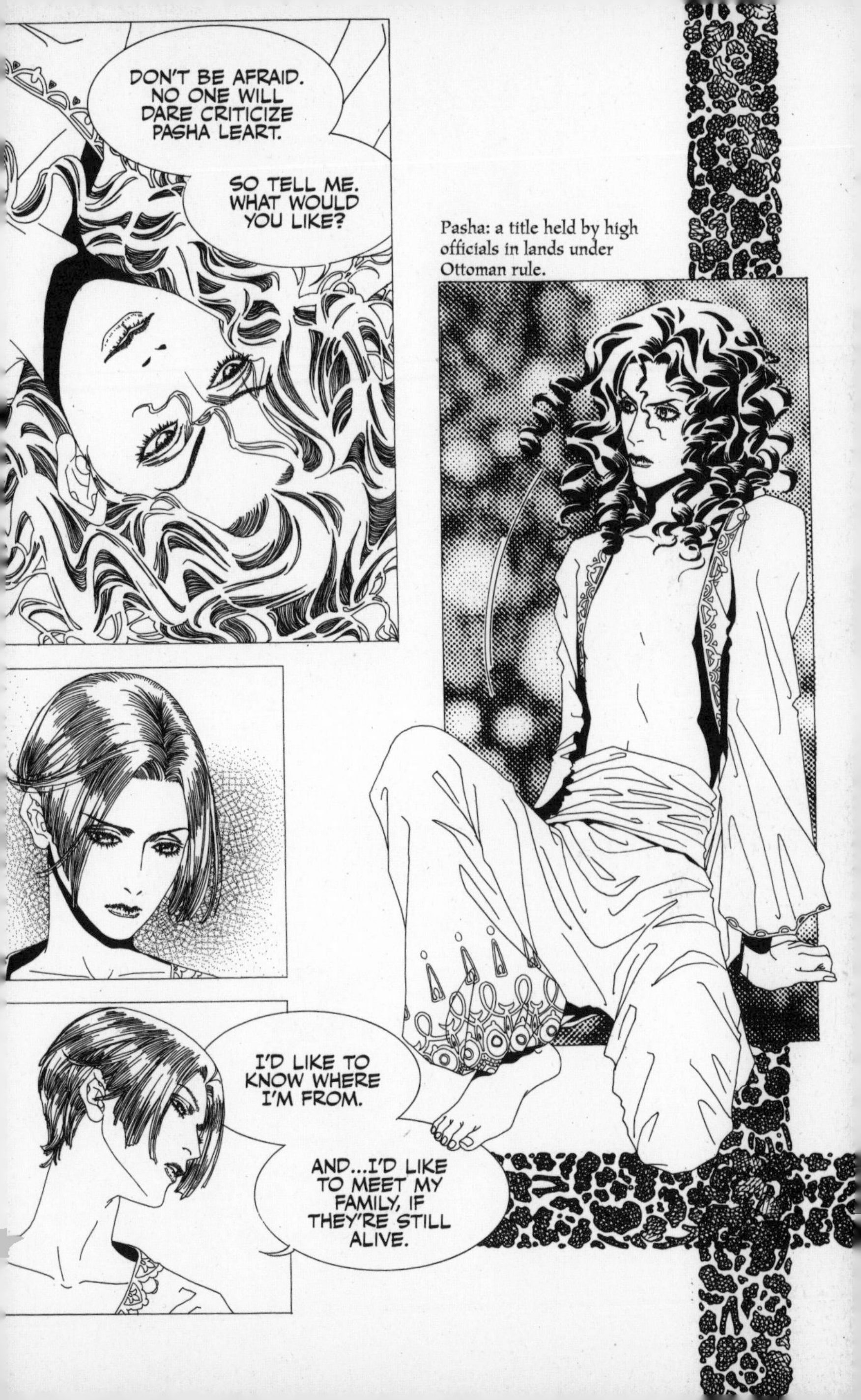
DON'T BE AFRAID. NO ONE WILL DARE CRITICIZE PASHA LEART.
SO TELL ME. WHAT WOULD YOU LIKE?
I'D LIKE TO KNOW WHERE I'M FROM.
AND...I'D LIKE TO MEET MY FAMILY, IF THEY'RE STILL ALIVE.
Pasha: a title held by high officials in lands under Ottoman rule.

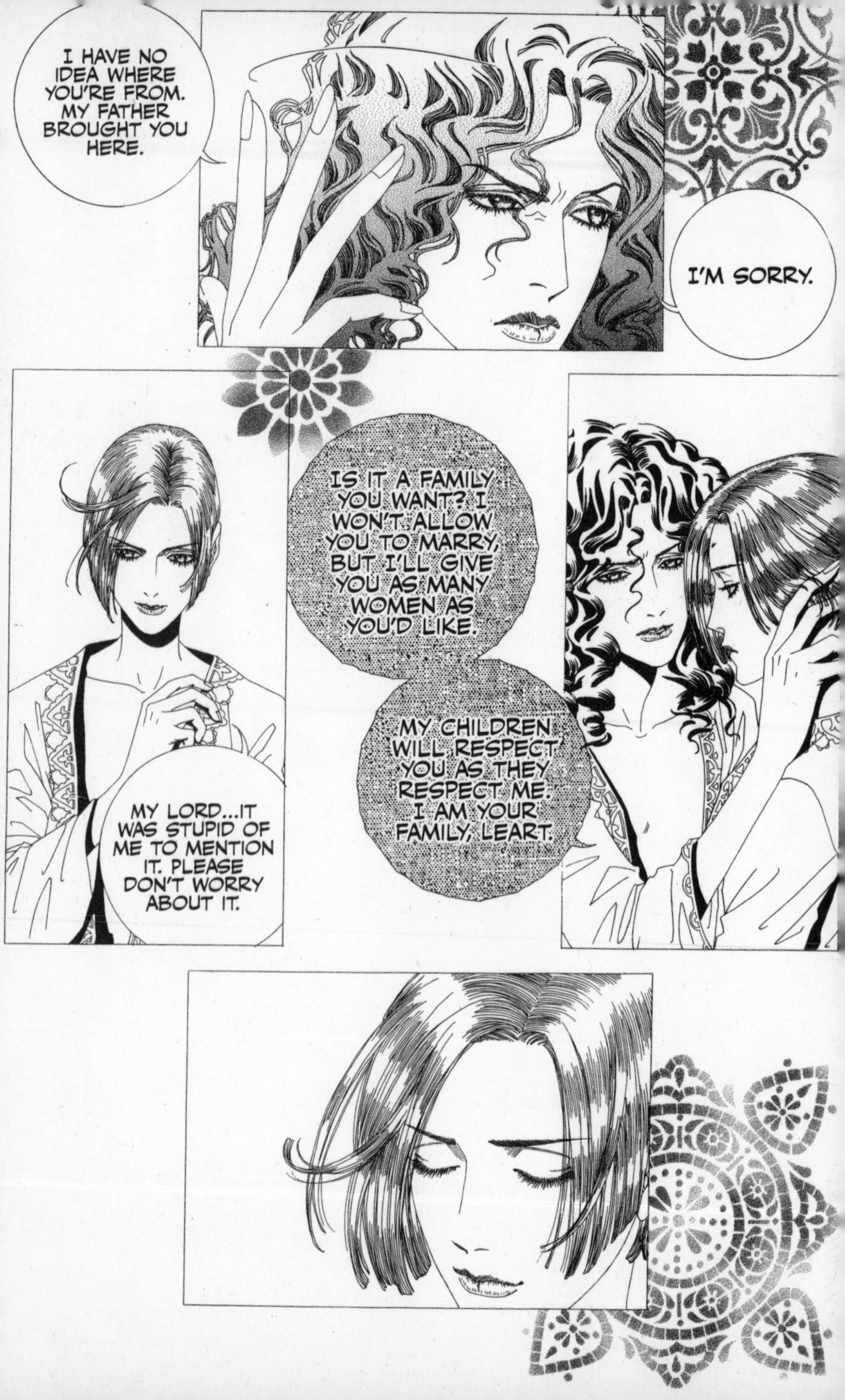
I HAVE NO IDEA WHERE YOU'RE FROM. MY FATHER BROUGHT YOU HERE.
I'M SORRY.
MY LORD...IT WAS STUPID OF ME TO MENTION IT. PLEASE DON'T WORRY ABOUT IT.
IS IT A FAMILY YOU WANT? I WON'T ALLOW YOU TO MARRY, BUT I'LL GIVE YOU AS MANY WOMEN AS YOU'D LIKE.
MY CHILDREN WILL RESPECT YOU AS THEY RESPECT ME. I AM YOUR FAMILY, LEART.

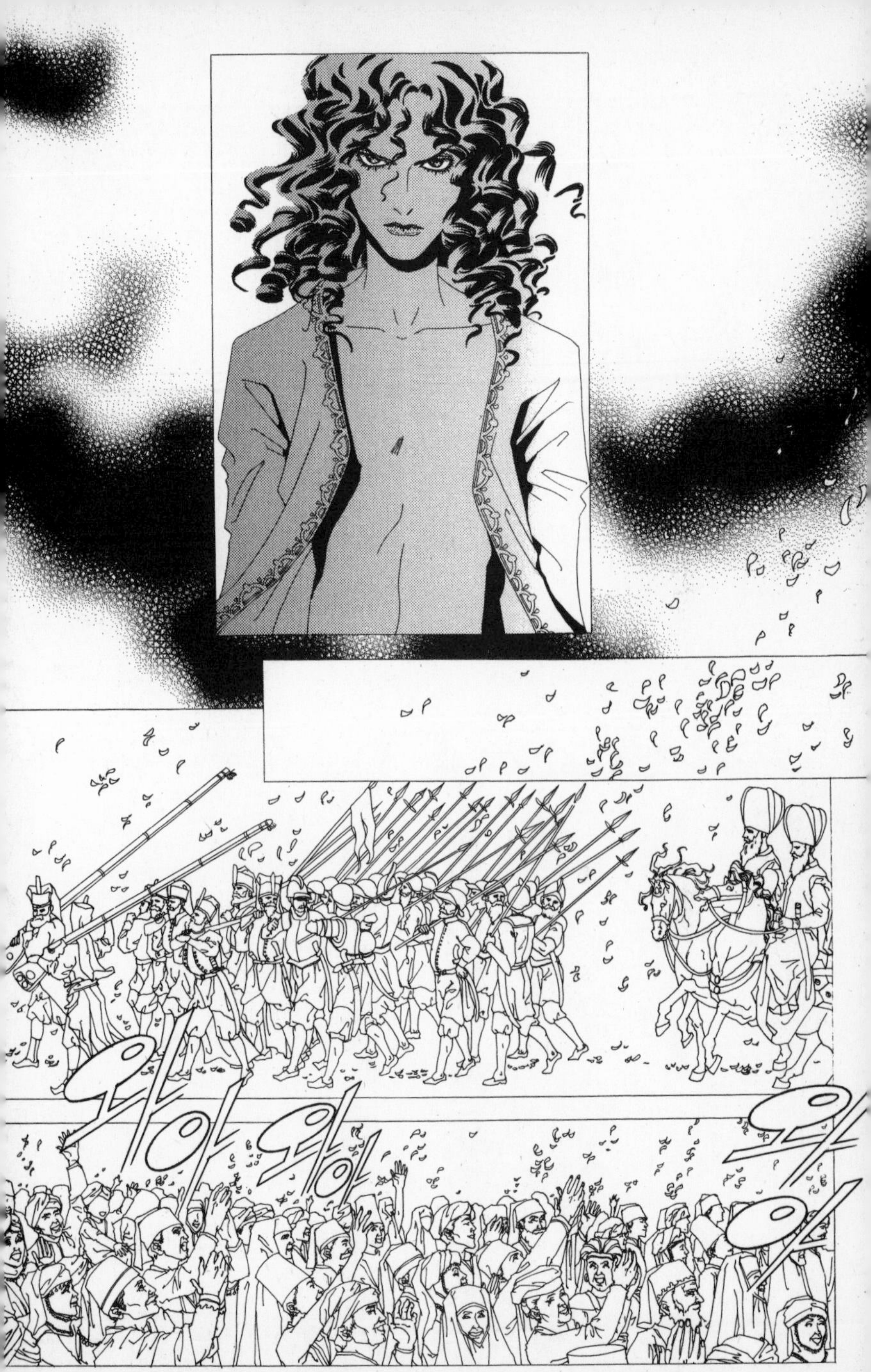
와아 와아
와아

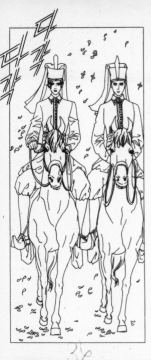

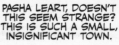

PASHA LEART, DOESN'T THIS SEEM STRANGE? THIS IS SUCH A SMALL, INSIGNIFICANT TOWN.

AND WE'RE SUPPOSED TO SLAUGHTER EVERY LIVING THING... INCLUDING WOMEN AND CHILDREN.

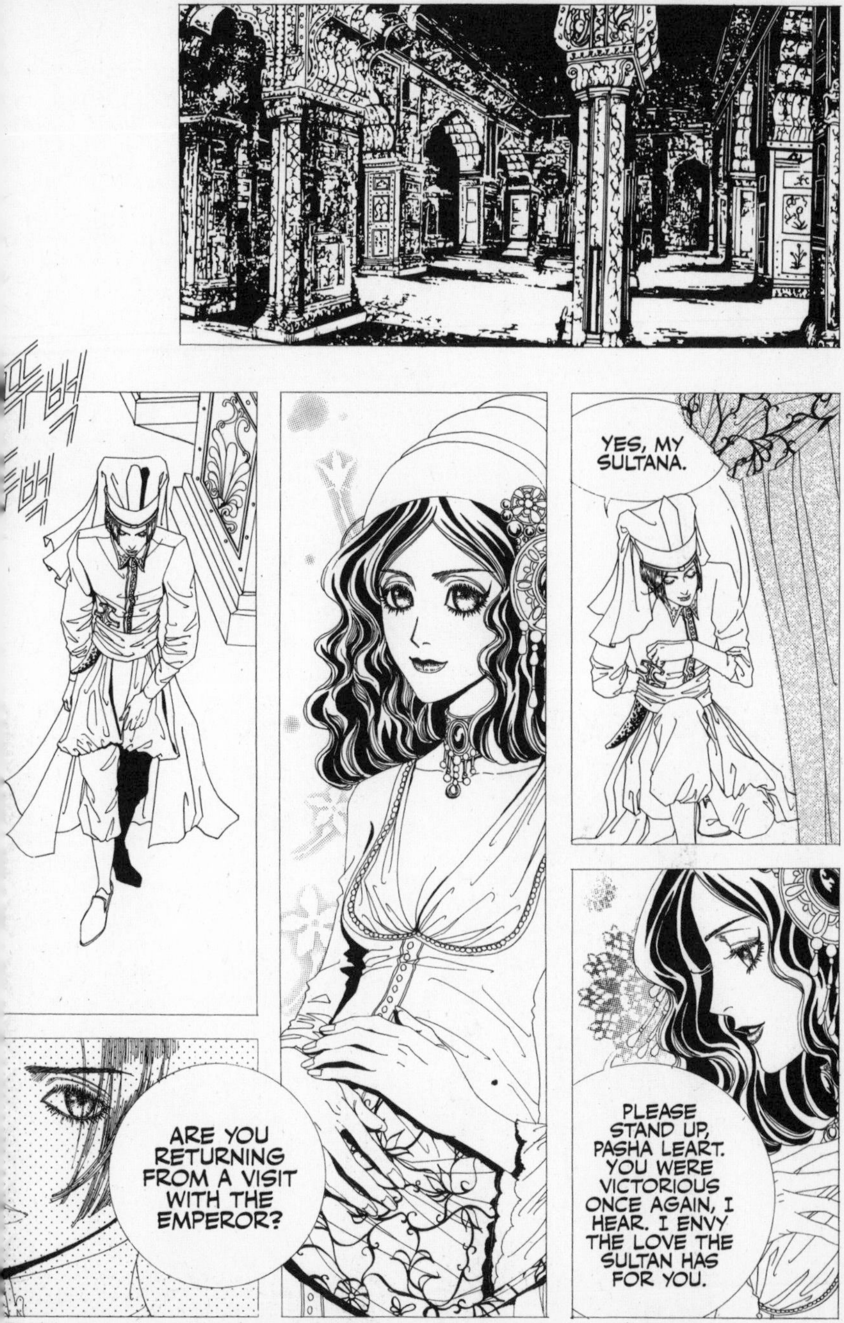
뚜벅
뚜벅
ARE YOU RETURNING FROM A VISIT WITH THE EMPEROR?
YES, MY SULTANA.
PLEASE STAND UP, PASHA LEART. YOU WERE VICTORIOUS ONCE AGAIN, I HEAR. I ENVY THE LOVE THE SULTAN HAS FOR YOU.

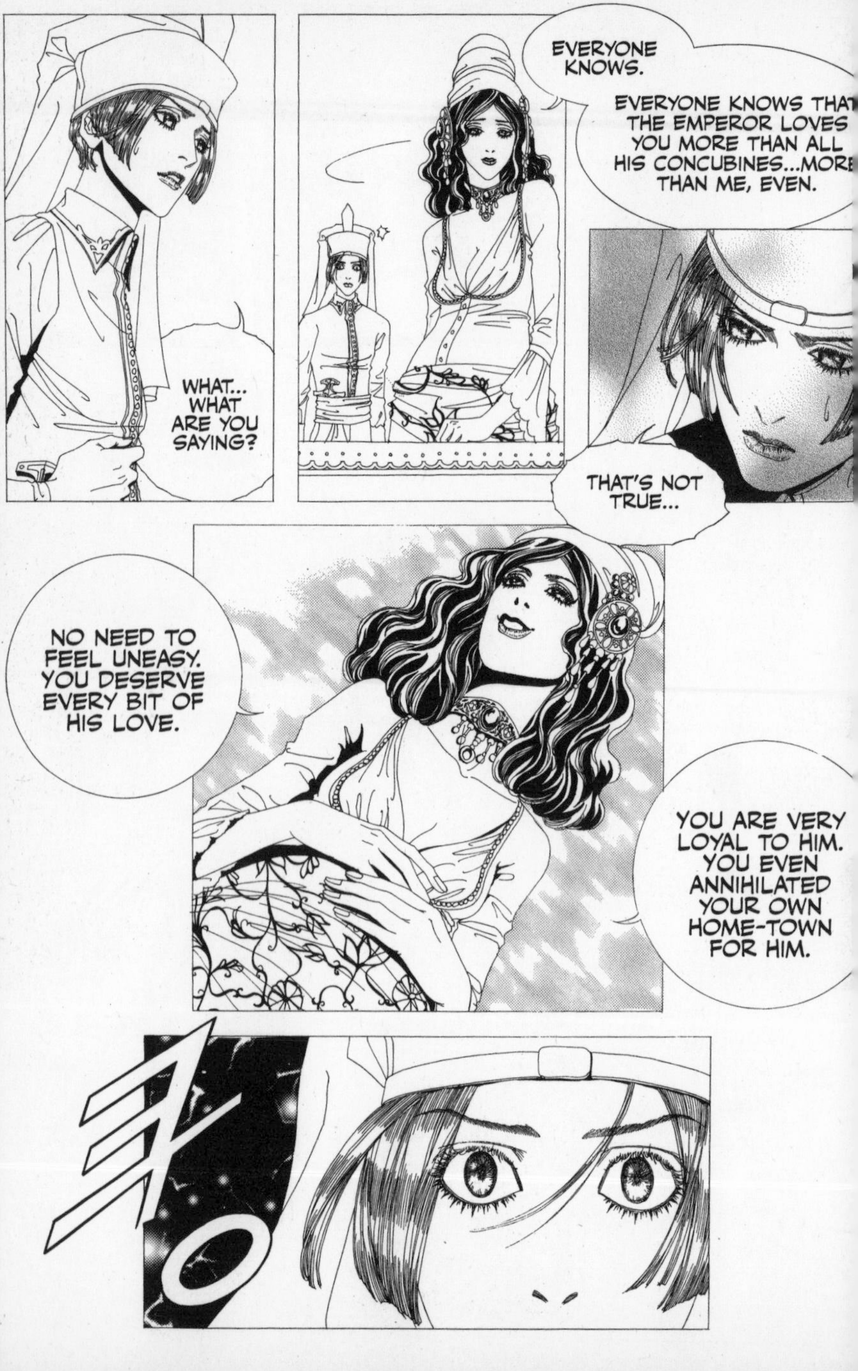
WHAT... WHAT ARE YOU SAYING?
EVERYONE KNOWS.
EVERYONE KNOWS THAT THE EMPEROR LOVES YOU MORE THAN ALL HIS CONCUBINES...MORE THAN ME, EVEN.
THAT'S NOT TRUE...
NO NEED TO FEEL UNEASY. YOU DESERVE EVERY BIT OF HIS LOVE.
YOU ARE VERY LOYAL TO HIM. YOU EVEN ANNIHILATED YOUR OWN HOME-TOWN FOR HIM.

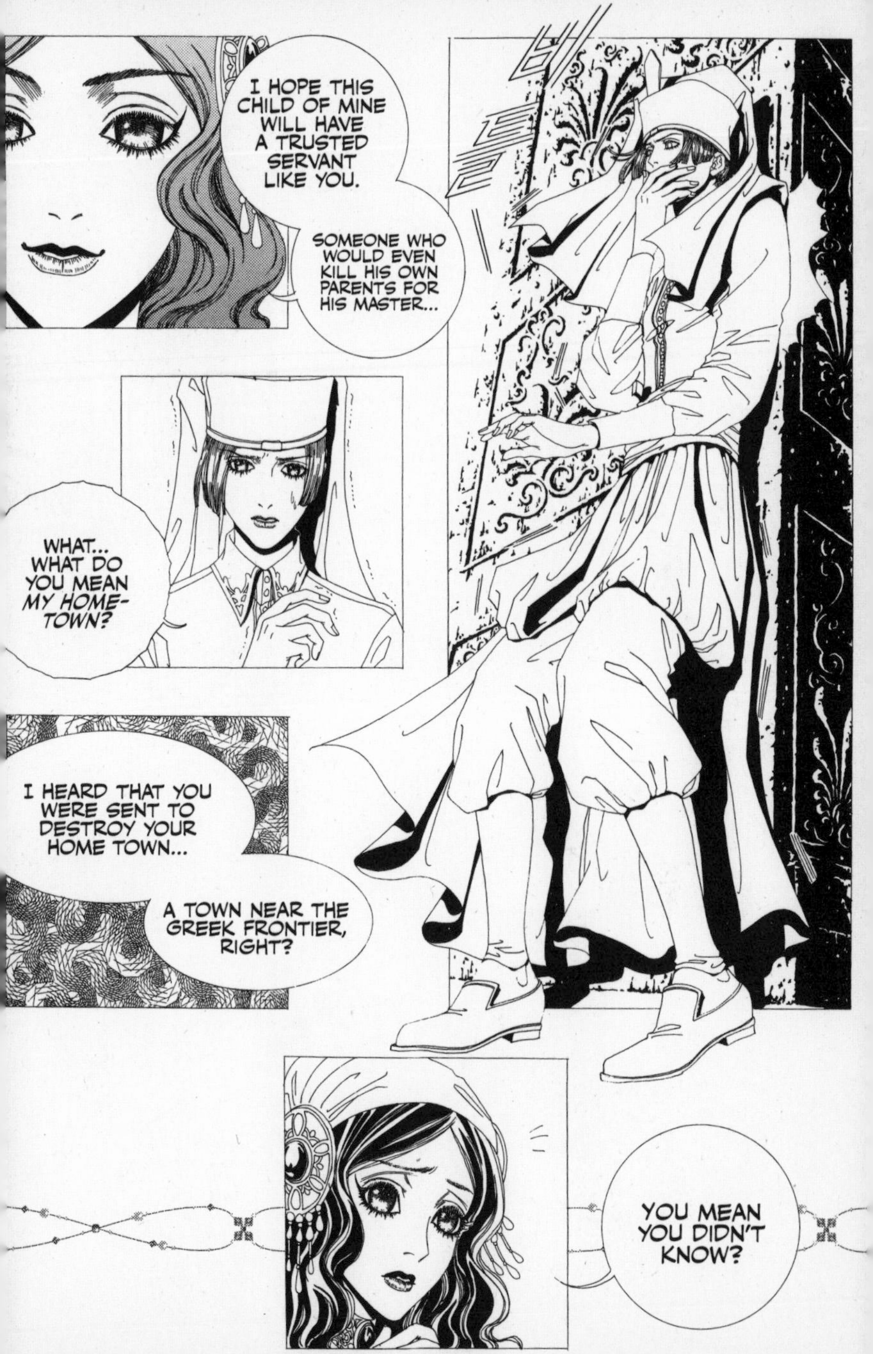
I HOPE THIS CHILD OF MINE WILL HAVE A TRUSTED SERVANT LIKE YOU.
SOMEONE WHO WOULD EVEN KILL HIS OWN PARENTS FOR HIS MASTER...
WHAT... WHAT DO YOU MEAN MY *HOME-TOWN*?
I HEARD THAT YOU WERE SENT TO DESTROY YOUR HOME TOWN...
A TOWN NEAR THE GREEK FRONTIER, RIGHT?
YOU MEAN YOU DIDN'T KNOW?

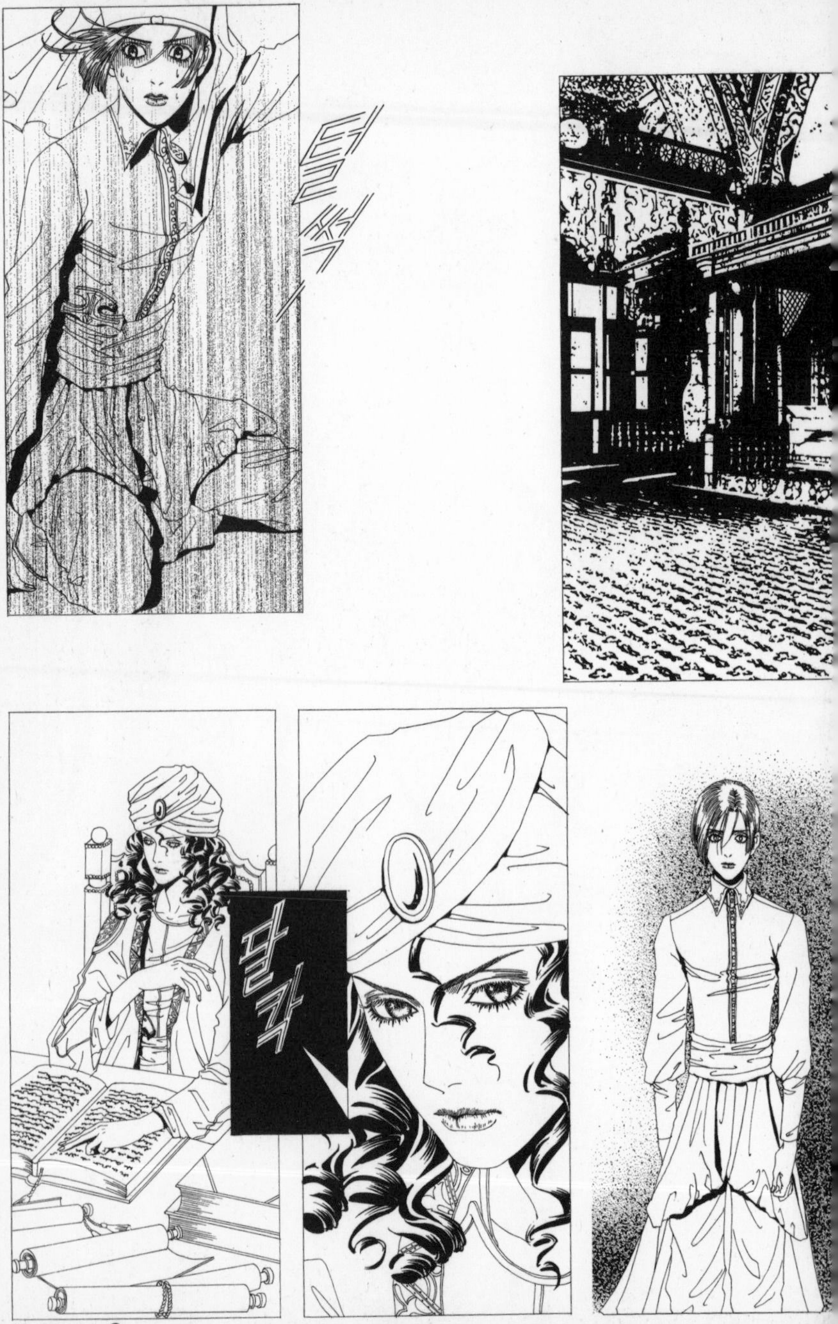
덜썩

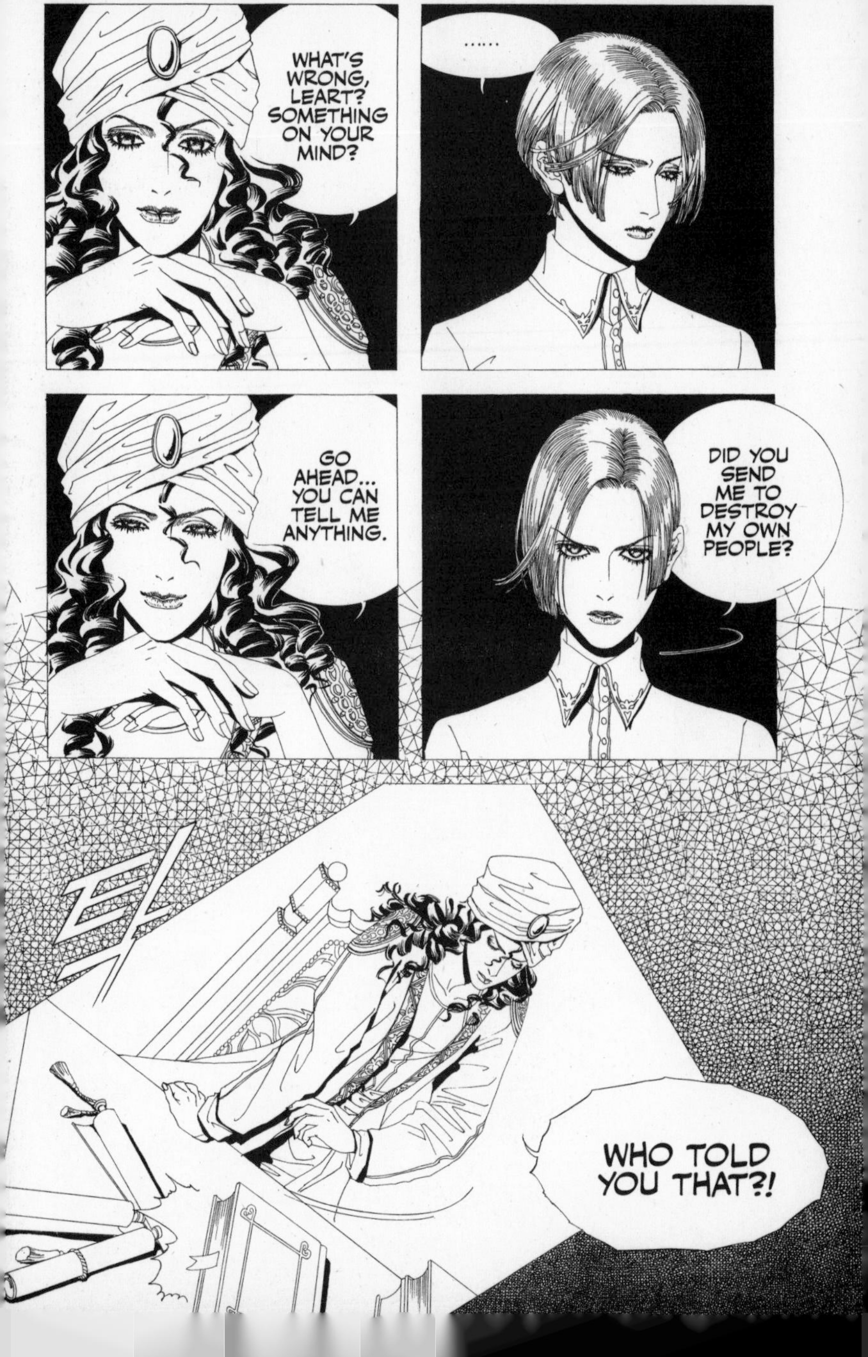
WHAT'S WRONG, LEART? SOMETHING ON YOUR MIND?
......
GO AHEAD... YOU CAN TELL ME ANYTHING.
DID YOU SEND ME TO DESTROY MY OWN PEOPLE?
WHO TOLD YOU THAT?!

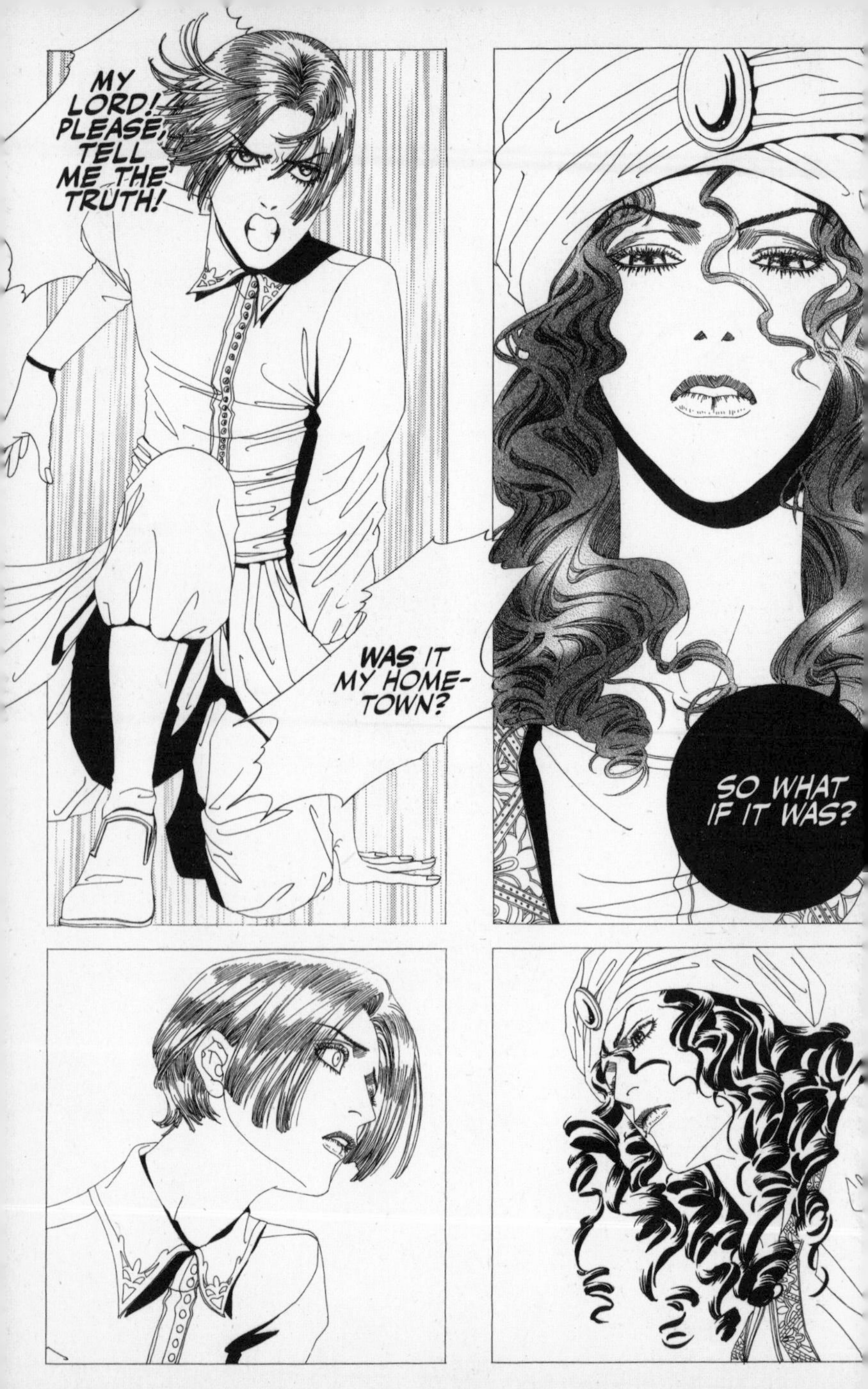
MY LORD! PLEASE, TELL ME THE TRUTH!
WAS IT MY HOME-TOWN?
SO WHAT IF IT WAS?

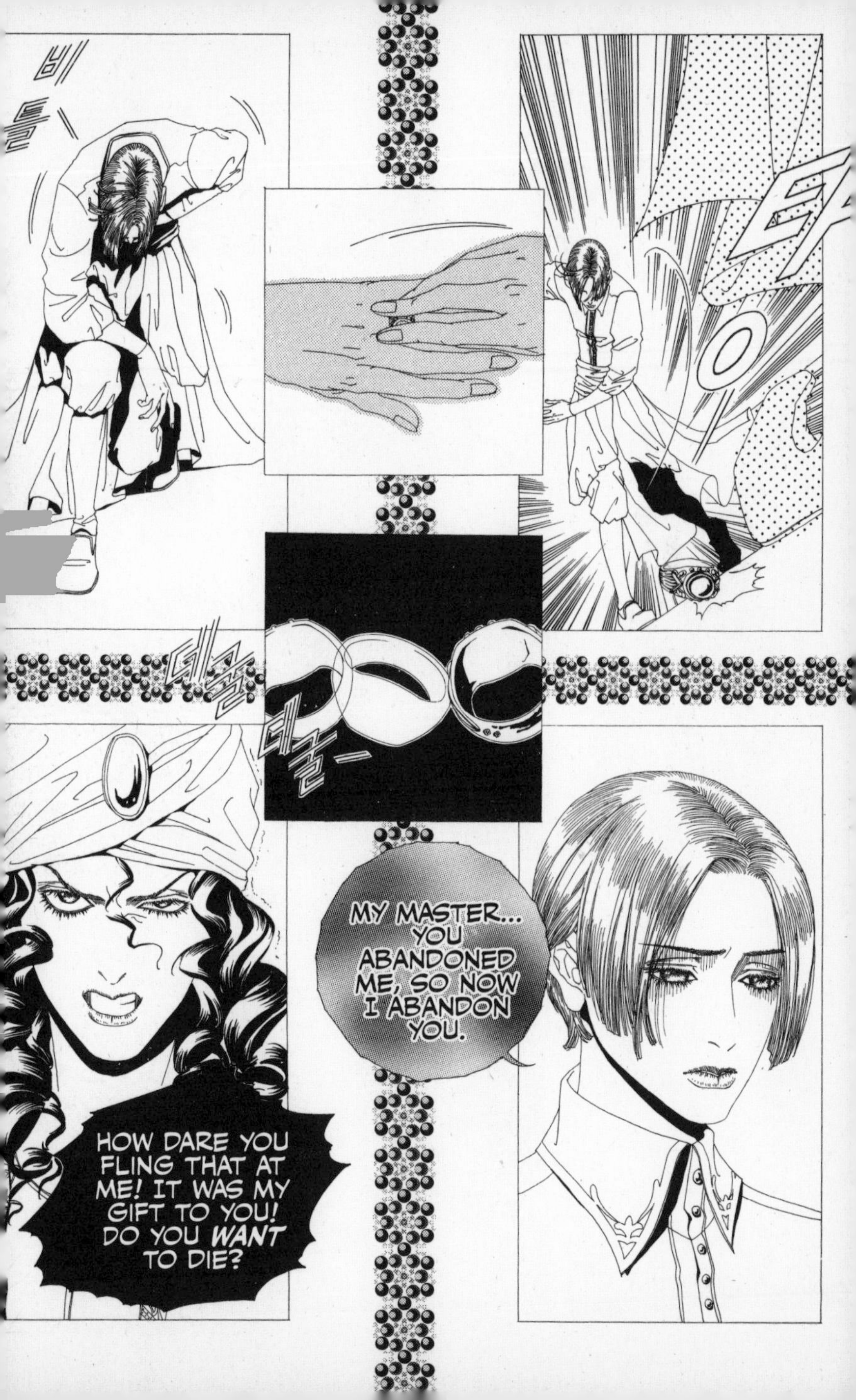
비틀
데굴
데굴—
HOW DARE YOU FLING THAT AT ME! IT WAS MY GIFT TO YOU! DO YOU *WANT* TO DIE?
MY MASTER... YOU ABANDONED ME, SO NOW I ABANDON YOU.

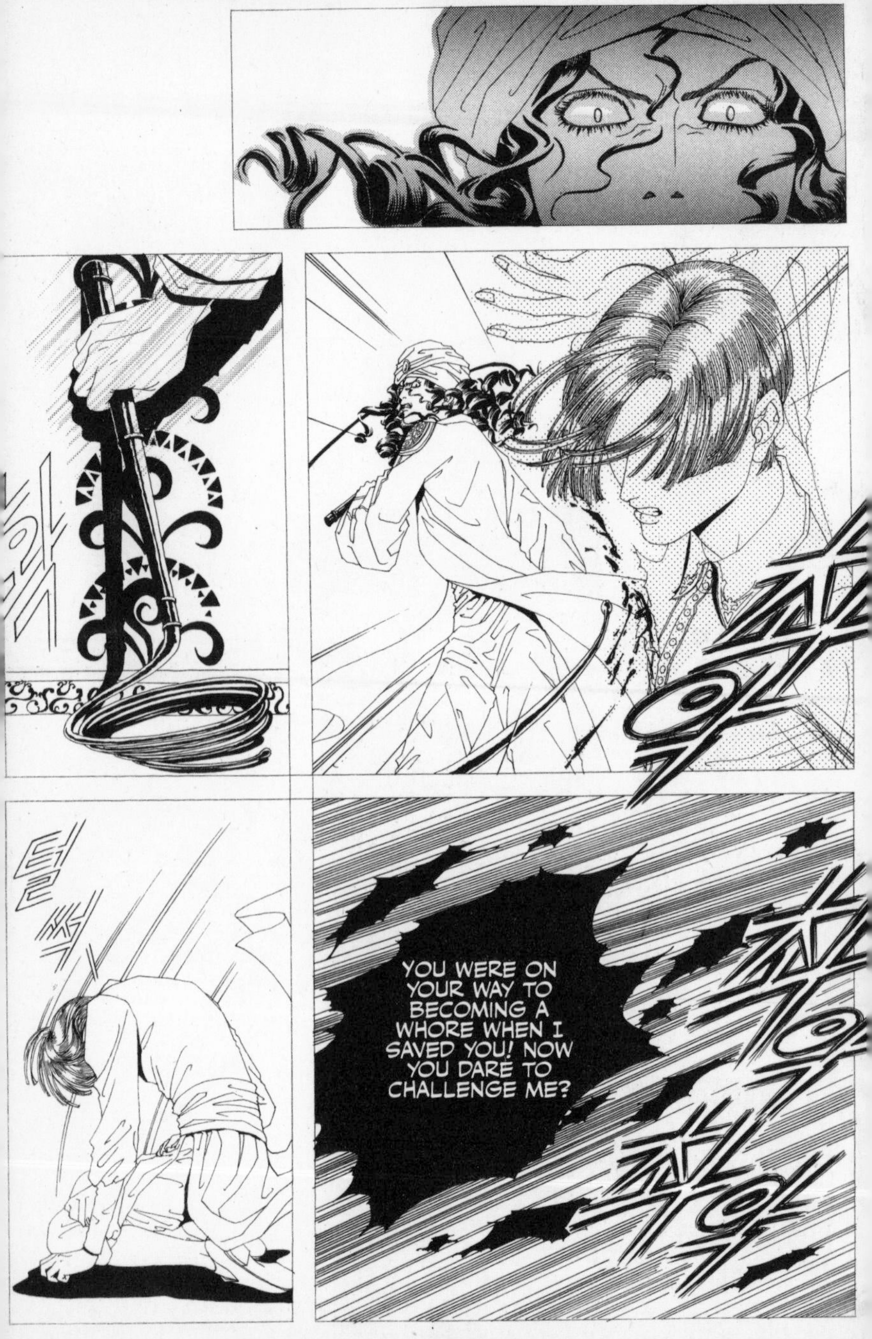
YOU WERE ON YOUR WAY TO BECOMING A WHORE WHEN I SAVED YOU! NOW YOU DARE TO CHALLENGE ME?

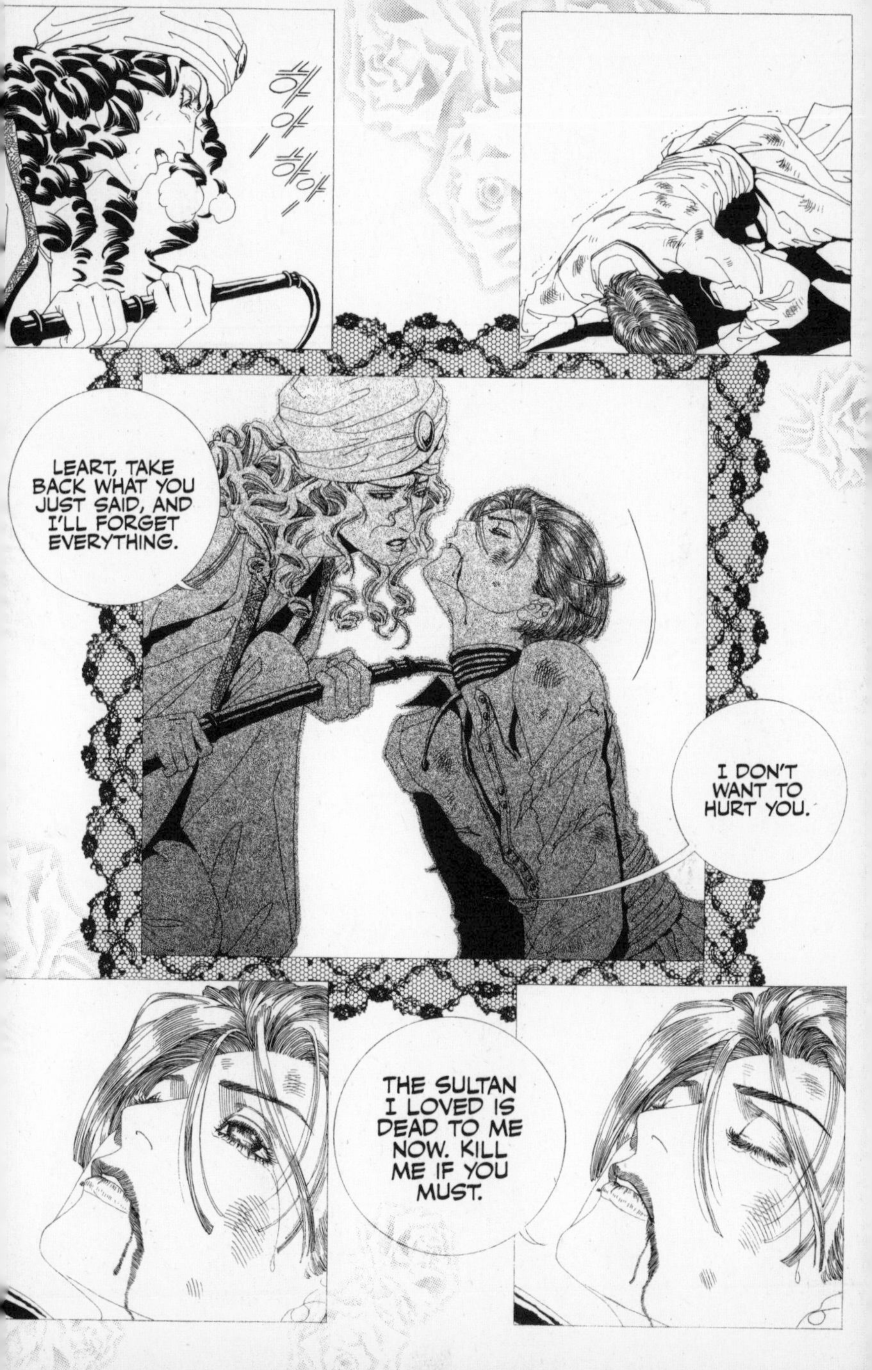

하아 하아
LEART, TAKE BACK WHAT YOU JUST SAID, AND I'LL FORGET EVERYTHING.
I DON'T WANT TO HURT YOU.
THE SULTAN I LOVED IS DEAD TO ME NOW. KILL ME IF YOU MUST.

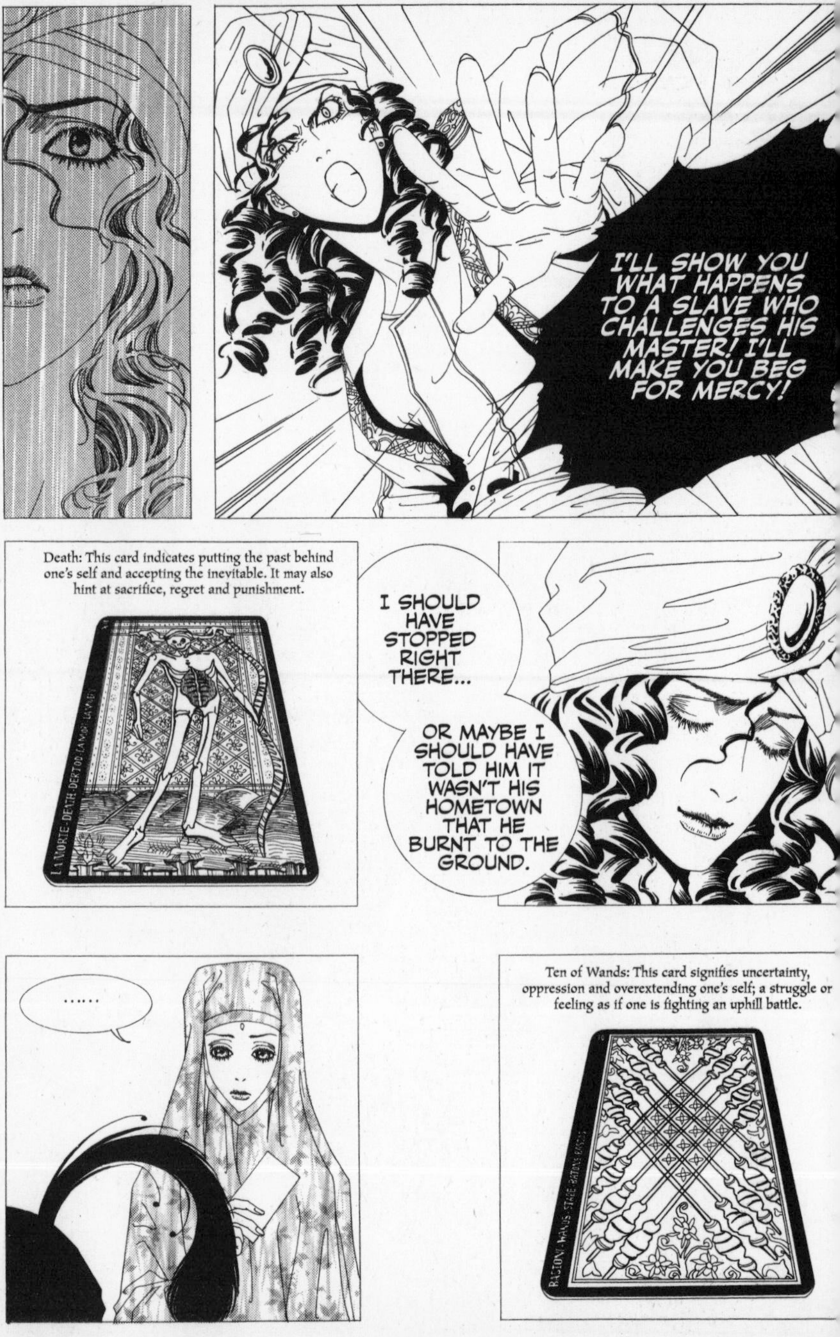
I'LL SHOW YOU WHAT HAPPENS TO A SLAVE WHO CHALLENGES HIS MASTER! I'LL MAKE YOU BEG FOR MERCY!
Death: This card indicates putting the past behind one's self and accepting the inevitable. It may also hint at sacrifice, regret and punishment.
I SHOULD HAVE STOPPED RIGHT THERE...
OR MAYBE I SHOULD HAVE TOLD HIM IT WASN'T HIS HOMETOWN THAT HE BURNT TO THE GROUND.
......
Ten of Wands: This card signifies uncertainty, oppression and overextending one's self; a struggle or feeling as if one is fighting an uphill battle.

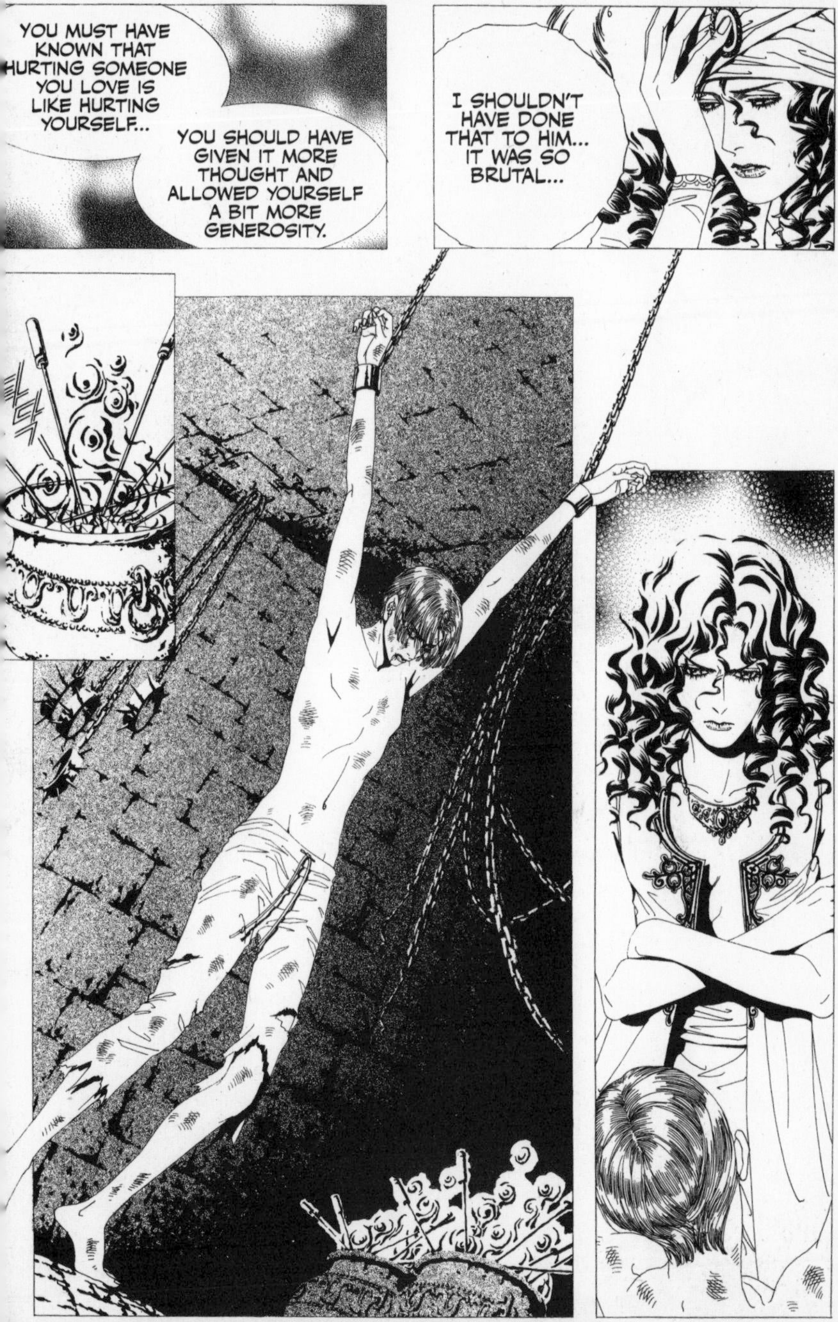
YOU MUST HAVE KNOWN THAT HURTING SOMEONE YOU LOVE IS LIKE HURTING YOURSELF...
YOU SHOULD HAVE GIVEN IT MORE THOUGHT AND ALLOWED YOURSELF A BIT MORE GENEROSITY.
I SHOULDN'T HAVE DONE THAT TO HIM... IT WAS SO BRUTAL...

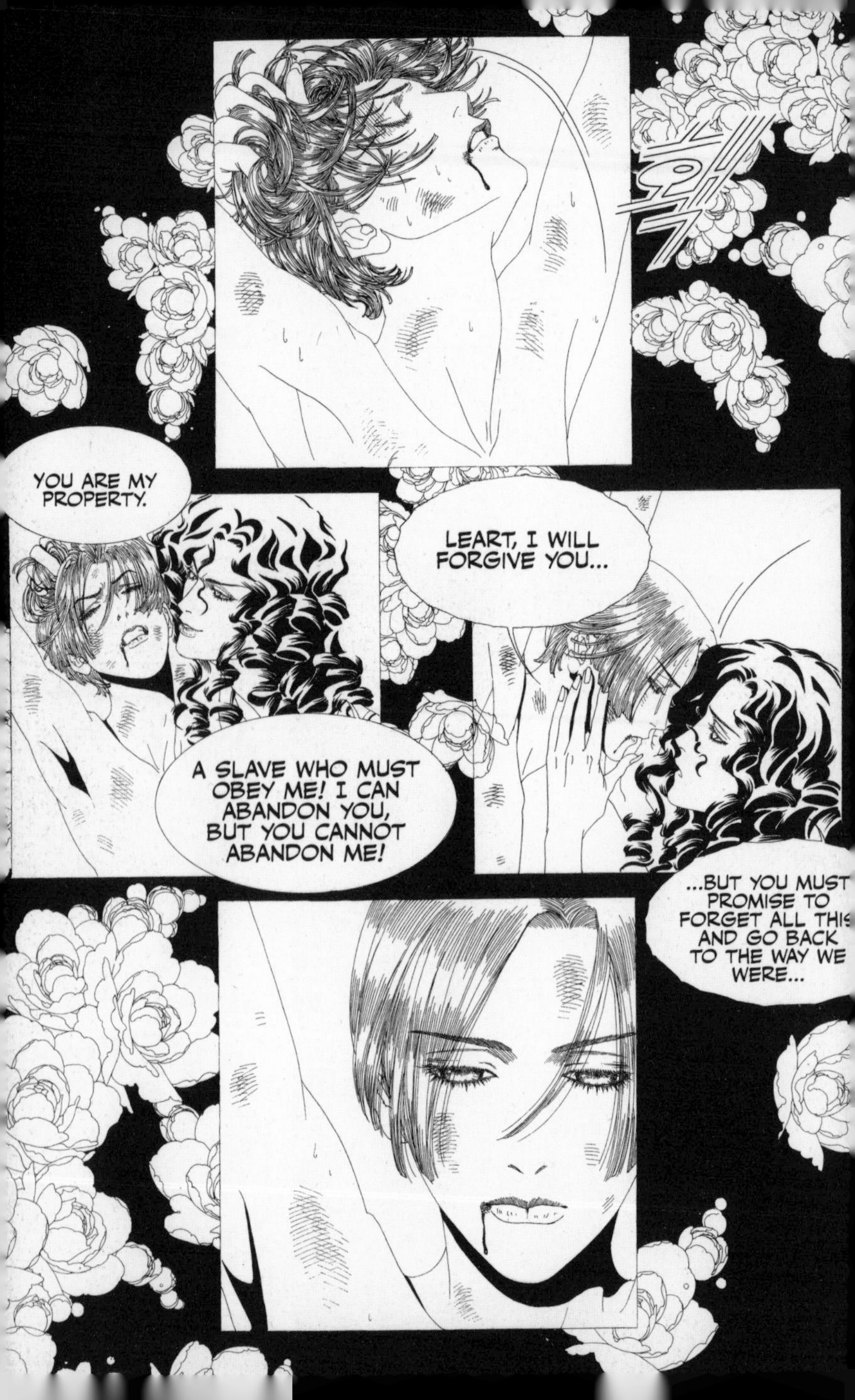
YOU ARE MY PROPERTY.
A SLAVE WHO MUST OBEY ME! I CAN ABANDON YOU, BUT YOU CANNOT ABANDON ME!
LEART, I WILL FORGIVE YOU...
...BUT YOU MUST PROMISE TO FORGET ALL THIS AND GO BACK TO THE WAY WE WERE...

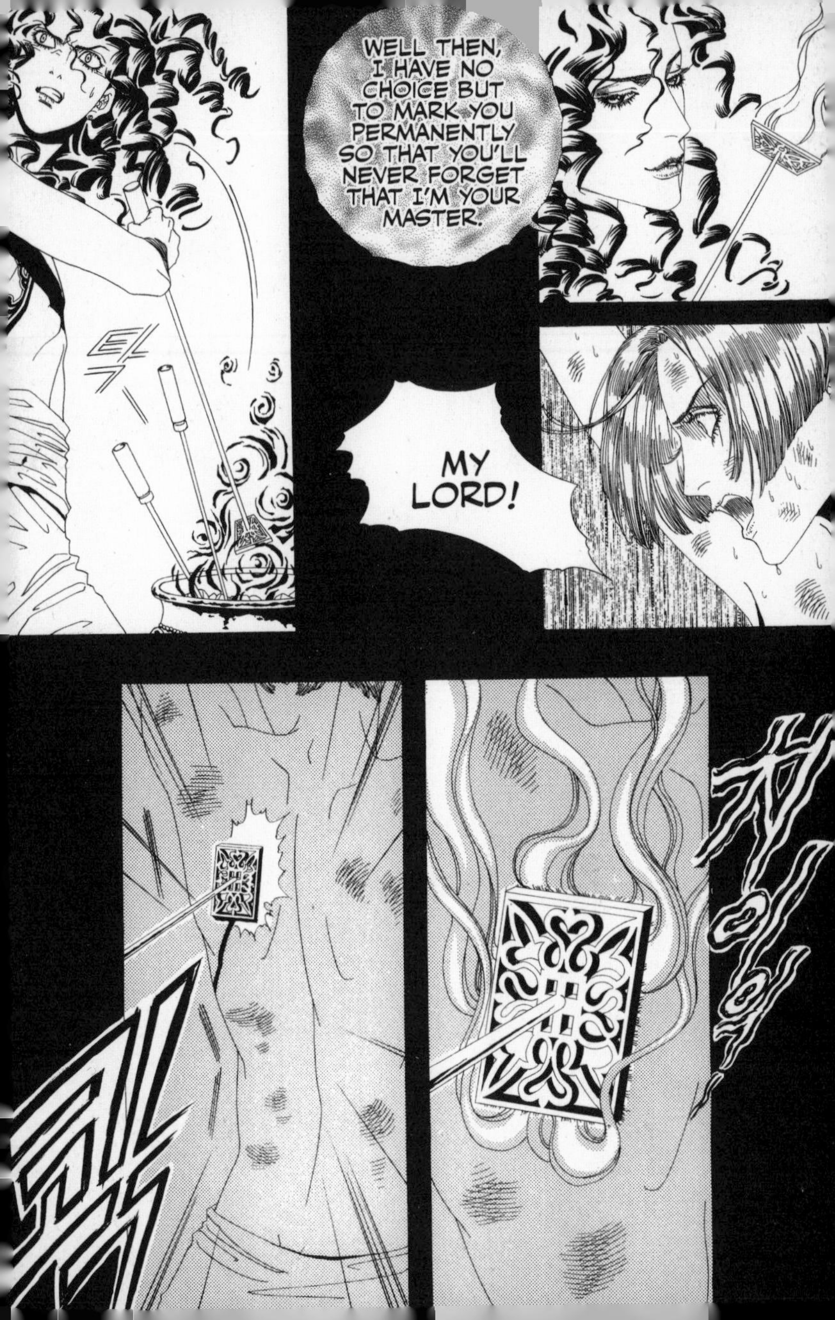
WELL THEN, I HAVE NO CHOICE BUT TO MARK YOU PERMANENTLY SO THAT YOU'LL NEVER FORGET THAT I'M YOUR MASTER.
MY LORD!

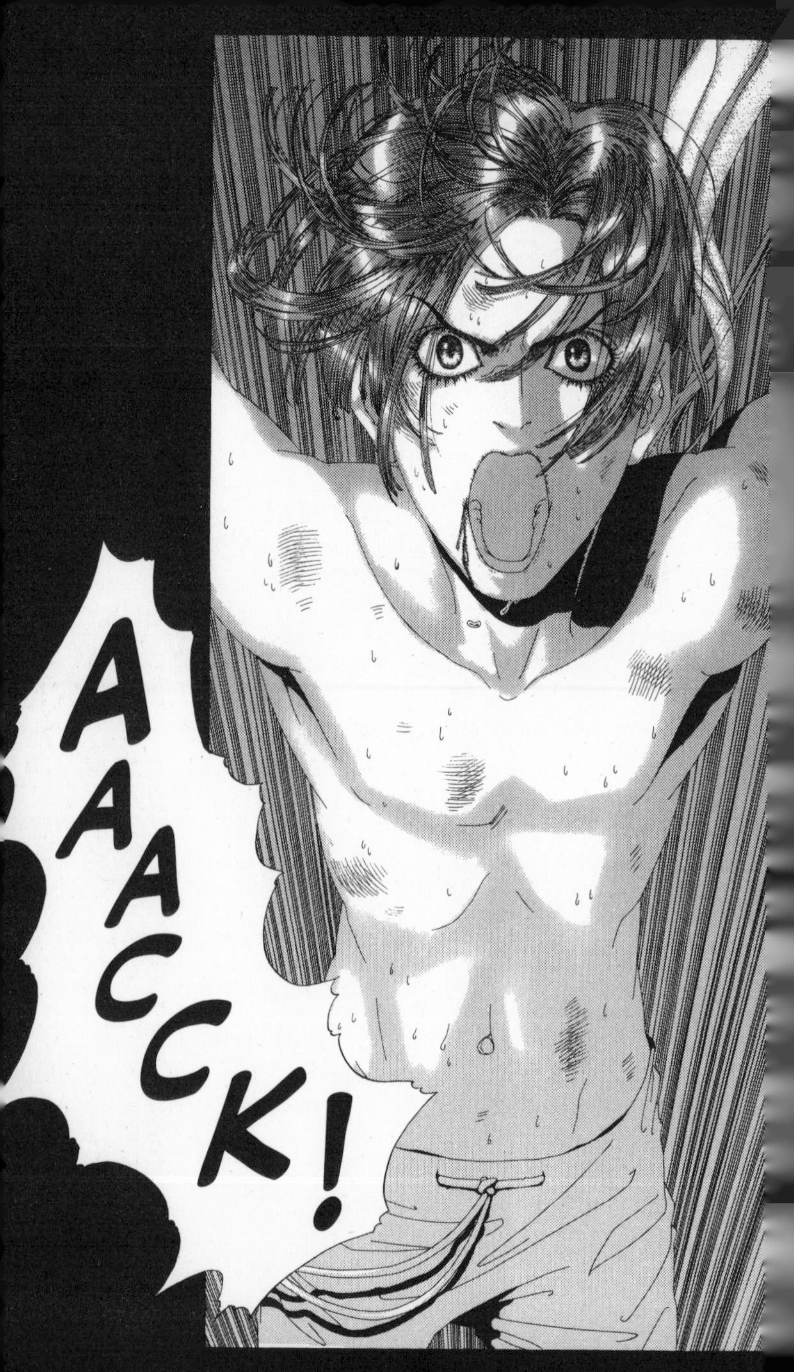
AAACCK!

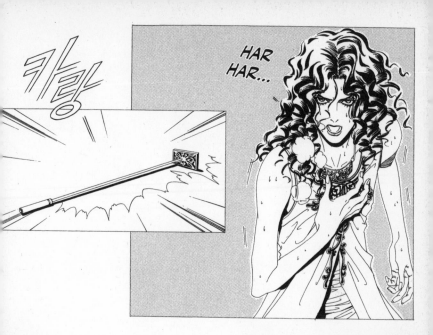

HAR HAR...

YOU EXCELLED IN EVERYTHING...

I WONDERED IF THERE WAS ANYTHING YOU COULDN'T DO.

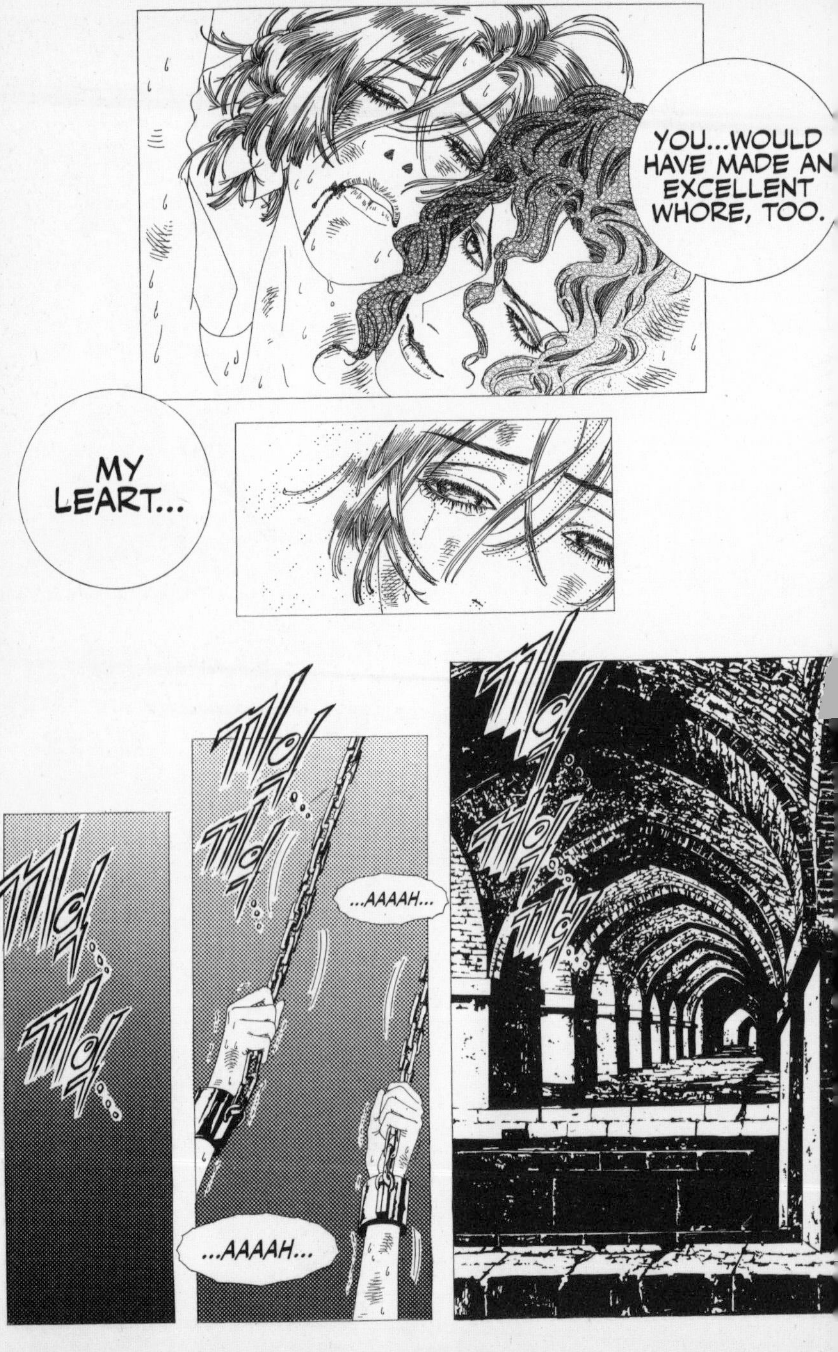

YOU...WOULD HAVE MADE AN EXCELLENT WHORE, TOO.
MY LEART...
...AAAAH...
...AAAAH...

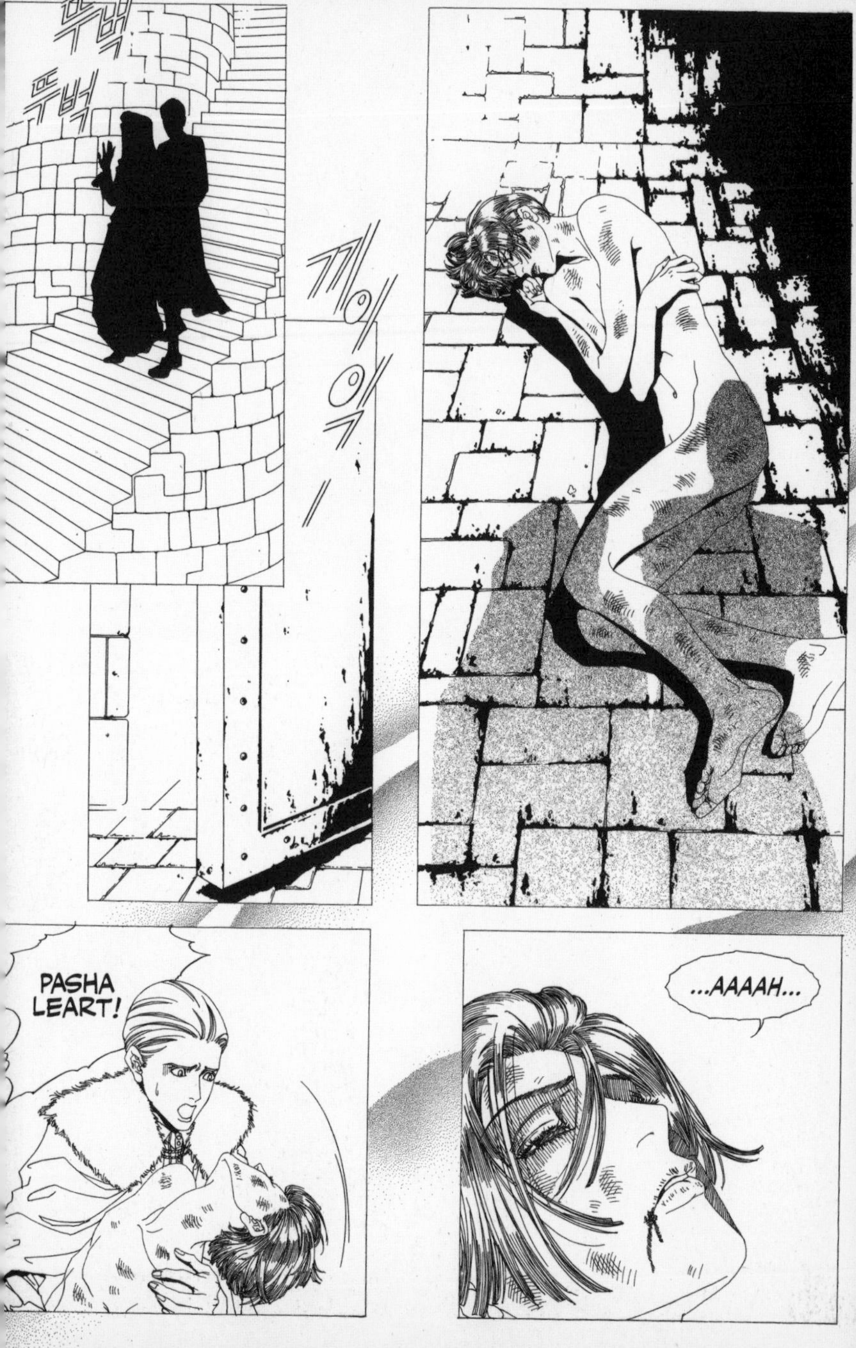
뚜벅
뚜벅
끼이익
PASHA LEART!
...AAAAH...

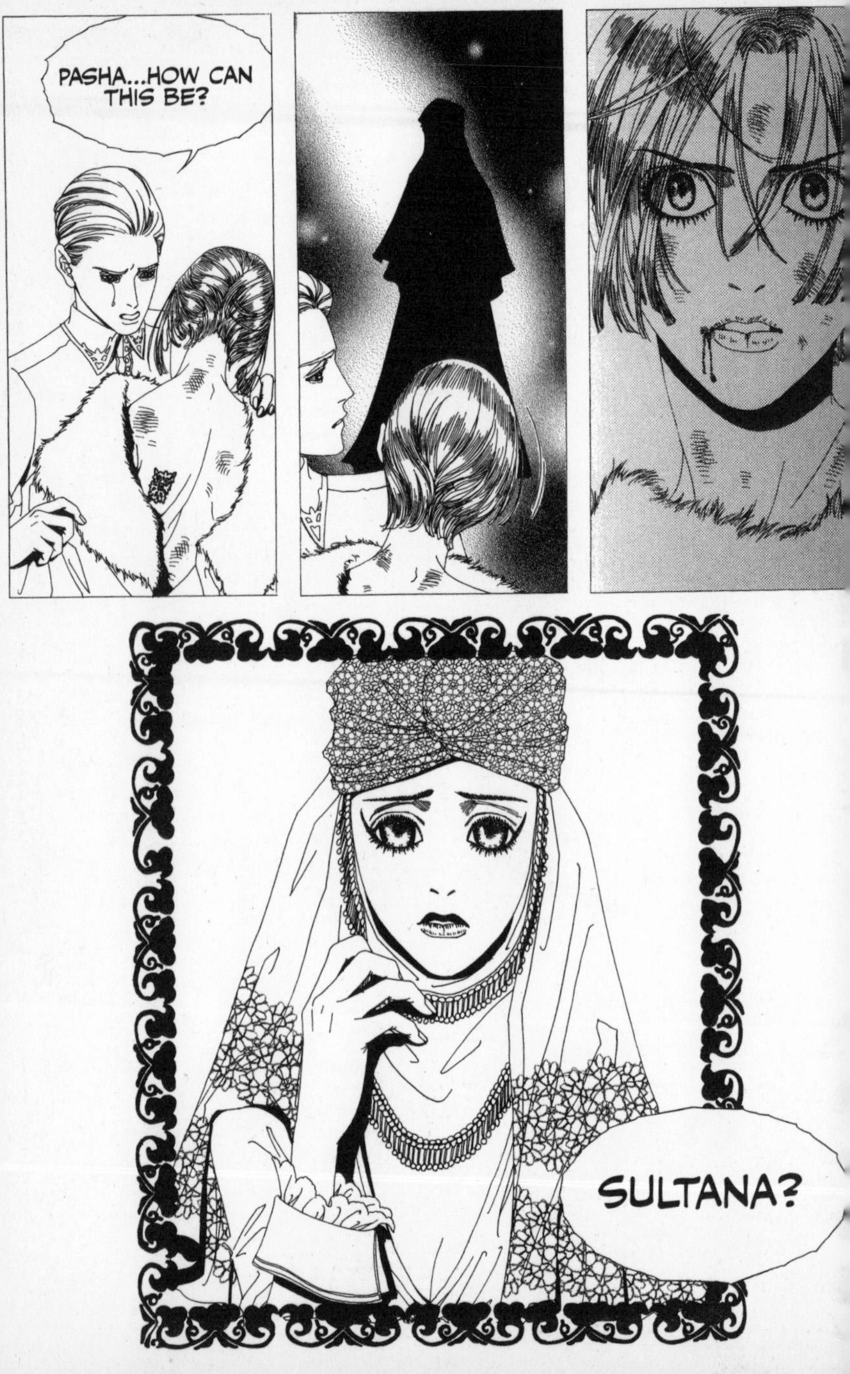
PASHA...HOW CAN THIS BE?
SULTANA?

ILLUSTRATION FROM ART NOUVEAU TAROT DECK

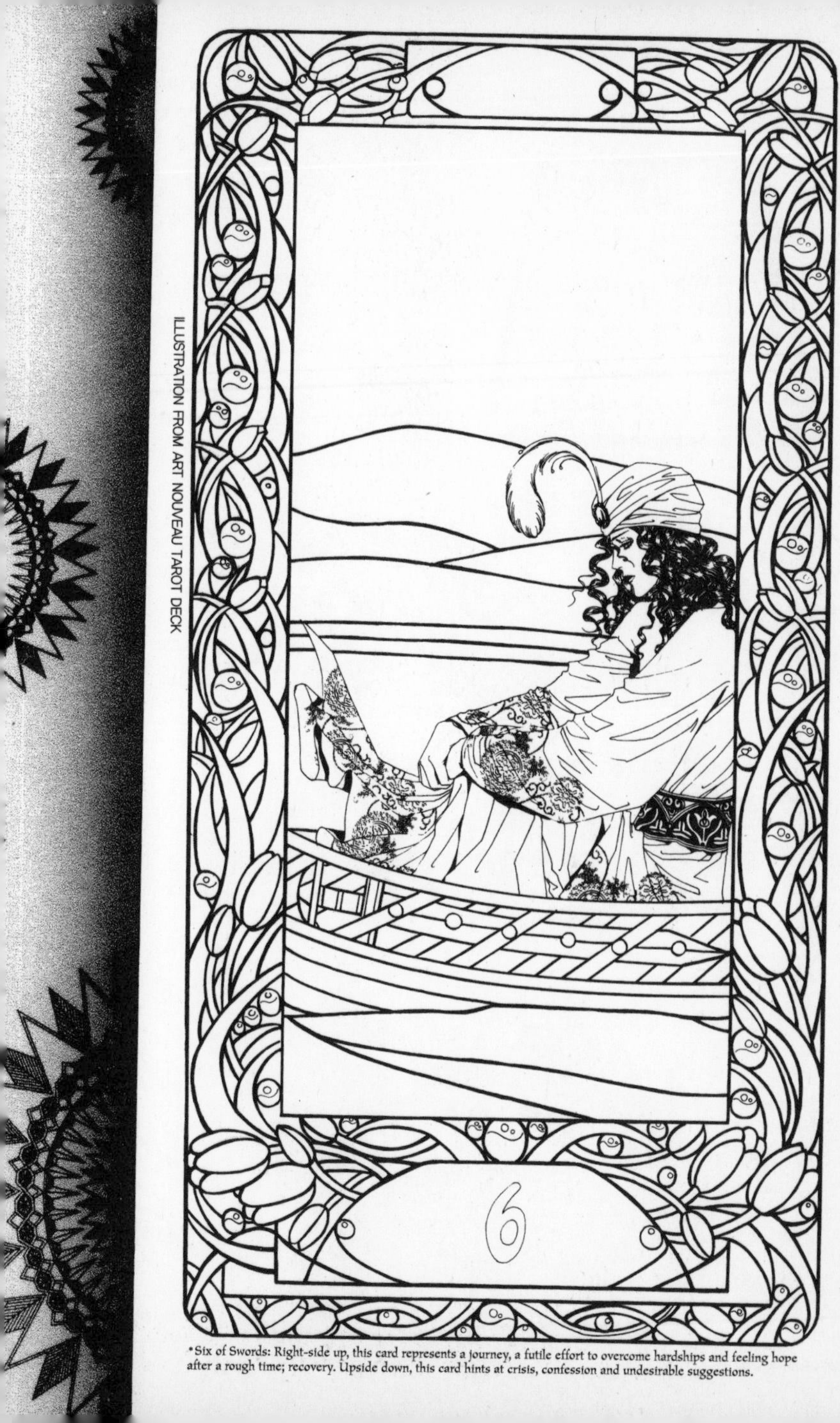
6

*Six of Swords: Right-side up, this card represents a journey, a futile effort to overcome hardships and feeling hope after a rough time; recovery. Upside down, this card hints at crisis, confession and undesirable suggestions.

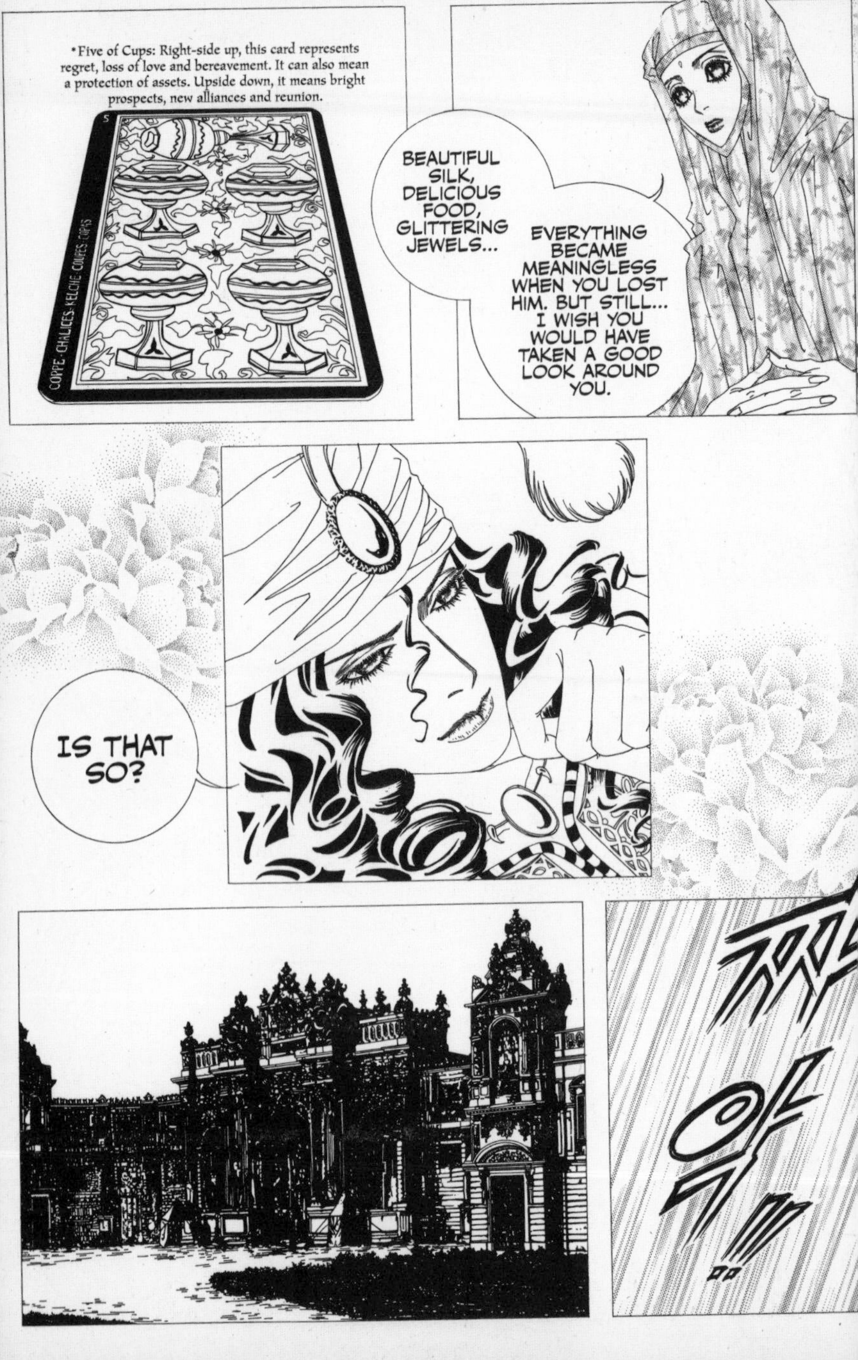
*Five of Cups: Right-side up, this card represents regret, loss of love and bereavement. It can also mean a protection of assets. Upside down, it means bright prospects, new alliances and reunion.
5
COPPE·CHALICES·KELCHE·COUPES·CUPS
BEAUTIFUL SILK, DELICIOUS FOOD, GLITTERING JEWELS...
EVERYTHING BECAME MEANINGLESS WHEN YOU LOST HIM. BUT STILL... I WISH YOU WOULD HAVE TAKEN A GOOD LOOK AROUND YOU.
IS THAT SO?

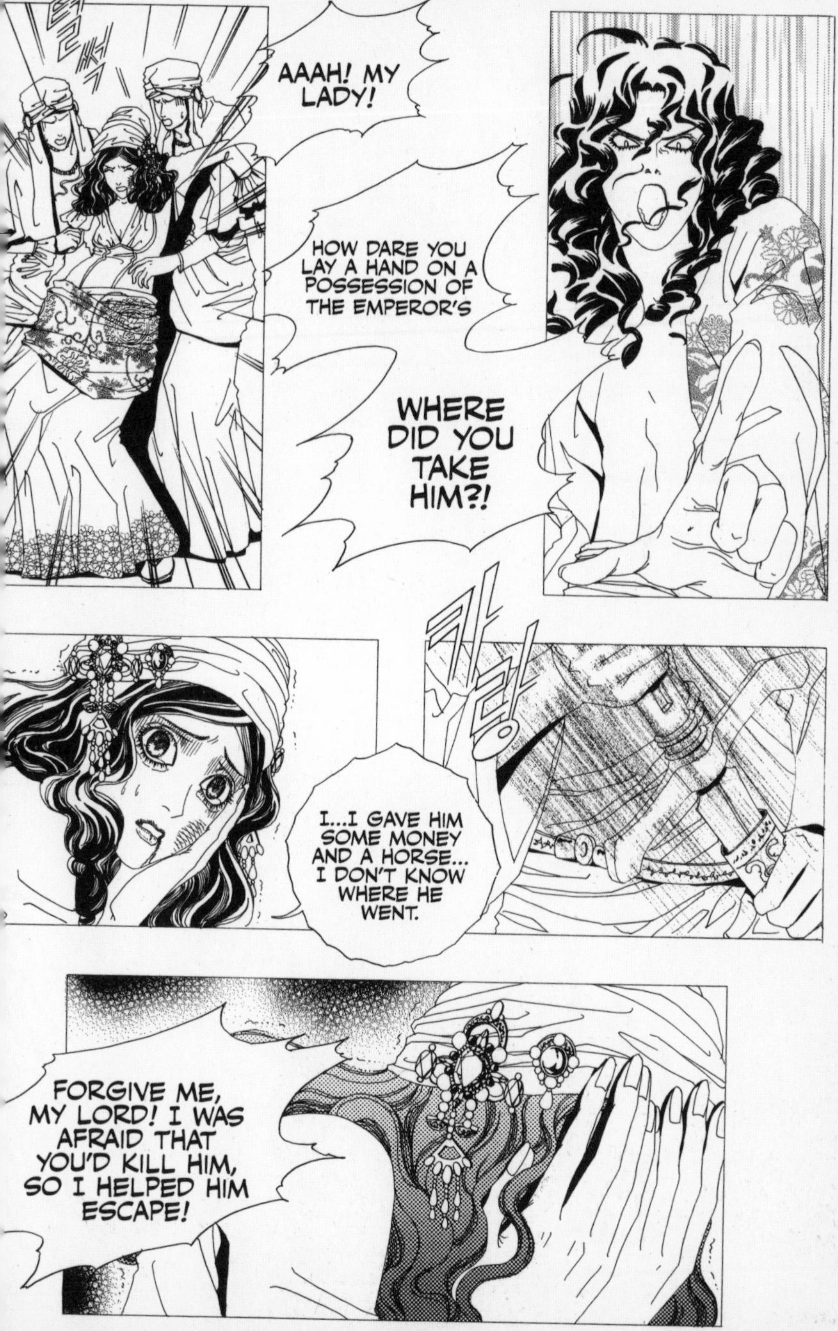
AAAH! MY LADY!
HOW DARE YOU LAY A HAND ON A POSSESSION OF THE EMPEROR'S
WHERE DID YOU TAKE HIM?!
I...I GAVE HIM SOME MONEY AND A HORSE... I DON'T KNOW WHERE HE WENT.
FORGIVE ME, MY LORD! I WAS AFRAID THAT YOU'D KILL HIM, SO I HELPED HIM ESCAPE!

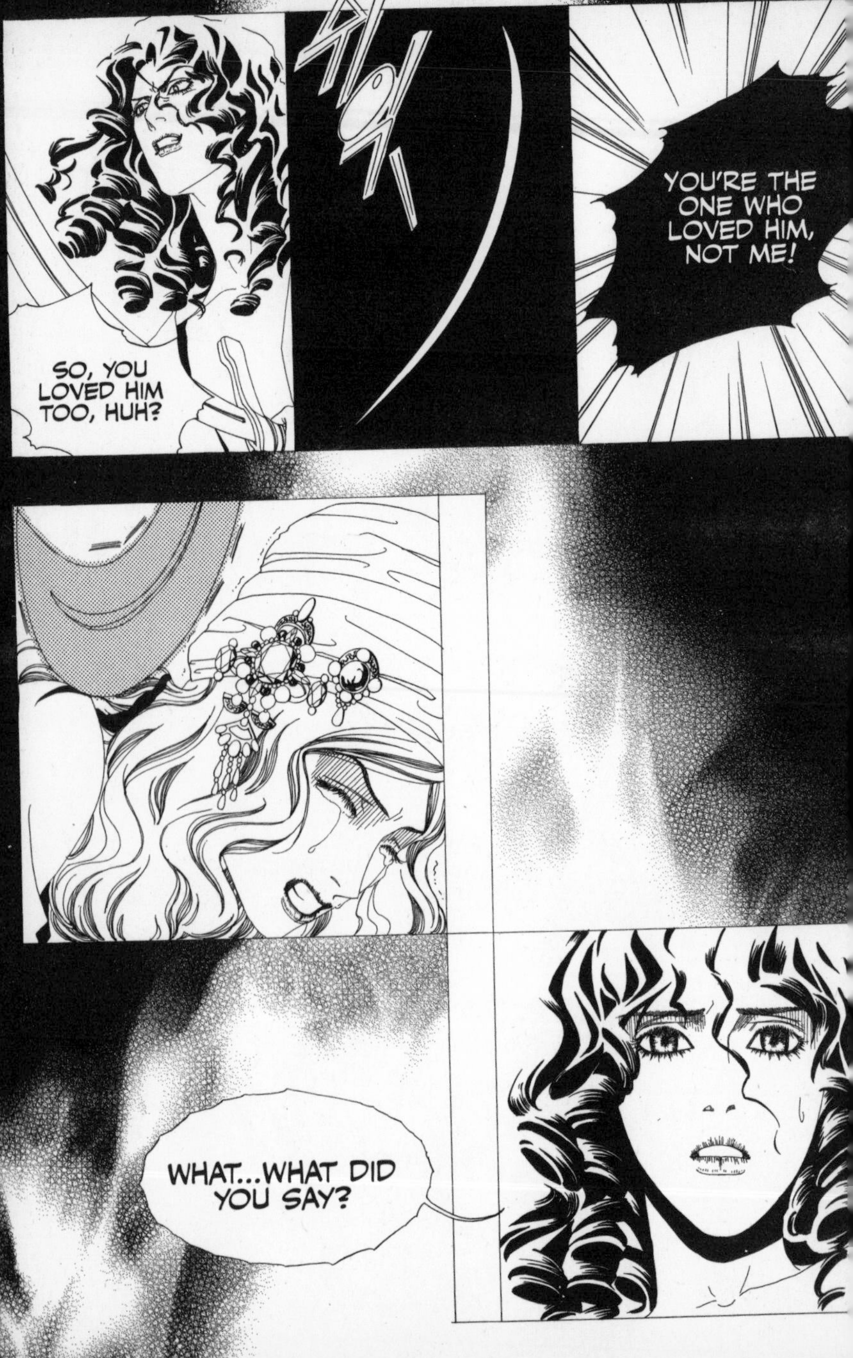
SO, YOU LOVED HIM TOO, HUH?
YOU'RE THE ONE WHO LOVED HIM, NOT ME!
WHAT...WHAT DID YOU SAY?

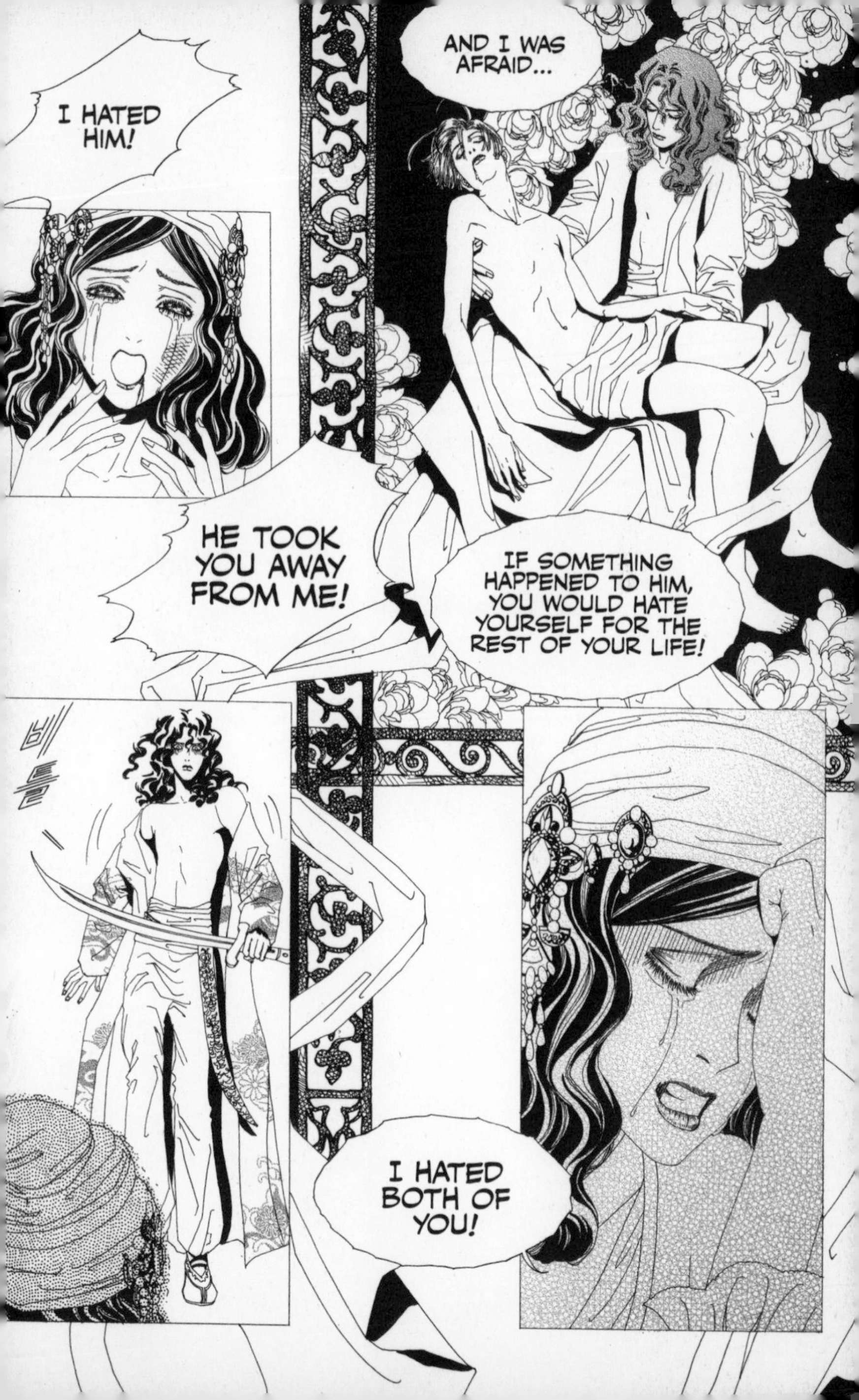
I HATED HIM!
HE TOOK YOU AWAY FROM ME!
AND I WAS AFRAID...
IF SOMETHING HAPPENED TO HIM, YOU WOULD HATE YOURSELF FOR THE REST OF YOUR LIFE!
비틀
I HATED BOTH OF YOU!

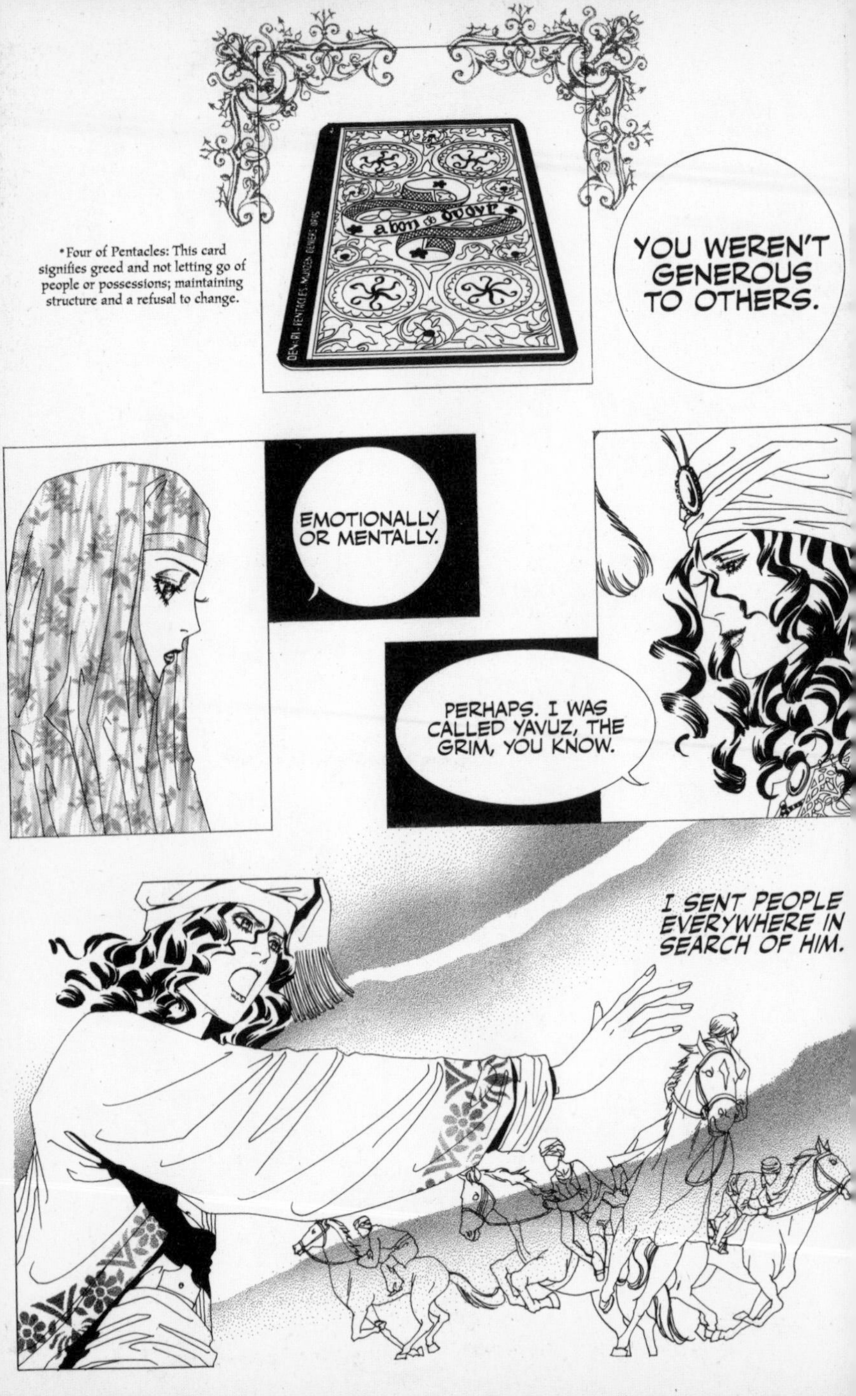
*Four of Pentacles: This card signifies greed and not letting go of people or possessions; maintaining structure and a refusal to change.
YOU WEREN'T GENEROUS TO OTHERS.
EMOTIONALLY OR MENTALLY.
PERHAPS. I WAS CALLED YAVUZ, THE GRIM, YOU KNOW.
I SENT PEOPLE EVERYWHERE IN SEARCH OF HIM.

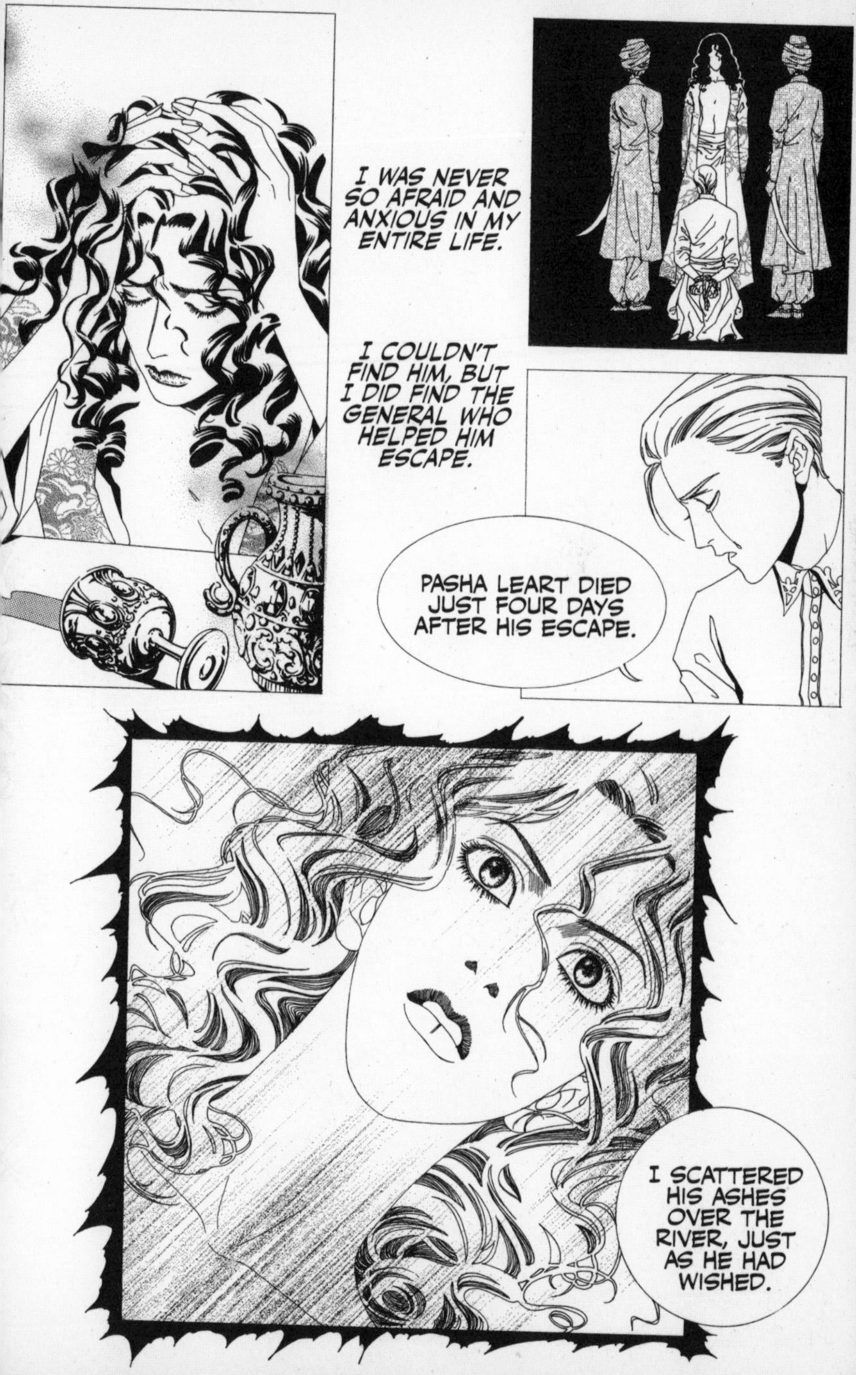
I WAS NEVER SO AFRAID AND ANXIOUS IN MY ENTIRE LIFE.
I COULDN'T FIND HIM, BUT I DID FIND THE GENERAL WHO HELPED HIM ESCAPE.
PASHA LEART DIED JUST FOUR DAYS AFTER HIS ESCAPE.
I SCATTERED HIS ASHES OVER THE RIVER, JUST AS HE HAD WISHED.

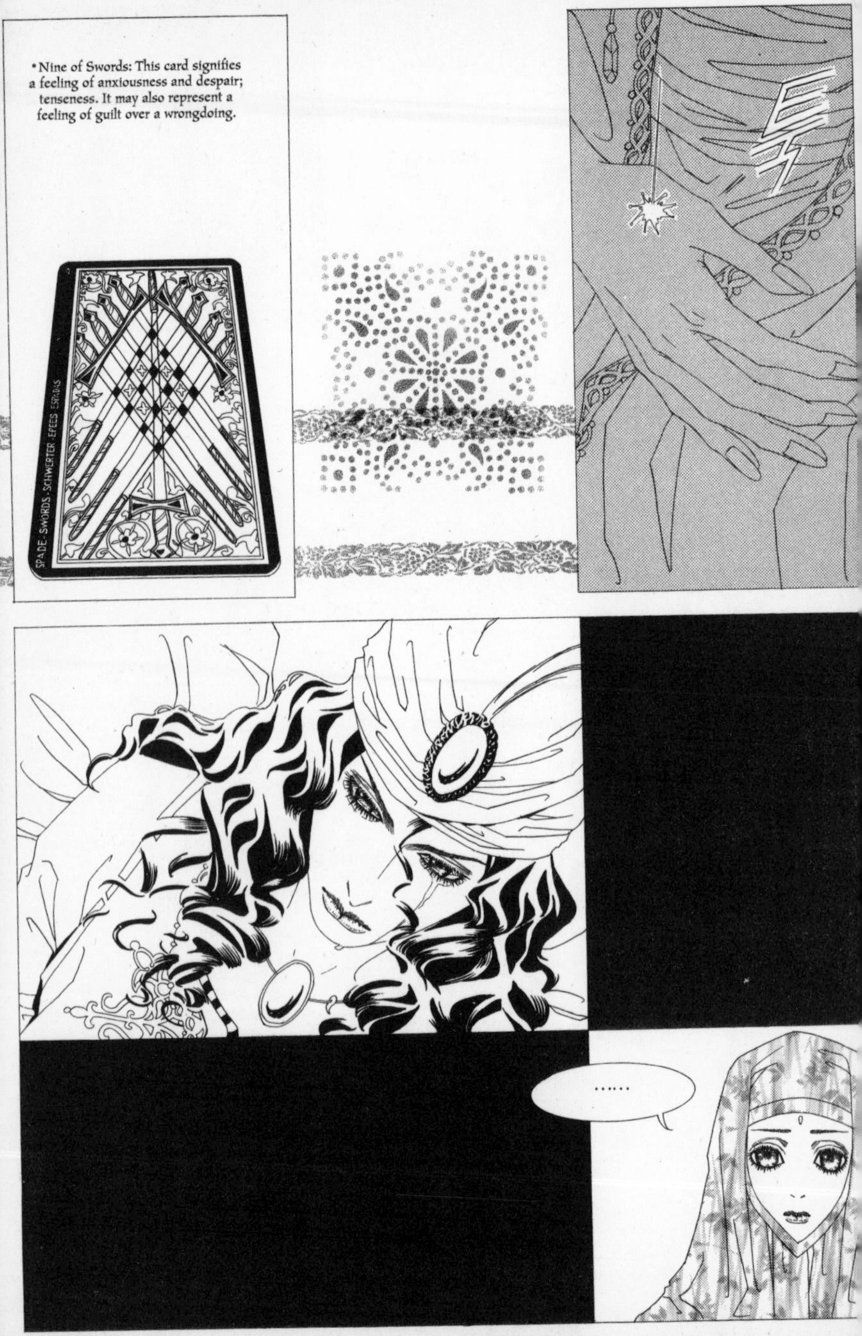
*Nine of Swords: This card signifies a feeling of anxiousness and despair; tenseness. It may also represent a feeling of guilt over a wrongdoing.
SPADE · SWORDS · SCHWERTER · EPEES · ESPADAS
......

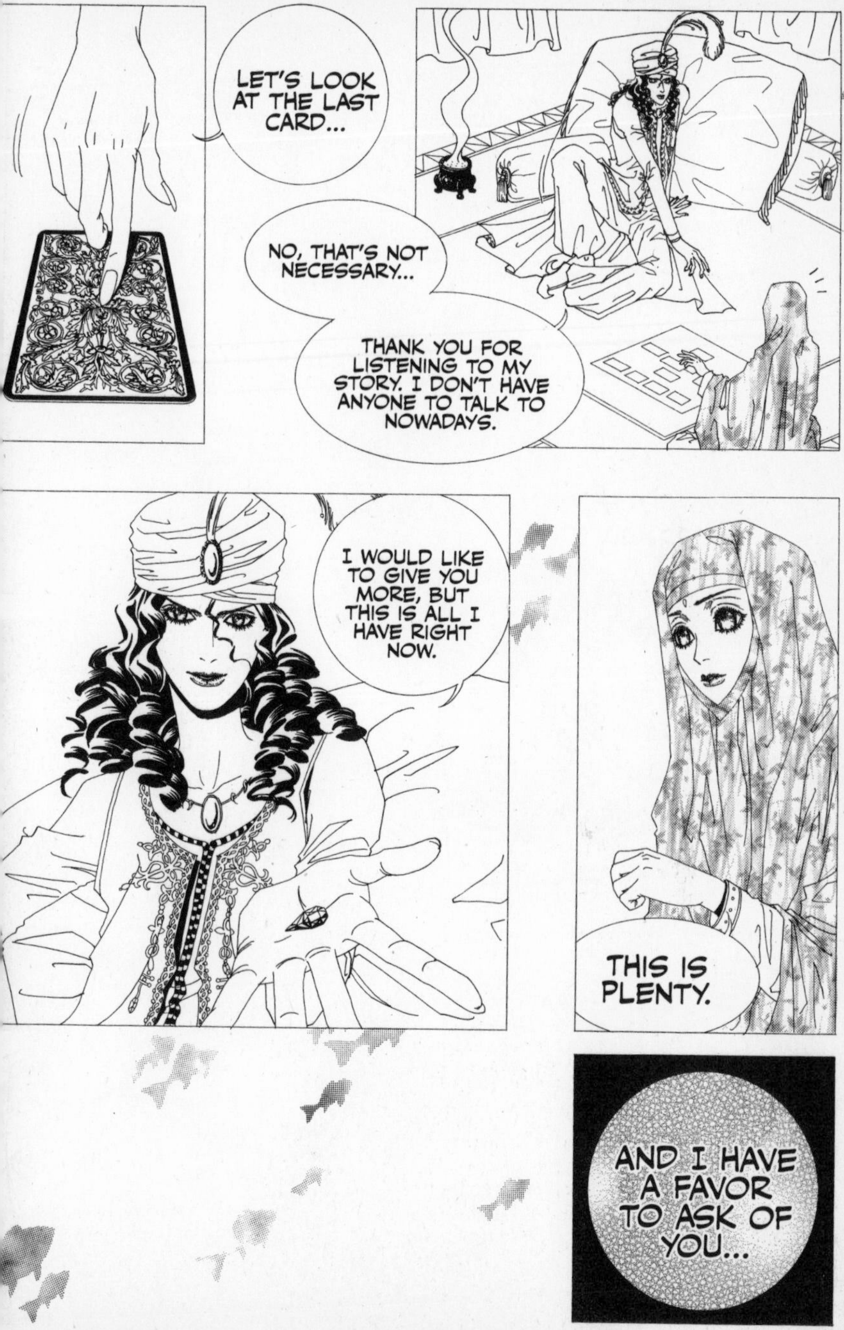
LET'S LOOK AT THE LAST CARD...
NO, THAT'S NOT NECESSARY...
THANK YOU FOR LISTENING TO MY STORY. I DON'T HAVE ANYONE TO TALK TO NOWADAYS.
I WOULD LIKE TO GIVE YOU MORE, BUT THIS IS ALL I HAVE RIGHT NOW.
THIS IS PLENTY.
AND I HAVE A FAVOR TO ASK OF YOU...

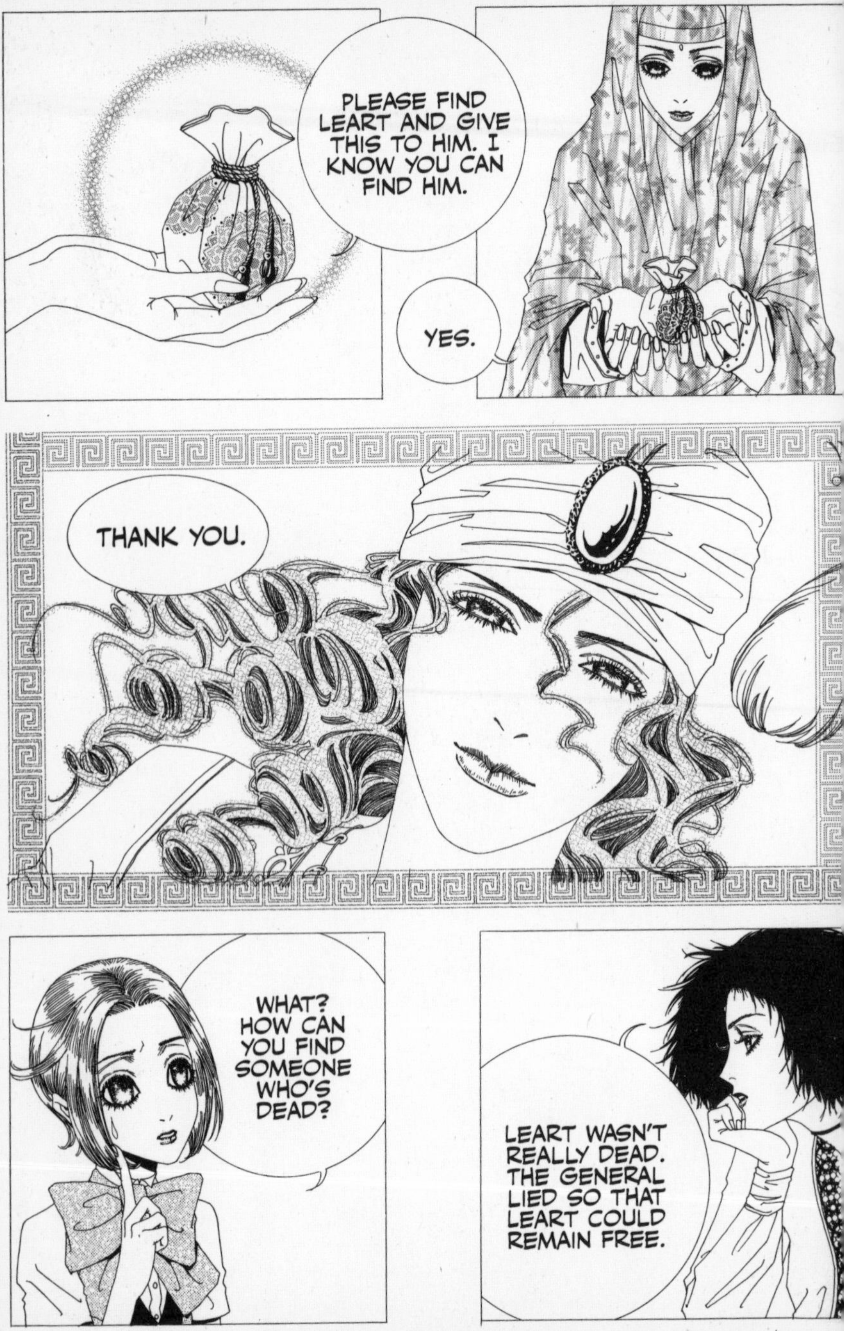
PLEASE FIND LEART AND GIVE THIS TO HIM. I KNOW YOU CAN FIND HIM.
YES.
THANK YOU.
WHAT? HOW CAN YOU FIND SOMEONE WHO'S DEAD?
LEART WASN'T REALLY DEAD. THE GENERAL LIED SO THAT LEART COULD REMAIN FREE.

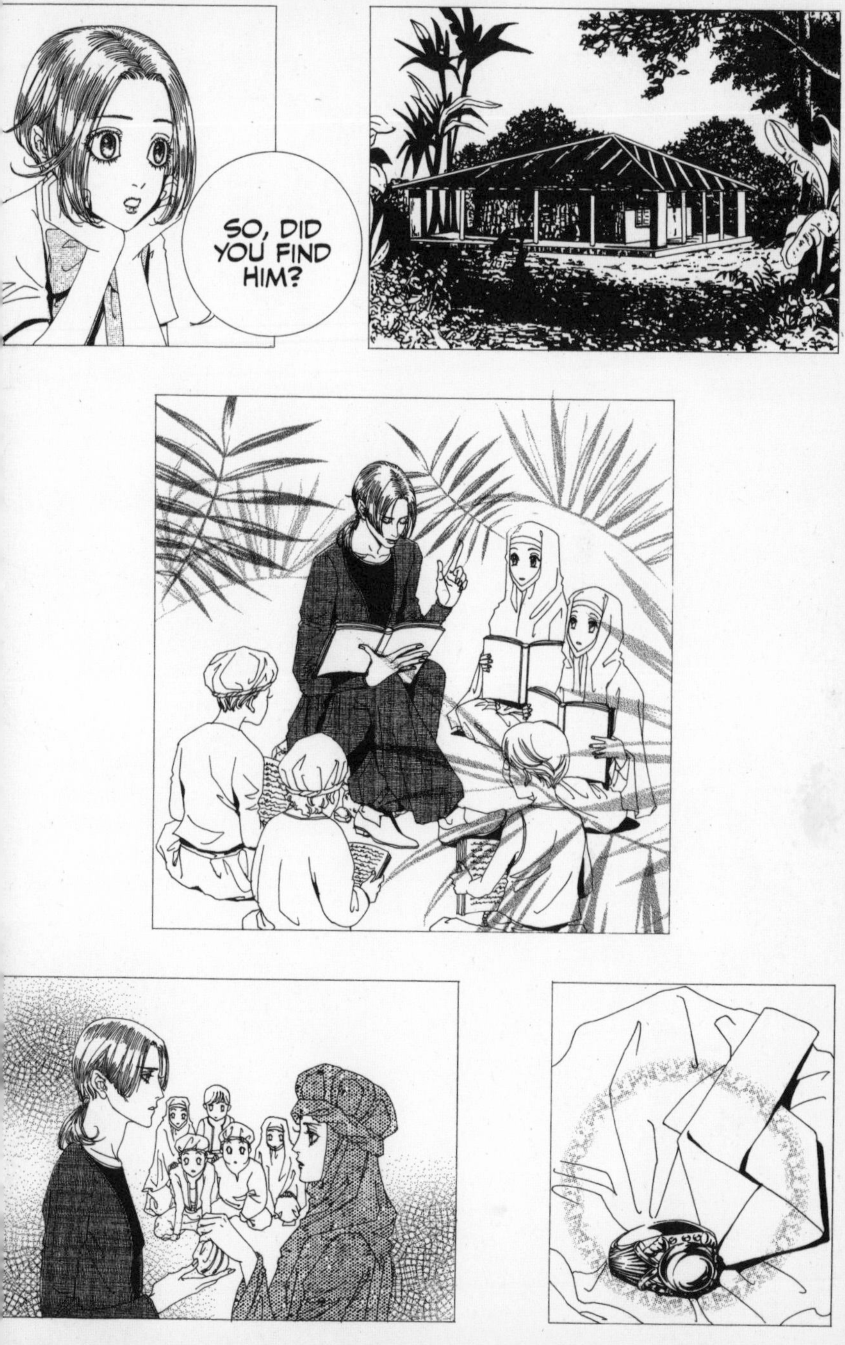
SO, DID YOU FIND HIM?

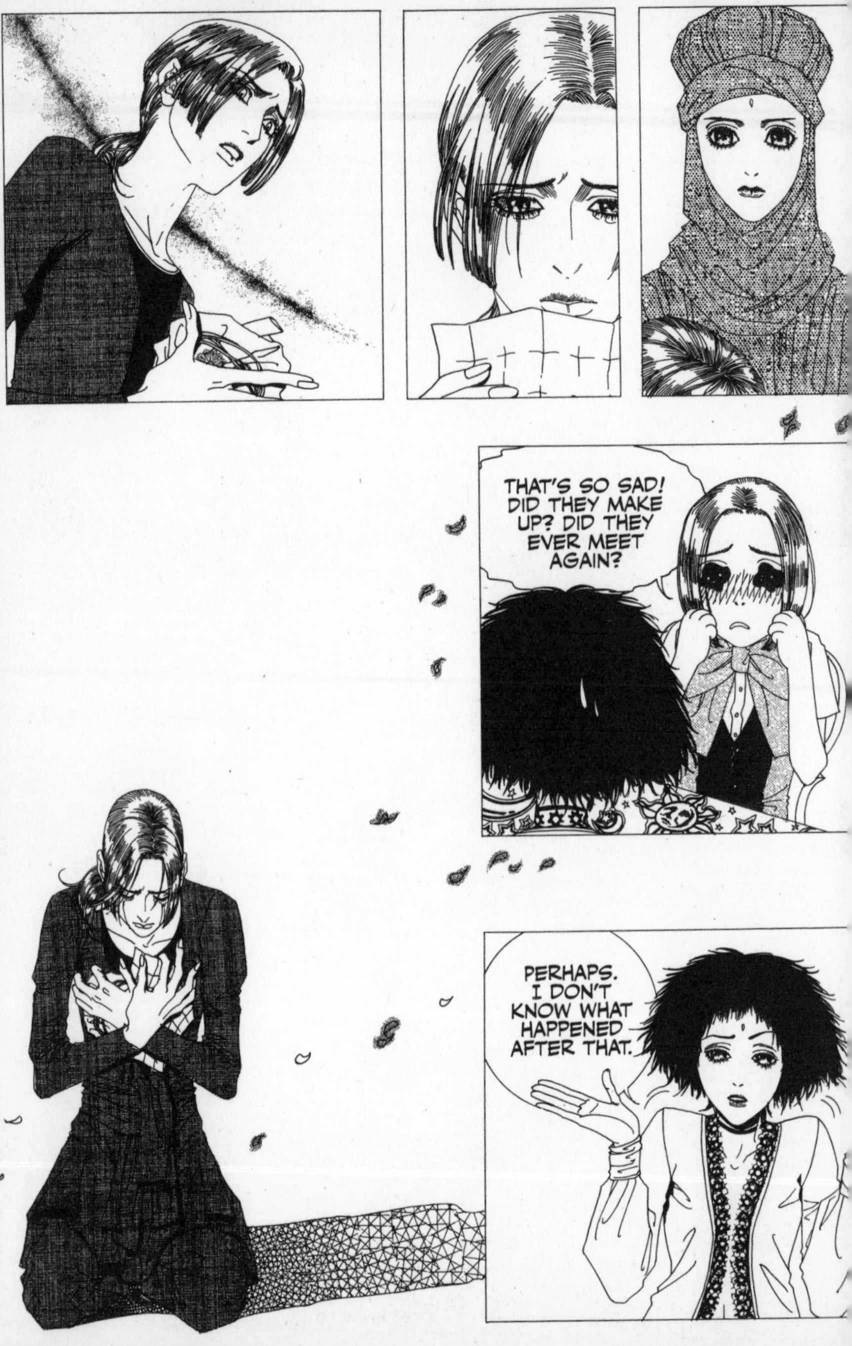
THAT'S SO SAD! DID THEY MAKE UP? DID THEY EVER MEET AGAIN?
PERHAPS. I DON'T KNOW WHAT HAPPENED AFTER THAT.

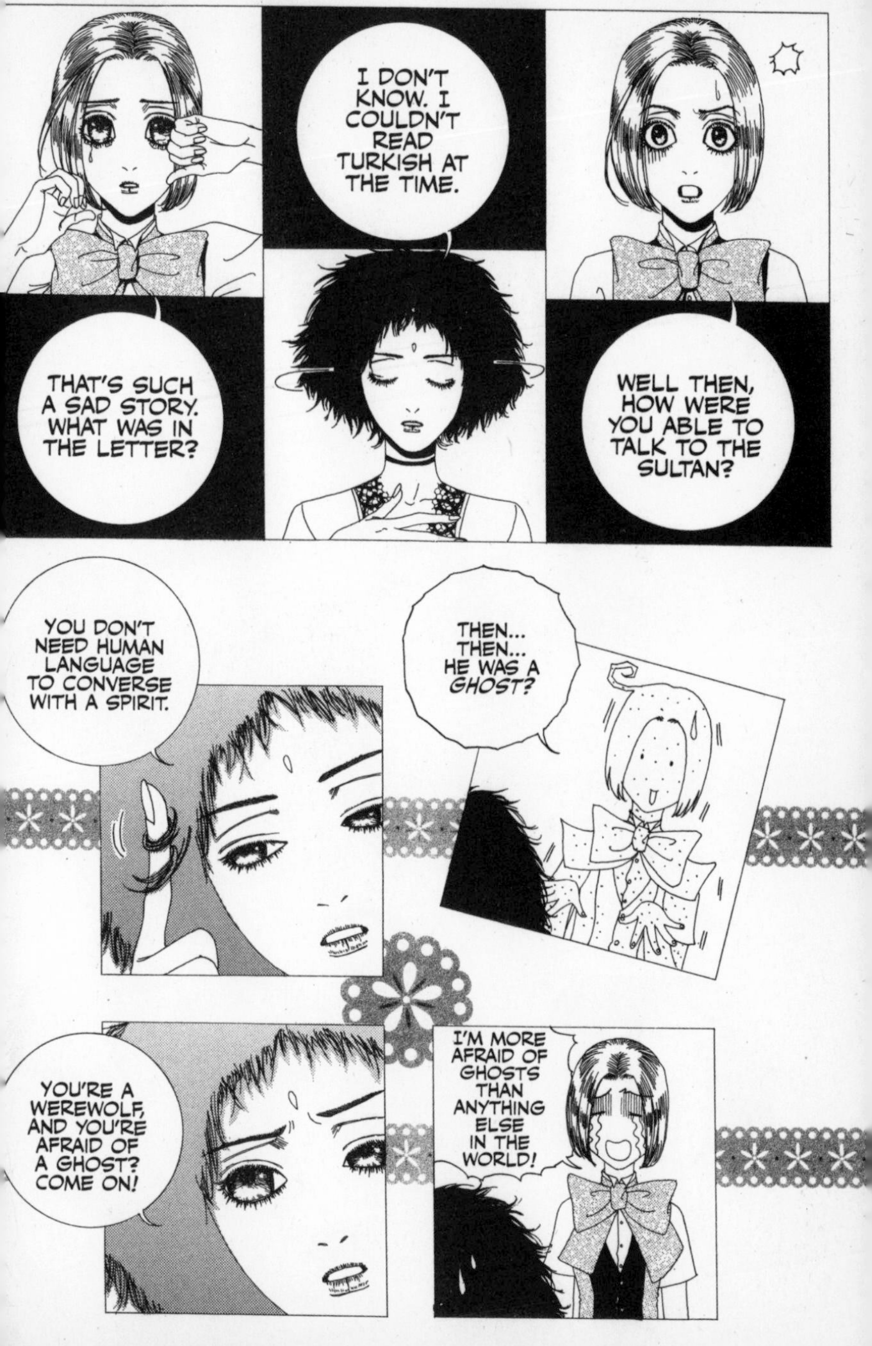
THAT'S SUCH A SAD STORY. WHAT WAS IN THE LETTER?
I DON'T KNOW. I COULDN'T READ TURKISH AT THE TIME.
WELL THEN, HOW WERE YOU ABLE TO TALK TO THE SULTAN?
YOU DON'T NEED HUMAN LANGUAGE TO CONVERSE WITH A SPIRIT.
THEN... THEN... HE WAS A *GHOST*?
YOU'RE A WEREWOLF, AND YOU'RE AFRAID OF A GHOST? COME ON!
I'M MORE AFRAID OF GHOSTS THAN ANYTHING ELSE IN THE WORLD!

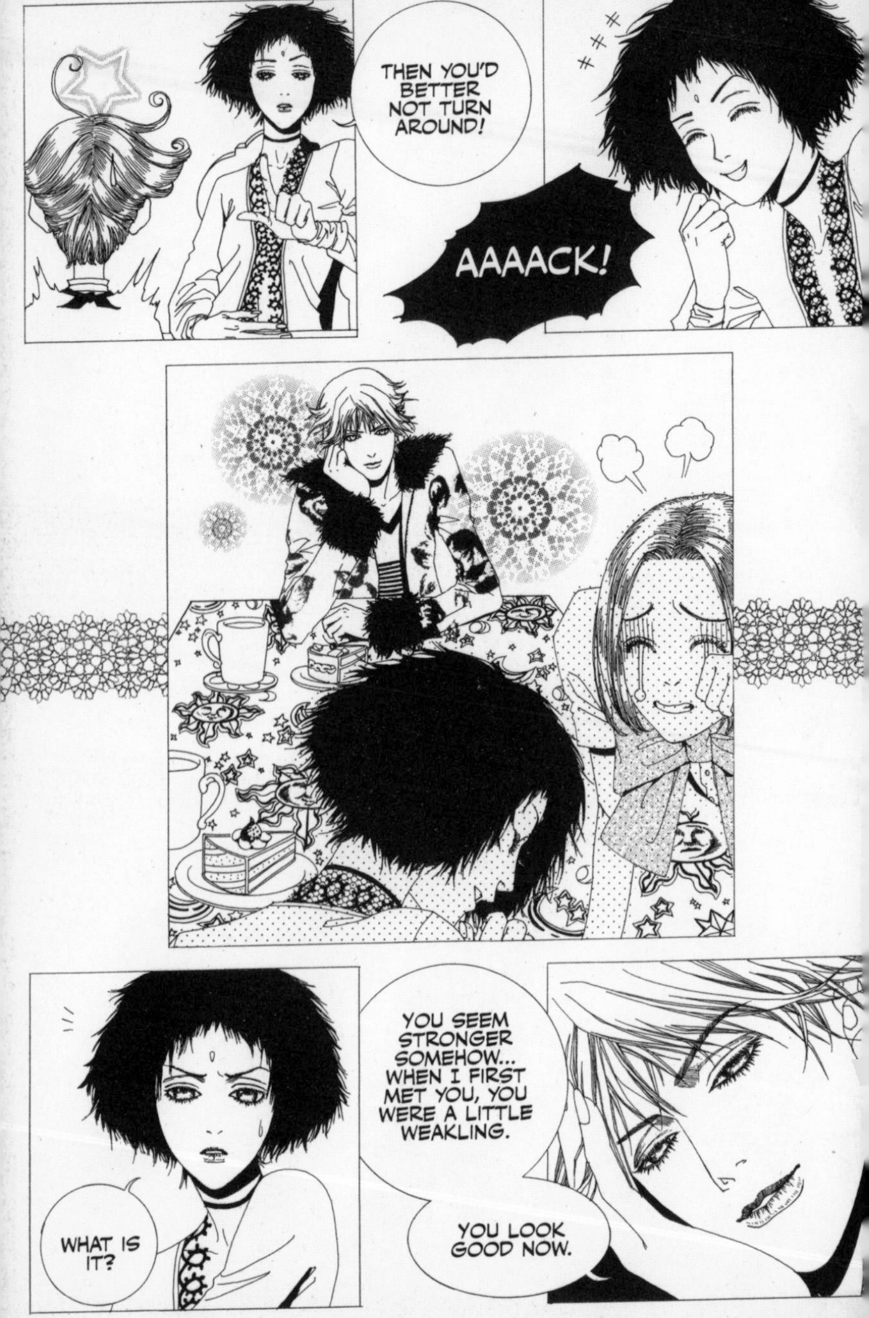
THEN YOU'D BETTER NOT TURN AROUND!
AAAACK!
WHAT IS IT?
YOU SEEM STRONGER SOMEHOW... WHEN I FIRST MET YOU, YOU WERE A LITTLE WEAKLING.
YOU LOOK GOOD NOW.

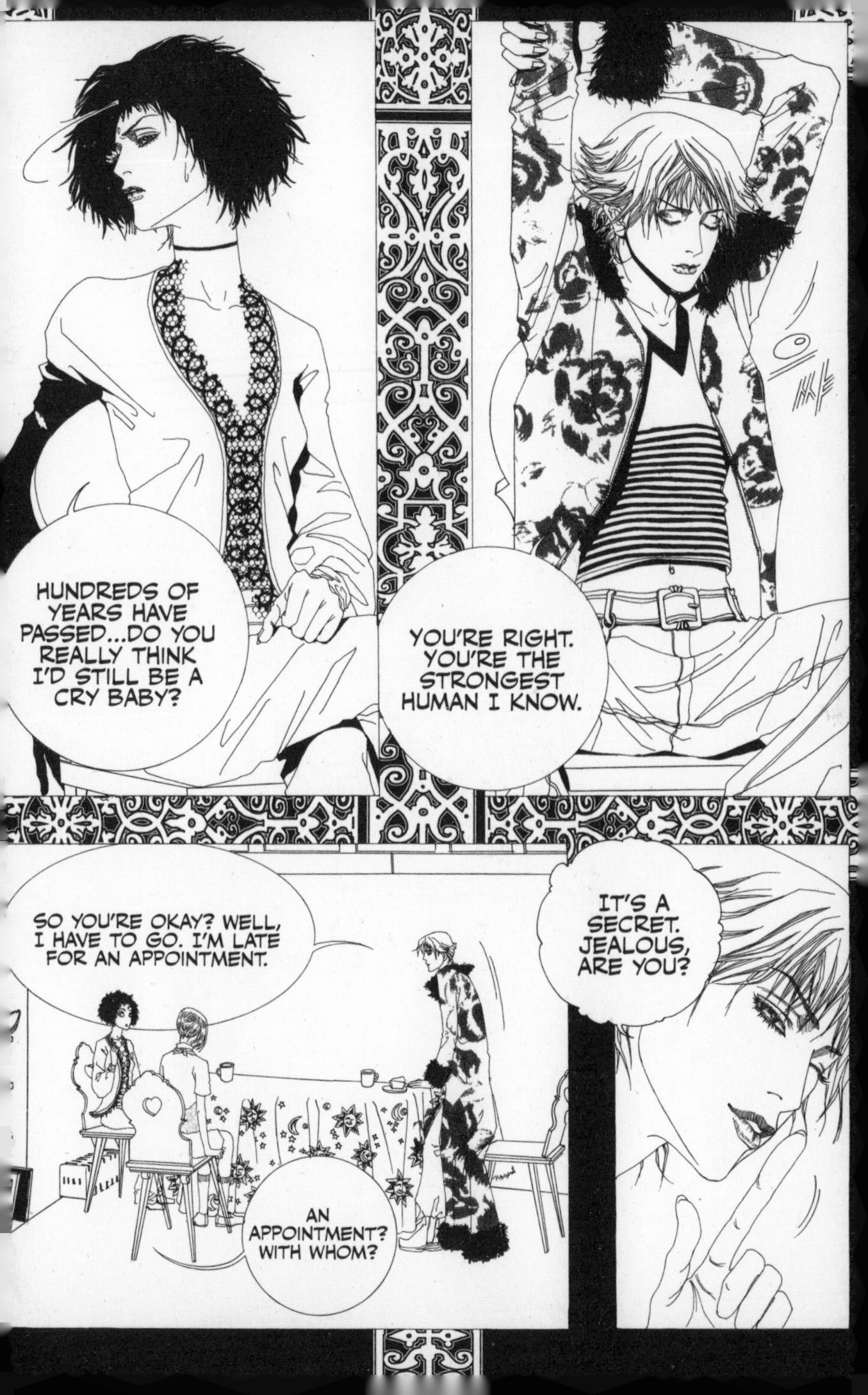
HUNDREDS OF YEARS HAVE PASSED...DO YOU REALLY THINK I'D STILL BE A CRY BABY?
YOU'RE RIGHT. YOU'RE THE STRONGEST HUMAN I KNOW.
SO YOU'RE OKAY? WELL, I HAVE TO GO. I'M LATE FOR AN APPOINTMENT.
AN APPOINTMENT? WITH WHOM?
IT'S A SECRET. JEALOUS, ARE YOU?

YUCK!

OH NO, IT'S RAINING!

HERE'S AN UMBRELLA.

THANK YOU!

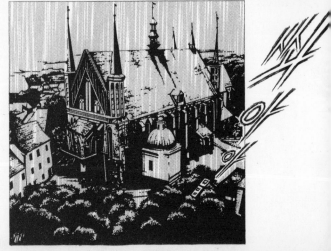

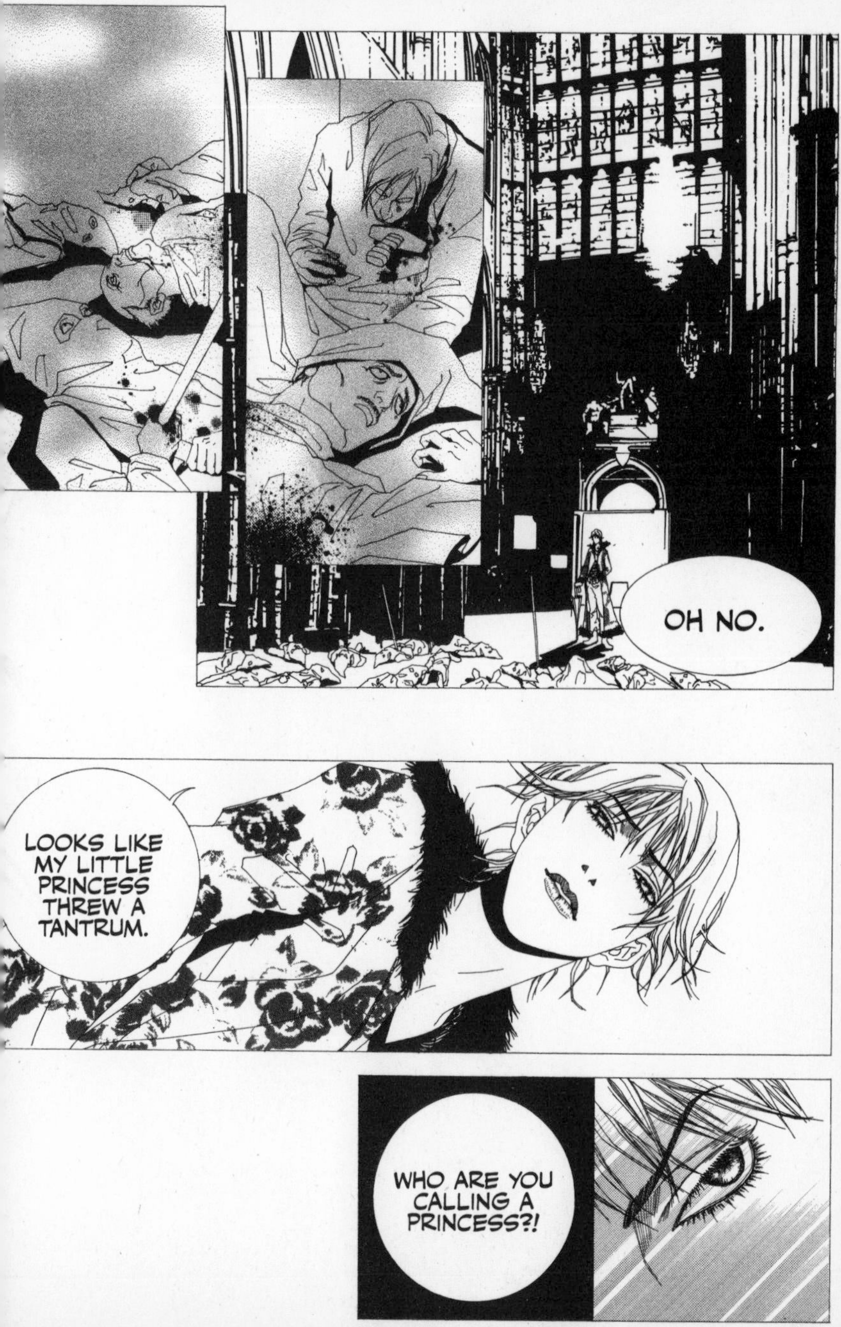
OH NO.
LOOKS LIKE MY LITTLE PRINCESS THREW A TANTRUM.
WHO ARE YOU CALLING A PRINCESS?!

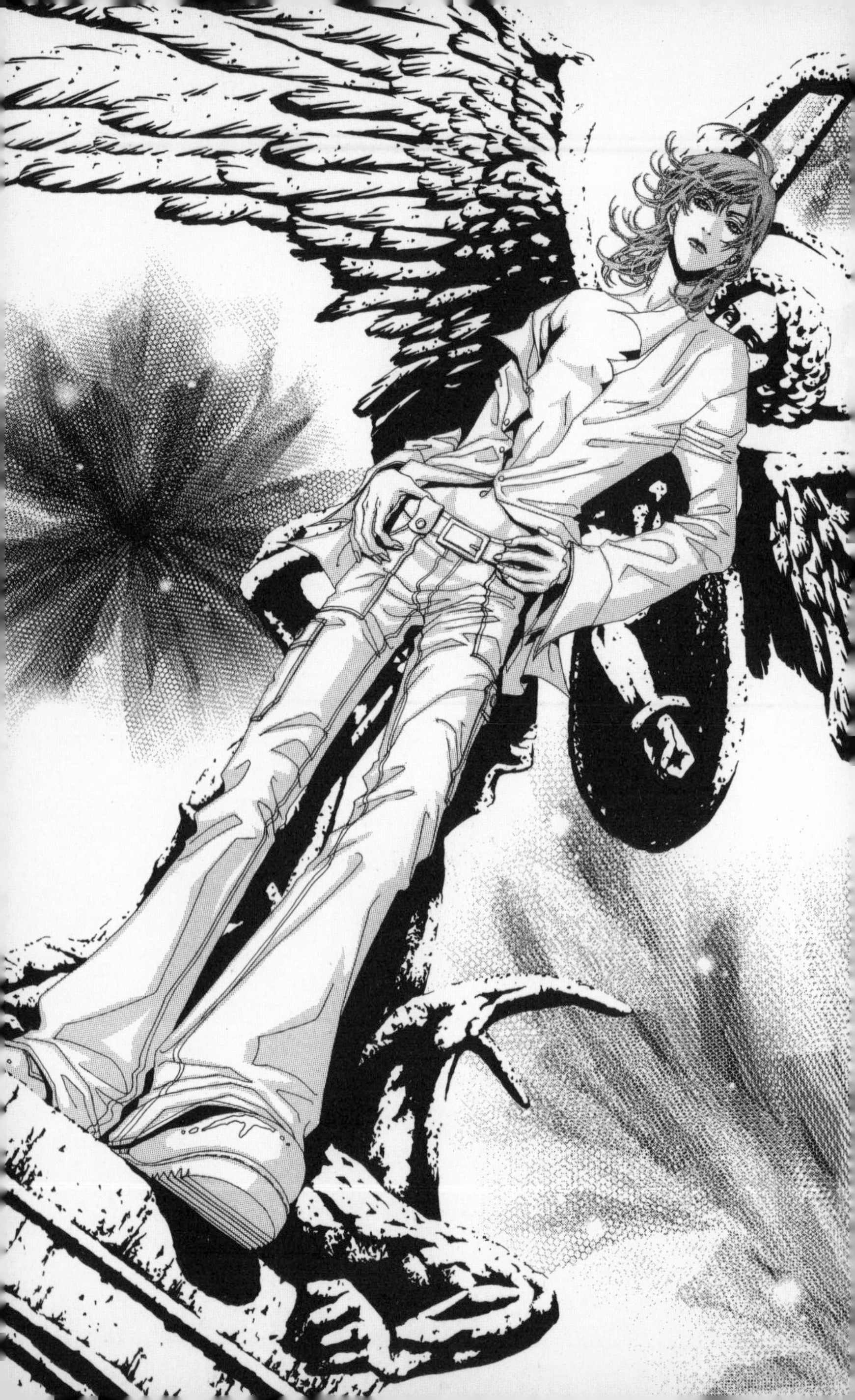

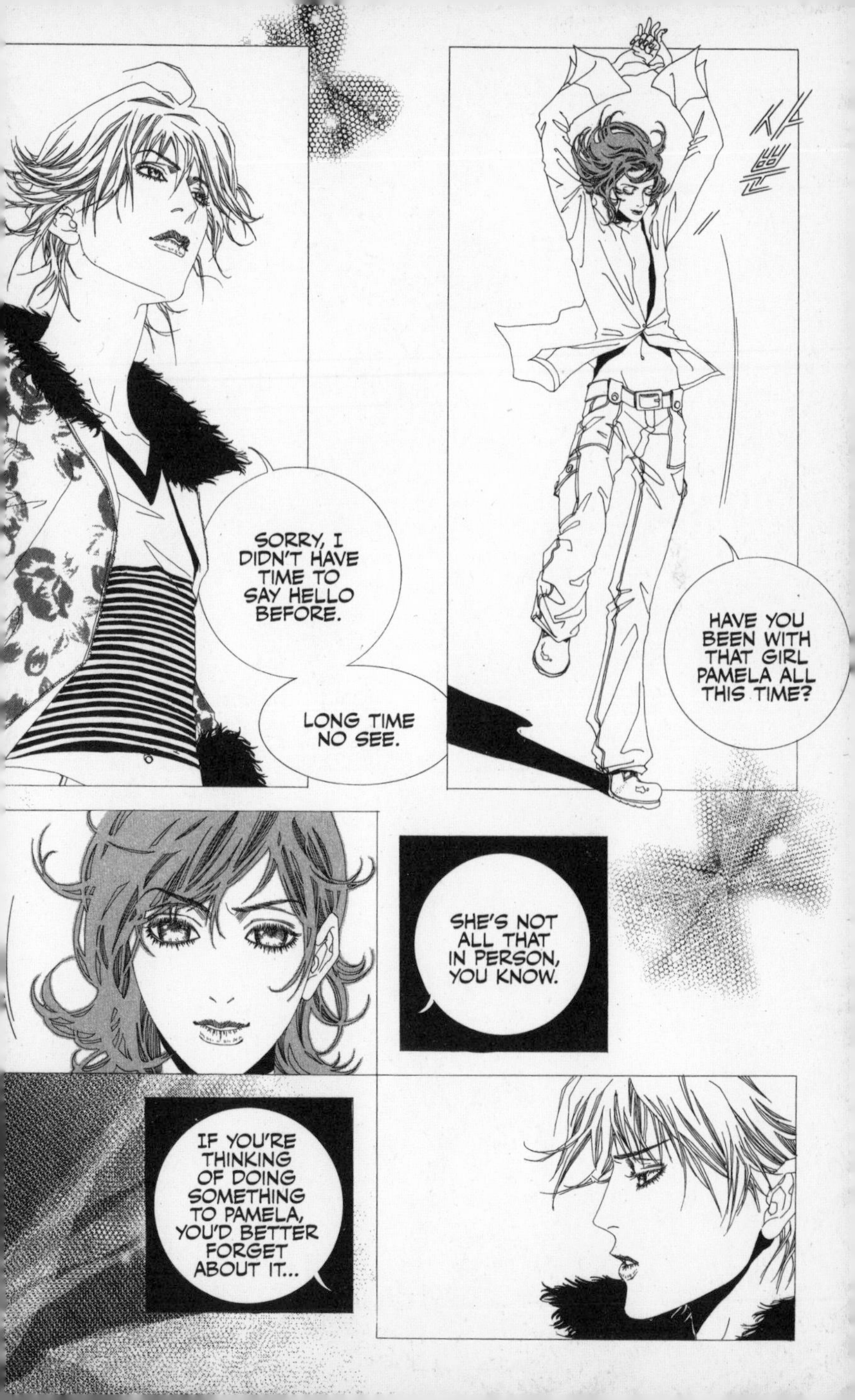
SORRY, I DIDN'T HAVE TIME TO SAY HELLO BEFORE.
LONG TIME NO SEE.
사뿐
HAVE YOU BEEN WITH THAT GIRL PAMELA ALL THIS TIME?
SHE'S NOT ALL THAT IN PERSON, YOU KNOW.
IF YOU'RE THINKING OF DOING SOMETHING TO PAMELA, YOU'D BETTER FORGET ABOUT IT...

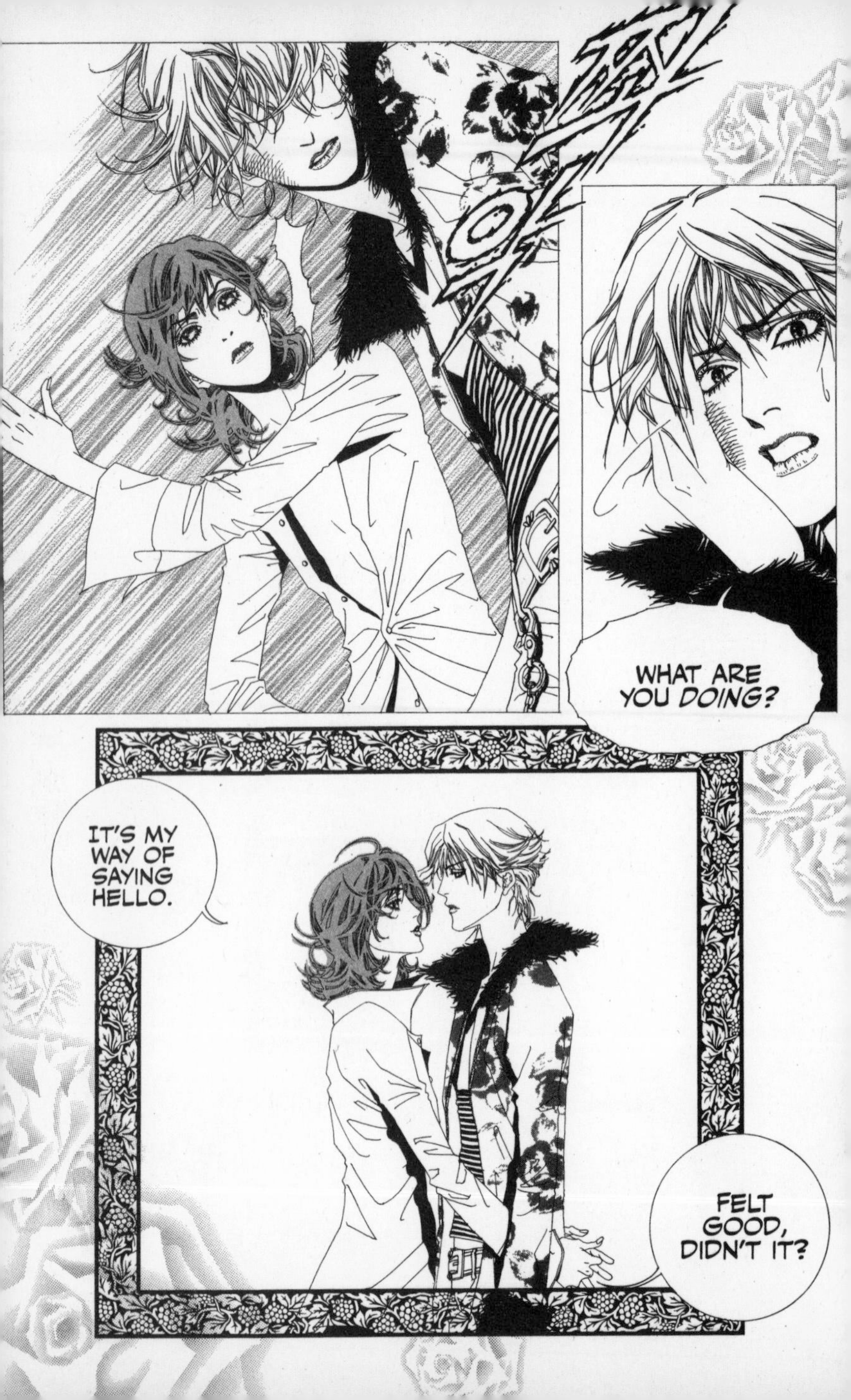
WHAT ARE YOU *DOING*?
IT'S MY WAY OF SAYING HELLO.
FELT GOOD, DIDN'T IT?

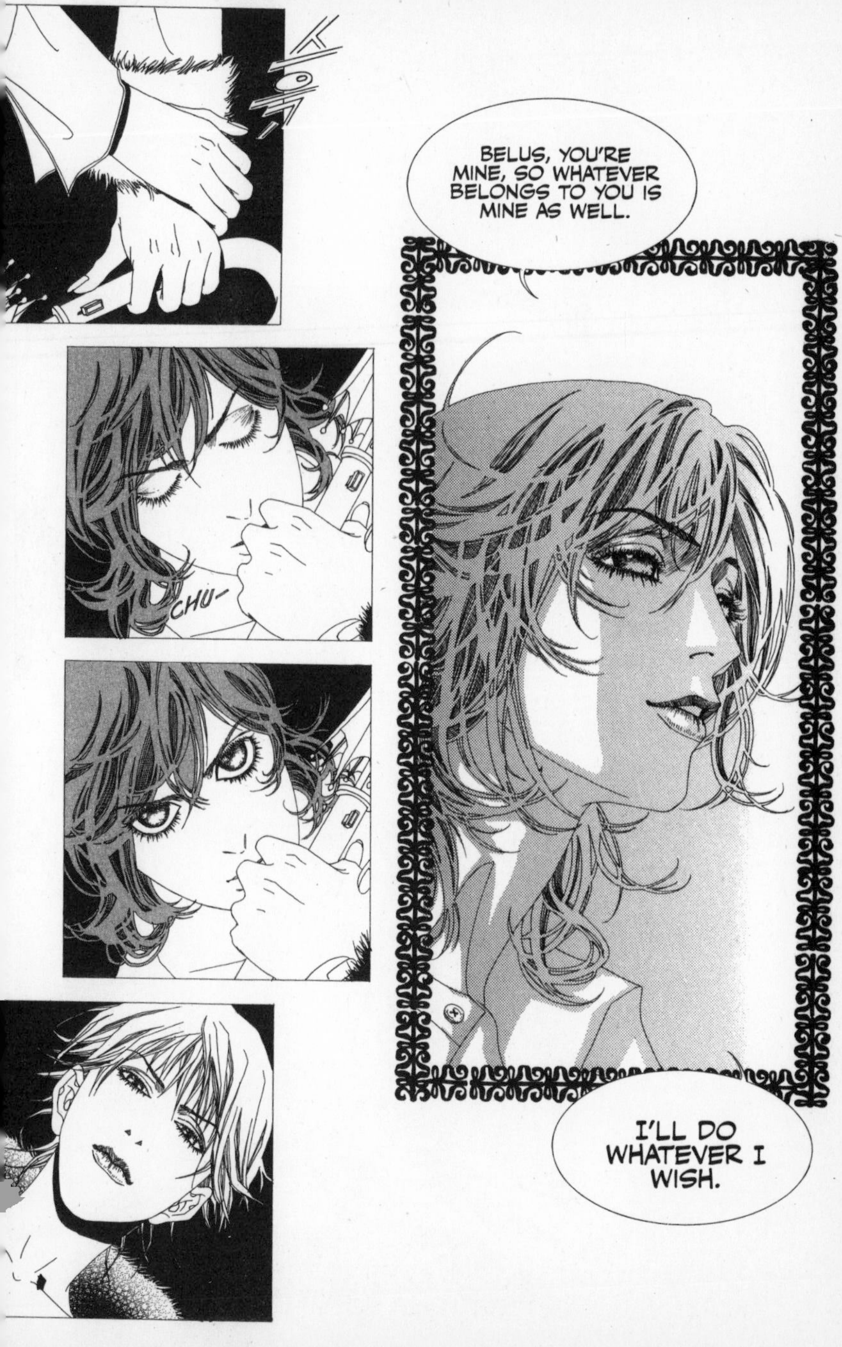
CHU-
BELUS, YOU'RE MINE, SO WHATEVER BELONGS TO YOU IS MINE AS WELL.
I'LL DO WHATEVER I WISH.

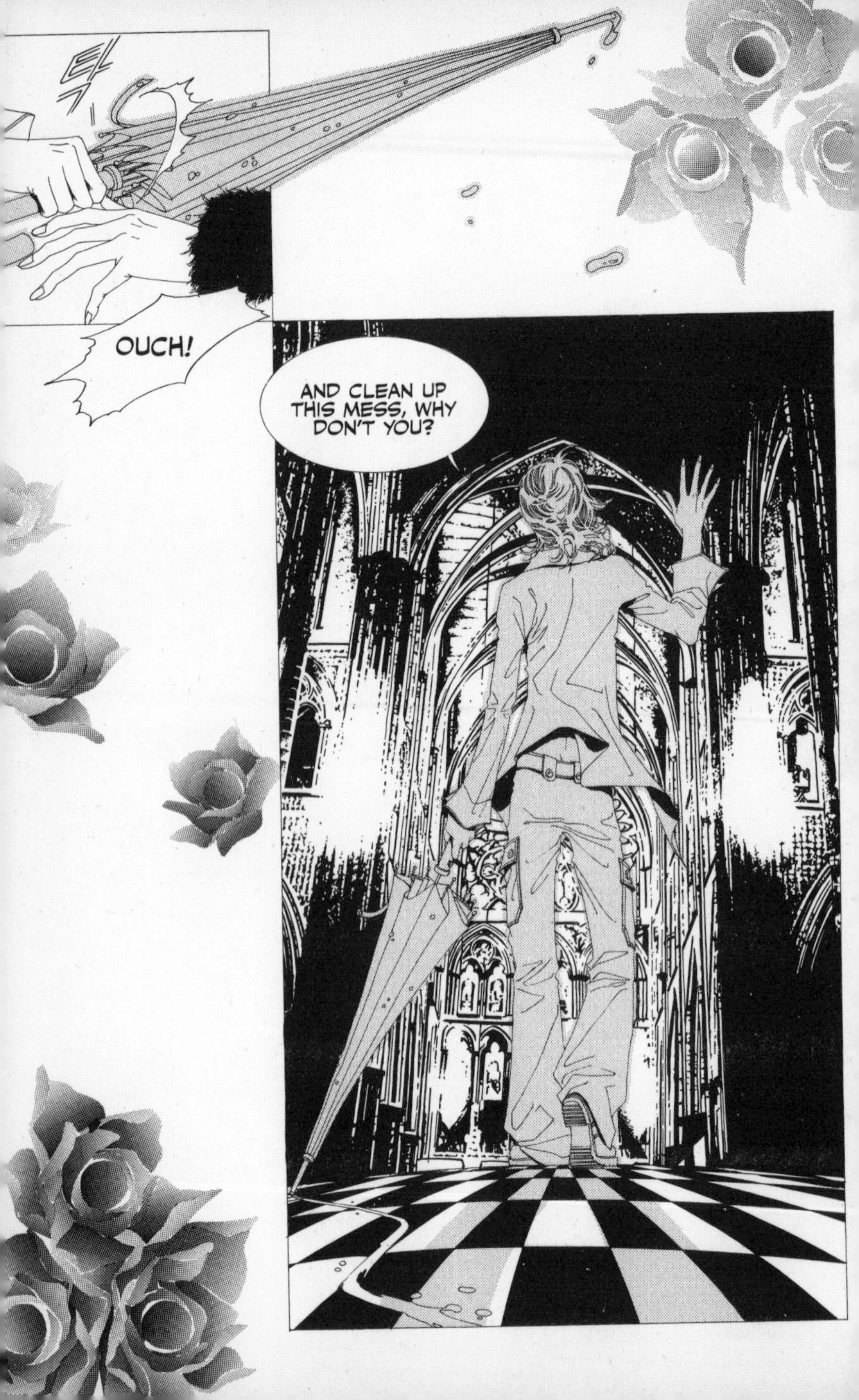
탁
OUCH!
AND CLEAN UP THIS MESS, WHY DON'T YOU?

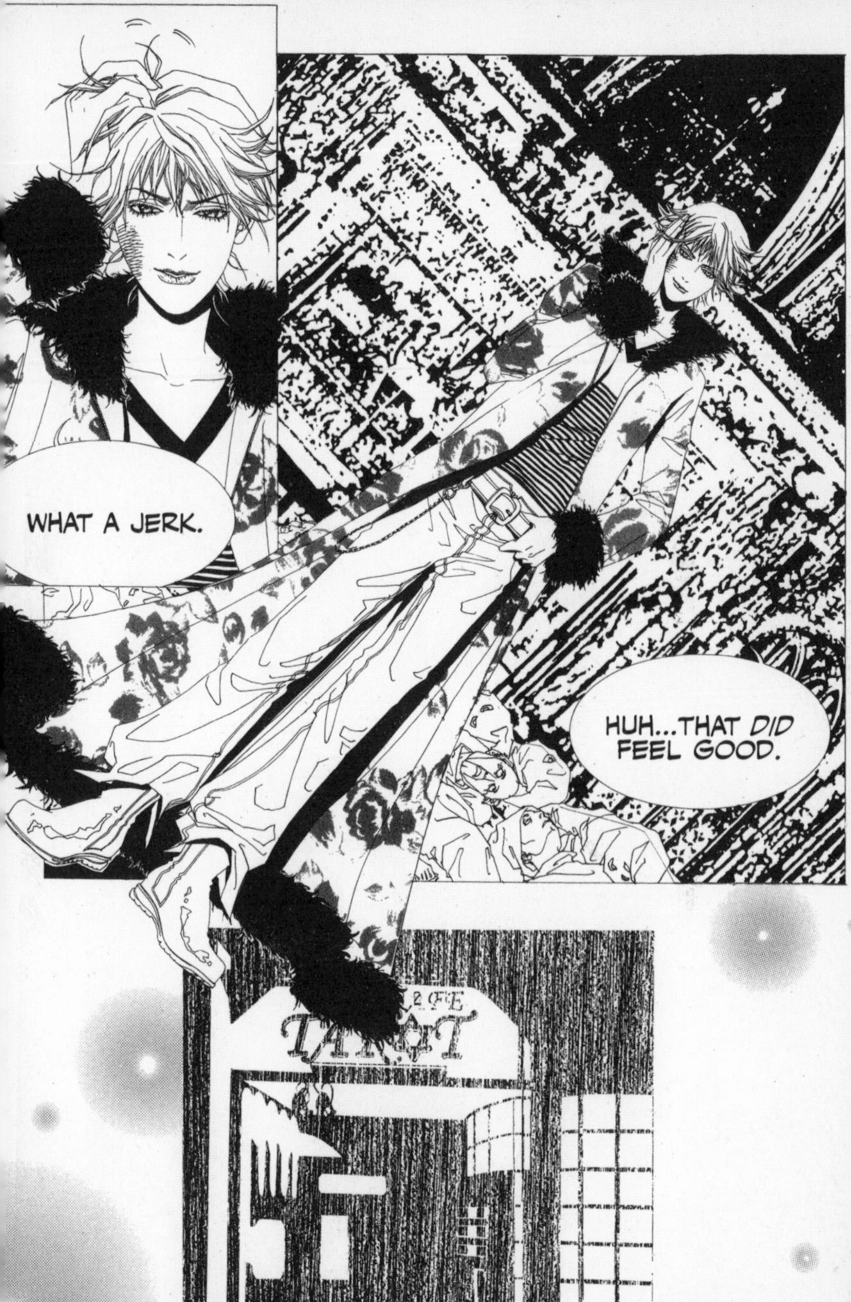
WHAT A JERK.
HUH...THAT *DID* FEEL GOOD.

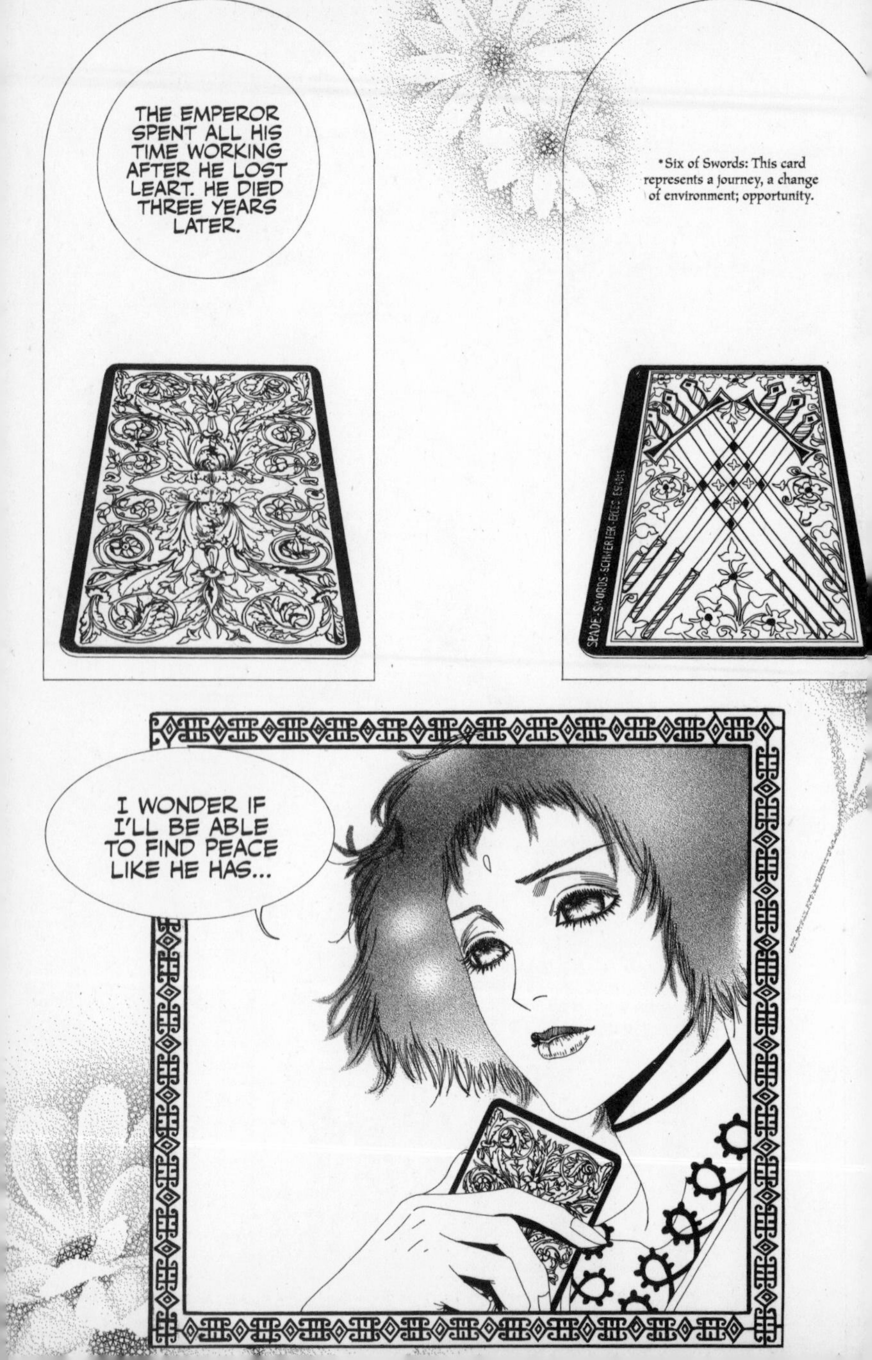
THE EMPEROR SPENT ALL HIS TIME WORKING AFTER HE LOST LEART. HE DIED THREE YEARS LATER.
*Six of Swords: This card represents a journey, a change of environment; opportunity.
I WONDER IF I'LL BE ABLE TO FIND PEACE LIKE HE HAS...

ILLUSTRATION FROM TAROT OF MOON GARDEN

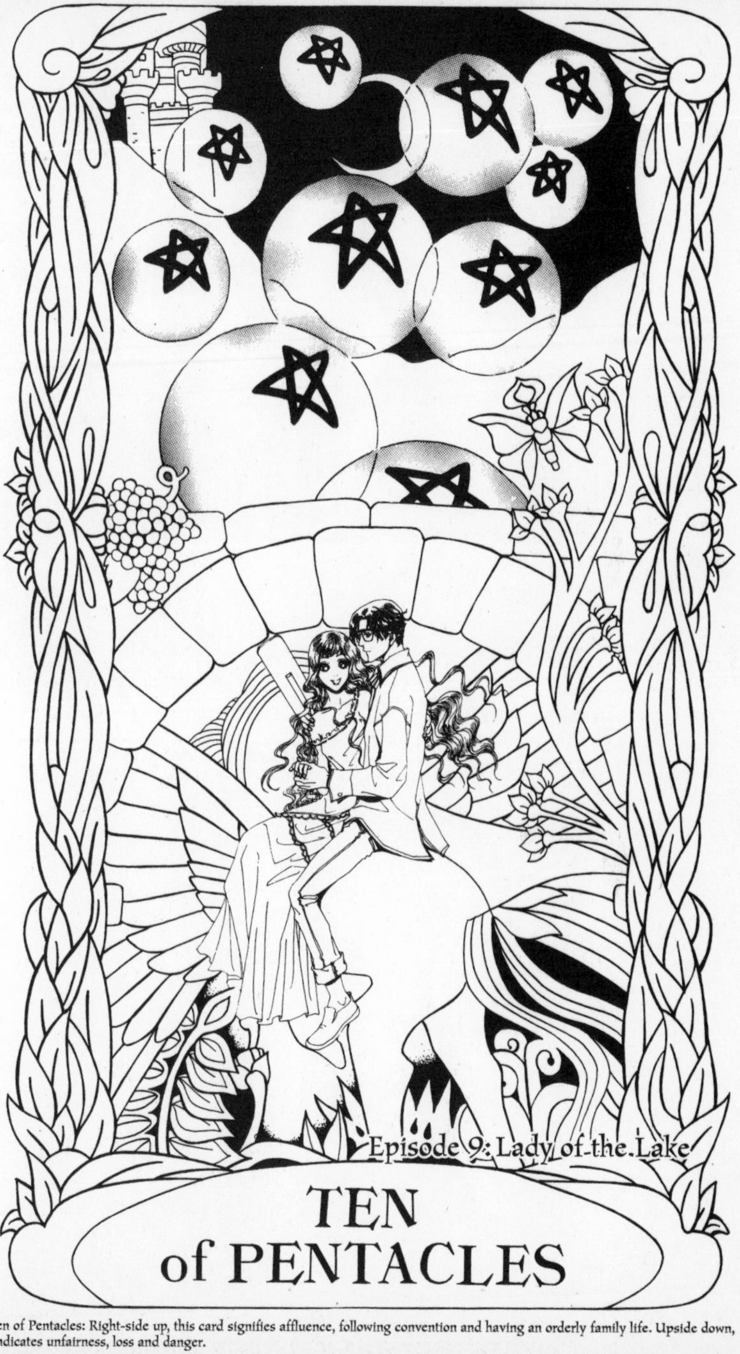
Episode 9: Lady of the Lake
TEN
of PENTACLES

*Ten of Pentacles: Right-side up, this card signifies affluence, following convention and having an orderly family life. Upside down, it indicates unfairness, loss and danger.

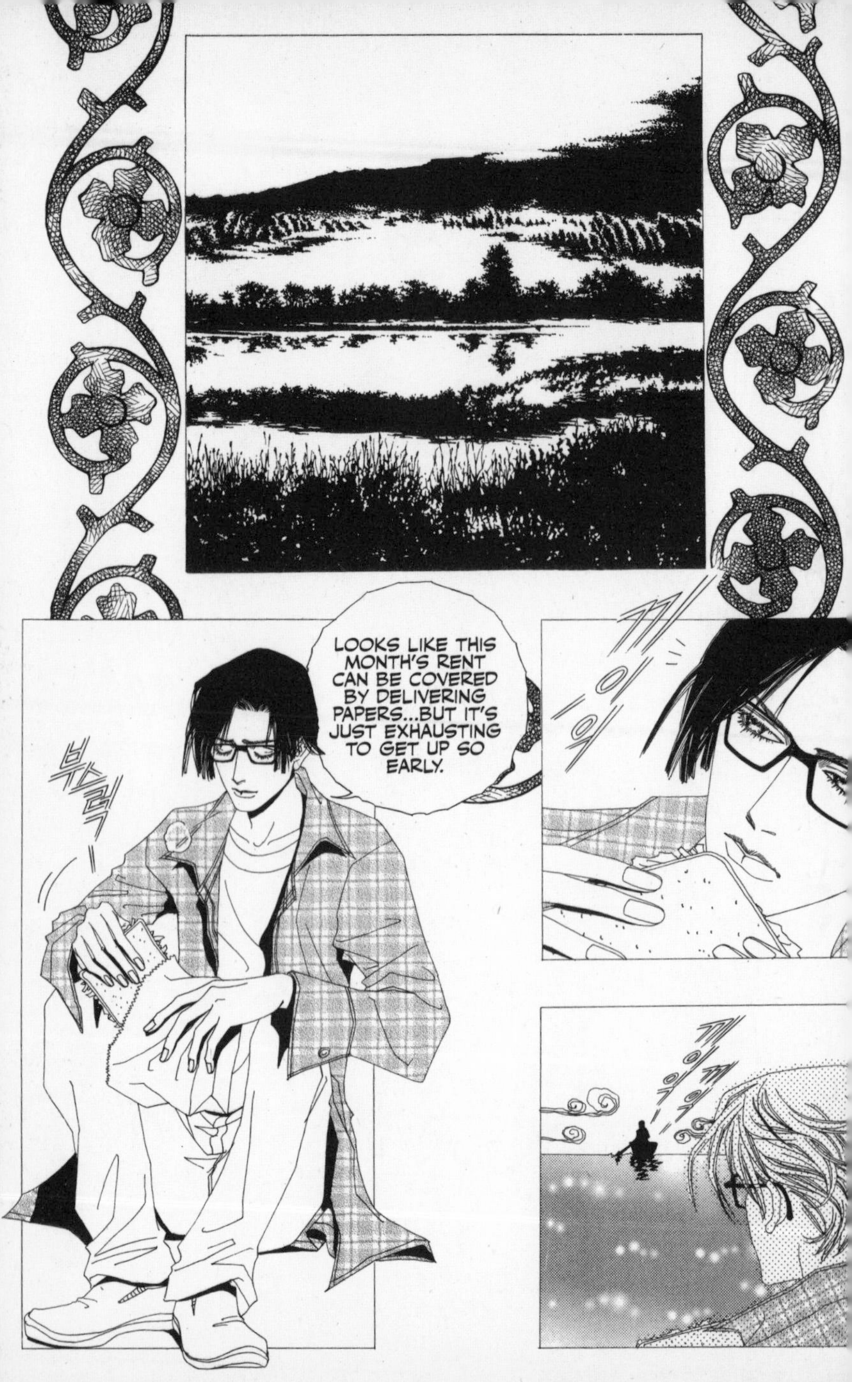
LOOKS LIKE THIS MONTH'S RENT CAN BE COVERED BY DELIVERING PAPERS...BUT IT'S JUST EXHAUSTING TO GET UP SO EARLY.

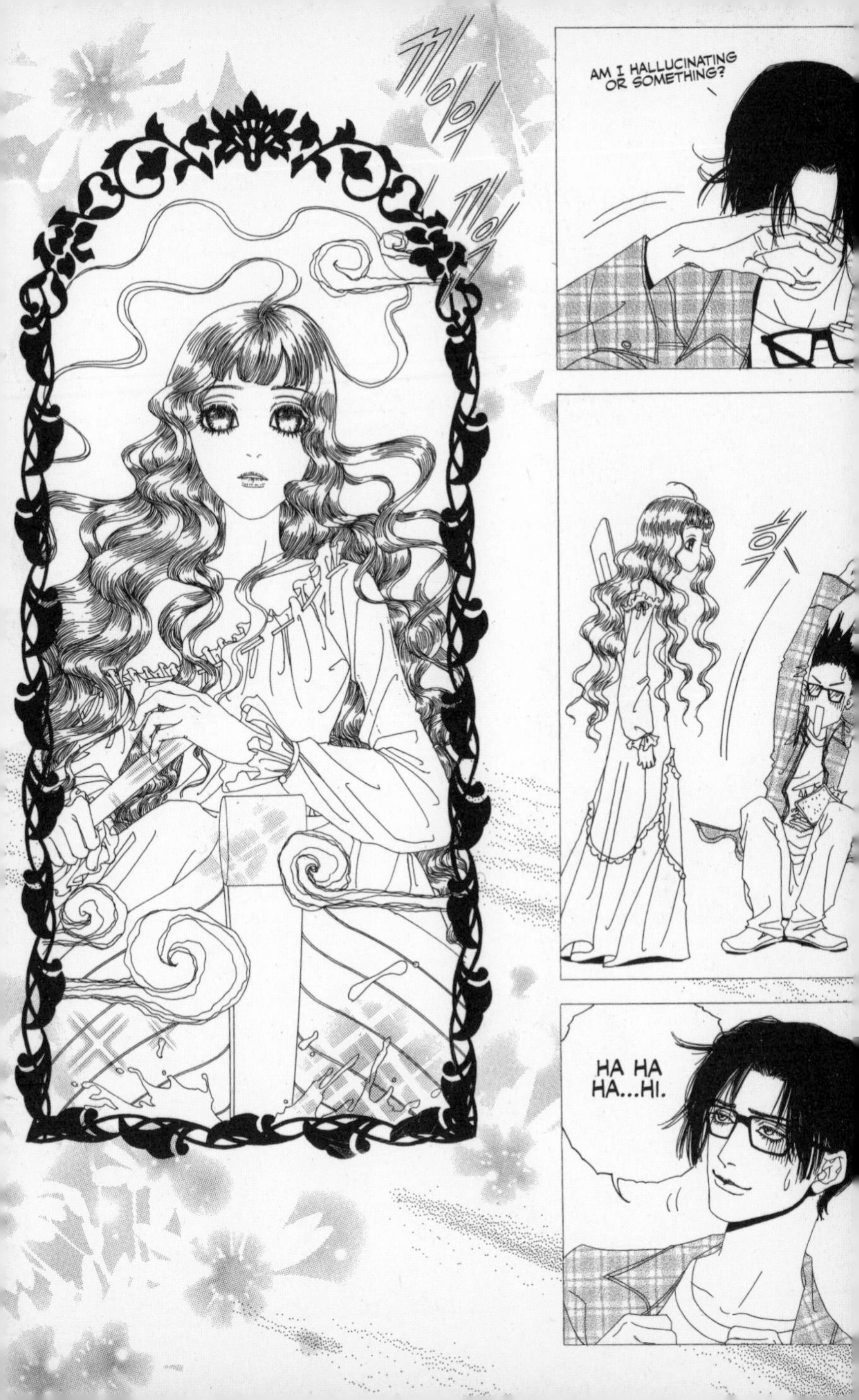
AM I HALLUCINATING OR SOMETHING?
HA HA HA...HI.

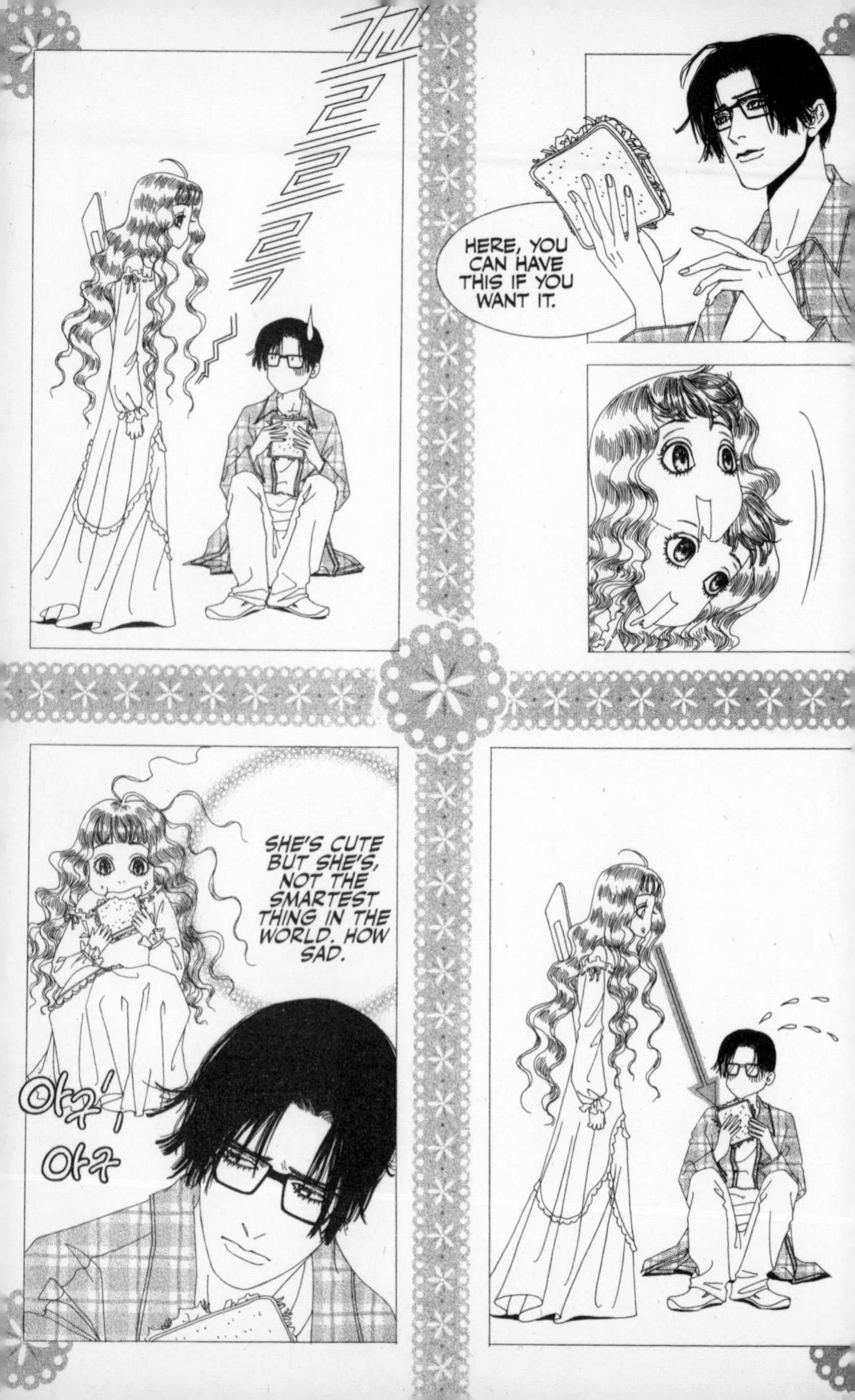
HERE, YOU CAN HAVE THIS IF YOU WANT IT.
SHE'S CUTE BUT SHE'S, NOT THE SMARTEST THING IN THE WORLD. HOW SAD.
아구 아구

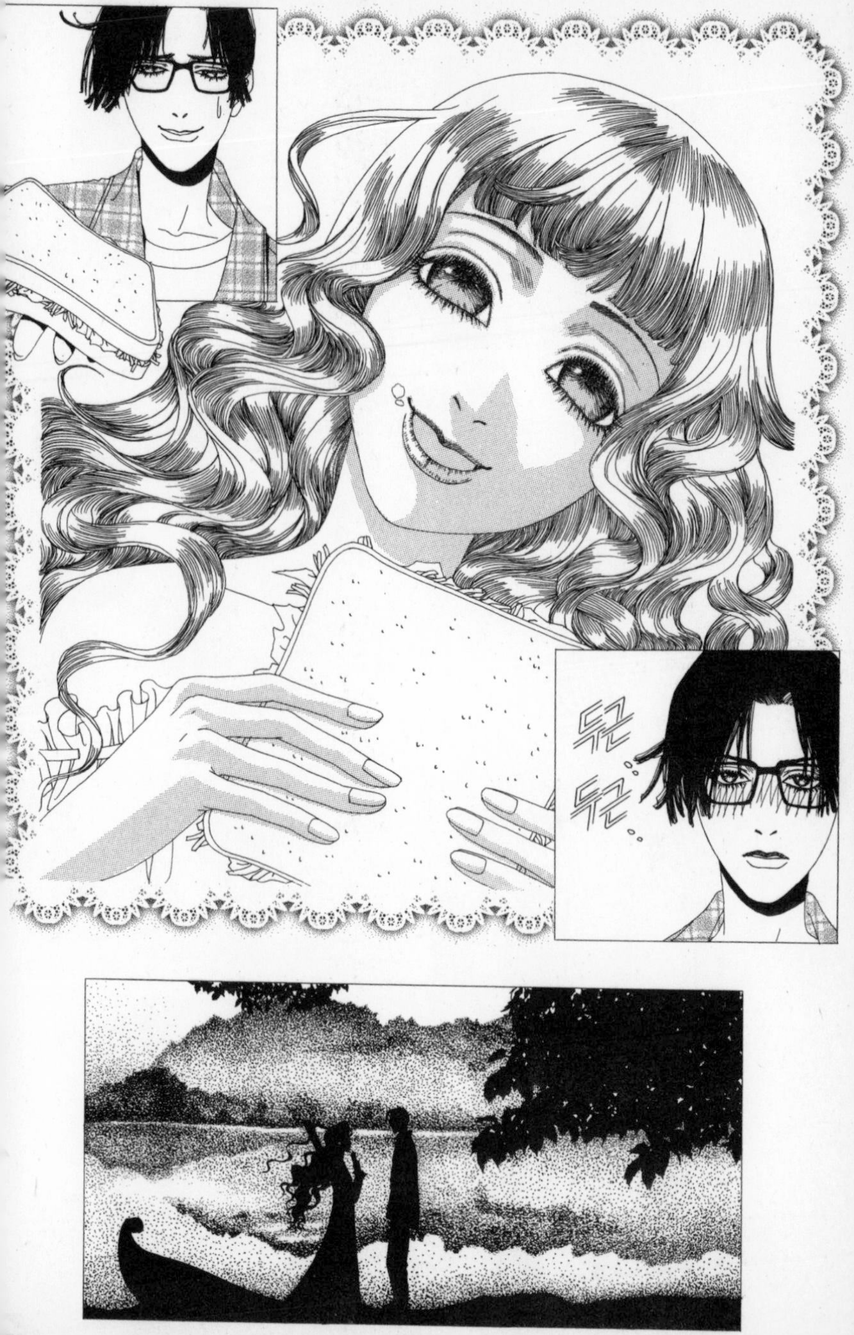
두근
두근

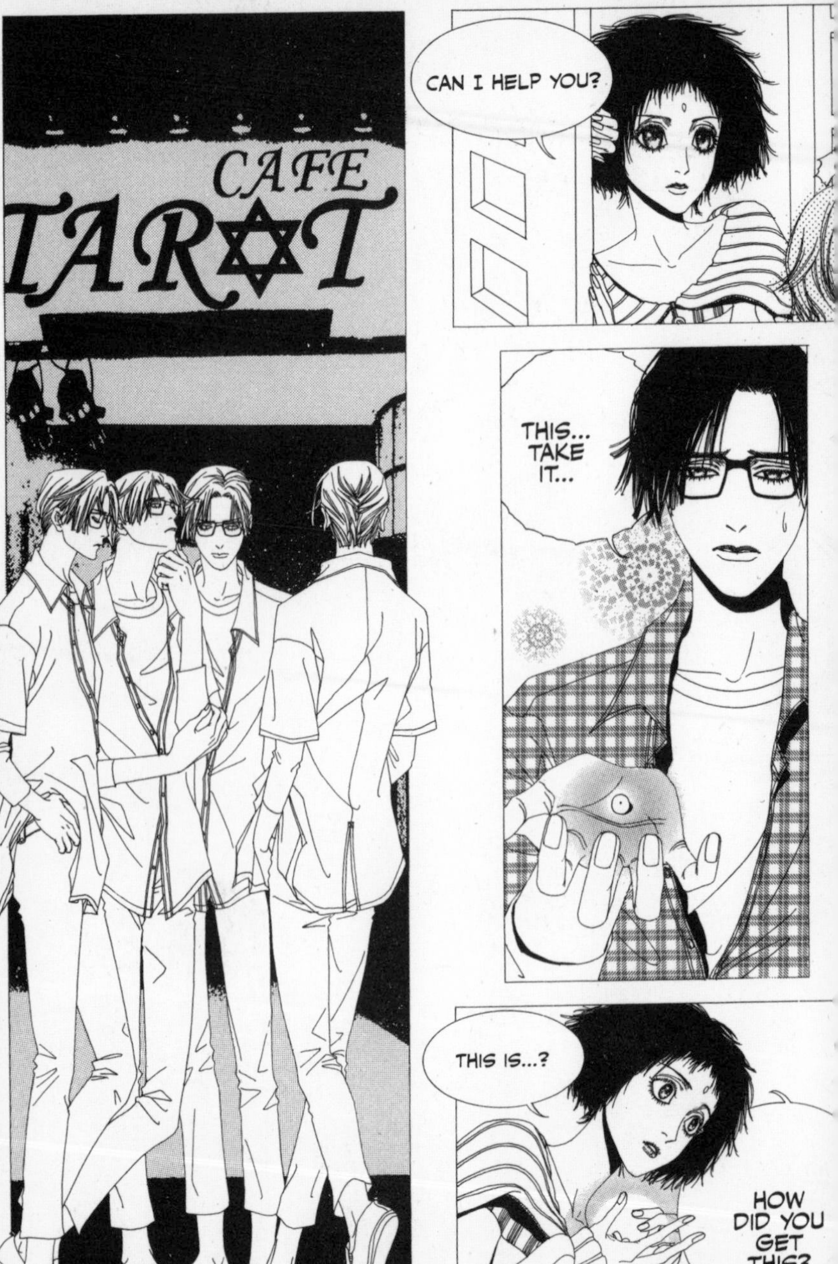
CAFE TAROT
CAN I HELP YOU?
THIS... TAKE IT...
THIS IS...?
HOW DID YOU GET THIS?

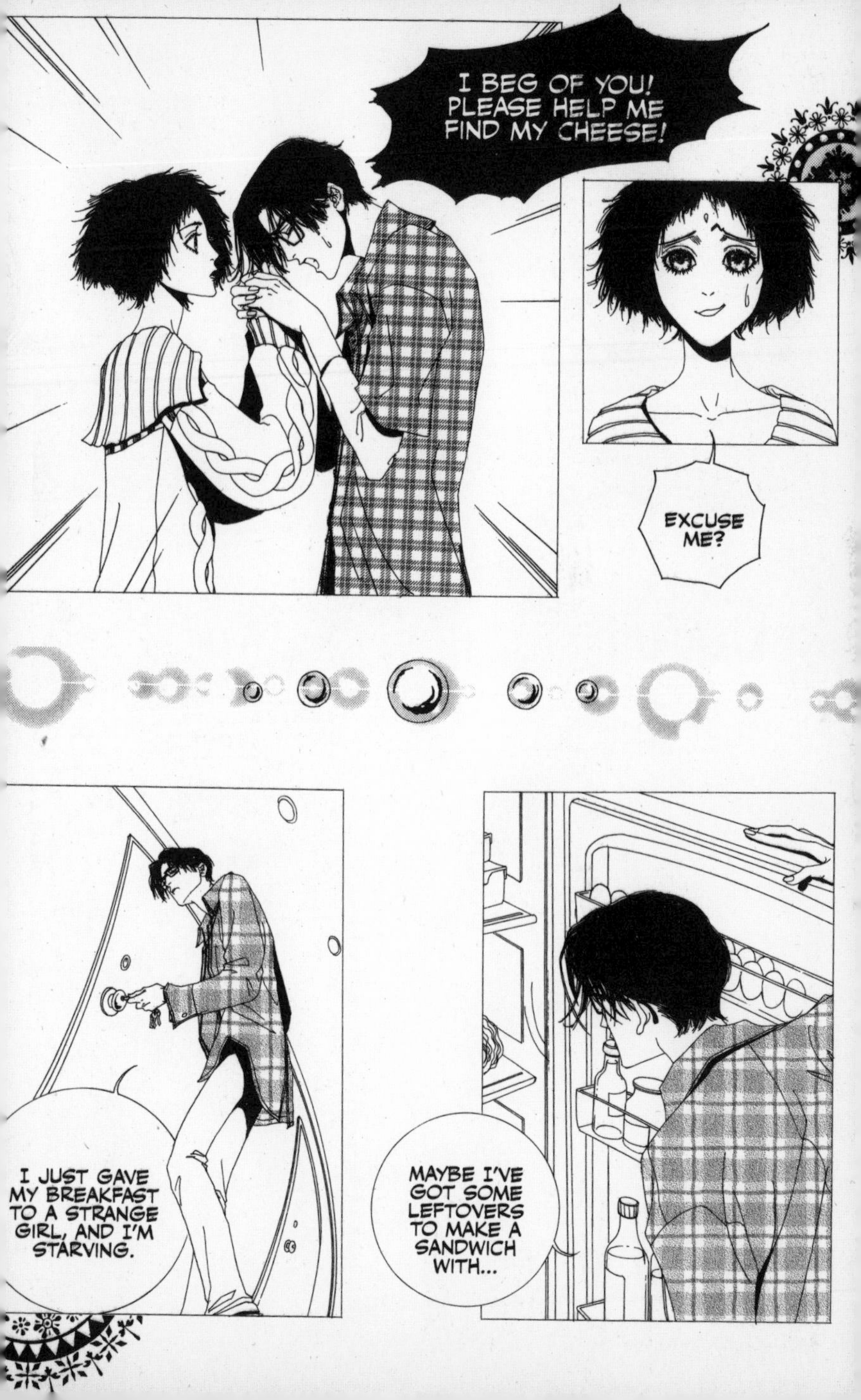
I BEG OF YOU! PLEASE HELP ME FIND MY CHEESE!
EXCUSE ME?
I JUST GAVE MY BREAKFAST TO A STRANGE GIRL, AND I'M STARVING.
MAYBE I'VE GOT SOME LEFTOVERS TO MAKE A SANDWICH WITH...

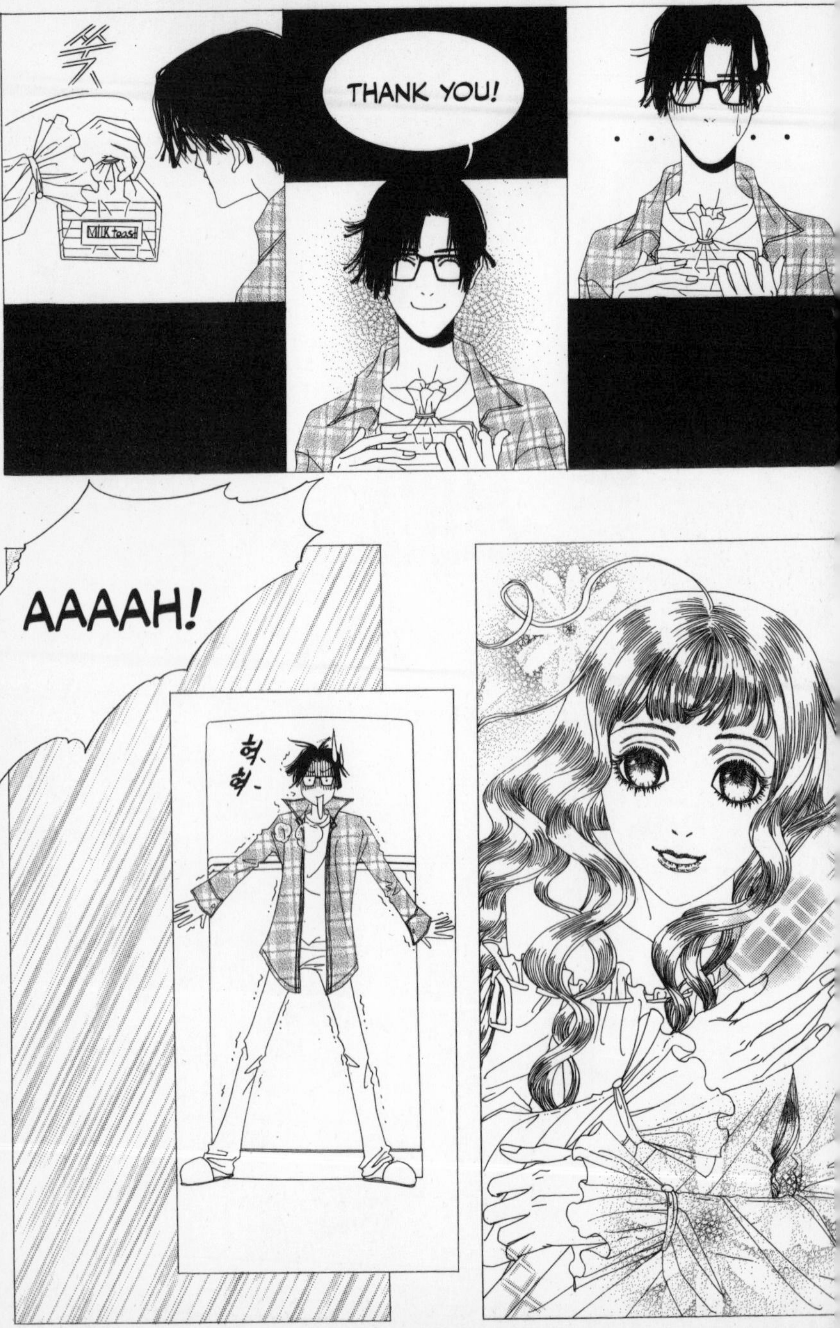

쓱
MILK toast
THANK YOU!
. . . . .
AAAAH!
허、
허-

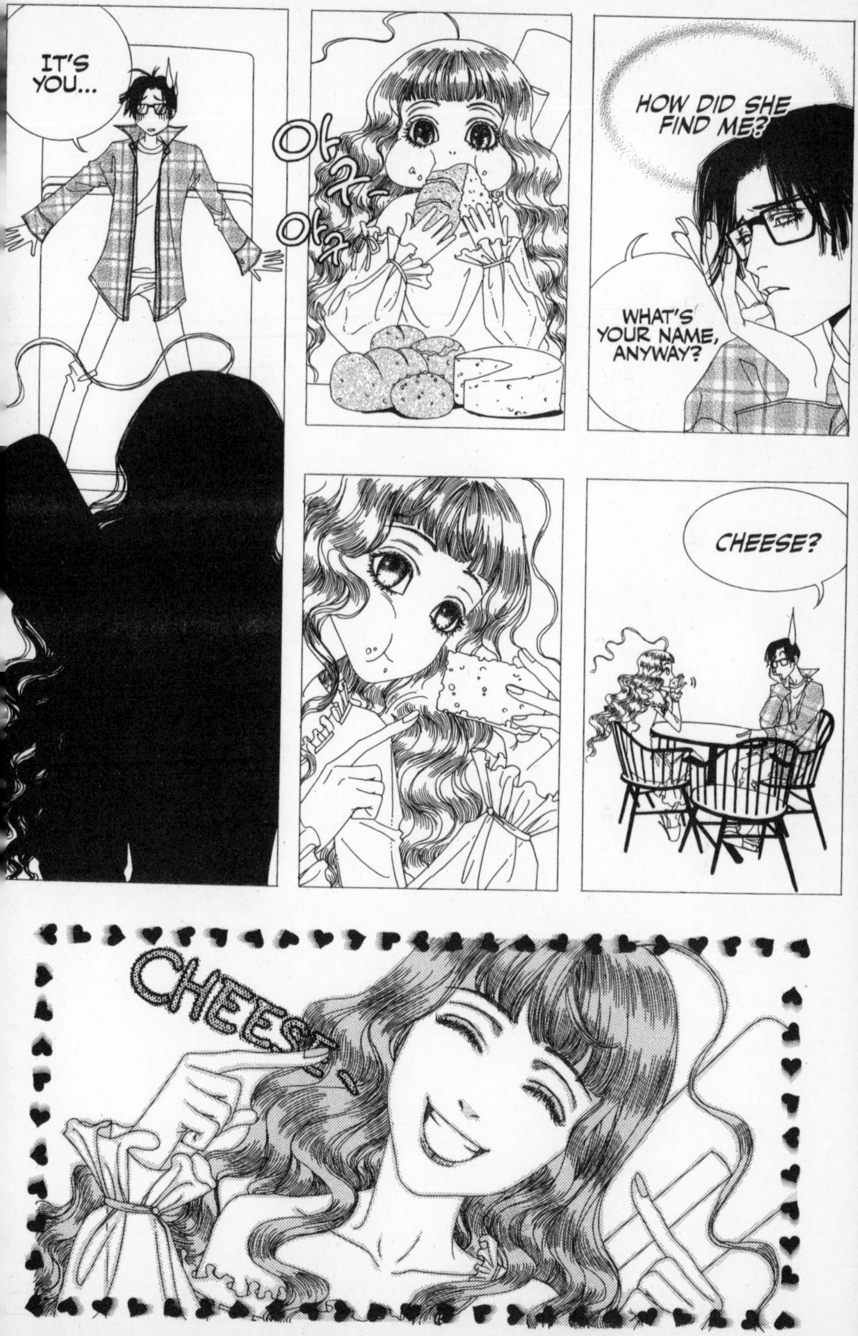
IT'S YOU...
HOW DID SHE FIND ME?
WHAT'S YOUR NAME, ANYWAY?
CHEESE?
CHEESE!

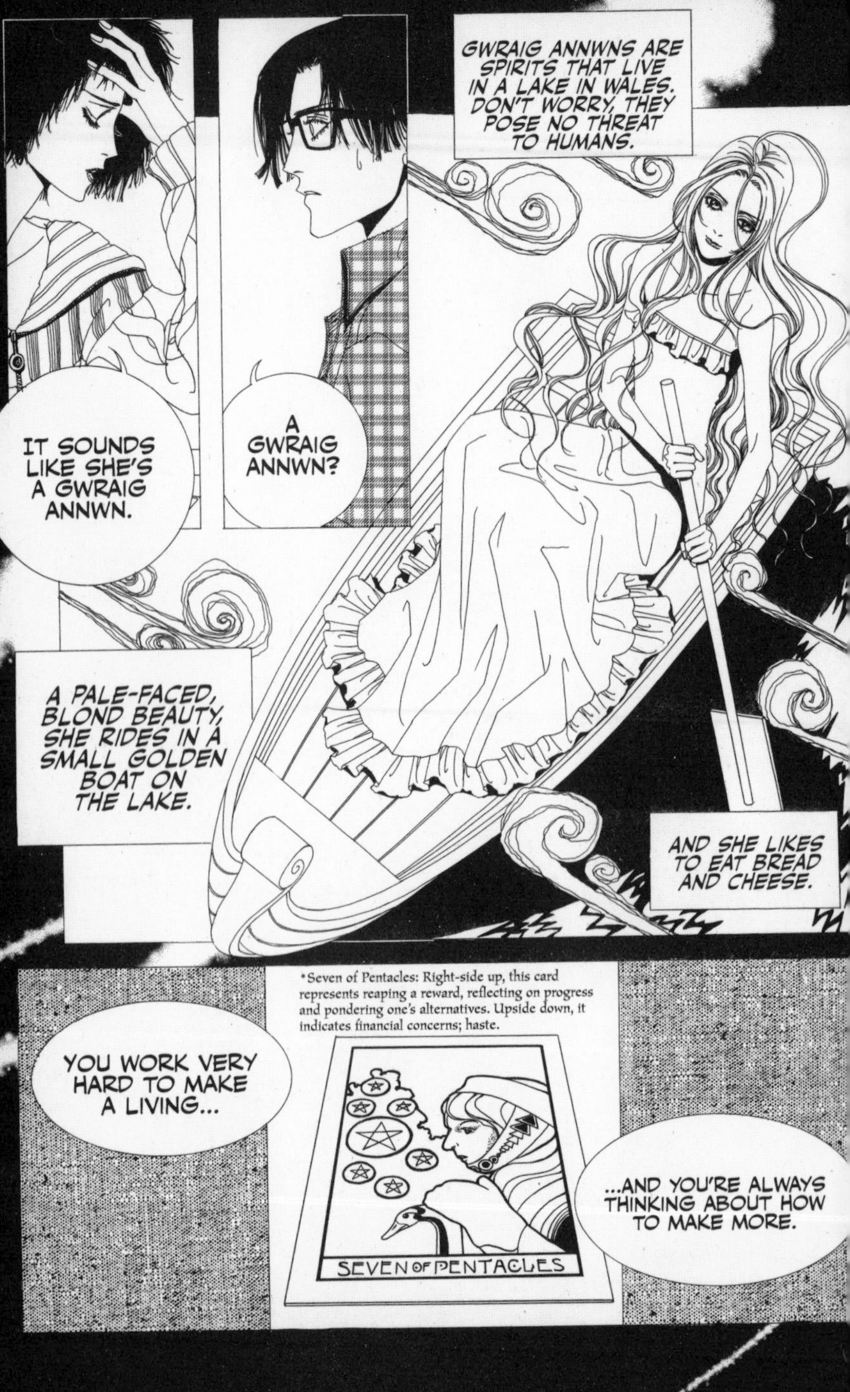
IT SOUNDS LIKE SHE'S A GWRAIG ANNWN.
A GWRAIG ANNWN?
GWRAIG ANNWNS ARE SPIRITS THAT LIVE IN A LAKE IN WALES. DON'T WORRY, THEY POSE NO THREAT TO HUMANS.
A PALE-FACED, BLOND BEAUTY, SHE RIDES IN A SMALL GOLDEN BOAT ON THE LAKE.
AND SHE LIKES TO EAT BREAD AND CHEESE.
YOU WORK VERY HARD TO MAKE A LIVING...
*Seven of Pentacles: Right-side up, this card represents reaping a reward, reflecting on progress and pondering one's alternatives. Upside down, it indicates financial concerns; haste.
SEVEN OF PENTACLES
...AND YOU'RE ALWAYS THINKING ABOUT HOW TO MAKE MORE.

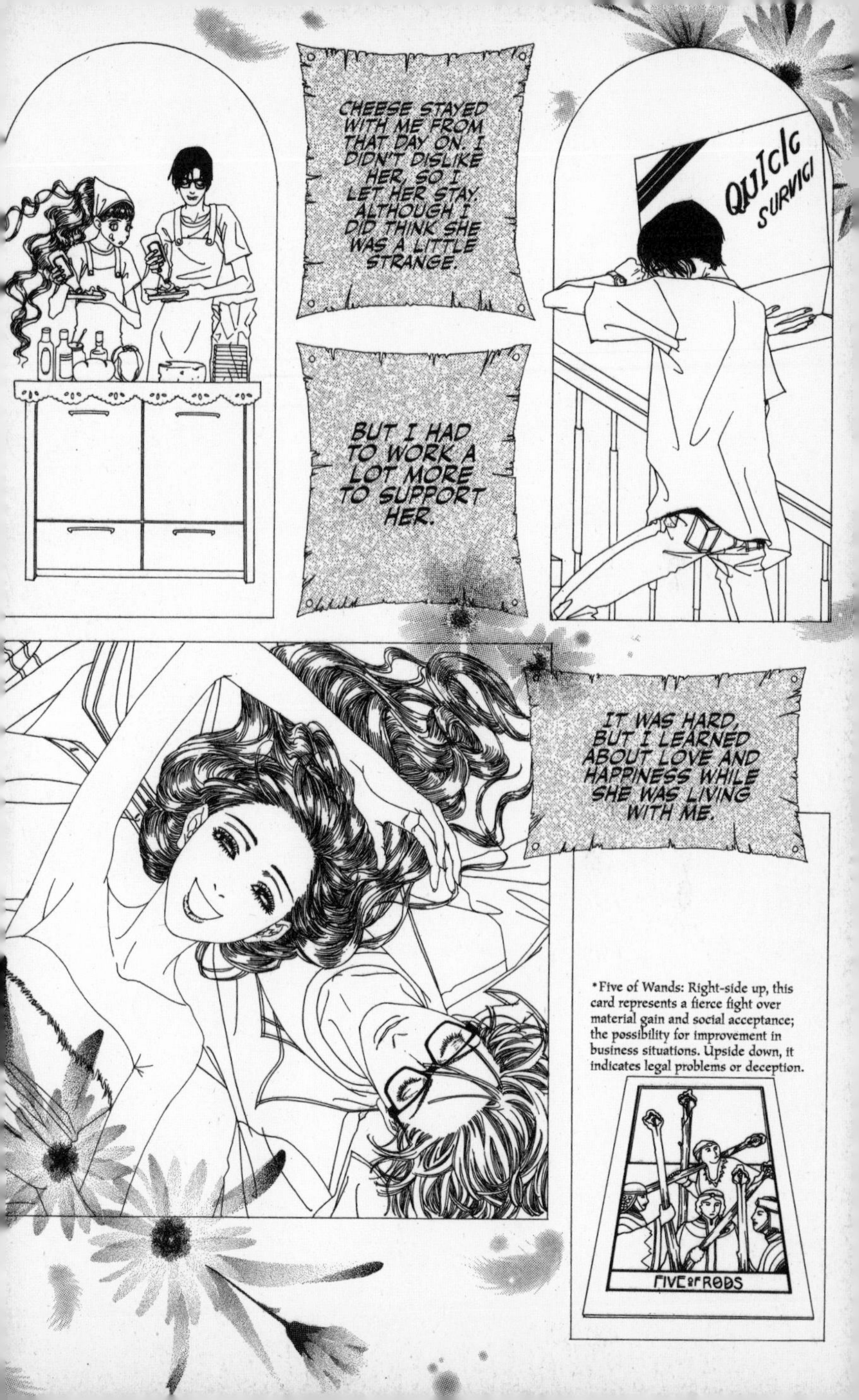
CHEESE STAYED WITH ME FROM THAT DAY ON. I DIDN'T DISLIKE HER, SO I LET HER STAY. ALTHOUGH I DID THINK SHE WAS A LITTLE STRANGE.
BUT I HAD TO WORK A LOT MORE TO SUPPORT HER.
IT WAS HARD, BUT I LEARNED ABOUT LOVE AND HAPPINESS WHILE SHE WAS LIVING WITH ME.
FIVE of RODS

*Five of Wands: Right-side up, this card represents a fierce fight over material gain and social acceptance; the possibility for improvement in business situations. Upside down, it indicates legal problems or deception.

BUT THEN TROUBLE BEGAN TO BREW IN YOUR RELATIONSHIP.

CHEESE... SHE WAS TOO GOOD FOR ME.

I THOUGHT SHE STAYED WITH ME WAS BECAUSE SHE LIKED THE FOOD AND GIFTS I GAVE HER, SO I WORKED HARDER TO MAKE EVEN MORE MONEY. BUT THAT GAVE ME LESS TIME TO SPEND WITH HER.

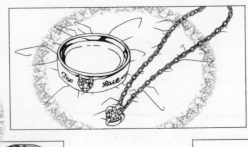

I CAN BUY THAT FOR HER WITH THIS MONTH'S PAYCHECK.

RING

DOES IT TASTE GOOD?

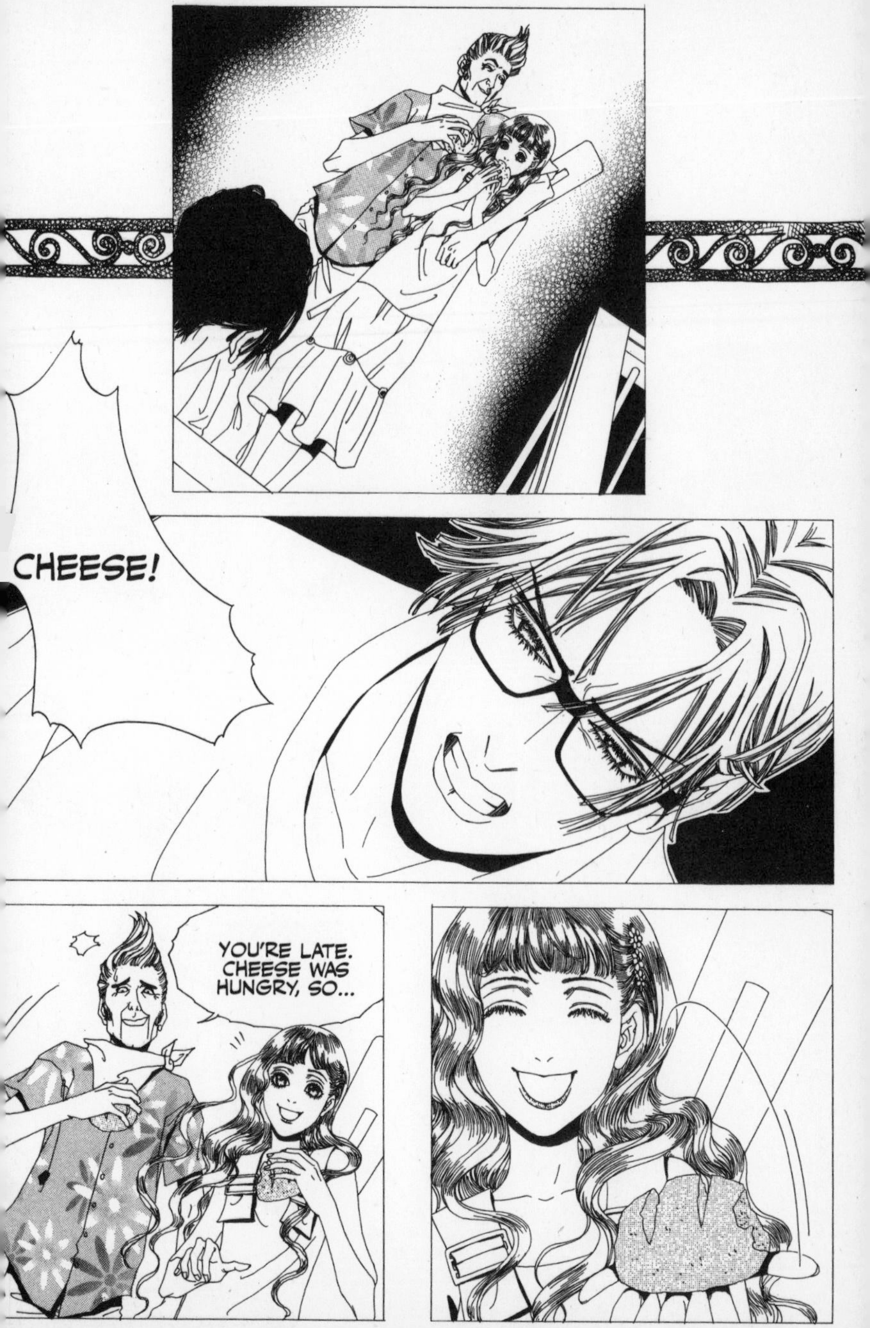
CHEESE!
YOU'RE LATE. CHEESE WAS HUNGRY, SO...

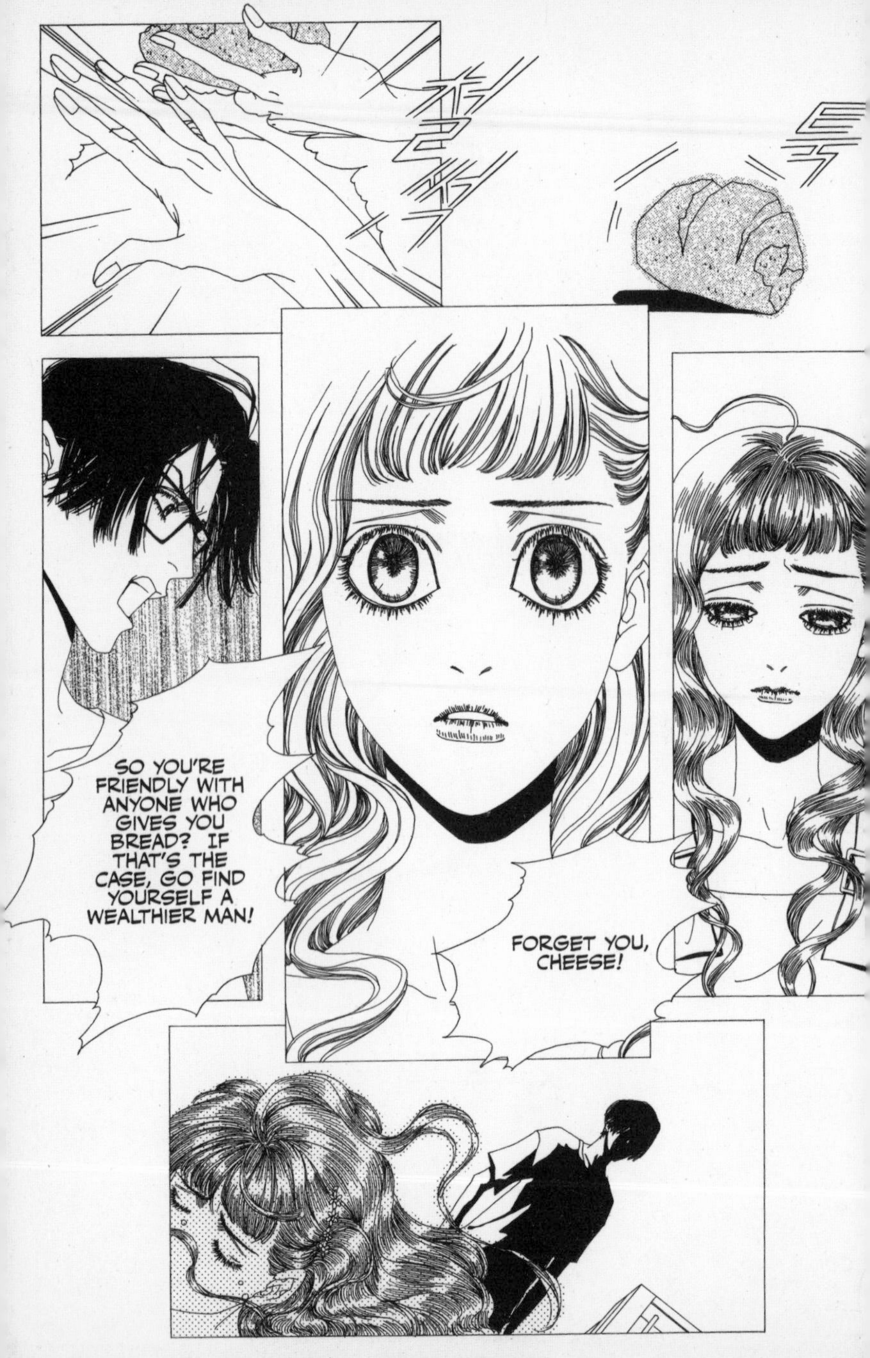
SO YOU'RE FRIENDLY WITH ANYONE WHO GIVES YOU BREAD? IF THAT'S THE CASE, GO FIND YOURSELF A WEALTHIER MAN!
FORGET YOU, CHEESE!

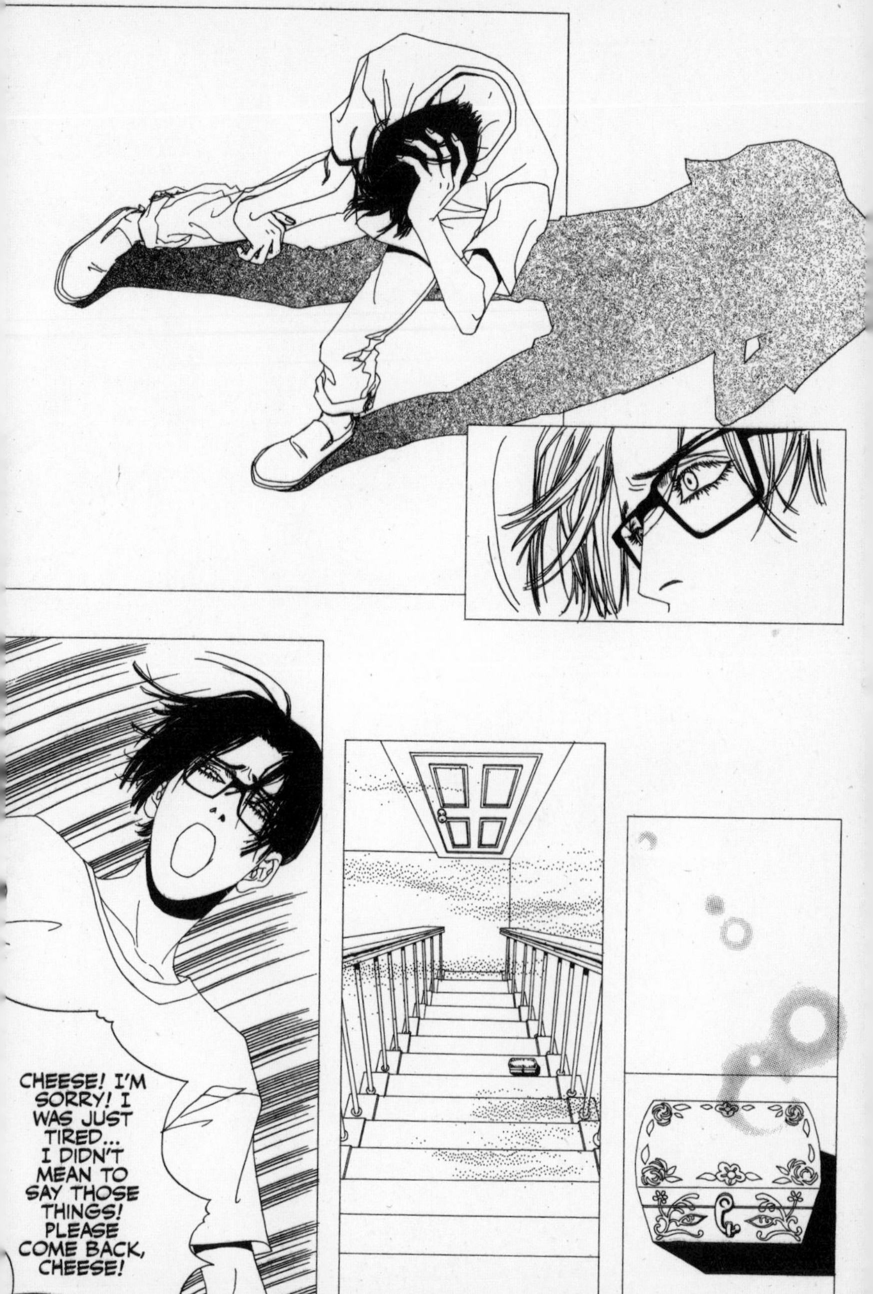
CHEESE! I'M SORRY! I WAS JUST TIRED... I DIDN'T MEAN TO SAY THOSE THINGS! PLEASE COME BACK, CHEESE!

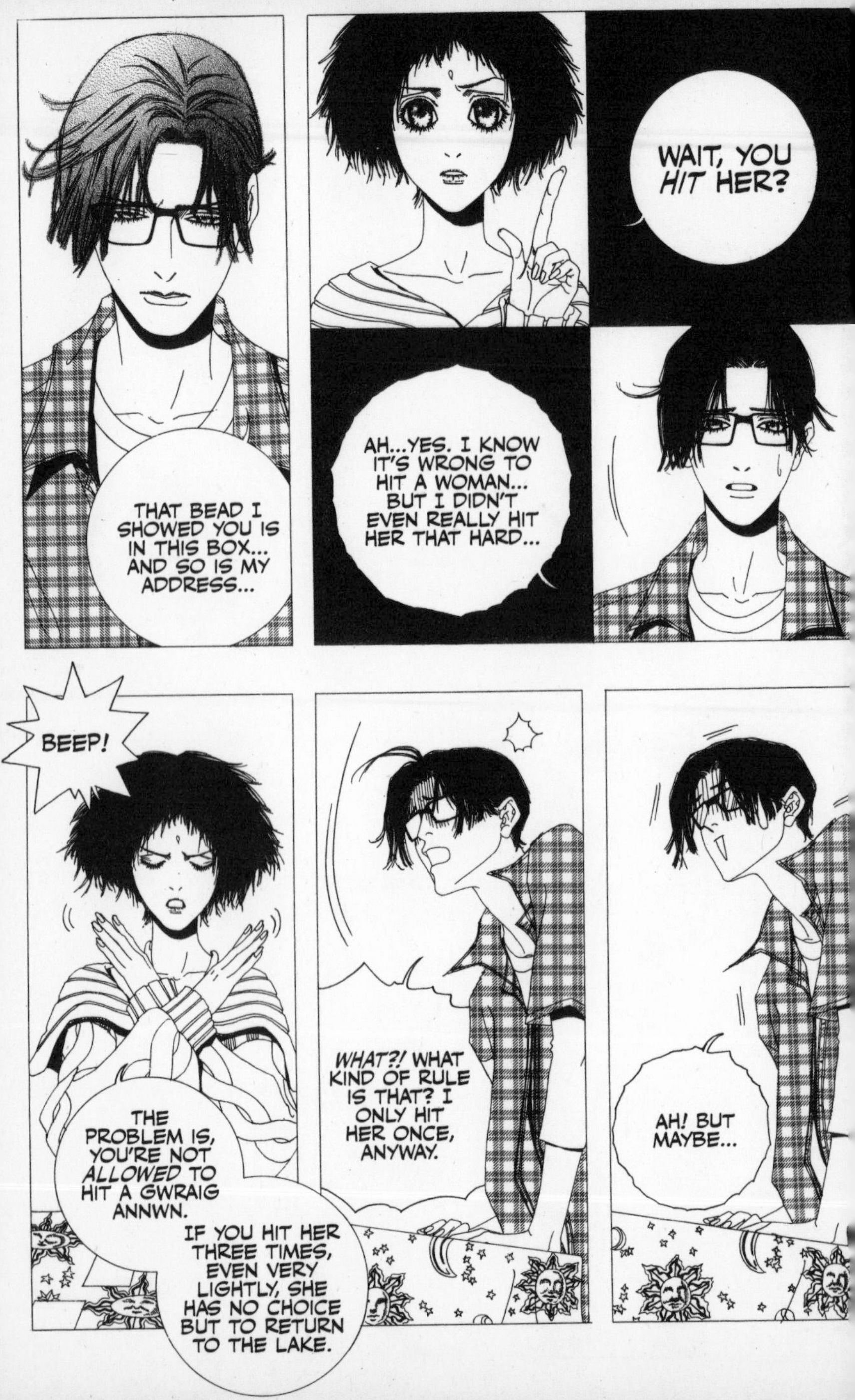
THAT BEAD I SHOWED YOU IS IN THIS BOX... AND SO IS MY ADDRESS...
WAIT, YOU *HIT* HER?
AH...YES. I KNOW IT'S WRONG TO HIT A WOMAN... BUT I DIDN'T EVEN REALLY HIT HER THAT HARD...
BEEP!
THE PROBLEM IS, YOU'RE NOT *ALLOWED* TO HIT A GWRAIG ANNWN.
IF YOU HIT HER THREE TIMES, EVEN VERY LIGHTLY, SHE HAS NO CHOICE BUT TO RETURN TO THE LAKE.
WHAT?! WHAT KIND OF RULE IS THAT? I ONLY HIT HER ONCE, ANYWAY.
AH! BUT MAYBE...

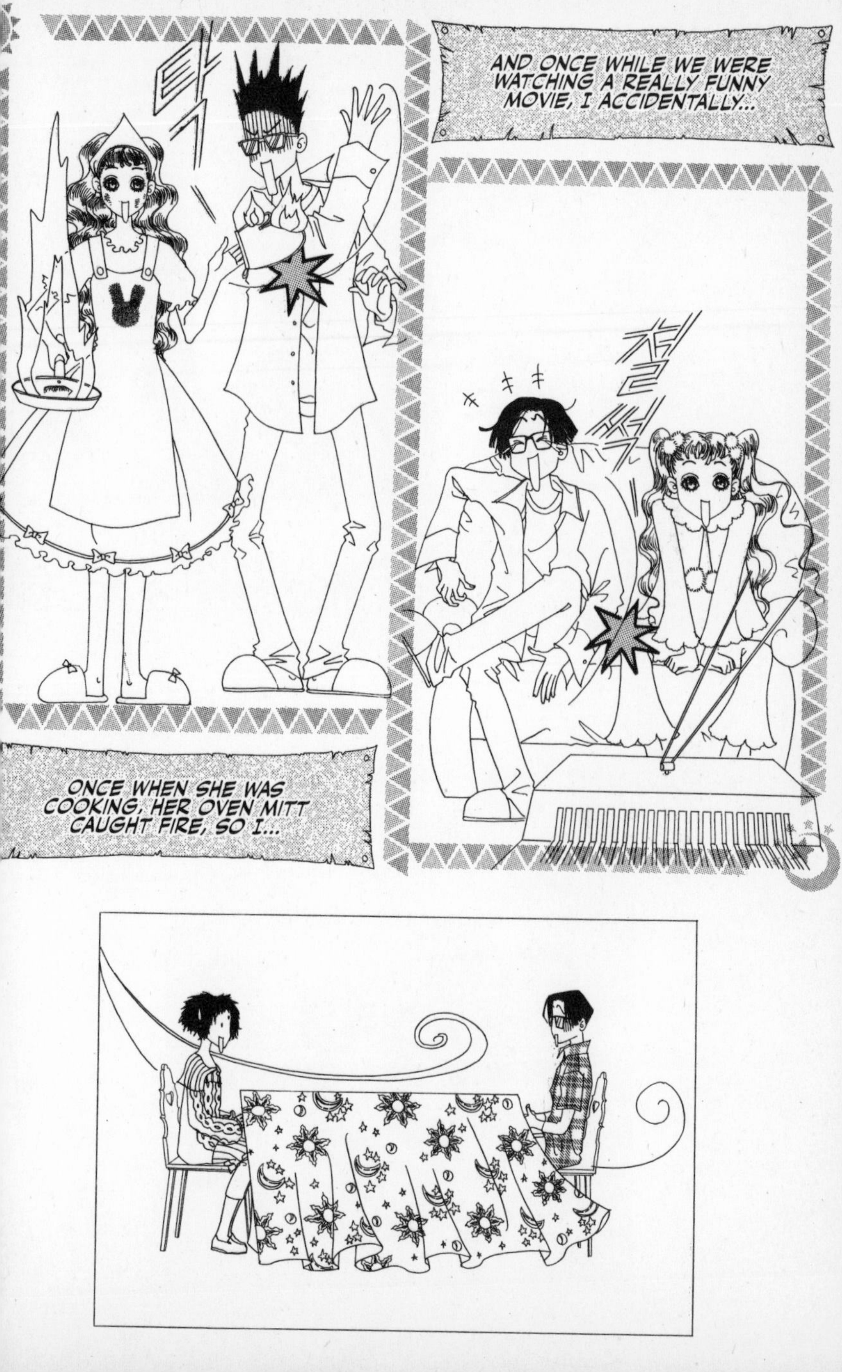
탁
ONCE WHEN SHE WAS COOKING, HER OVEN MITT CAUGHT FIRE, SO I...
AND ONCE WHILE WE WERE WATCHING A REALLY FUNNY MOVIE, I ACCIDENTALLY...
철썩

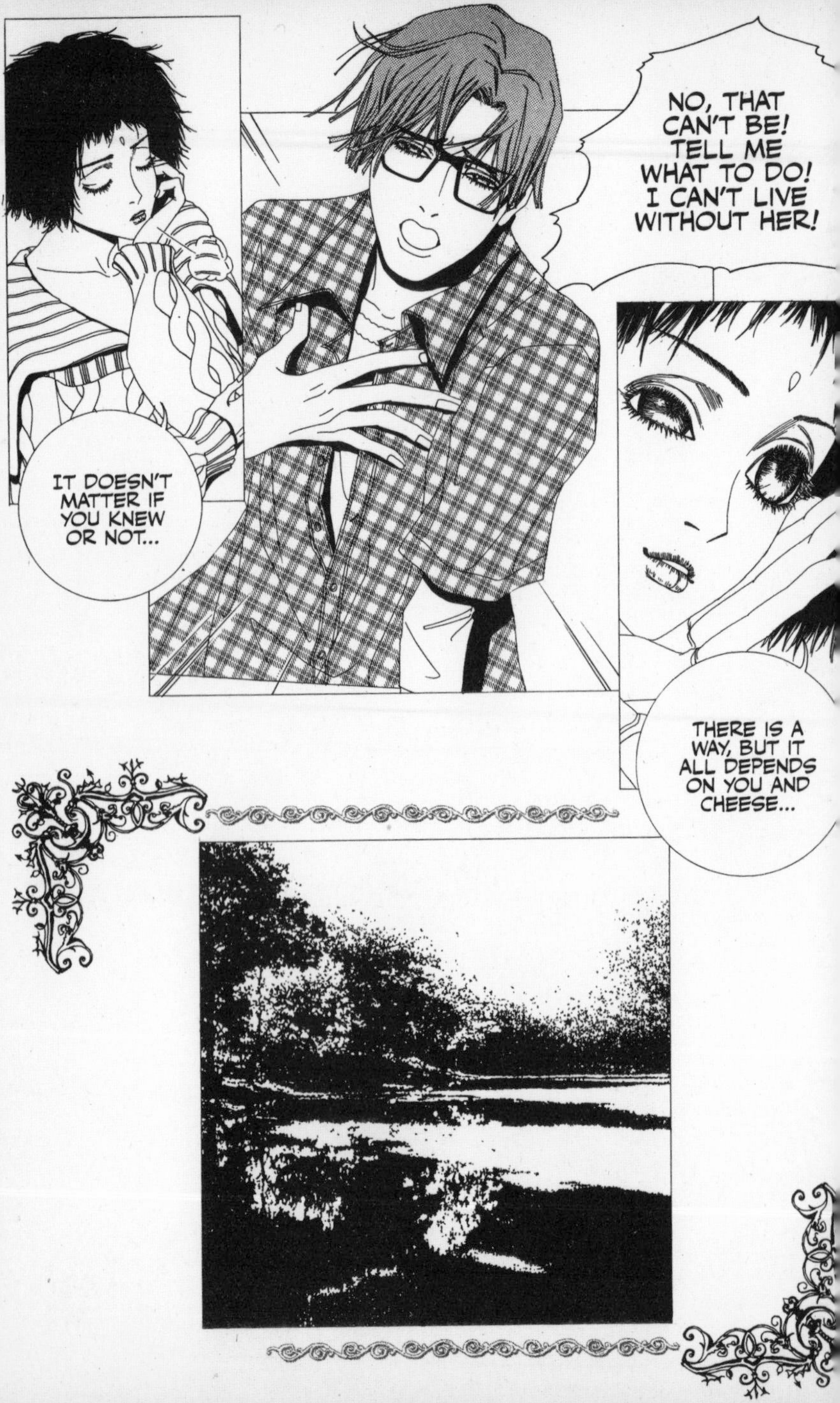
IT DOESN'T MATTER IF YOU KNEW OR NOT...
NO, THAT CAN'T BE! TELL ME WHAT TO DO! I CAN'T LIVE WITHOUT HER!
THERE IS A WAY, BUT IT ALL DEPENDS ON YOU AND CHEESE...

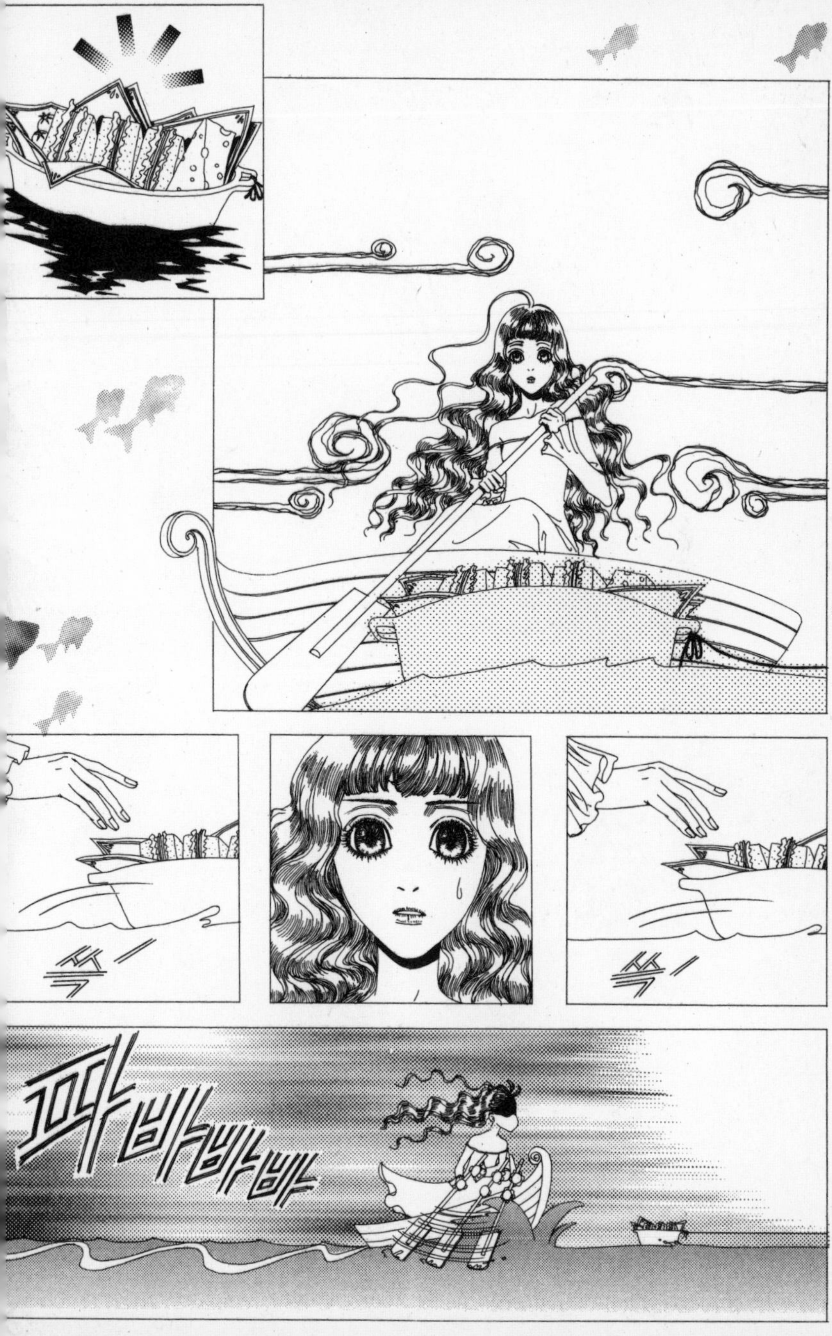

쓱-
쓱-
파바바바

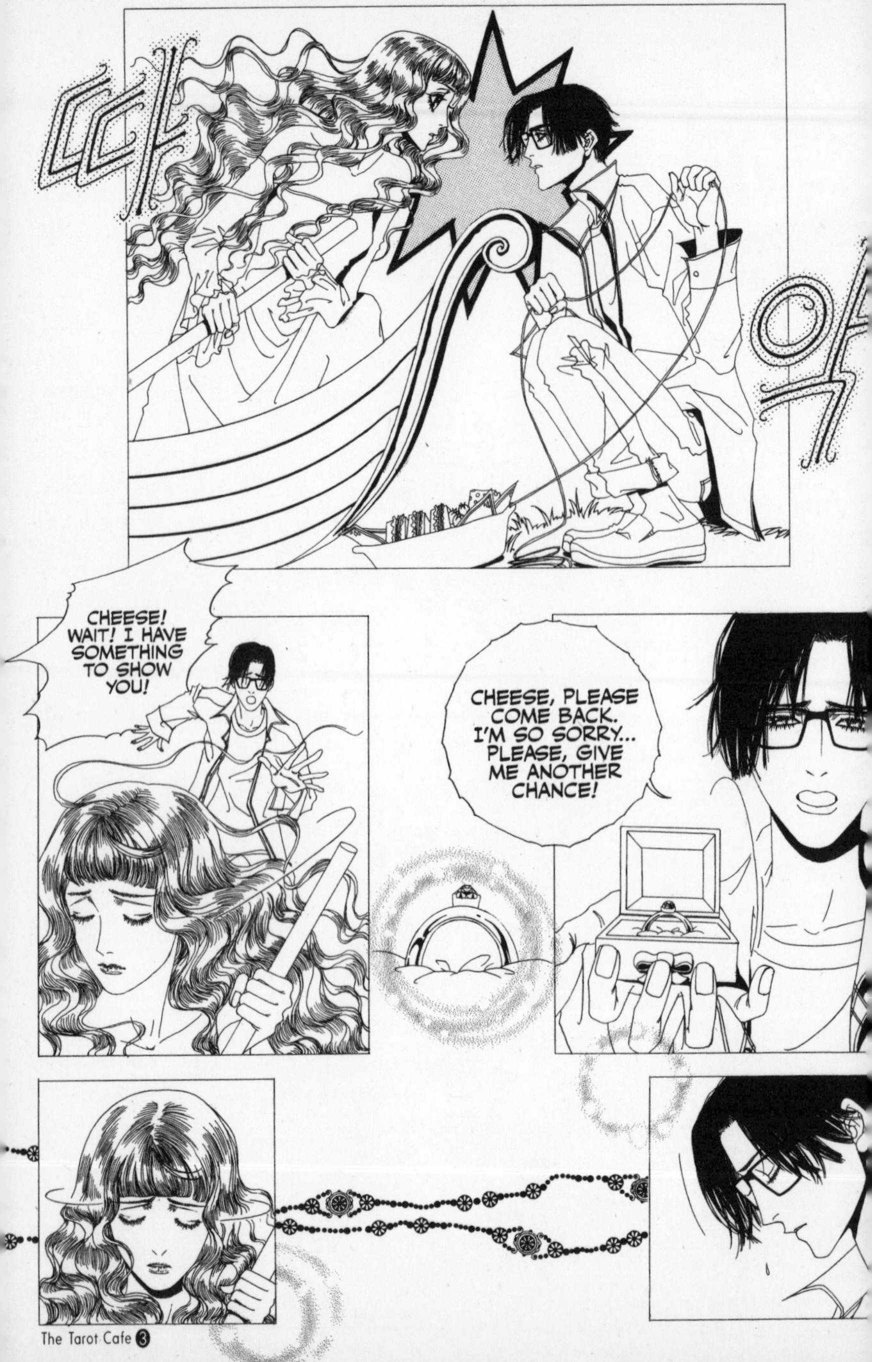
CHEESE! WAIT! I HAVE SOMETHING TO SHOW YOU!
CHEESE, PLEASE COME BACK. I'M SO SORRY... PLEASE, GIVE ME ANOTHER CHANCE!

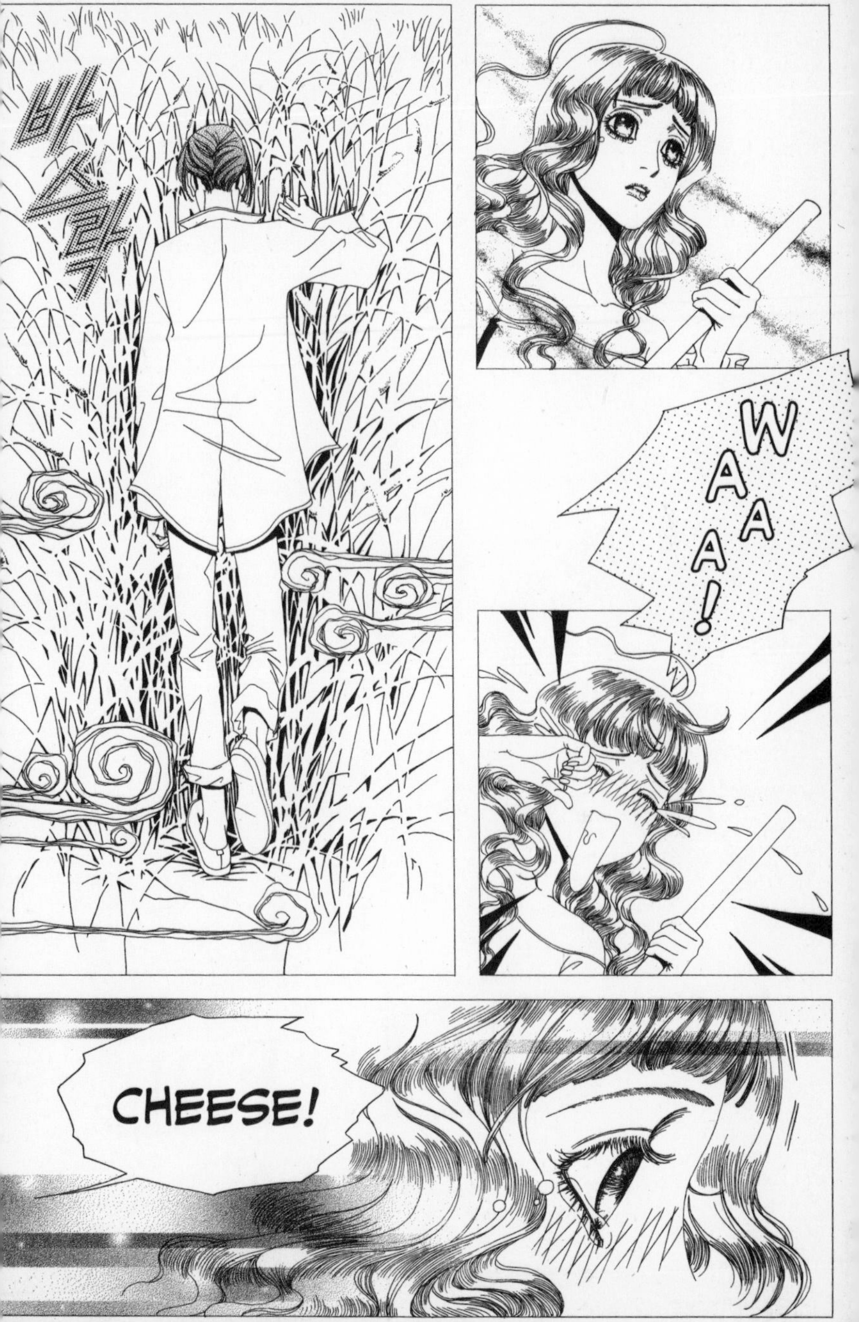
바스락
WAAA!
CHEESE!

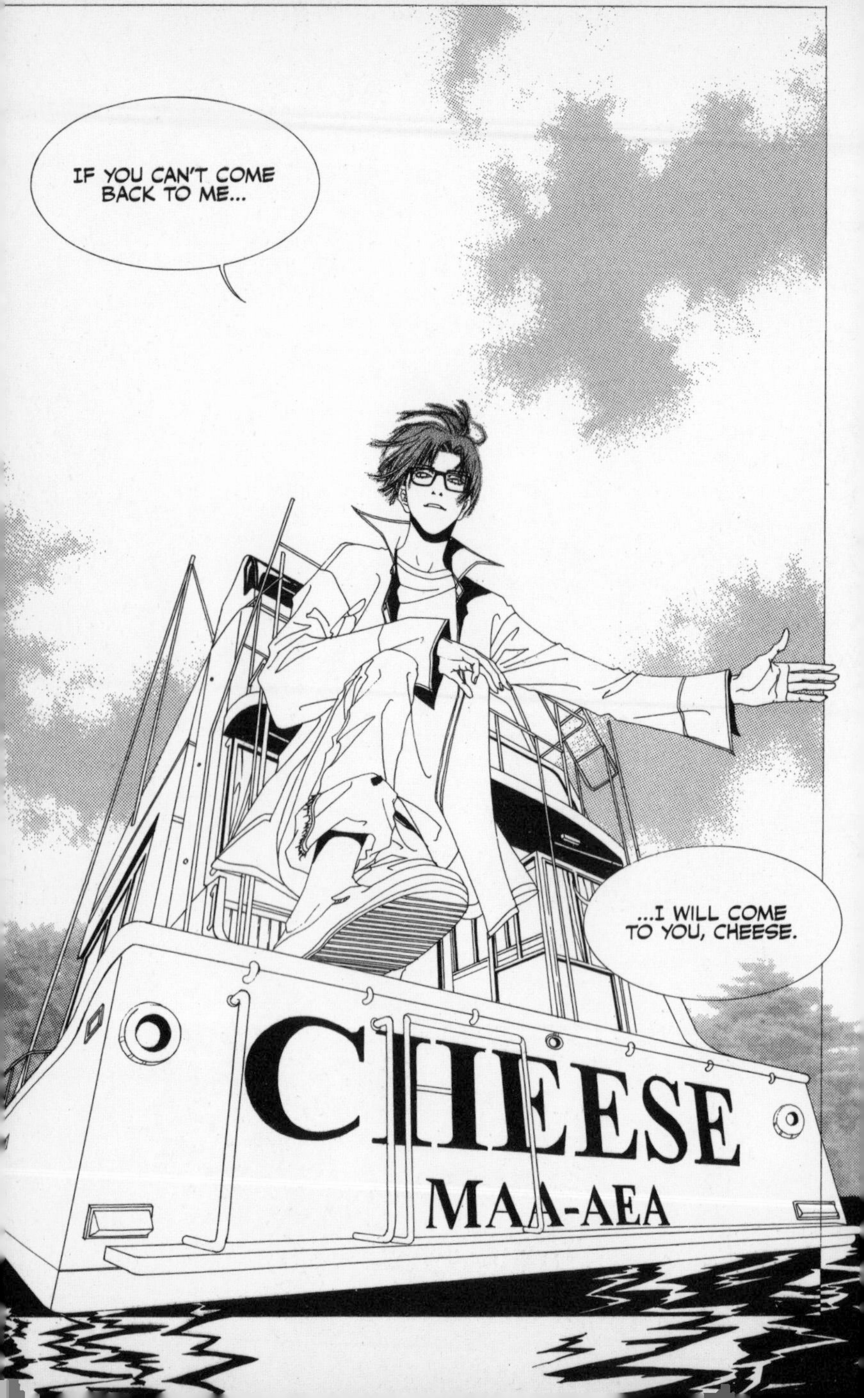
IF YOU CAN'T COME BACK TO ME...
...I WILL COME TO YOU, CHEESE.
CHEESE
MAA-AEA

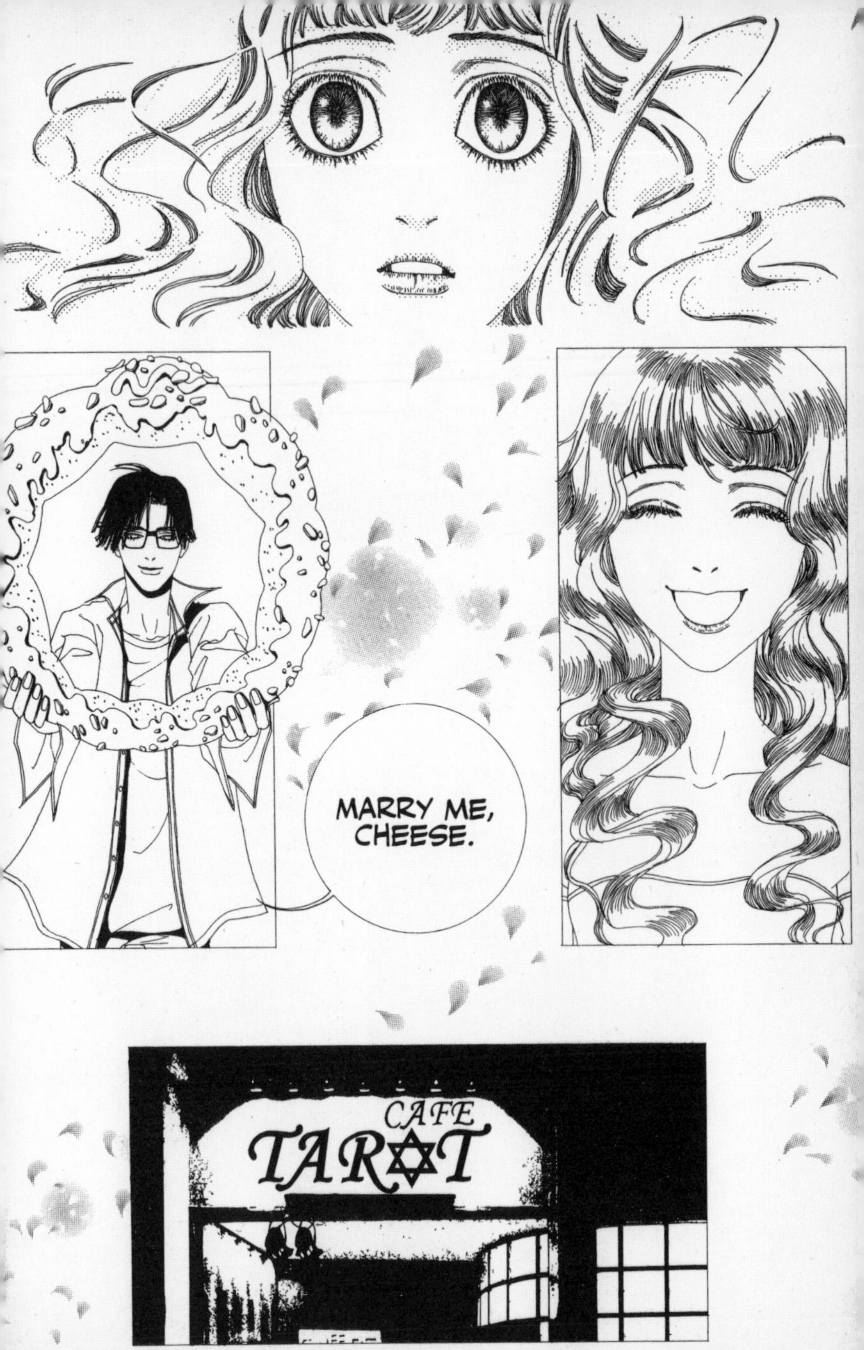
MARRY ME, CHEESE.
CAFE
TAROT

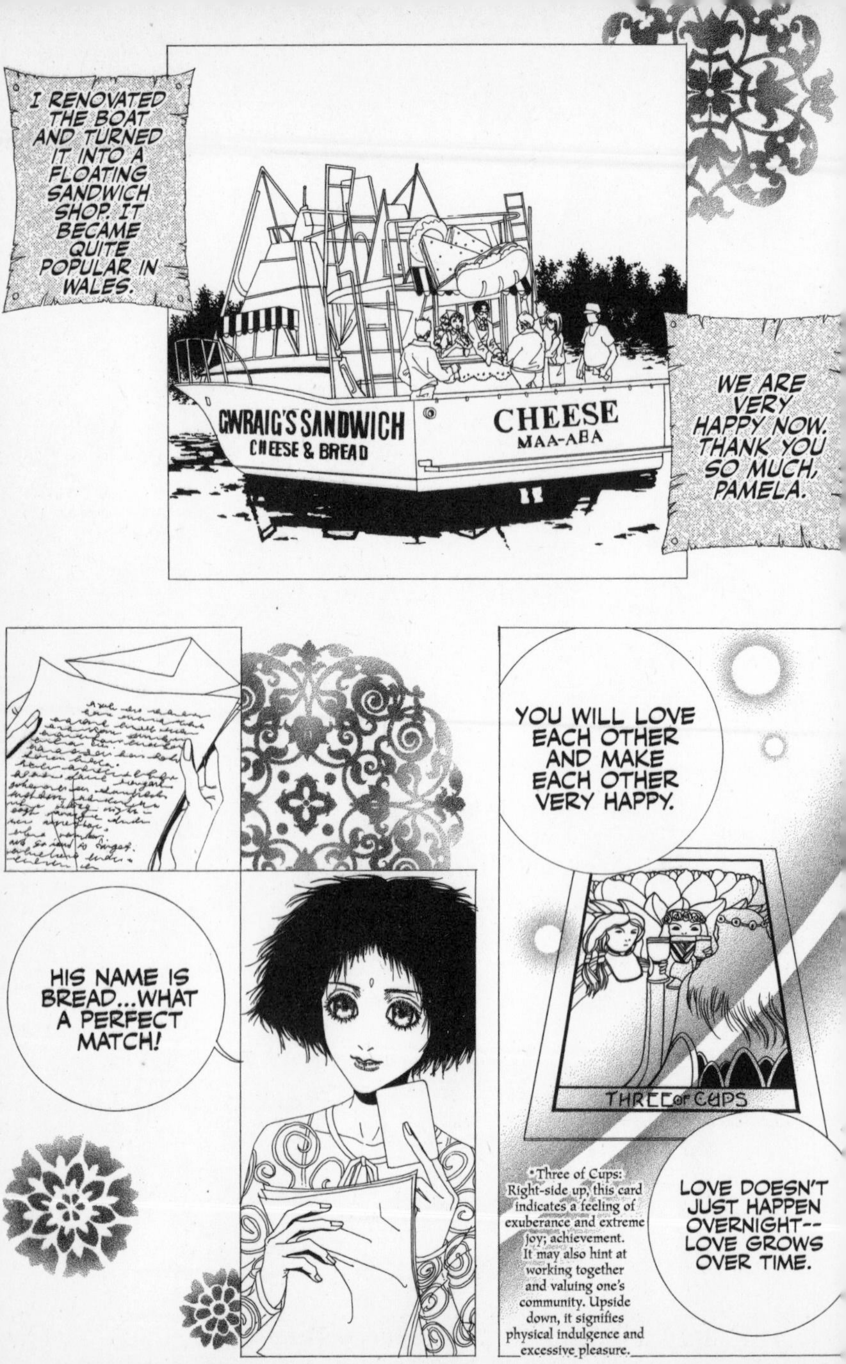
I RENOVATED THE BOAT AND TURNED IT INTO A FLOATING SANDWICH SHOP. IT BECAME QUITE POPULAR IN WALES.
GWRAIG'S SANDWICH
CHEESE & BREAD
CHEESE
MAA-ABA
WE ARE VERY HAPPY NOW. THANK YOU SO MUCH, PAMELA.
YOU WILL LOVE EACH OTHER AND MAKE EACH OTHER VERY HAPPY.
HIS NAME IS BREAD...WHAT A PERFECT MATCH!
THREE of CUPS
*Three of Cups: Right-side up, this card indicates a feeling of exuberance and extreme joy; achievement. It may also hint at working together and valuing one's community. Upside down, it signifies physical indulgence and excessive pleasure.
LOVE DOESN'T JUST HAPPEN OVERNIGHT-- LOVE GROWS OVER TIME.

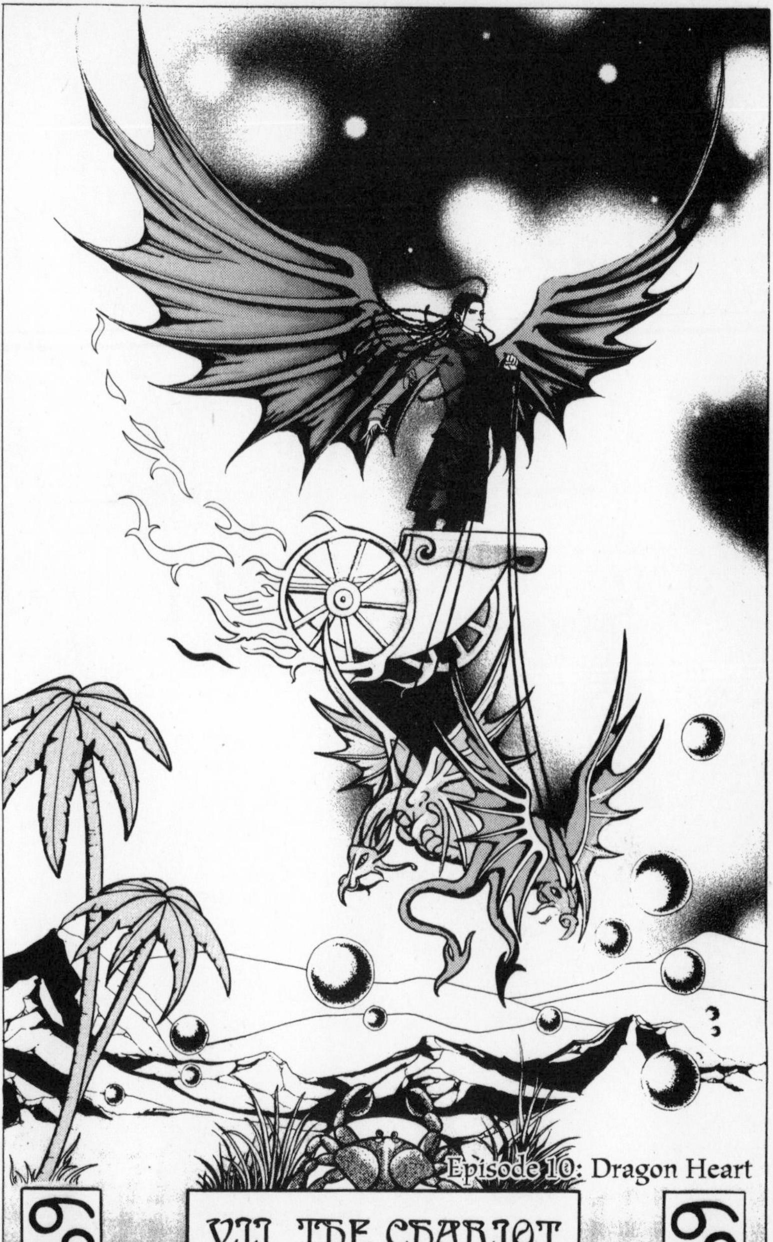
Episode 10: Dragon Heart
VII THE CHARIOT

*The Chariot: Right-side up, this card indicates a determination to succeed and achieve victory; focus. Upside down, it indicates a feeling of being blocked or restricted; being denied.

ILLUSTRATION FROM THE DRAGON TAROT

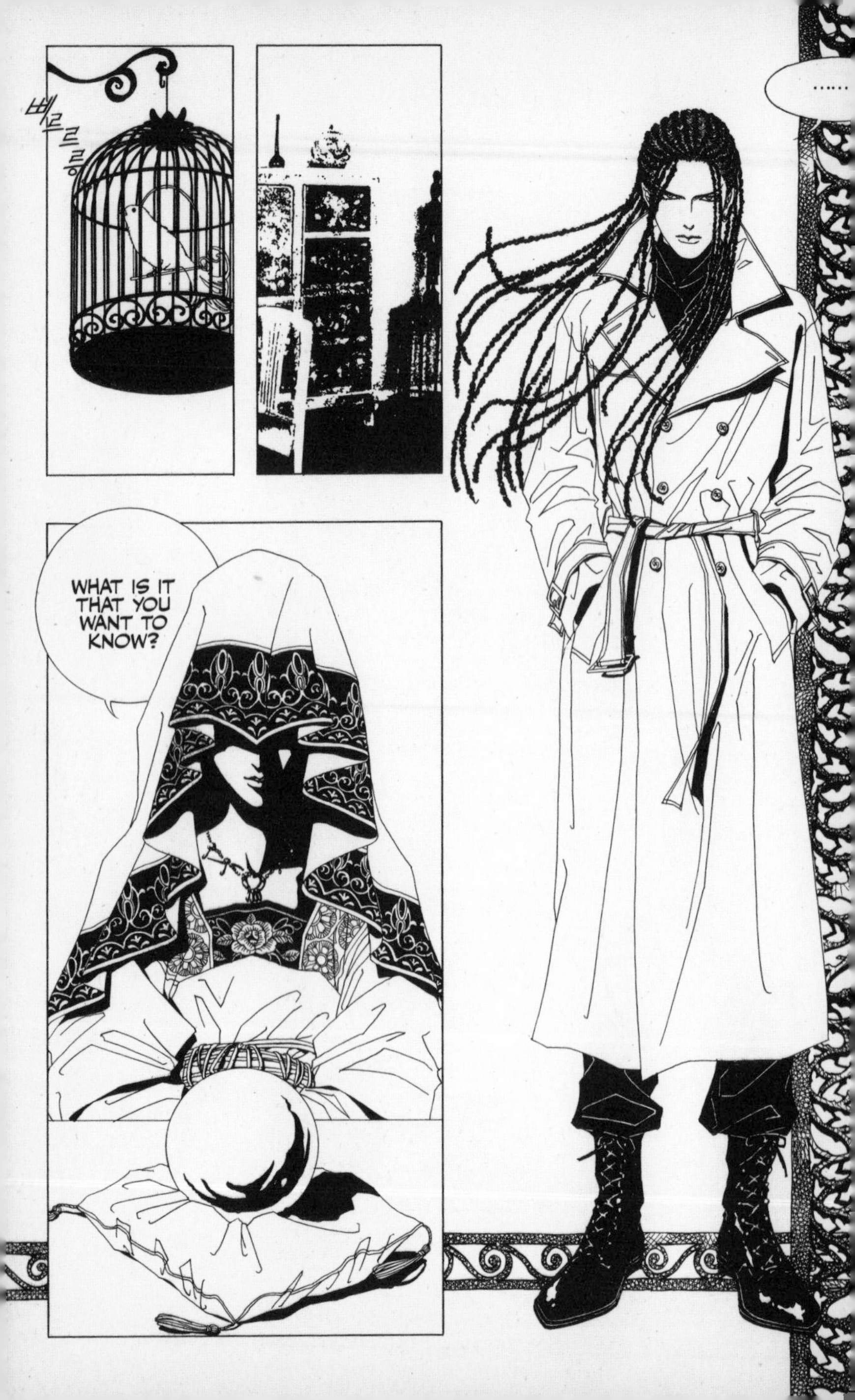
삐르르릉
WHAT IS IT THAT YOU WANT TO KNOW?
......

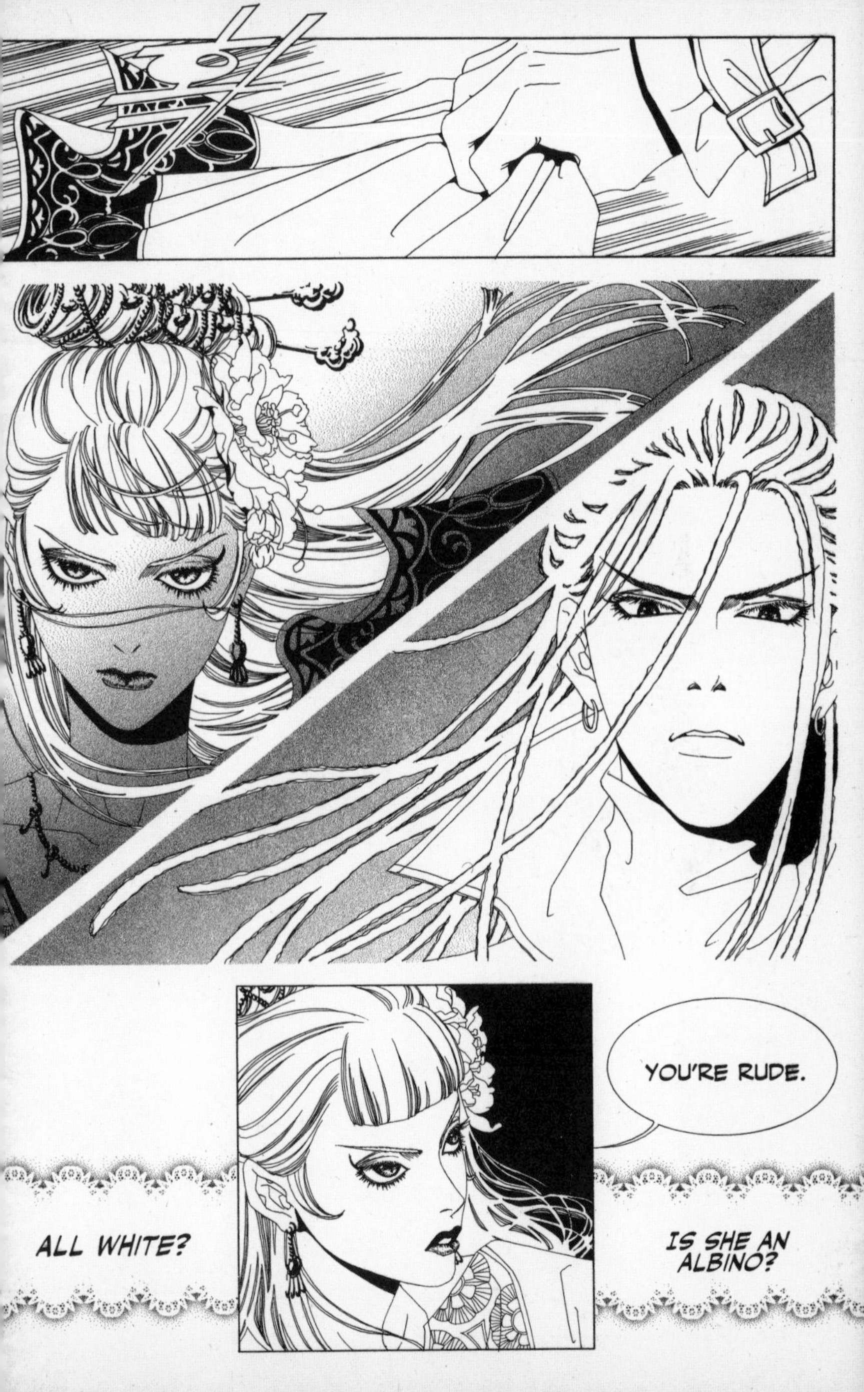
ALL WHITE?
YOU'RE RUDE.
IS SHE AN ALBINO?

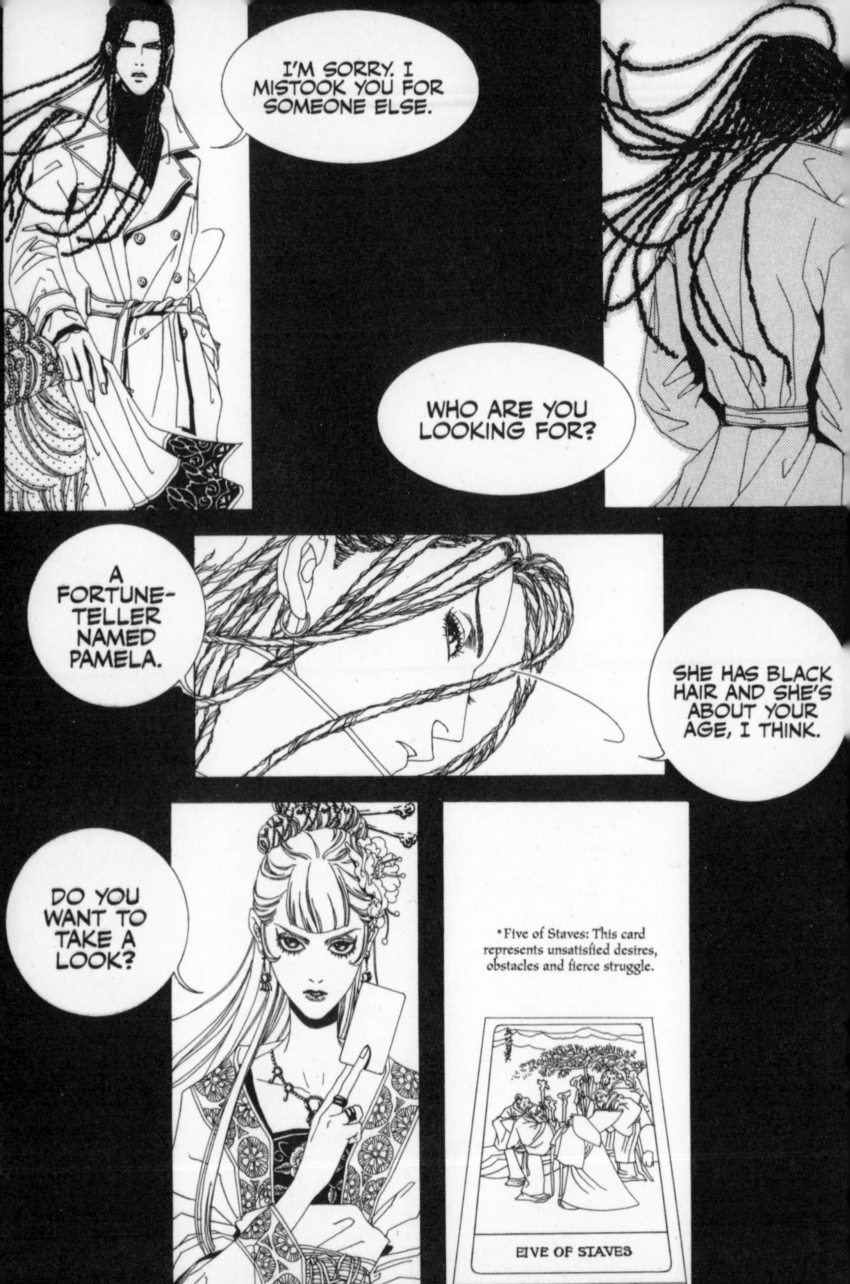
I'M SORRY. I MISTOOK YOU FOR SOMEONE ELSE.
WHO ARE YOU LOOKING FOR?
A FORTUNE-TELLER NAMED PAMELA.
SHE HAS BLACK HAIR AND SHE'S ABOUT YOUR AGE, I THINK.
DO YOU WANT TO TAKE A LOOK?
*Five of Staves: This card represents unsatisfied desires, obstacles and fierce struggle.
FIVE OF STAVES

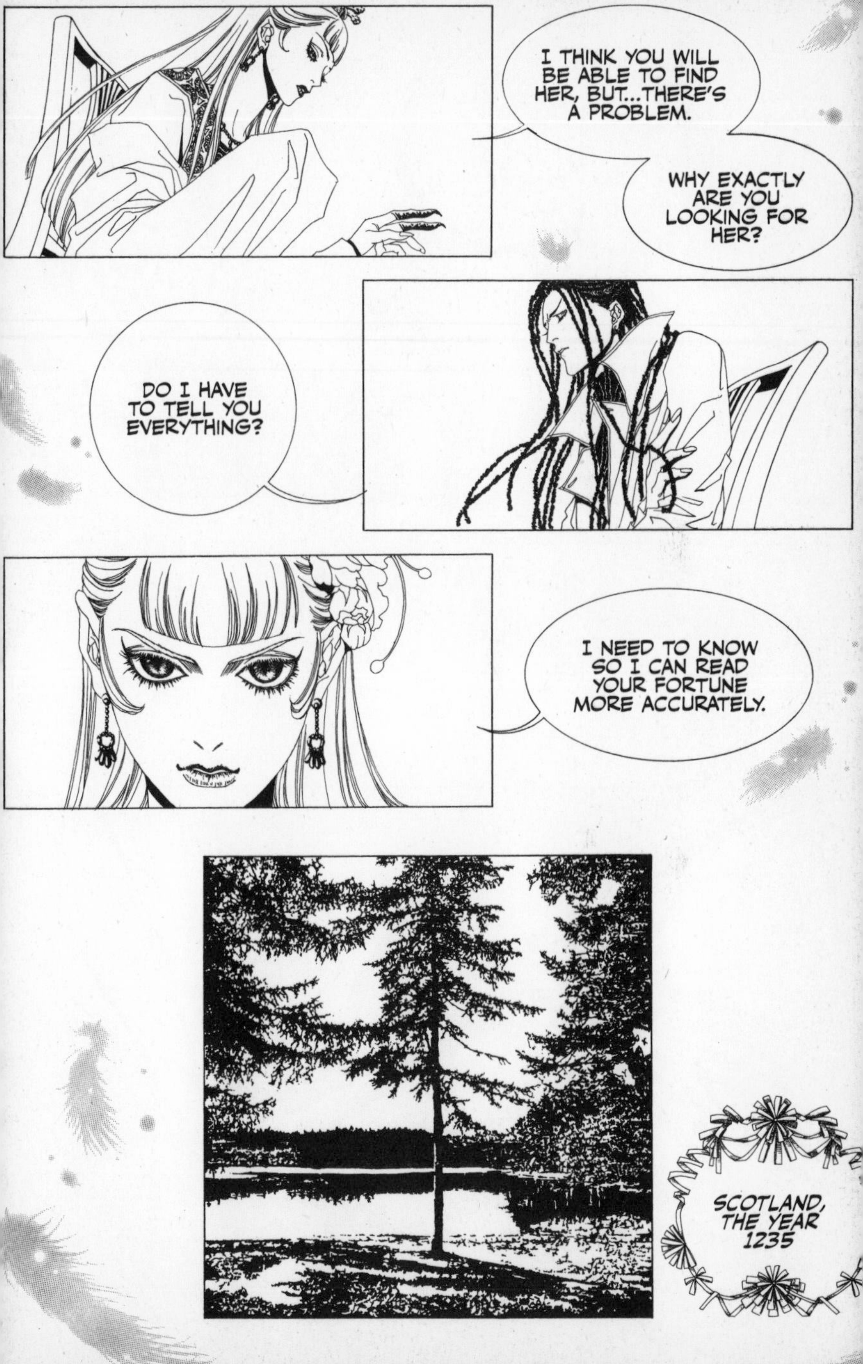
I THINK YOU WILL BE ABLE TO FIND HER, BUT...THERE'S A PROBLEM.
WHY EXACTLY ARE YOU LOOKING FOR HER?
DO I HAVE TO TELL YOU EVERYTHING?
I NEED TO KNOW SO I CAN READ YOUR FORTUNE MORE ACCURATELY.
SCOTLAND, THE YEAR 1235

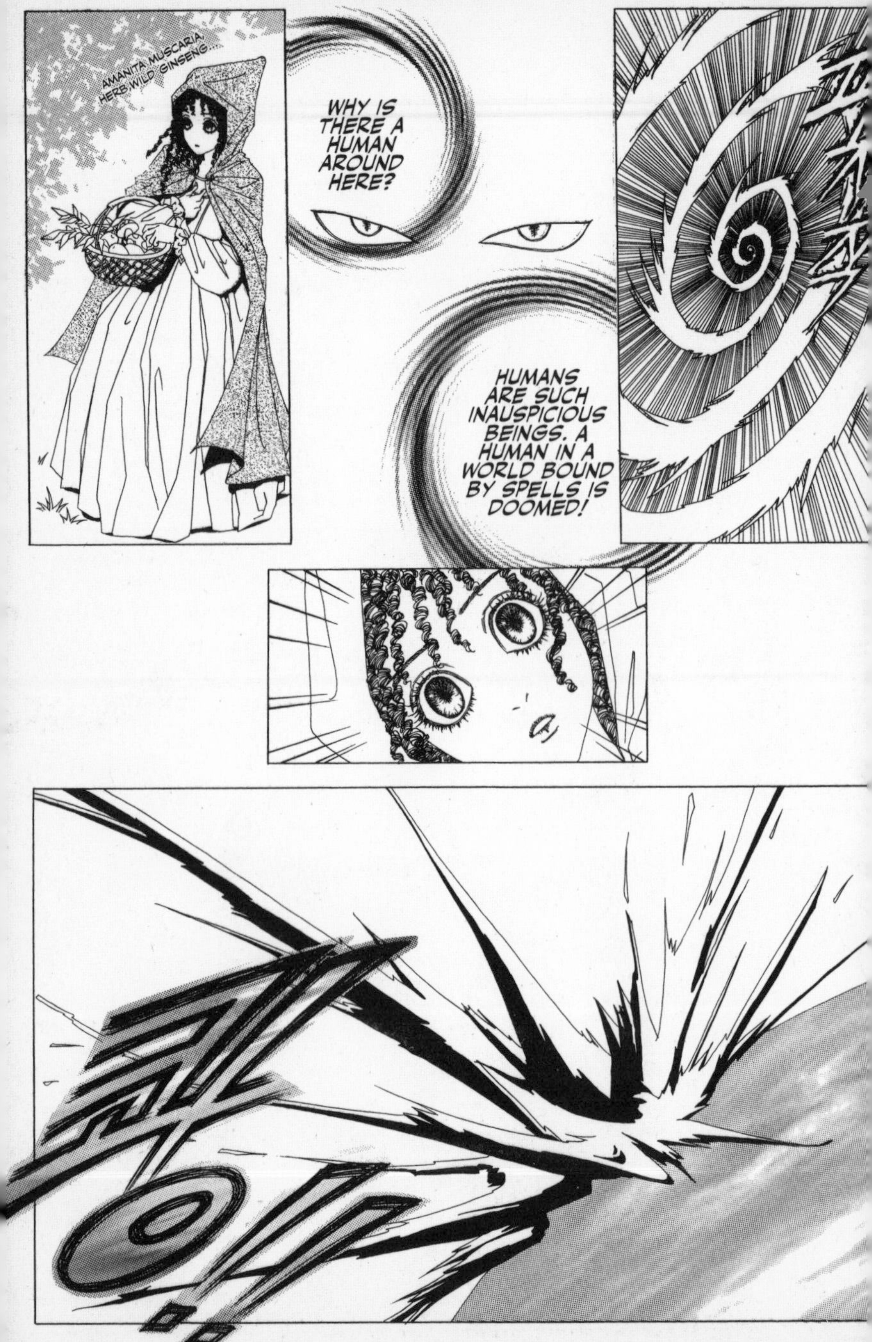
AMANITA MUSCARIA, HERB, WILD GINSENG...
WHY IS THERE A HUMAN AROUND HERE?
HUMANS ARE SUCH INAUSPICIOUS BEINGS. A HUMAN IN A WORLD BOUND BY SPELLS IS DOOMED!

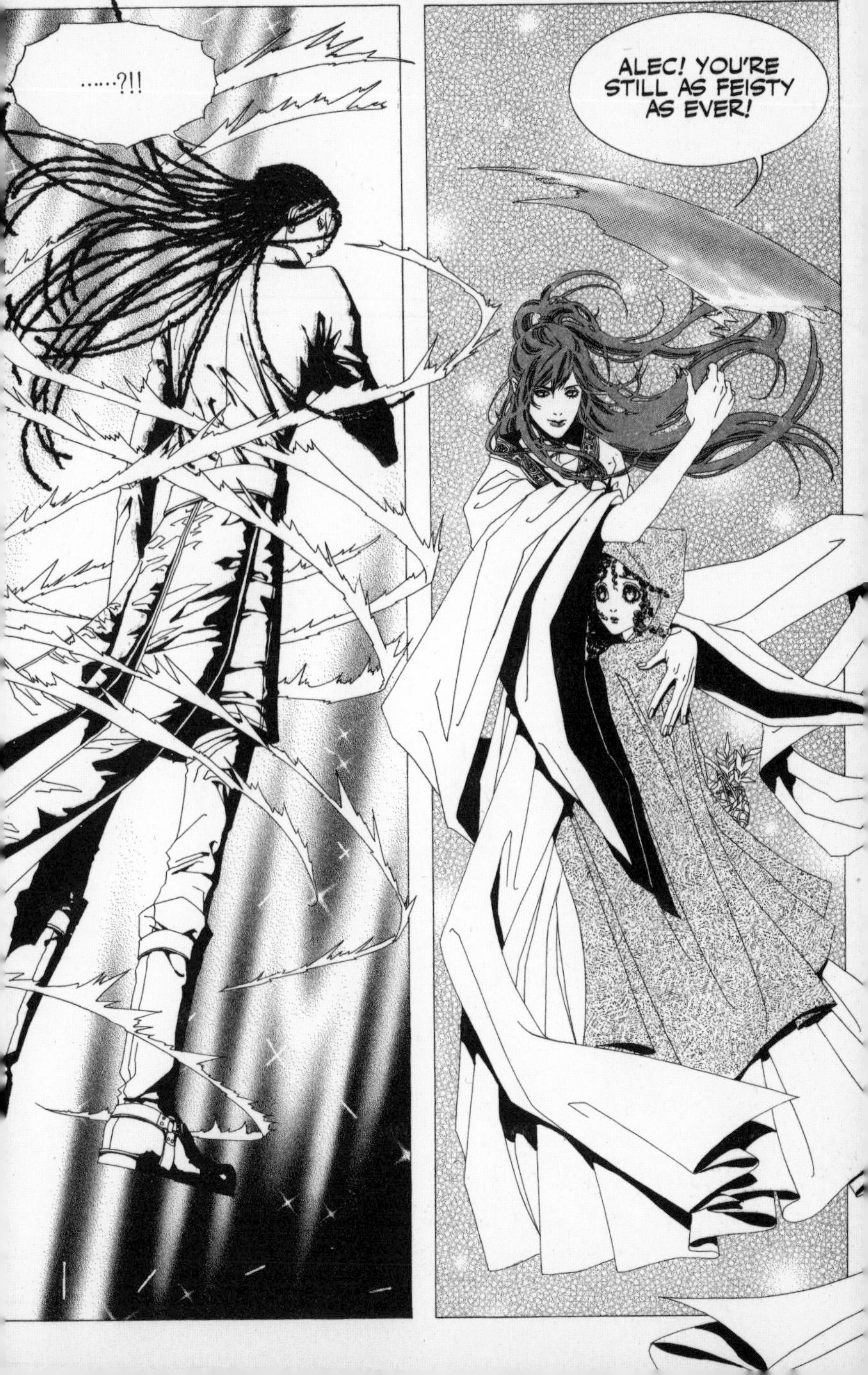
......?!!
ALEC! YOU'RE STILL AS FEISTY AS EVER!

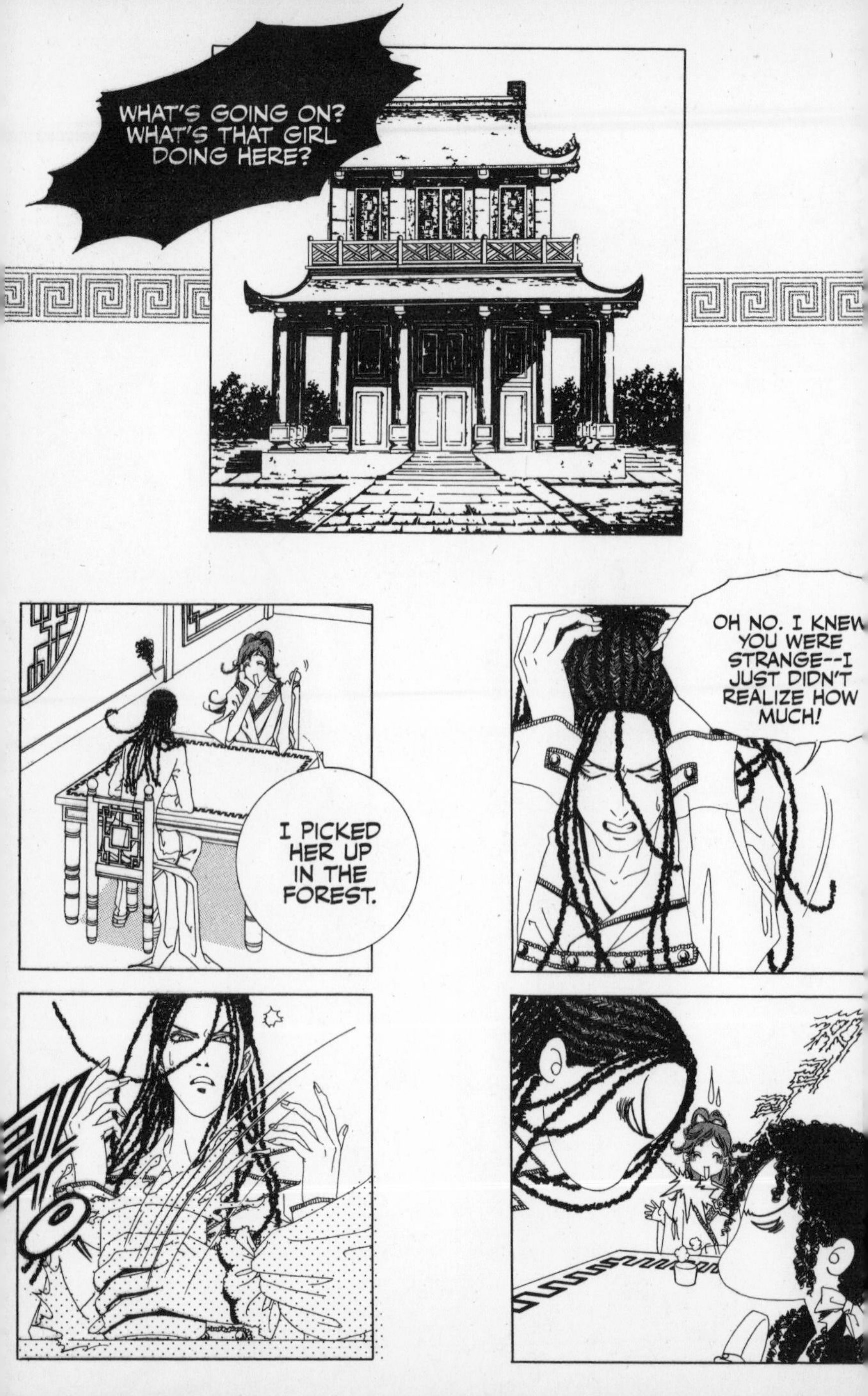
WHAT'S GOING ON? WHAT'S THAT GIRL DOING HERE?
I PICKED HER UP IN THE FOREST.
OH NO. I KNEW YOU WERE STRANGE--I JUST DIDN'T REALIZE HOW MUCH!

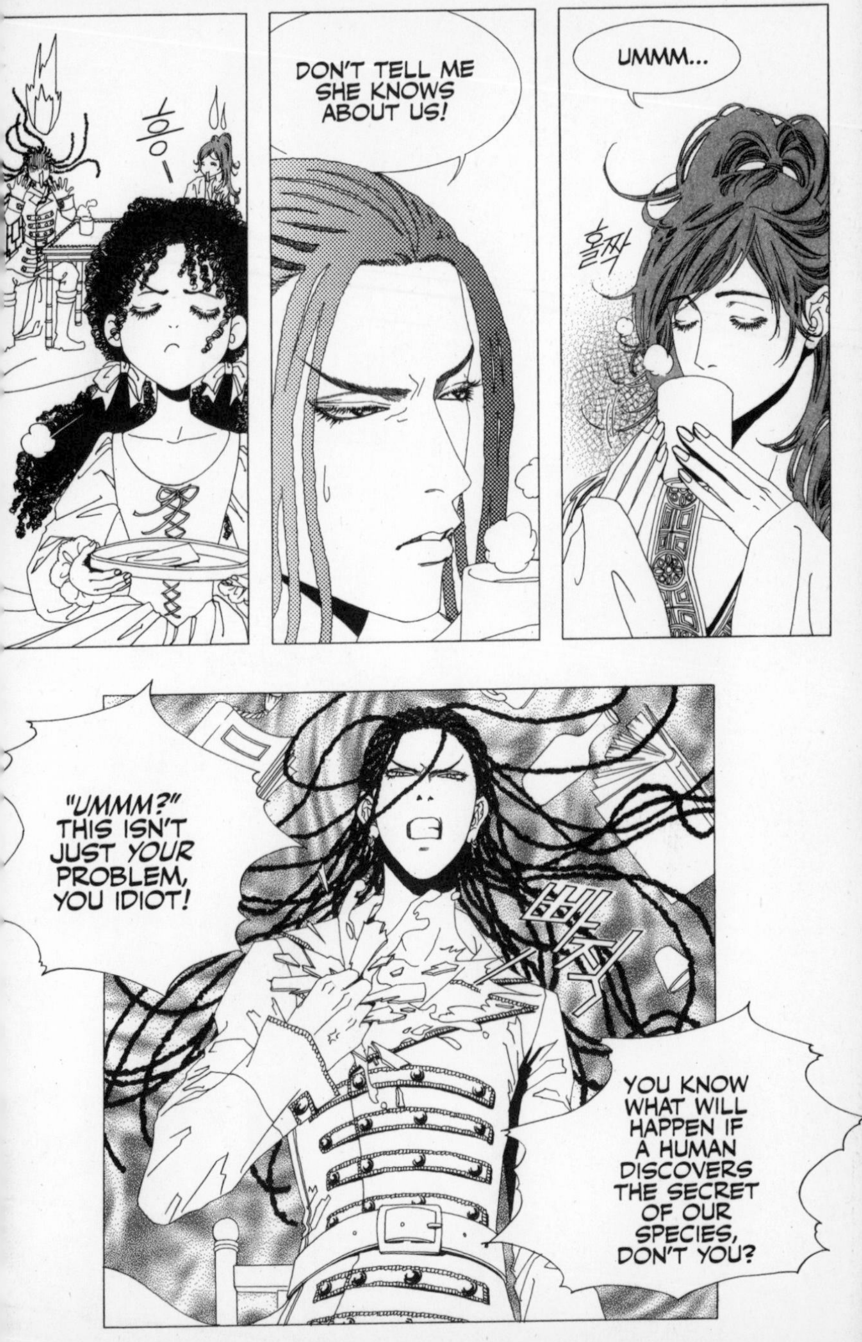
흥
DON'T TELL ME SHE KNOWS ABOUT US!
UMMM...
훌쩍
"UMMM?" THIS ISN'T JUST YOUR PROBLEM, YOU IDIOT!
빠직
YOU KNOW WHAT WILL HAPPEN IF A HUMAN DISCOVERS THE SECRET OF OUR SPECIES, DON'T YOU?

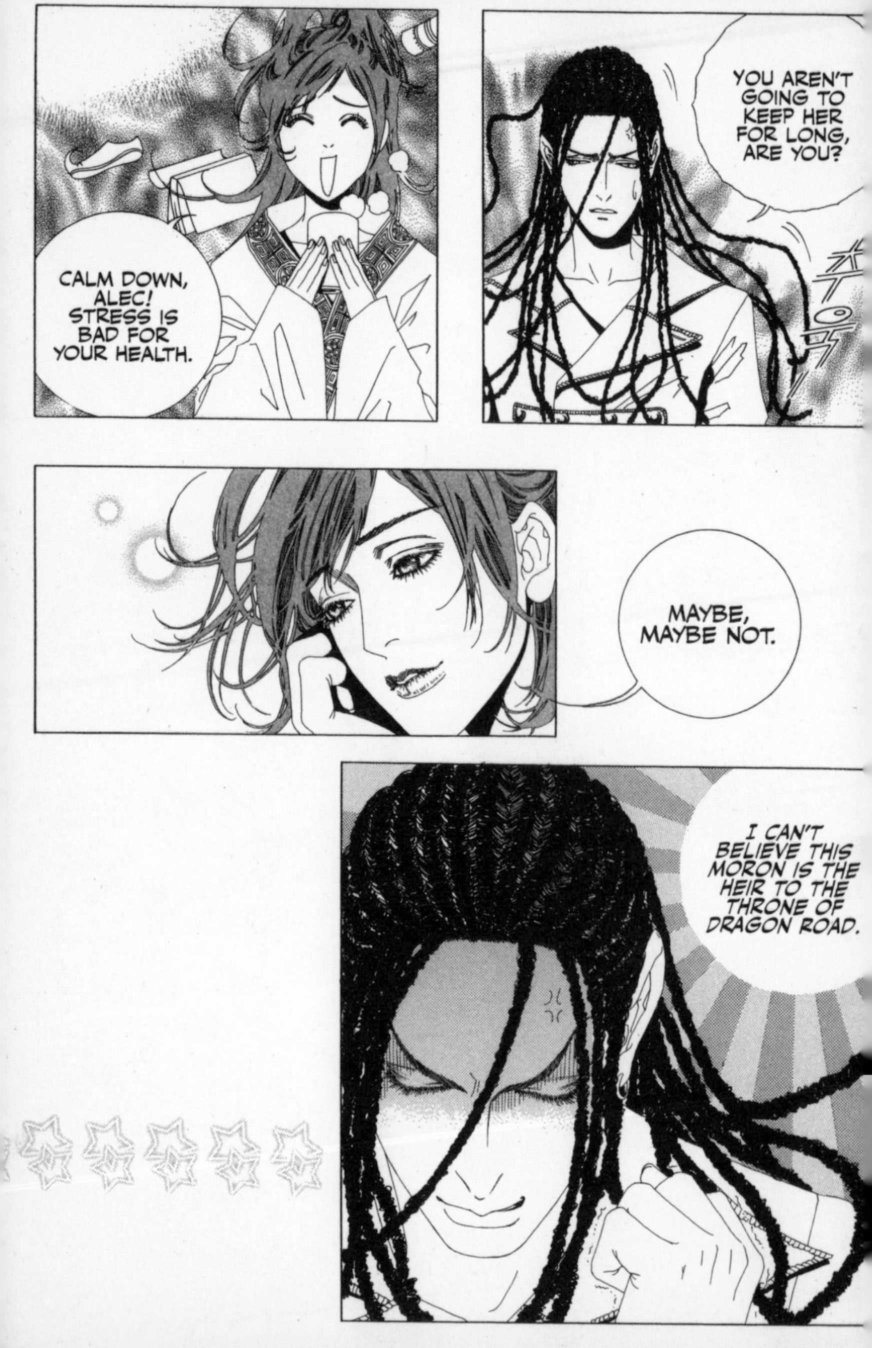
CALM DOWN, ALEC! STRESS IS BAD FOR YOUR HEALTH.
YOU AREN'T GOING TO KEEP HER FOR LONG, ARE YOU?
MAYBE, MAYBE NOT.
I CAN'T BELIEVE THIS MORON IS THE HEIR TO THE THRONE OF DRAGON ROAD.

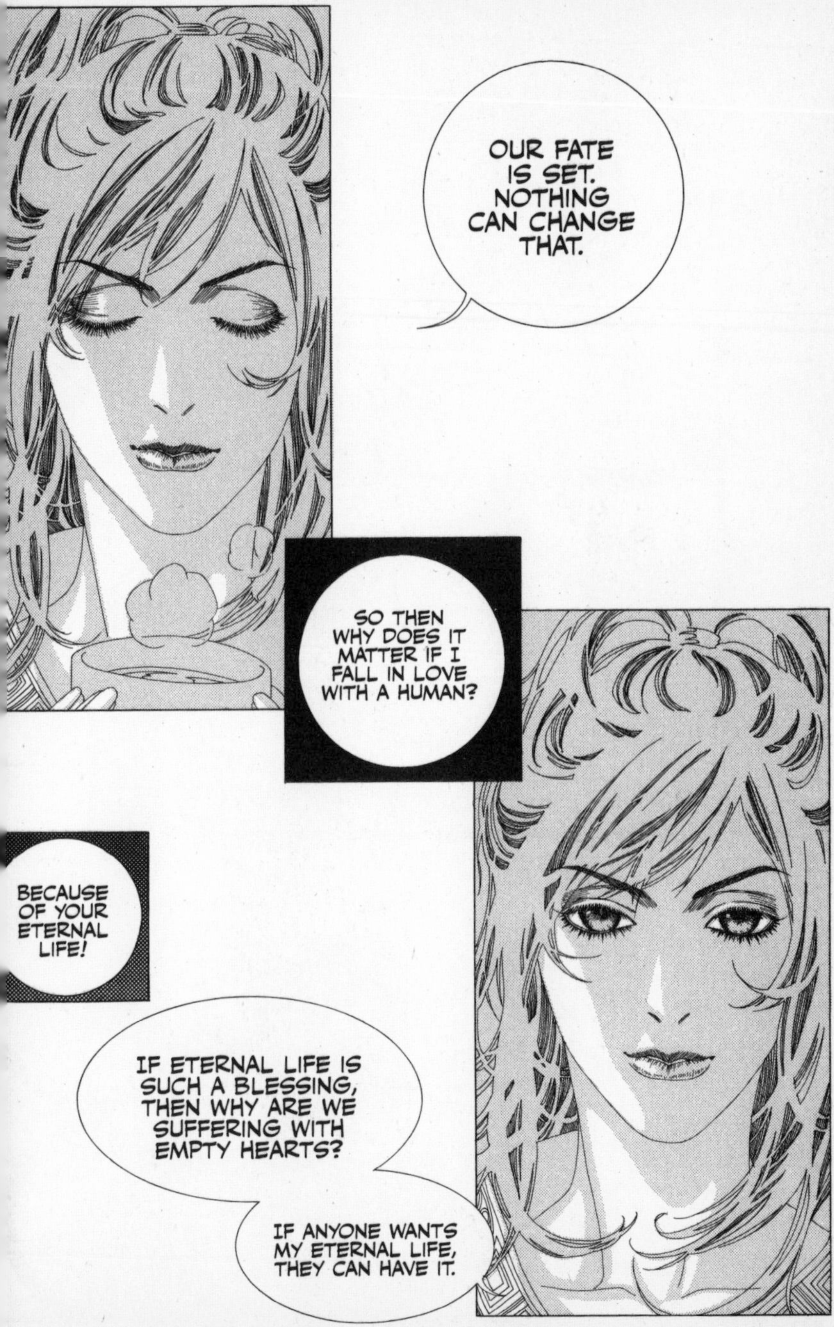
OUR FATE IS SET. NOTHING CAN CHANGE THAT.
SO THEN WHY DOES IT MATTER IF I FALL IN LOVE WITH A HUMAN?
BECAUSE OF YOUR ETERNAL LIFE!
IF ETERNAL LIFE IS SUCH A BLESSING, THEN WHY ARE WE SUFFERING WITH EMPTY HEARTS?
IF ANYONE WANTS MY ETERNAL LIFE, THEY CAN HAVE IT.

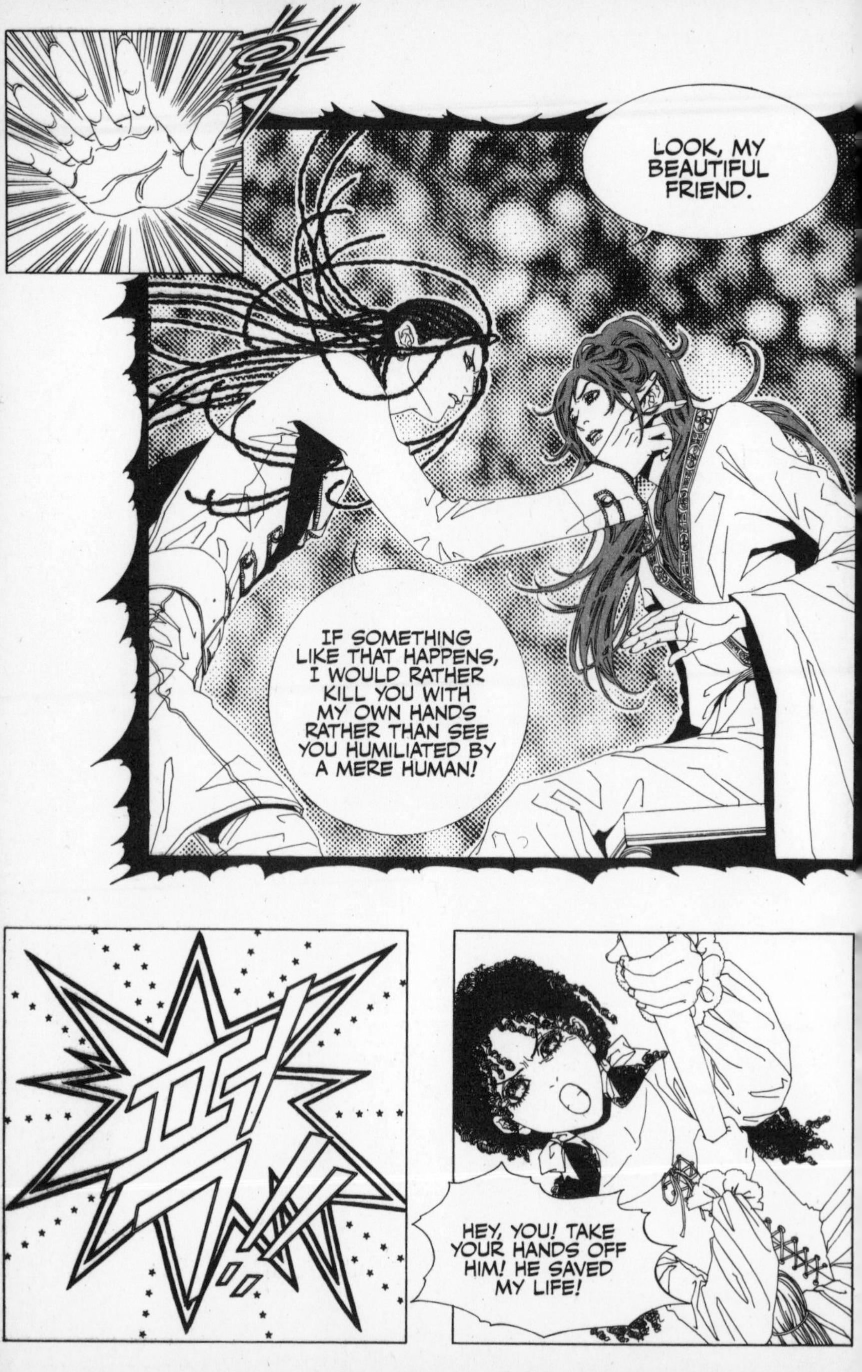
LOOK, MY BEAUTIFUL FRIEND.
IF SOMETHING LIKE THAT HAPPENS, I WOULD RATHER KILL YOU WITH MY OWN HANDS RATHER THAN SEE YOU HUMILIATED BY A MERE HUMAN!
HEY, YOU! TAKE YOUR HANDS OFF HIM! HE SAVED MY LIFE!

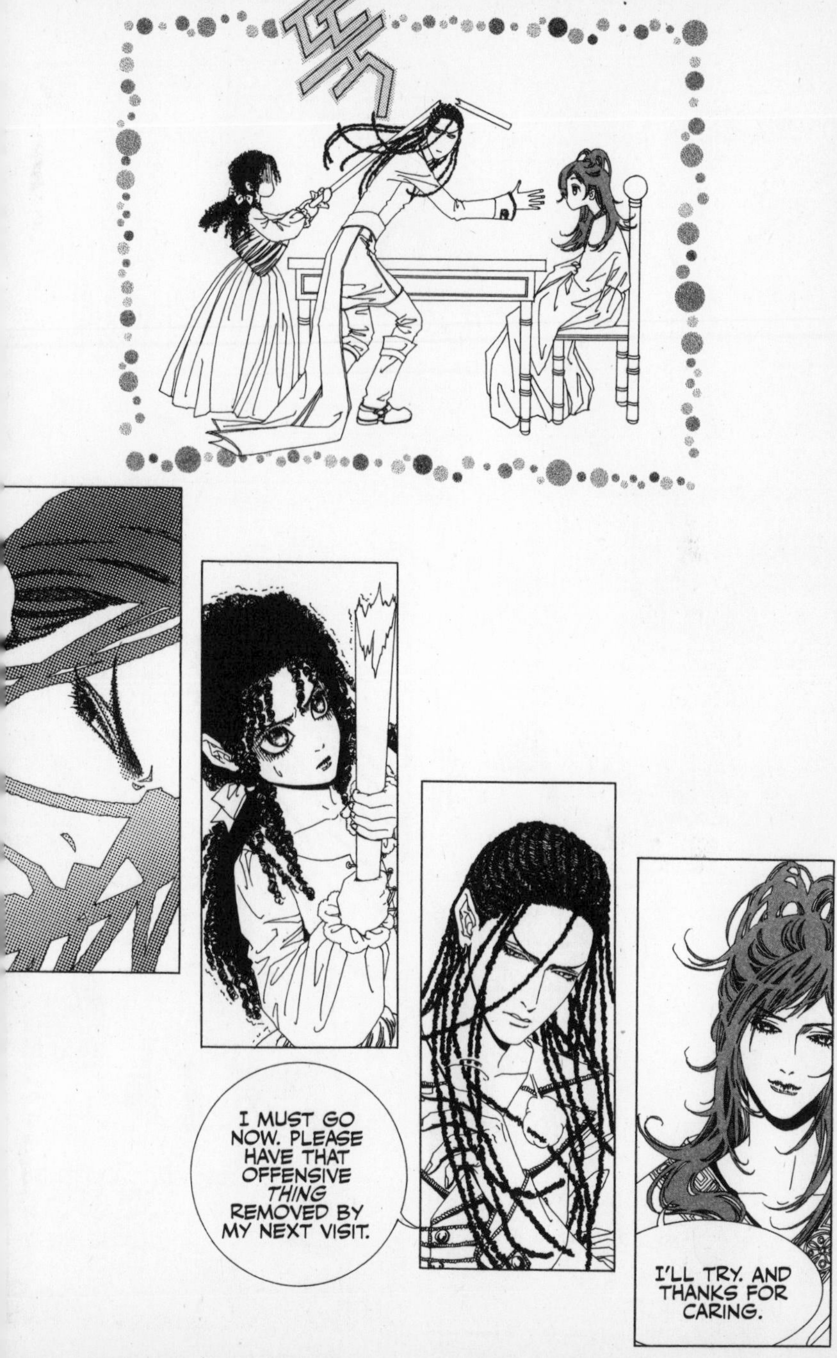
I MUST GO NOW. PLEASE HAVE THAT OFFENSIVE *THING* REMOVED BY MY NEXT VISIT.
I'LL TRY. AND THANKS FOR CARING.

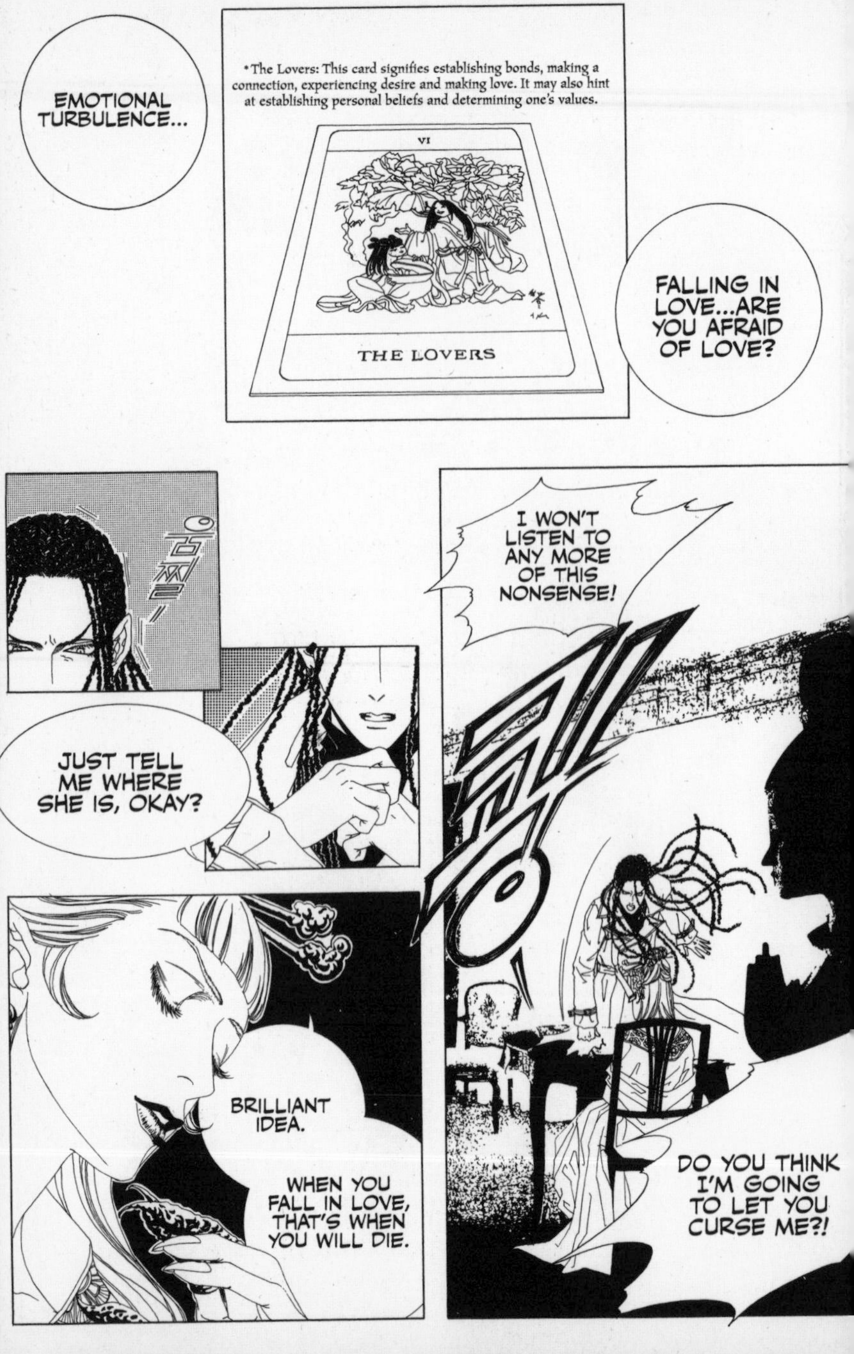
EMOTIONAL TURBULENCE...
*The Lovers: This card signifies establishing bonds, making a connection, experiencing desire and making love. It may also hint at establishing personal beliefs and determining one's values.
VI
THE LOVERS
FALLING IN LOVE...ARE YOU AFRAID OF LOVE?
JUST TELL ME WHERE SHE IS, OKAY?
BRILLIANT IDEA.
WHEN YOU FALL IN LOVE, THAT'S WHEN YOU WILL DIE.
I WON'T LISTEN TO ANY MORE OF THIS NONSENSE!
DO YOU THINK I'M GOING TO LET YOU CURSE ME?!

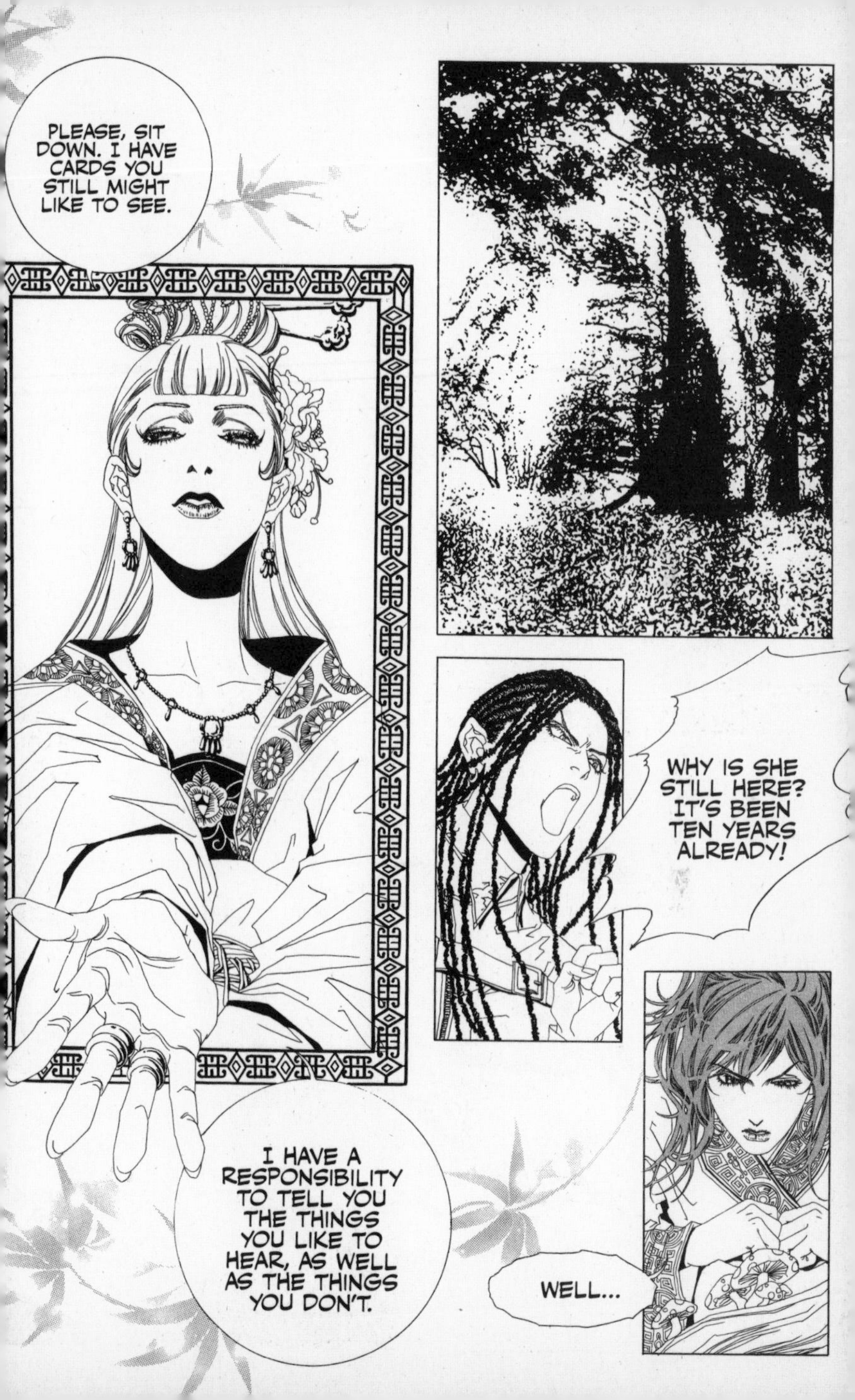
PLEASE, SIT DOWN. I HAVE CARDS YOU STILL MIGHT LIKE TO SEE.
I HAVE A RESPONSIBILITY TO TELL YOU THE THINGS YOU LIKE TO HEAR, AS WELL AS THE THINGS YOU DON'T.
WHY IS SHE STILL HERE? IT'S BEEN TEN YEARS ALREADY!
WELL...

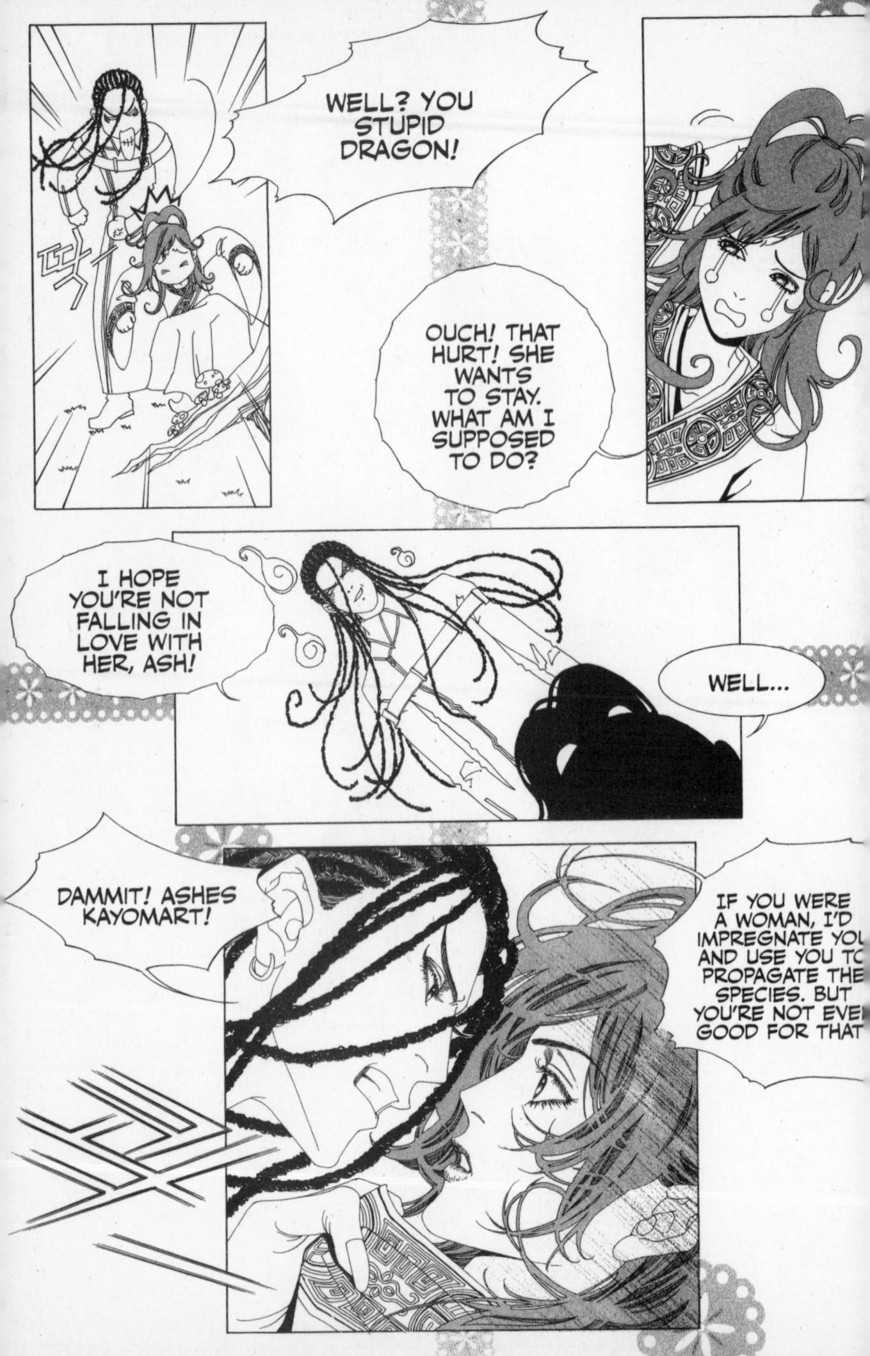
WELL? YOU STUPID DRAGON!
OUCH! THAT HURT! SHE WANTS TO STAY. WHAT AM I SUPPOSED TO DO?
I HOPE YOU'RE NOT FALLING IN LOVE WITH HER, ASH!
WELL...
DAMMIT! ASHES KAYOMART!
IF YOU WERE A WOMAN, I'D IMPREGNATE YO AND USE YOU T PROPAGATE THE SPECIES. BUT YOU'RE NOT EVE GOOD FOR THAT

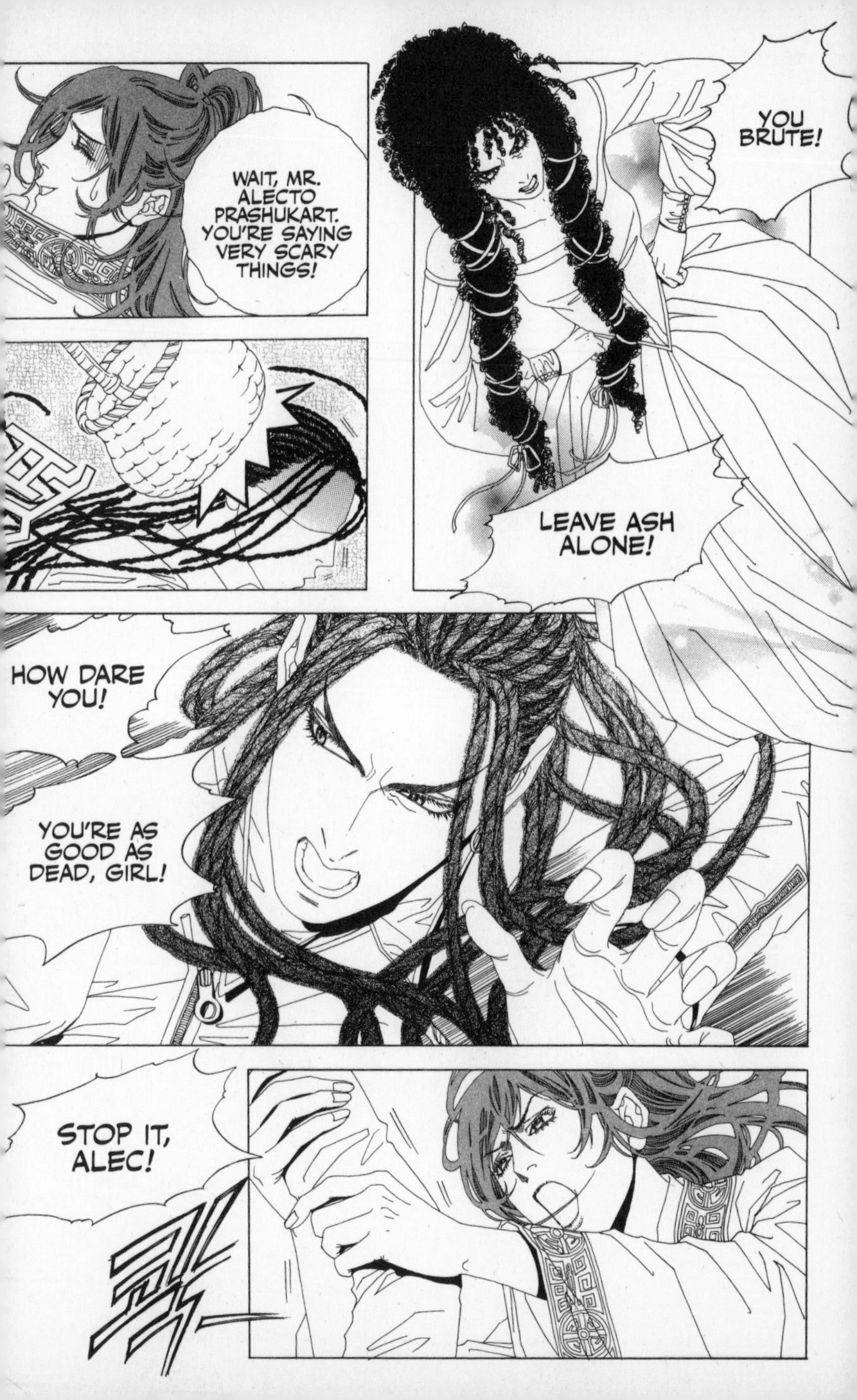
WAIT, MR. ALECTO PRASHUKART. YOU'RE SAYING VERY SCARY THINGS!
YOU BRUTE!
LEAVE ASH ALONE!
HOW DARE YOU!
YOU'RE AS GOOD AS DEAD, GIRL!
STOP IT, ALEC!

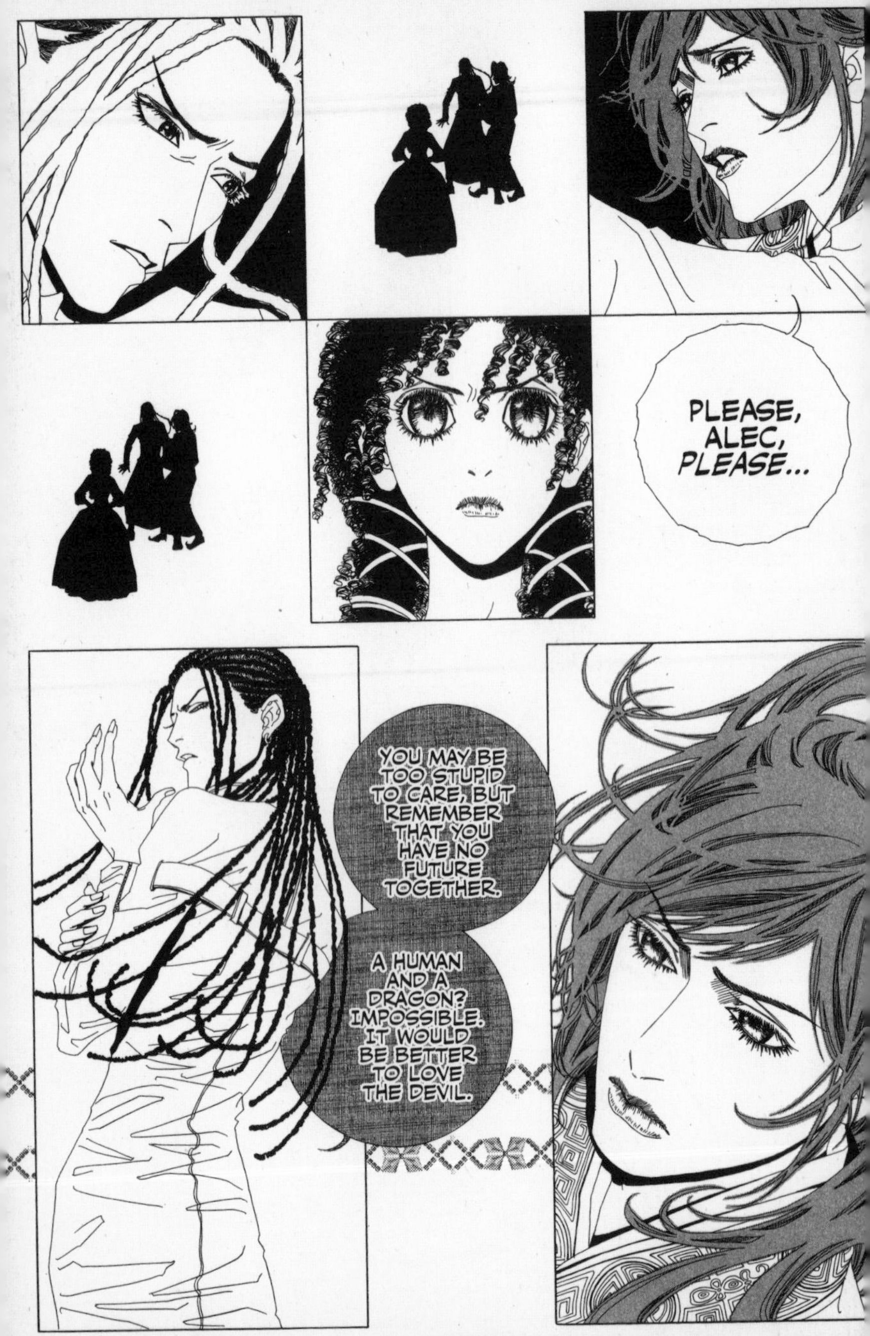
PLEASE, ALEC, PLEASE...
YOU MAY BE TOO STUPID TO CARE, BUT REMEMBER THAT YOU HAVE NO FUTURE TOGETHER.
A HUMAN AND A DRAGON? IMPOSSIBLE. IT WOULD BE BETTER TO LOVE THE DEVIL.

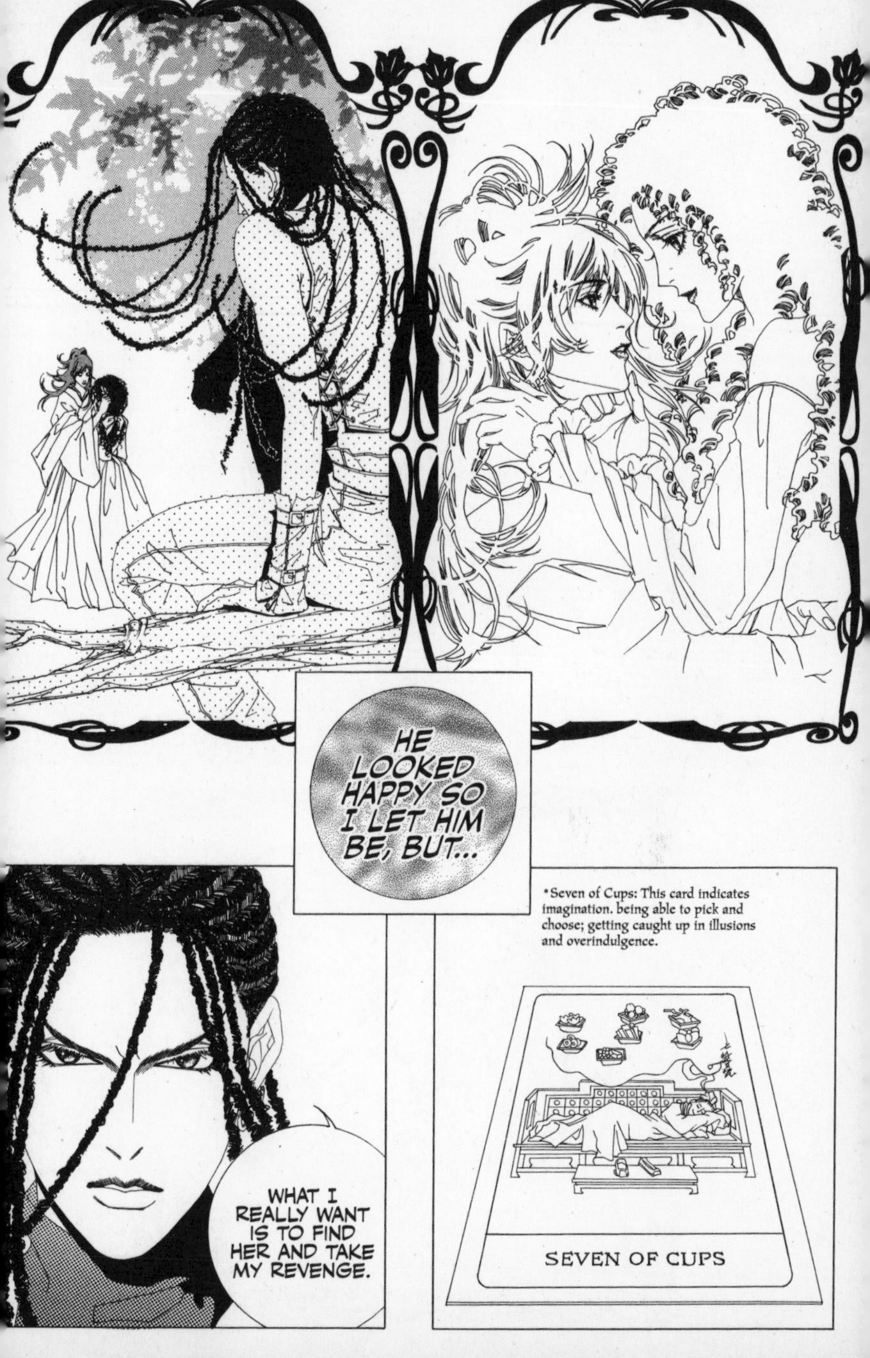
HE LOOKED HAPPY SO I LET HIM BE, BUT...
WHAT I REALLY WANT IS TO FIND HER AND TAKE MY REVENGE.
*Seven of Cups: This card indicates imagination. being able to pick and choose; getting caught up in illusions and overindulgence.
SEVEN OF CUPS

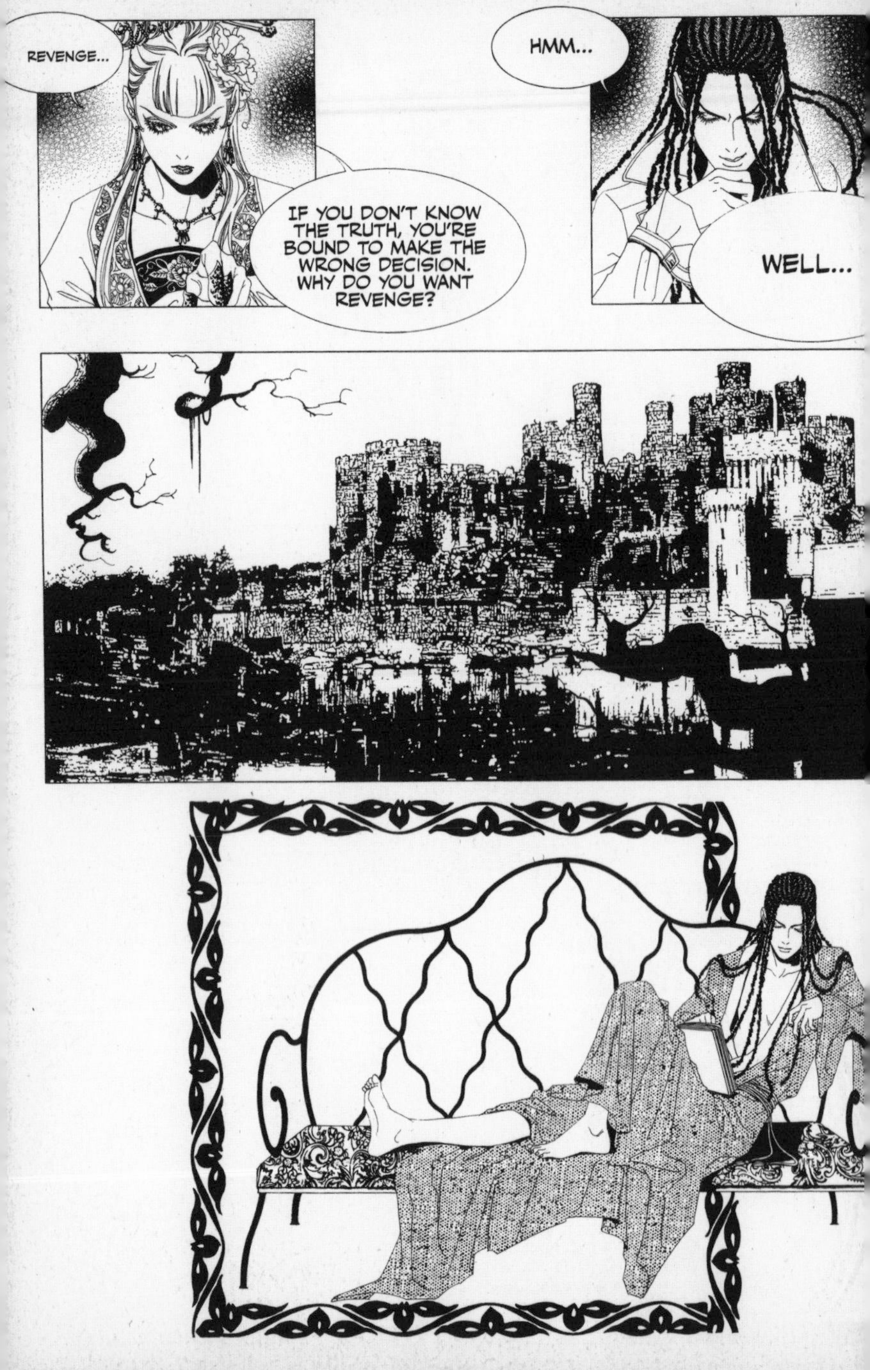
REVENGE...
IF YOU DON'T KNOW THE TRUTH, YOU'RE BOUND TO MAKE THE WRONG DECISION. WHY DO YOU WANT REVENGE?
HMM...
WELL...

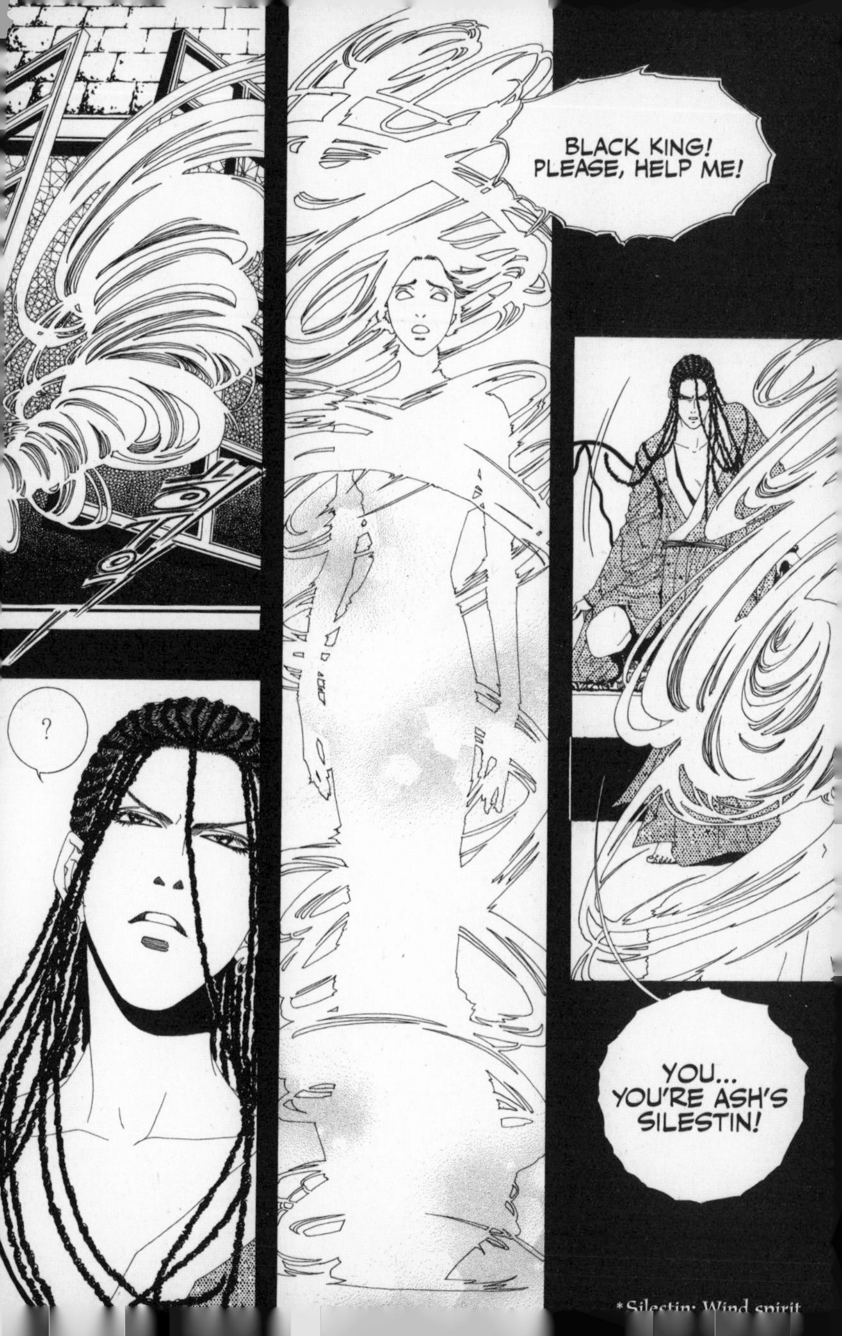
?
BLACK KING! PLEASE, HELP ME!
YOU... YOU'RE ASH'S SILESTIN!

*Silestin: Wind spirit

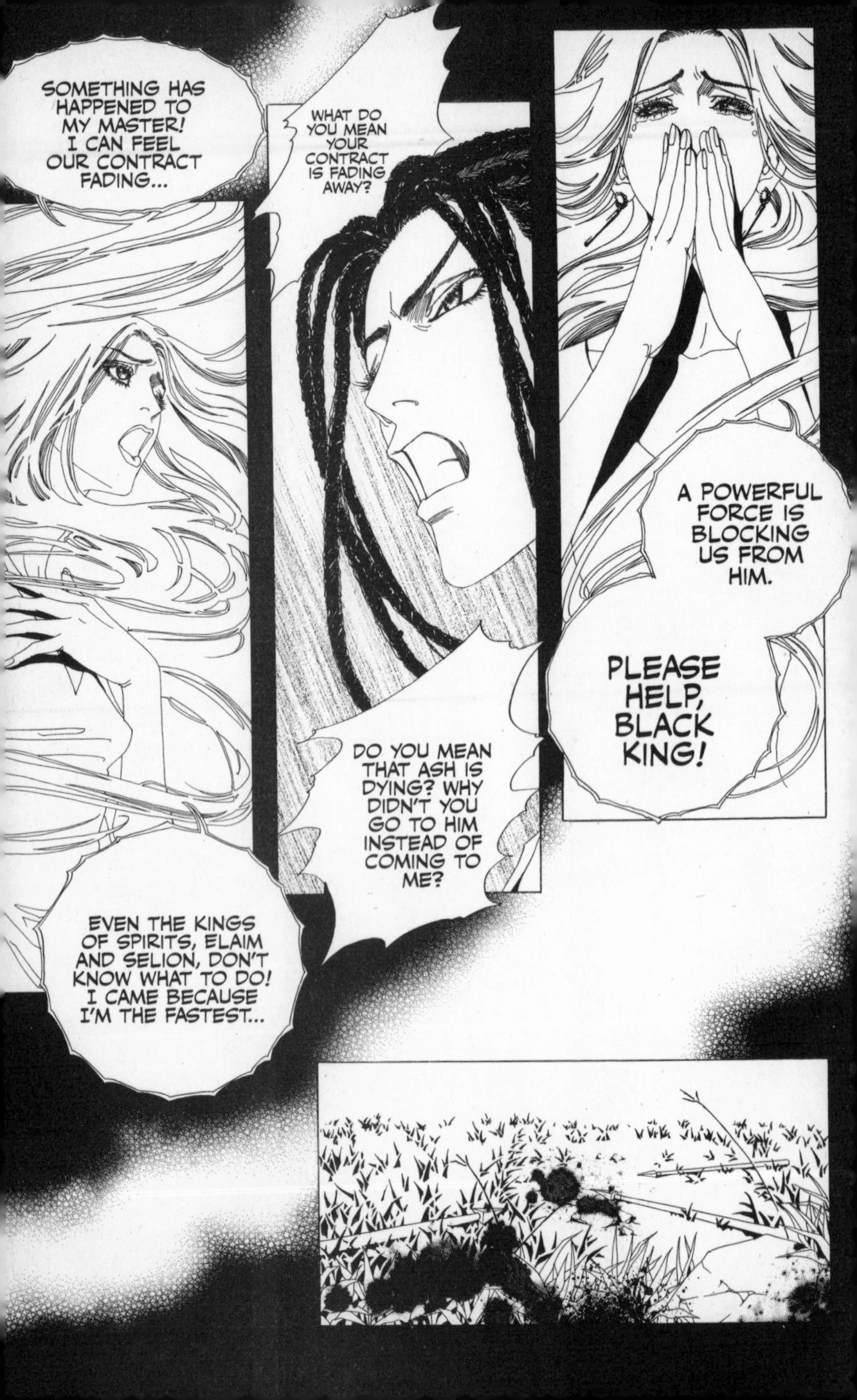
SOMETHING HAS HAPPENED TO MY MASTER! I CAN FEEL OUR CONTRACT FADING...
WHAT DO YOU MEAN YOUR CONTRACT IS FADING AWAY?
DO YOU MEAN THAT ASH IS DYING? WHY DIDN'T YOU GO TO HIM INSTEAD OF COMING TO ME?
EVEN THE KINGS OF SPIRITS, ELAIM AND SELION, DON'T KNOW WHAT TO DO! I CAME BECAUSE I'M THE FASTEST...
A POWERFUL FORCE IS BLOCKING US FROM HIM.
PLEASE HELP, BLACK KING!

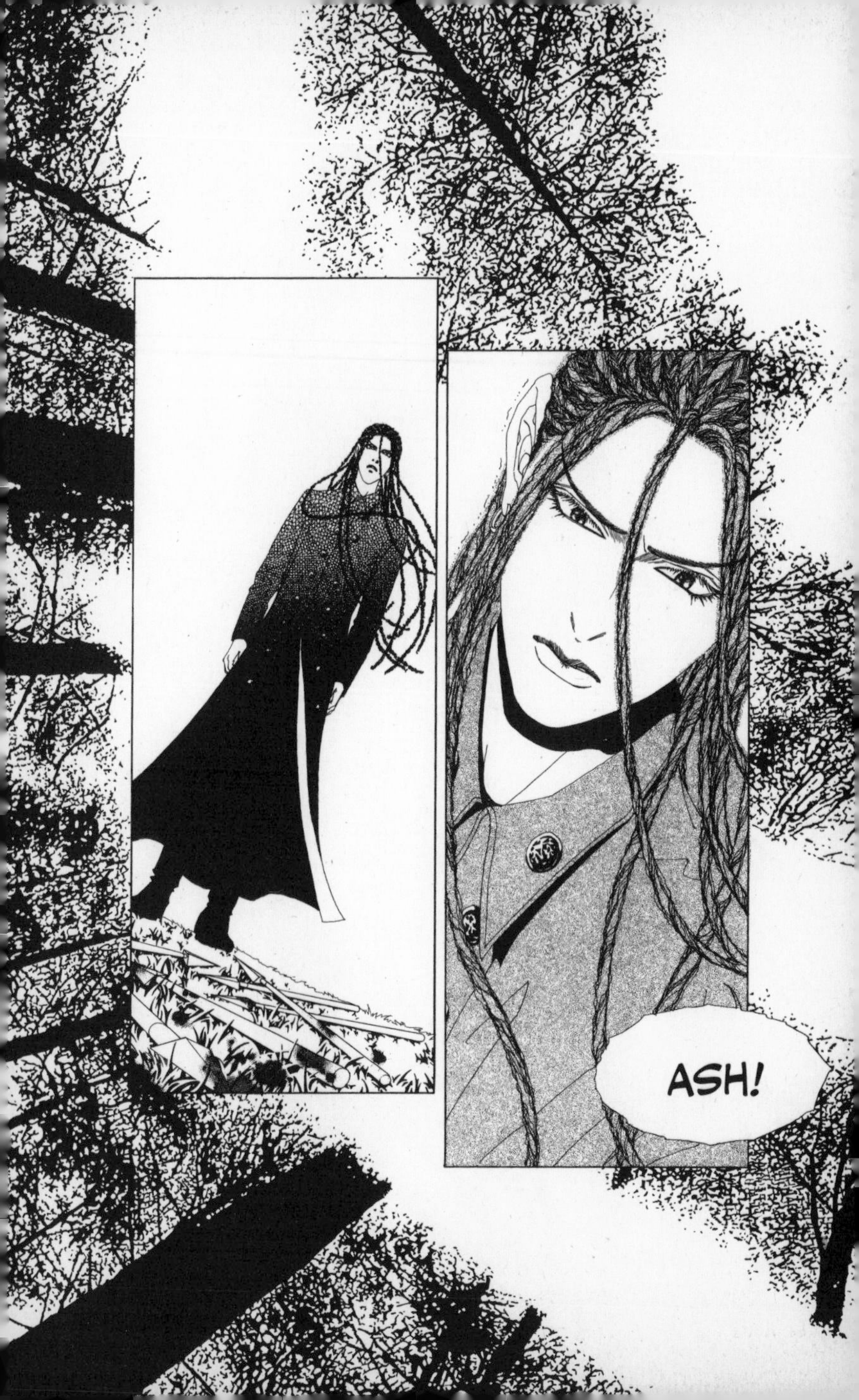
ASH!

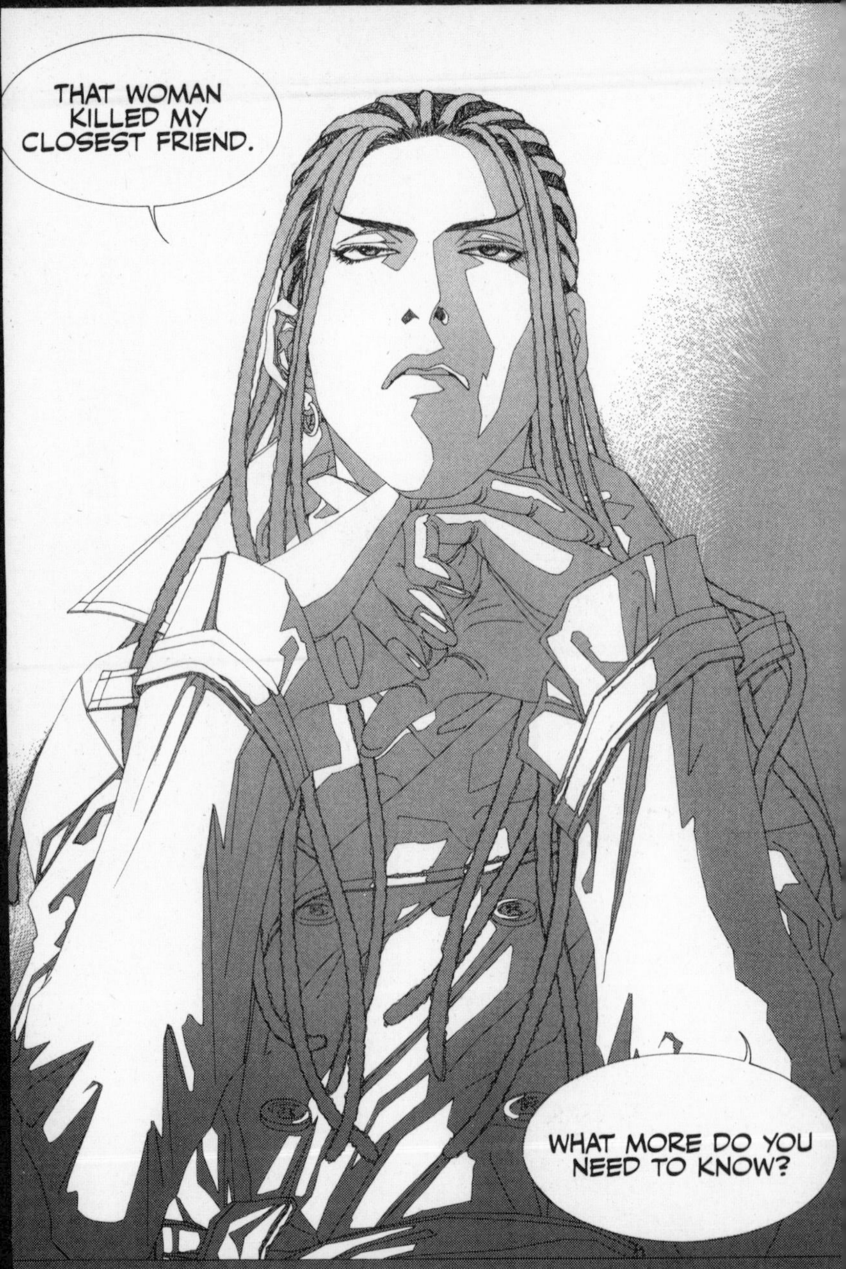
THAT WOMAN KILLED MY CLOSEST FRIEND.
WHAT MORE DO YOU NEED TO KNOW?

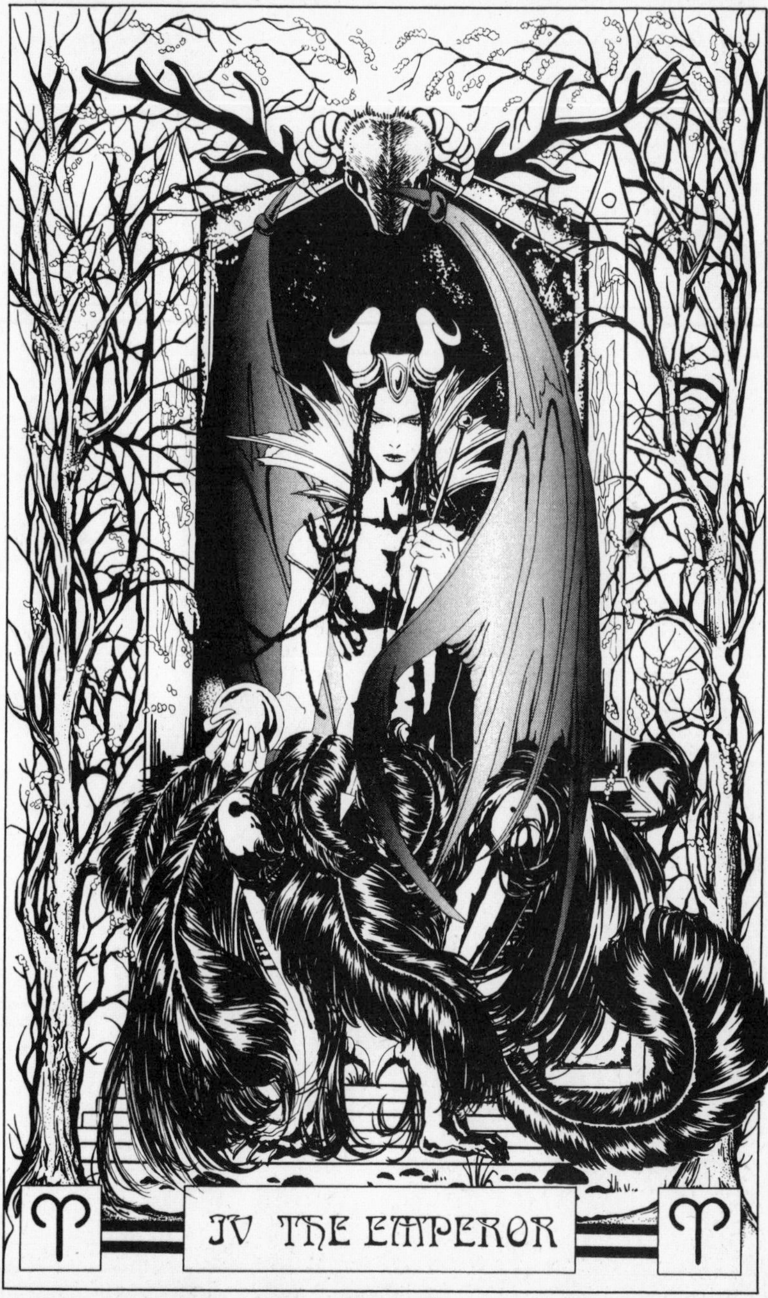
IV THE EMPEROR

•IV The Emperor: Right-side up, this card indicates a struggle for personal independence. Upside down, it can indicate arrogance and exclusivity.

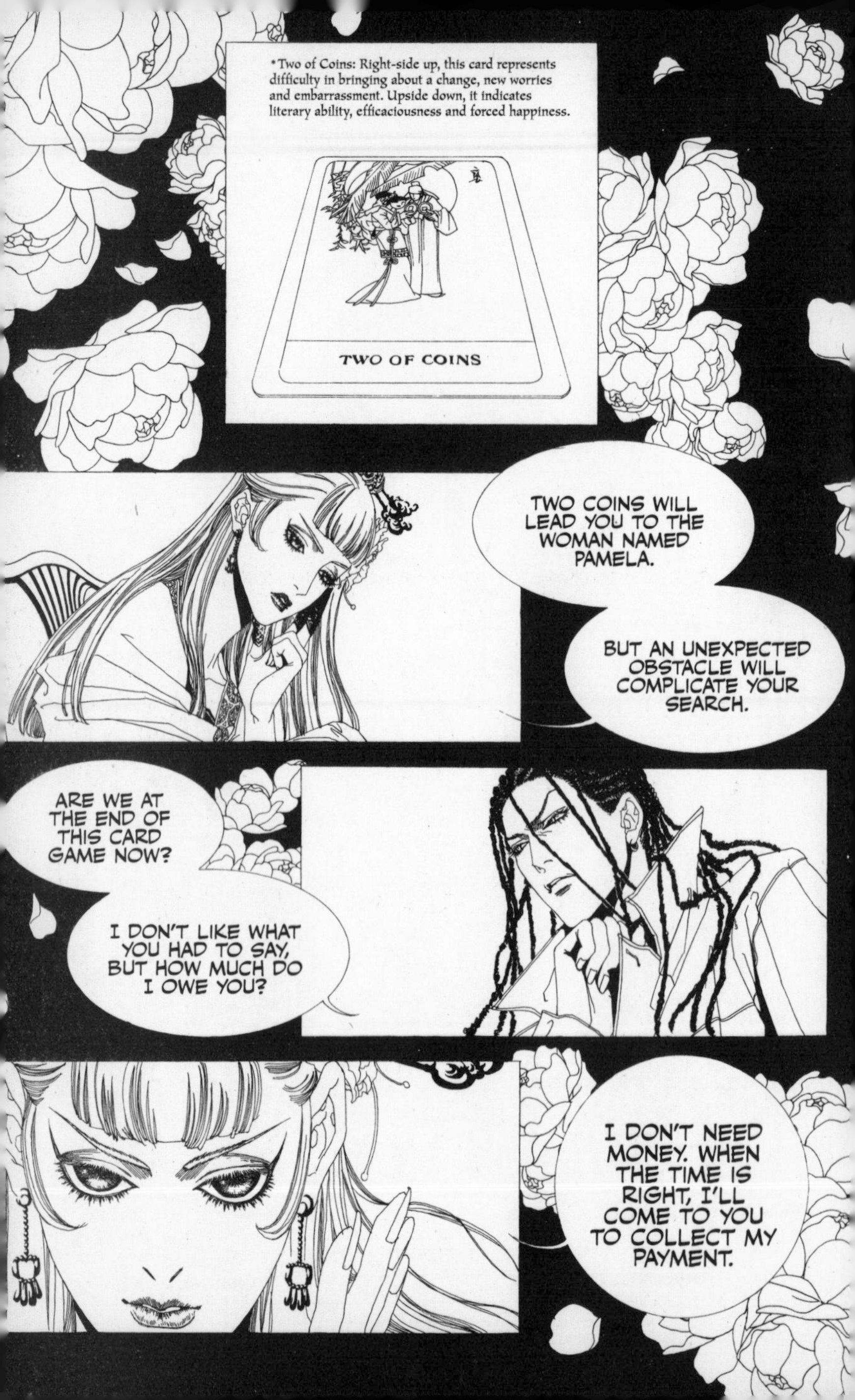
*Two of Coins: Right-side up, this card represents difficulty in bringing about a change, new worries and embarrassment. Upside down, it indicates literary ability, efficaciousness and forced happiness.
TWO OF COINS
TWO COINS WILL LEAD YOU TO THE WOMAN NAMED PAMELA.
BUT AN UNEXPECTED OBSTACLE WILL COMPLICATE YOUR SEARCH.
ARE WE AT THE END OF THIS CARD GAME NOW?
I DON'T LIKE WHAT YOU HAD TO SAY, BUT HOW MUCH DO I OWE YOU?
I DON'T NEED MONEY. WHEN THE TIME IS RIGHT, I'LL COME TO YOU TO COLLECT MY PAYMENT.

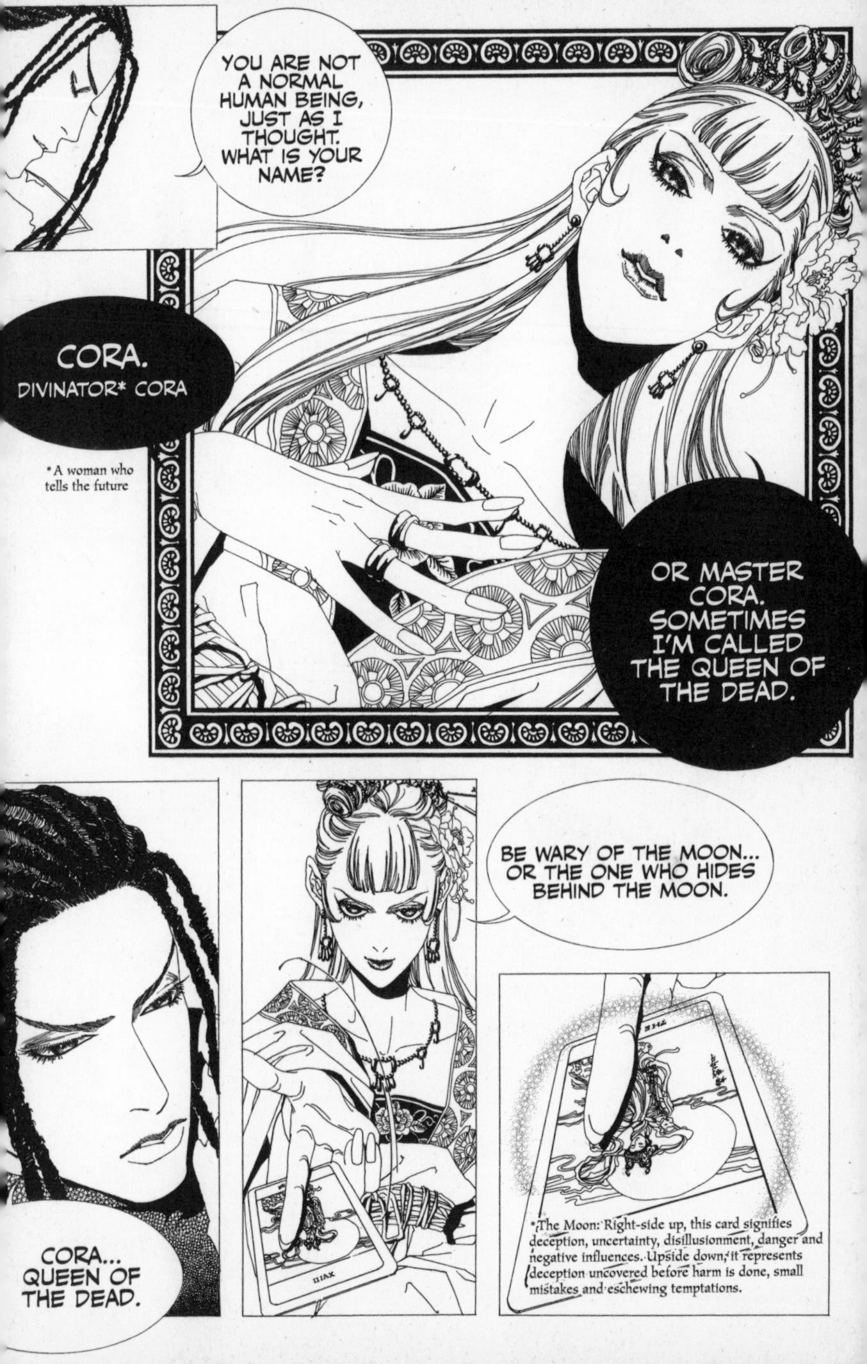
YOU ARE NOT A NORMAL HUMAN BEING, JUST AS I THOUGHT. WHAT IS YOUR NAME?
CORA.
DIVINATOR* CORA
*A woman who tells the future
OR MASTER CORA. SOMETIMES I'M CALLED THE QUEEN OF THE DEAD.
CORA... QUEEN OF THE DEAD.
BE WARY OF THE MOON... OR THE ONE WHO HIDES BEHIND THE MOON.
*The Moon: Right-side up, this card signifies deception, uncertainty, disillusionment, danger and negative influences. Upside down, it represents deception uncovered before harm is done, small mistakes and eschewing temptations.

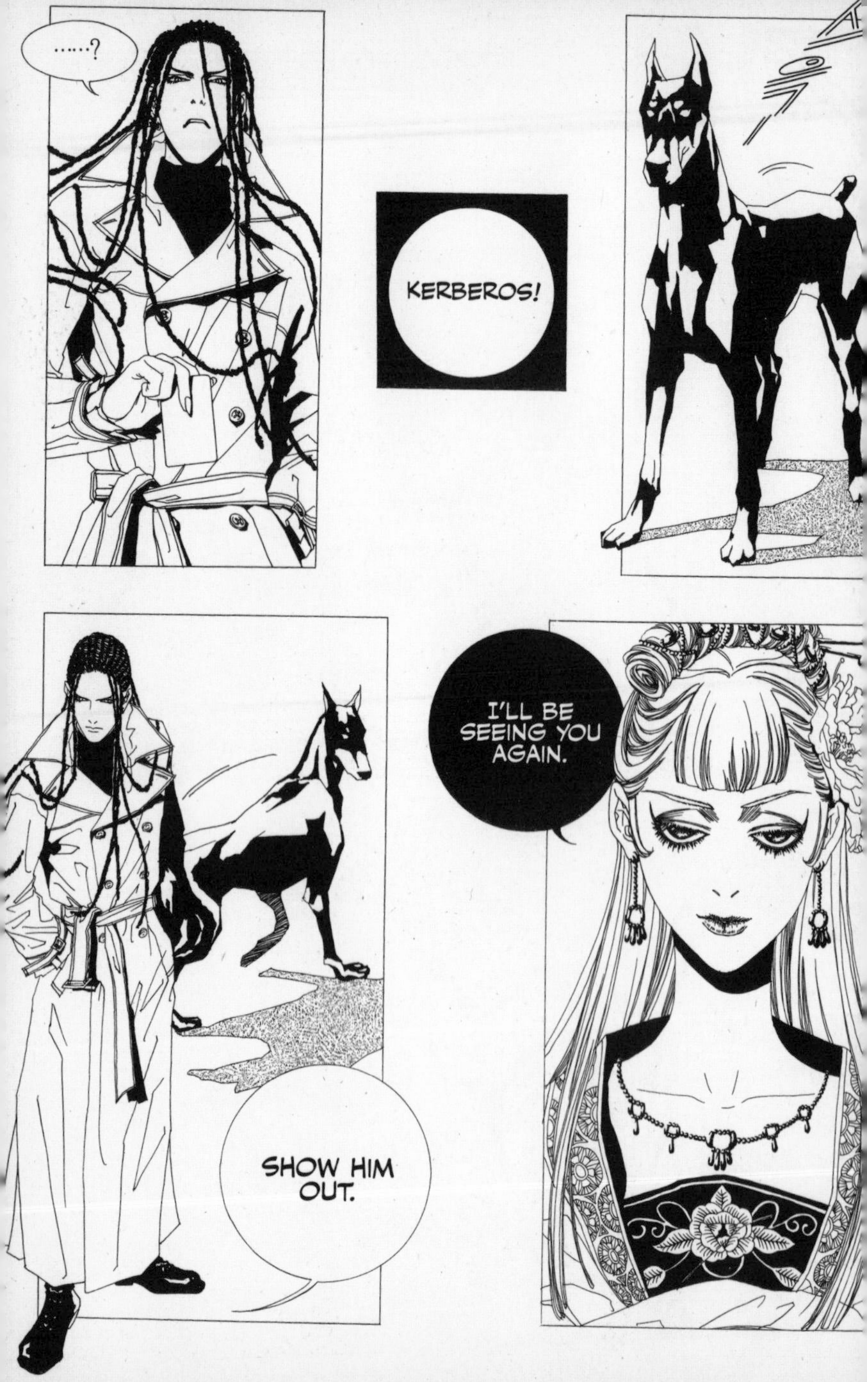
......?
KERBEROS!
SHOW HIM OUT.
I'LL BE SEEING YOU AGAIN.

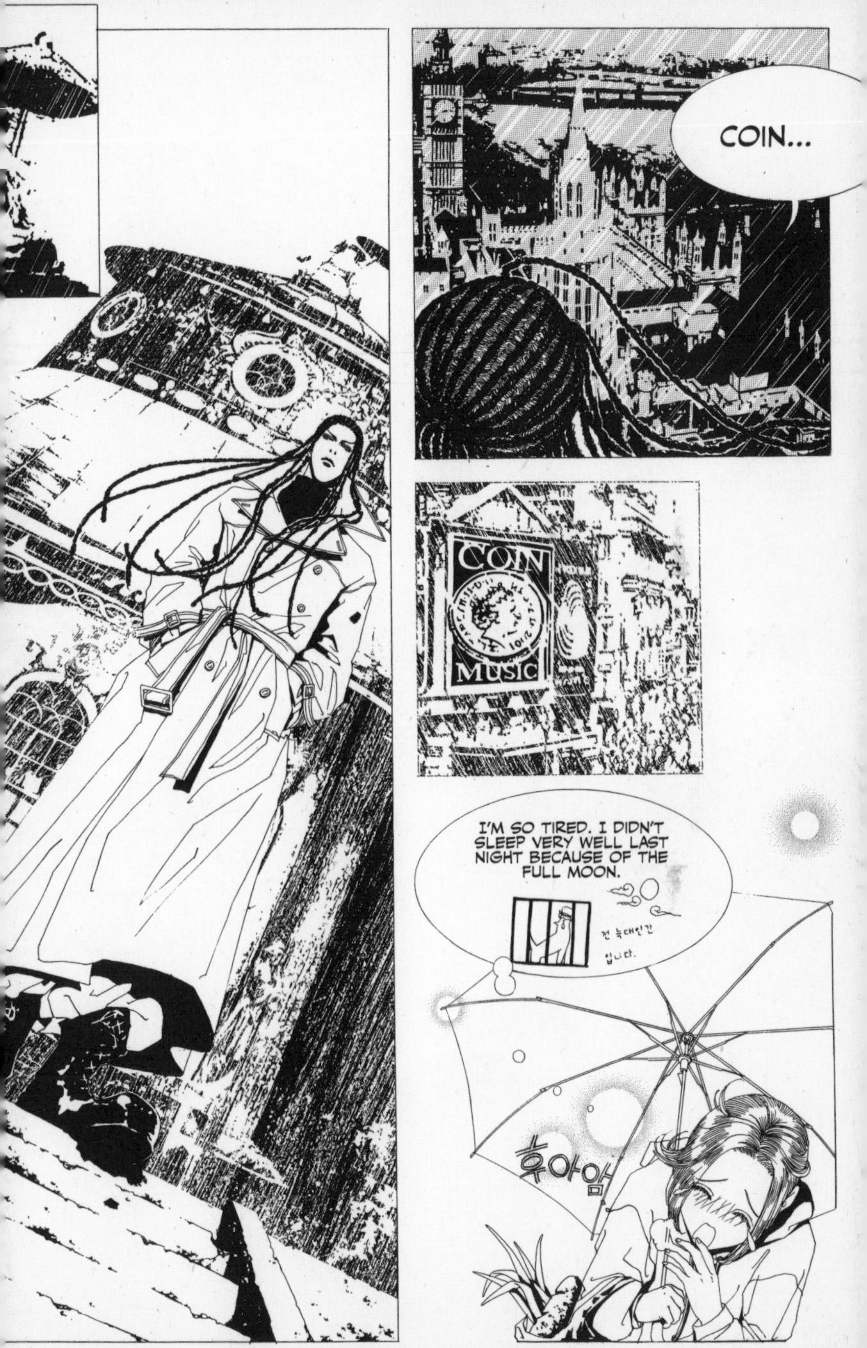
COIN...
CON
MUSIC
I'M SO TIRED. I DIDN'T SLEEP VERY WELL LAST NIGHT BECAUSE OF THE FULL MOON.
전 늑대인간 입니다.
후아암

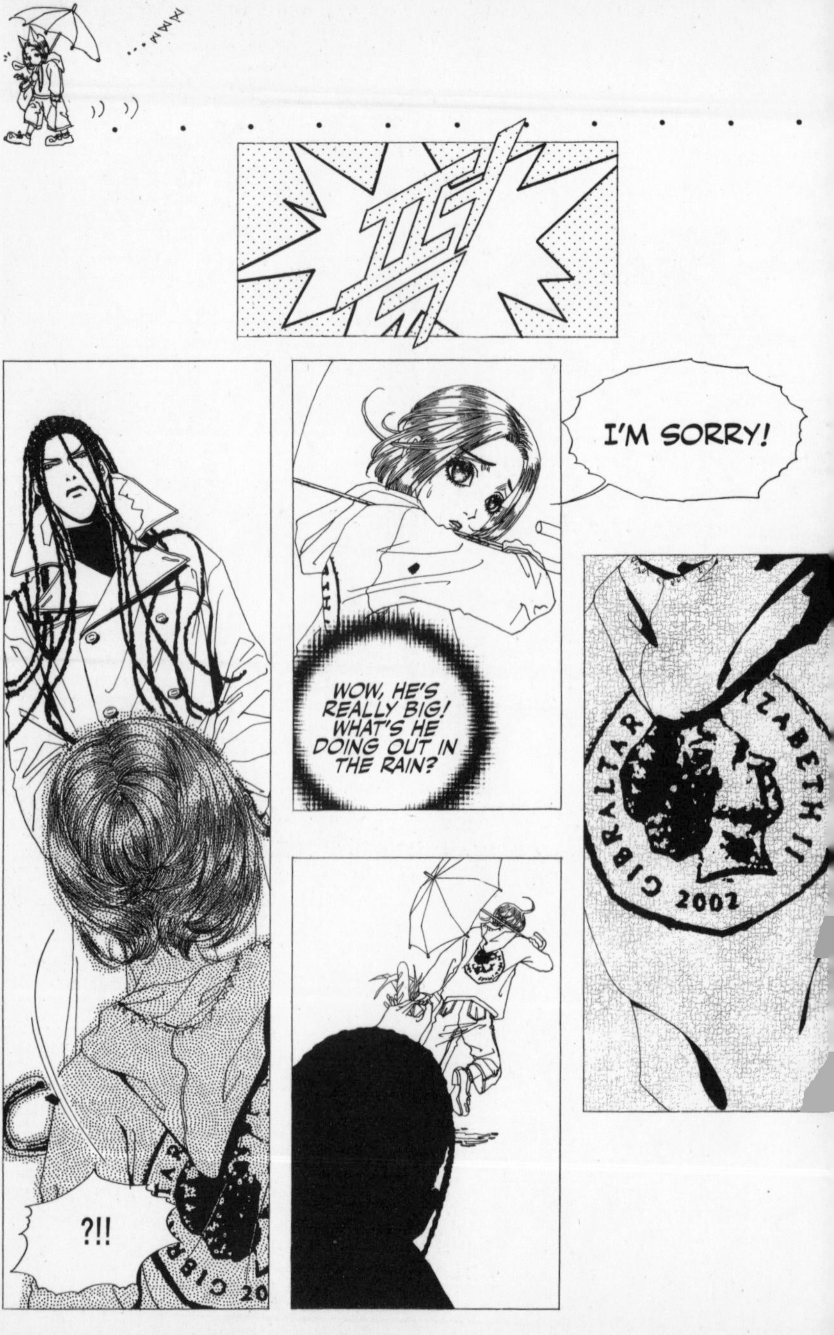
MMM...
?!!
I'M SORRY!
WOW, HE'S REALLY BIG! WHAT'S HE DOING OUT IN THE RAIN?
GIBRALTAR ZABETH II 2002

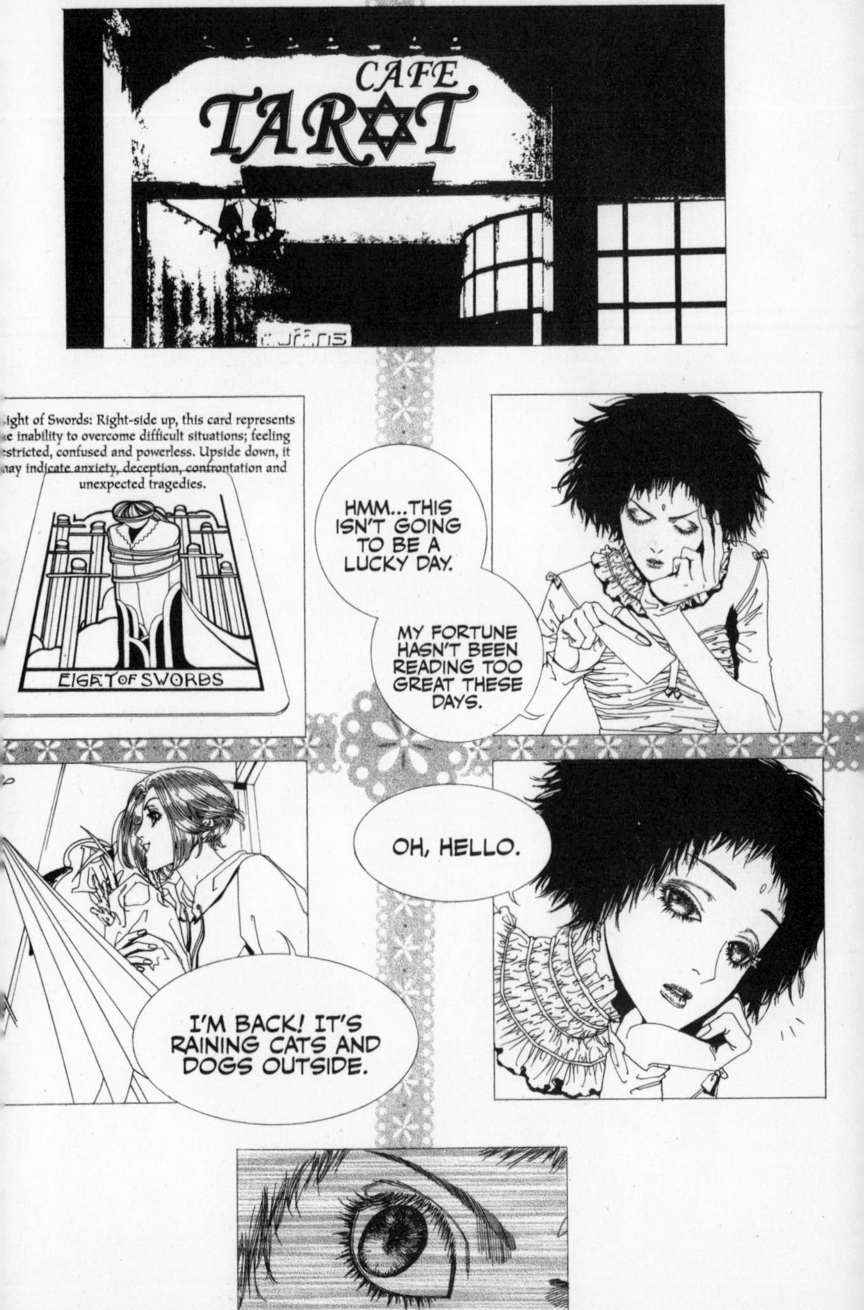
CAFE TAROT
ight of Swords: Right-side up, this card represents e inability to overcome difficult situations; feeling estricted, confused and powerless. Upside down, it nay indicate anxiety, deception, confrontation and unexpected tragedies.
EIGHT OF SWORDS
HMM...THIS ISN'T GOING TO BE A LUCKY DAY.
MY FORTUNE HASN'T BEEN READING TOO GREAT THESE DAYS.
I'M BACK! IT'S RAINING CATS AND DOGS OUTSIDE.
OH, HELLO.

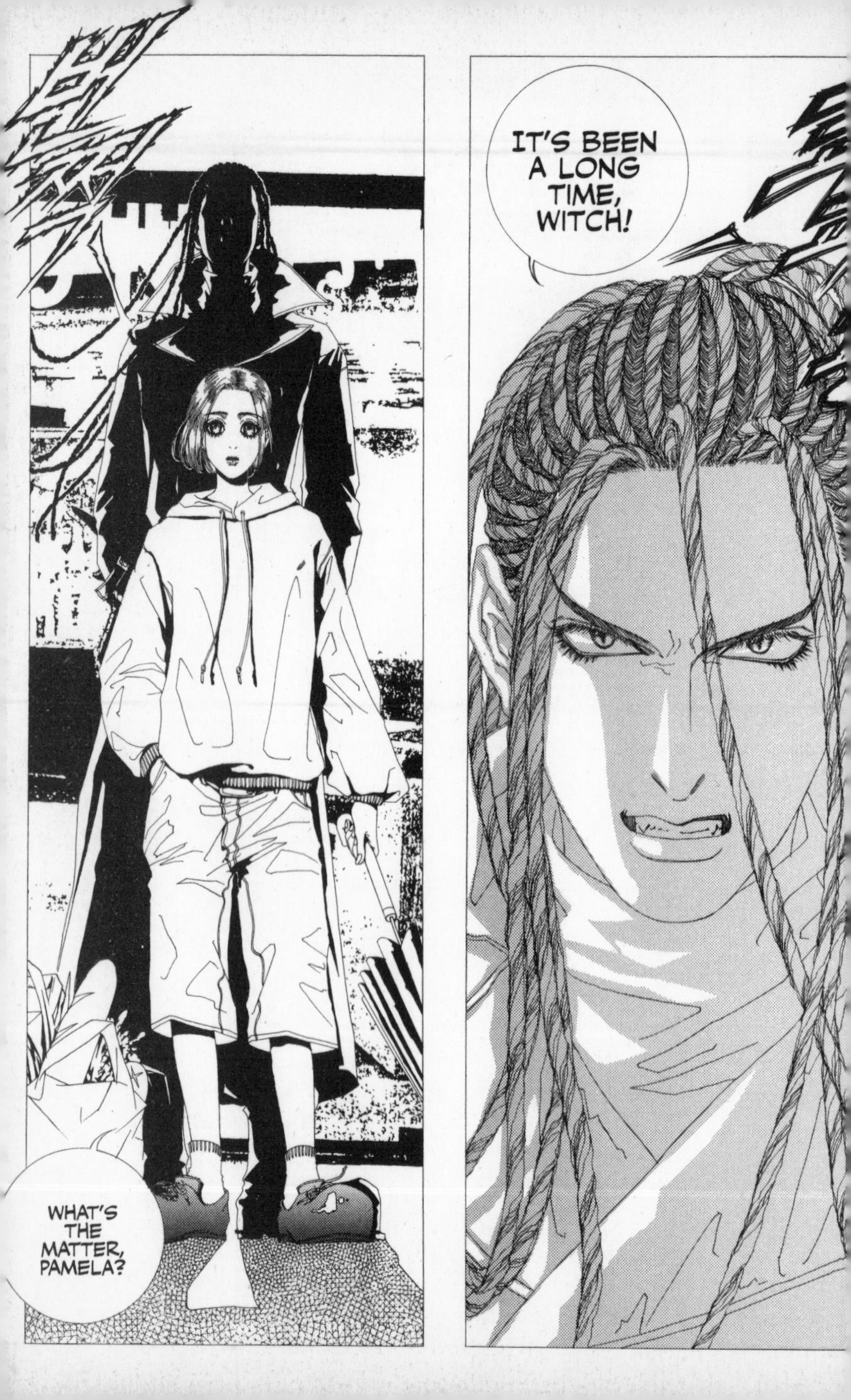
WHAT'S THE MATTER, PAMELA?
IT'S BEEN A LONG TIME, WITCH!

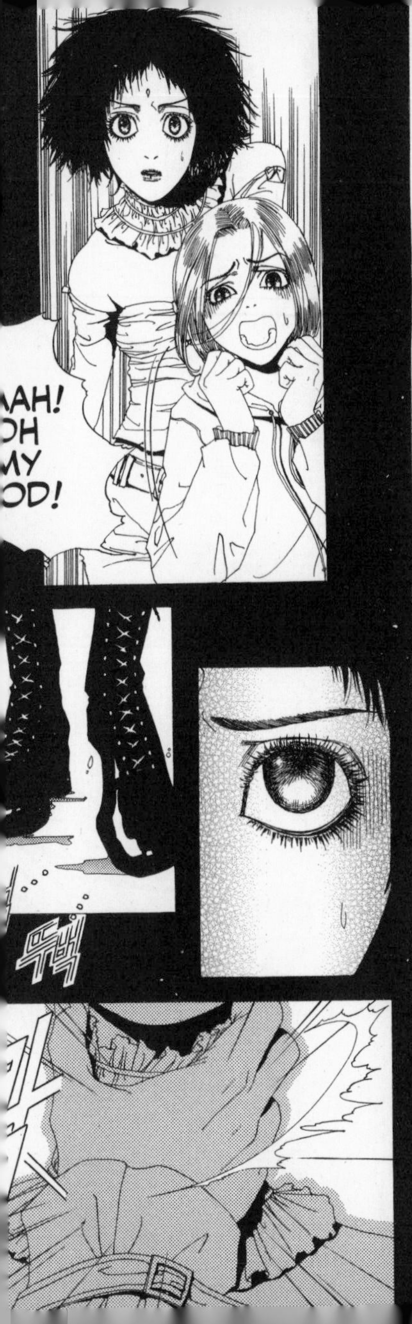
AH! OH MY OD!

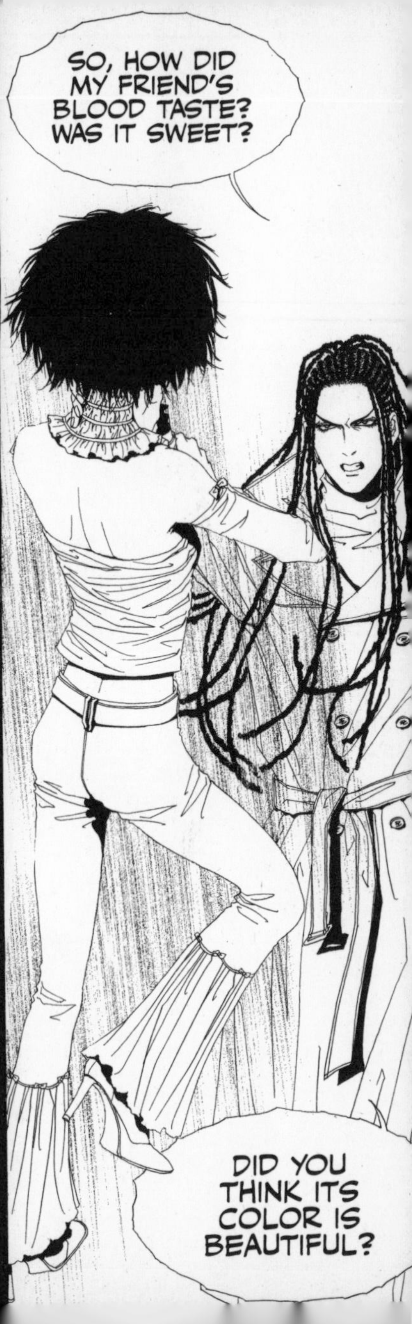
SO, HOW DID MY FRIEND'S BLOOD TASTE? WAS IT SWEET?
DID YOU THINK ITS COLOR IS BEAUTIFUL?

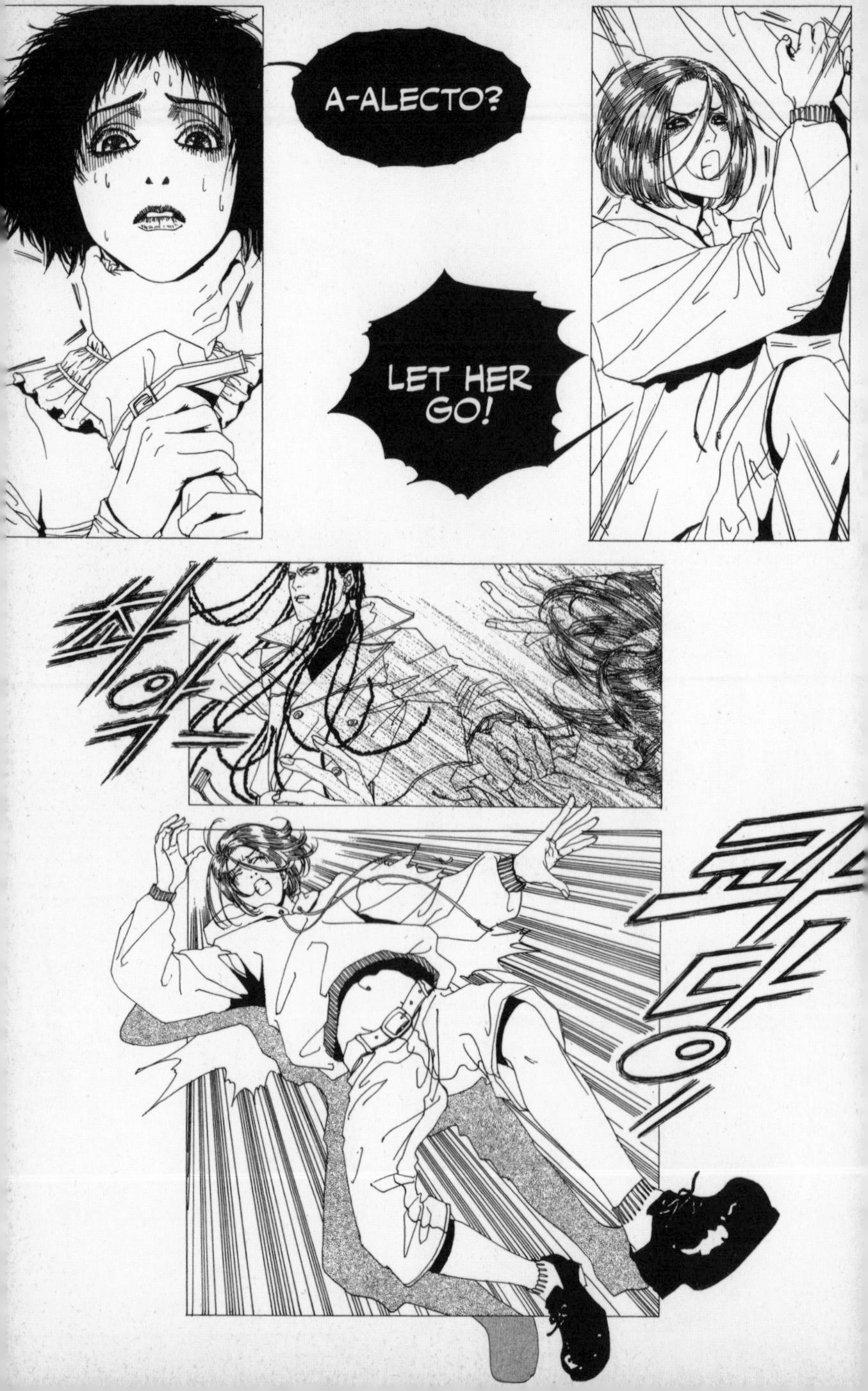
A-ALECTO?
LET HER GO!

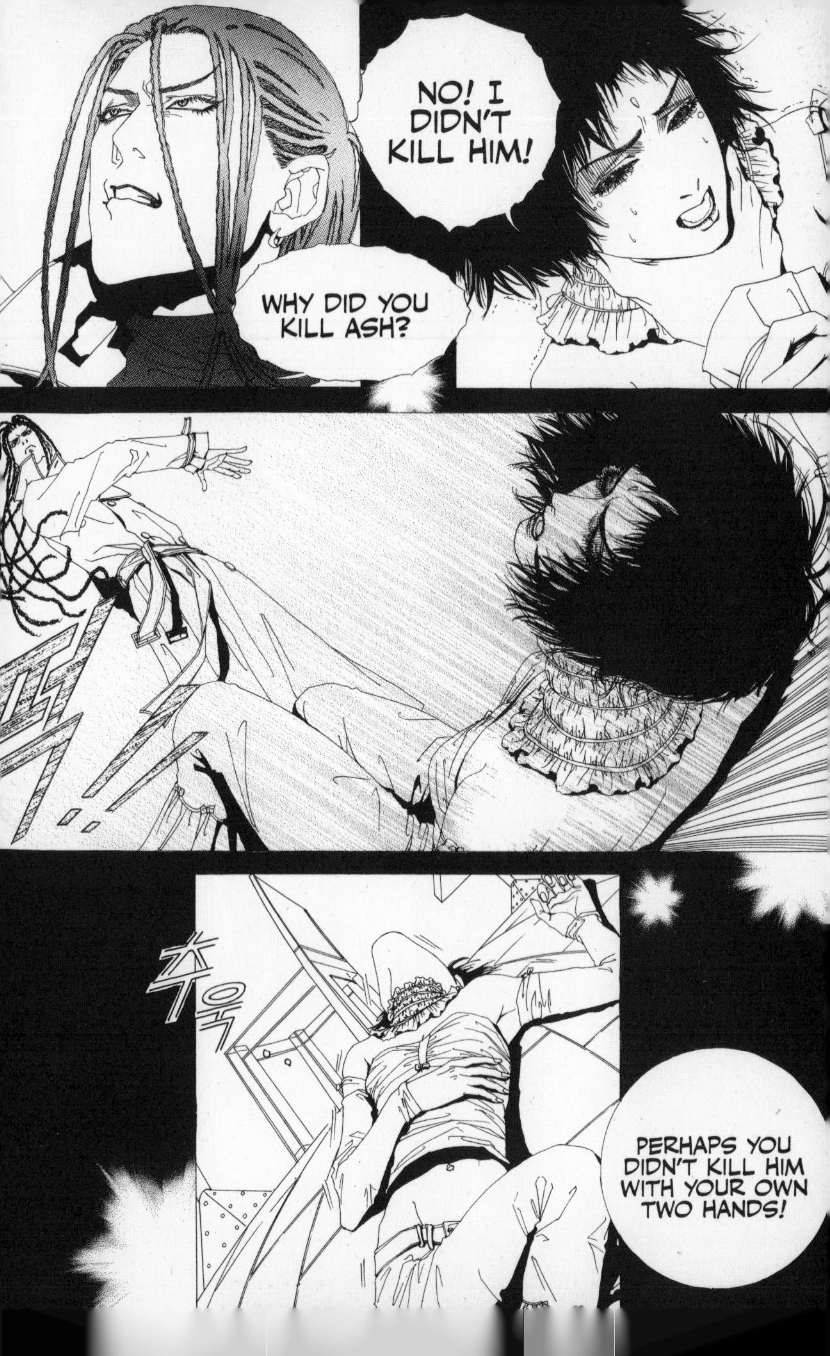
WHY DID YOU KILL ASH?
NO! I DIDN'T KILL HIM!
PERHAPS YOU DIDN'T KILL HIM WITH YOUR OWN TWO HANDS!

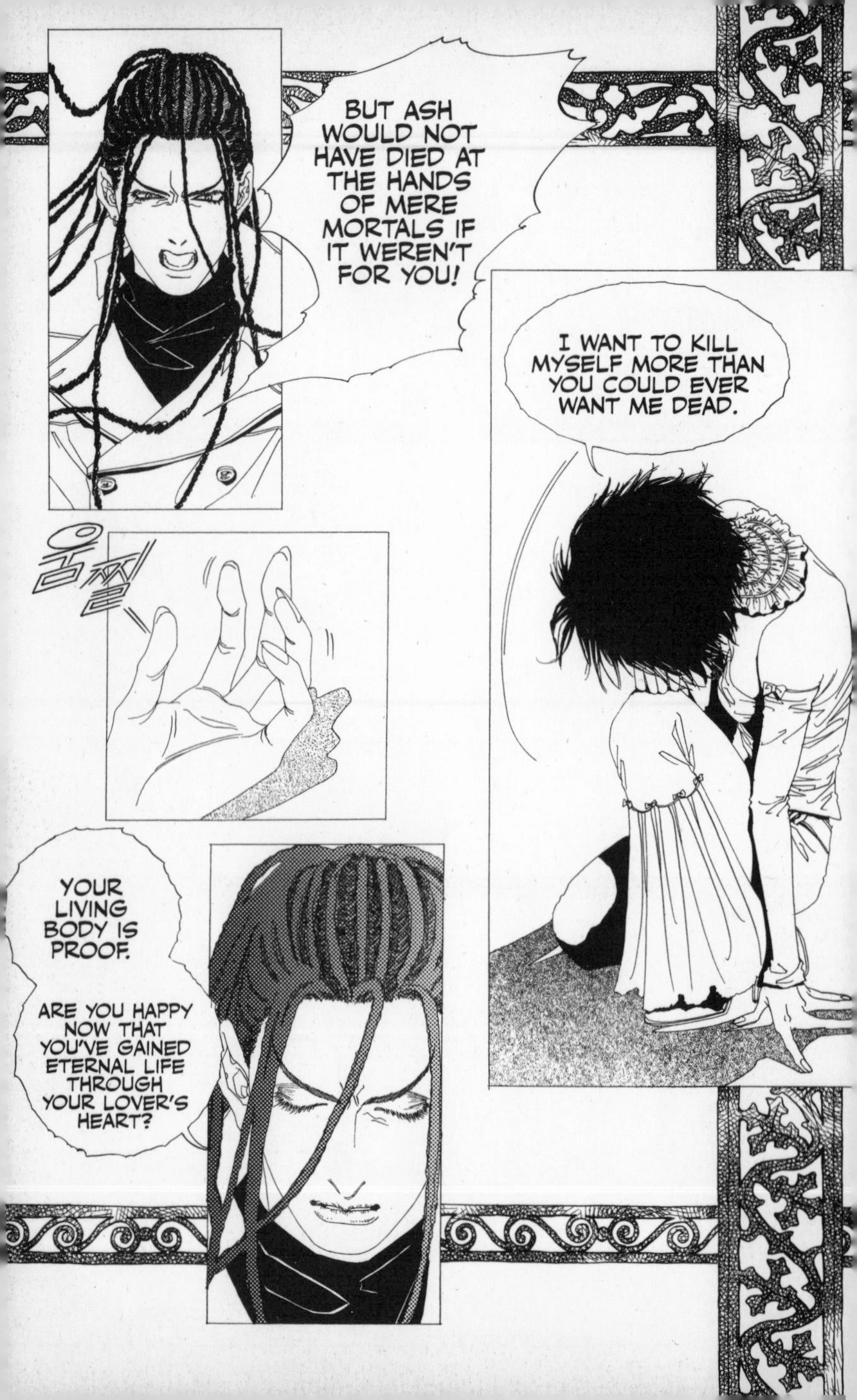
BUT ASH WOULD NOT HAVE DIED AT THE HANDS OF MERE MORTALS IF IT WEREN'T FOR YOU!
움찔
YOUR LIVING BODY IS PROOF.
ARE YOU HAPPY NOW THAT YOU'VE GAINED ETERNAL LIFE THROUGH YOUR LOVER'S HEART?
I WANT TO KILL MYSELF MORE THAN YOU COULD EVER WANT ME DEAD.

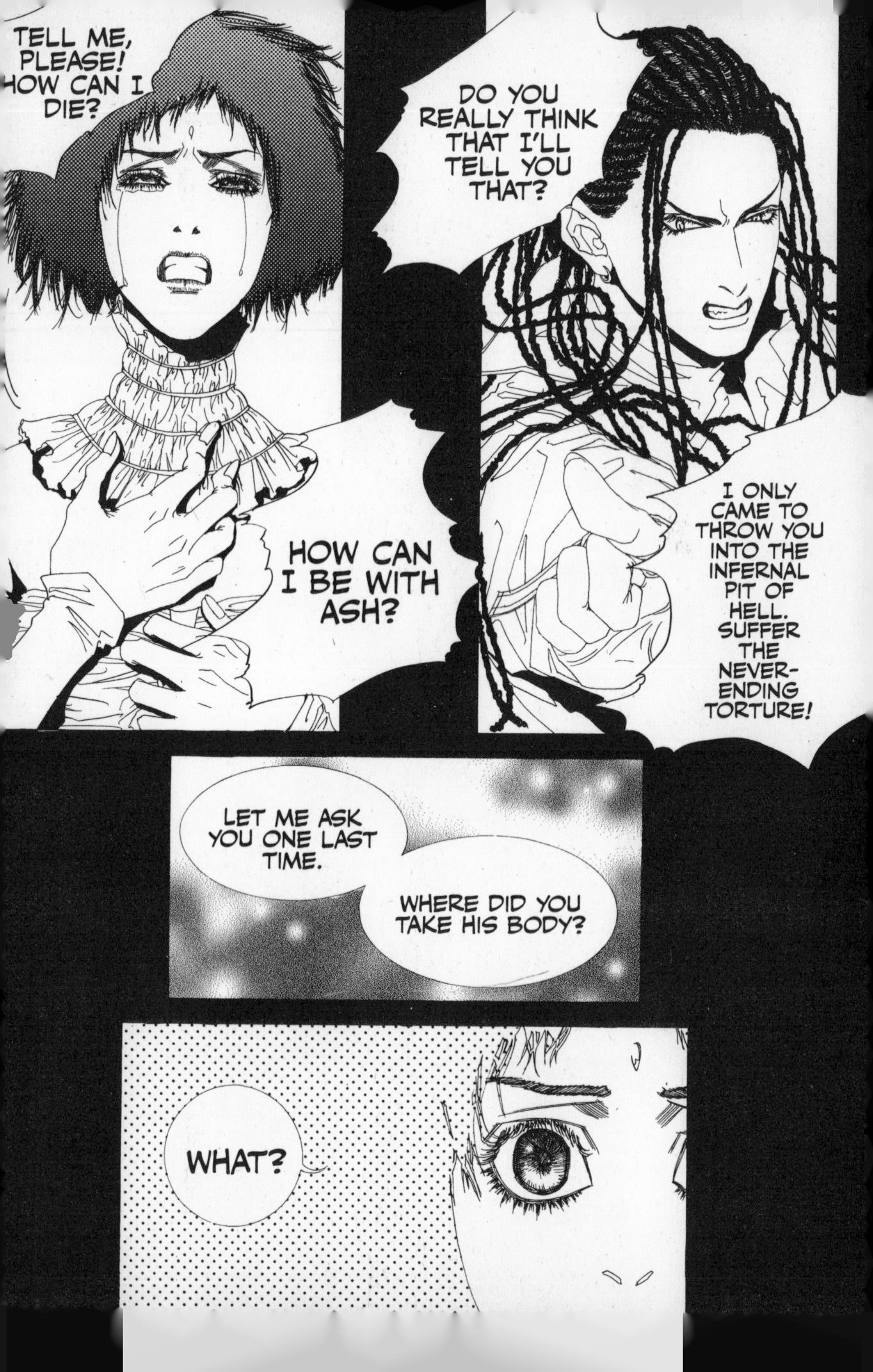
TELL ME, PLEASE! HOW CAN I DIE?
DO YOU REALLY THINK THAT I'LL TELL YOU THAT?
HOW CAN I BE WITH ASH?
I ONLY CAME TO THROW YOU INTO THE INFERNAL PIT OF HELL. SUFFER THE NEVER-ENDING TORTURE!
LET ME ASK YOU ONE LAST TIME.
WHERE DID YOU TAKE HIS BODY?
WHAT?

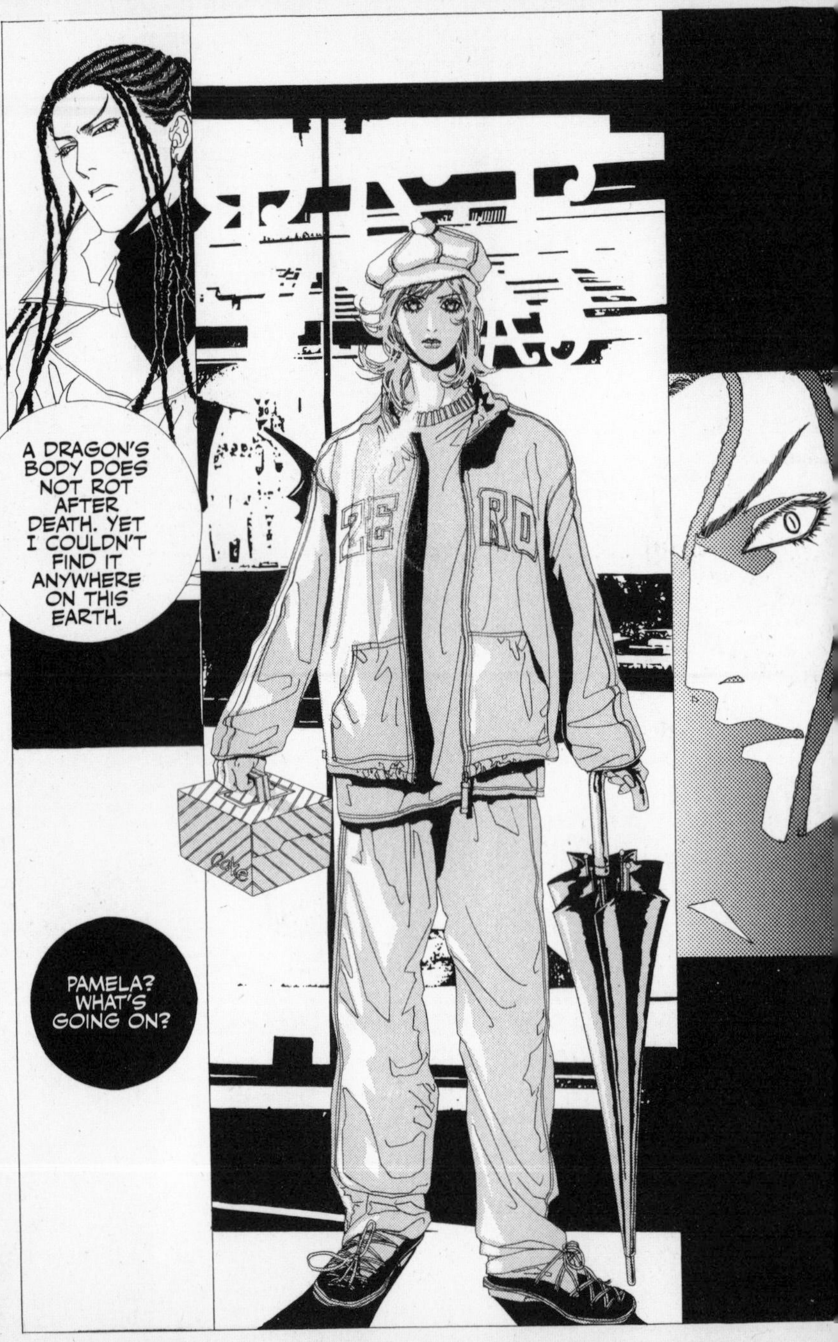
A DRAGON'S BODY DOES NOT ROT AFTER DEATH. YET I COULDN'T FIND IT ANYWHERE ON THIS EARTH.
PAMELA? WHAT'S GOING ON?

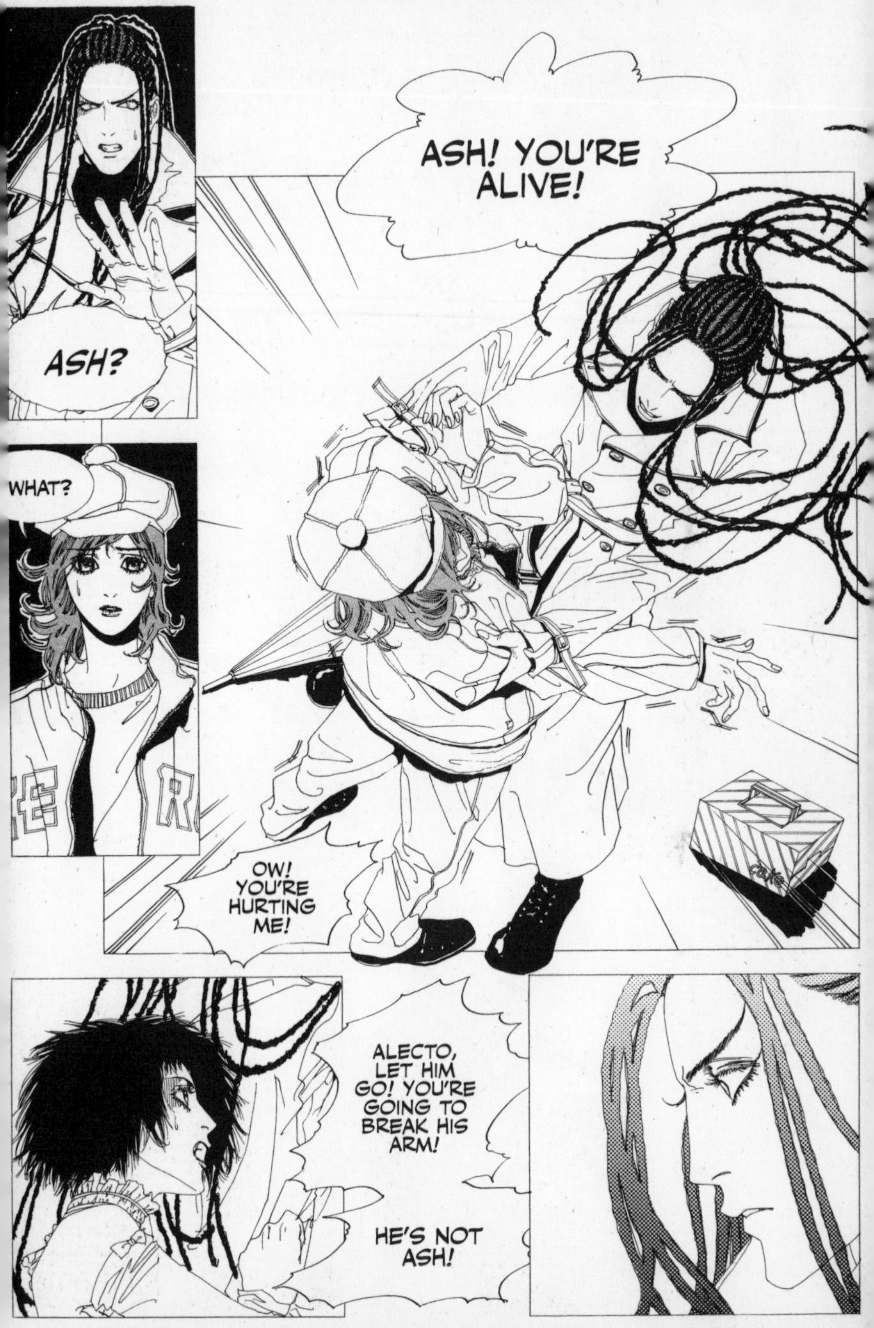
ASH?
WHAT?
ASH! YOU'RE ALIVE!
OW! YOU'RE HURTING ME!
ALECTO, LET HIM GO! YOU'RE GOING TO BREAK HIS ARM!
HE'S NOT ASH!

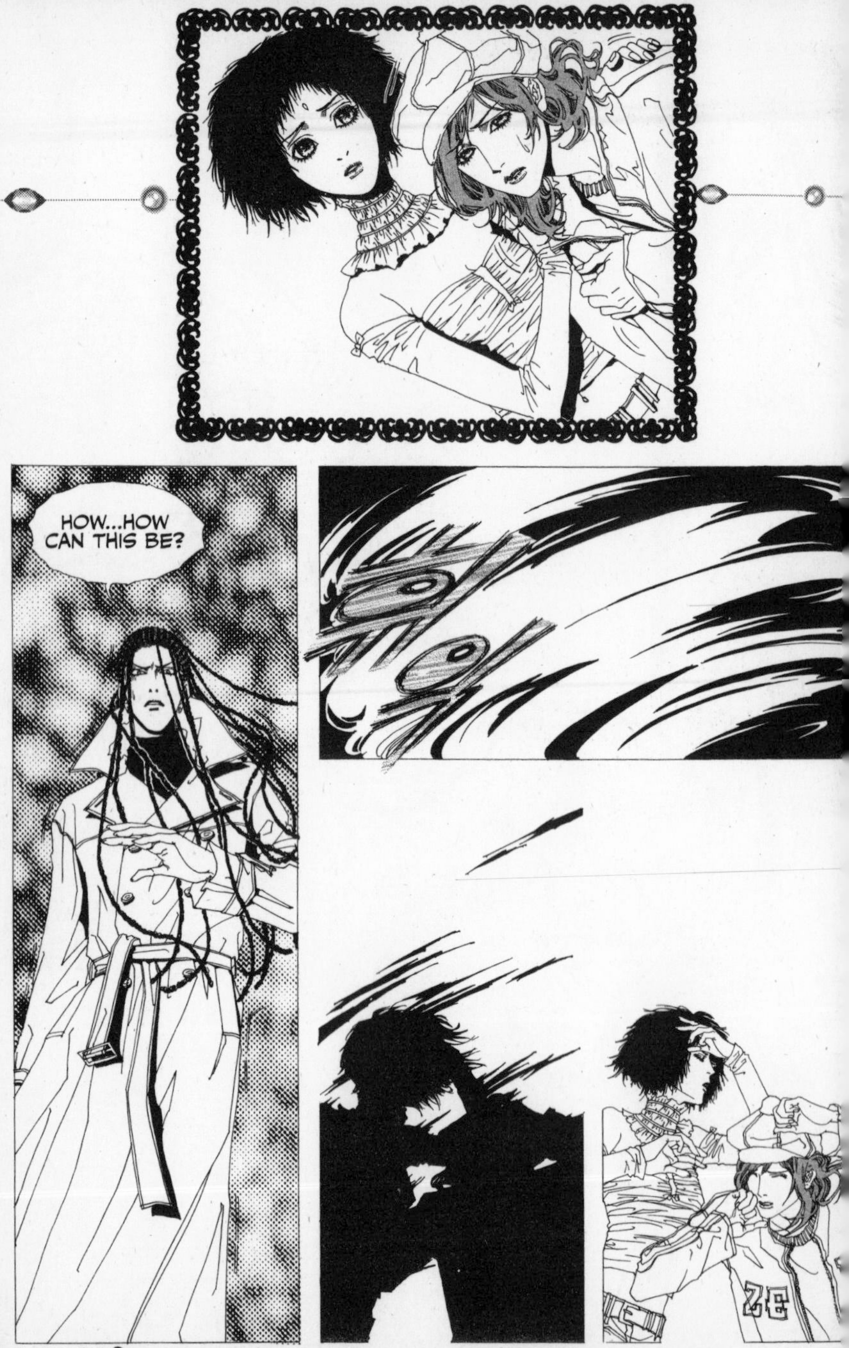
HOW...HOW CAN THIS BE?

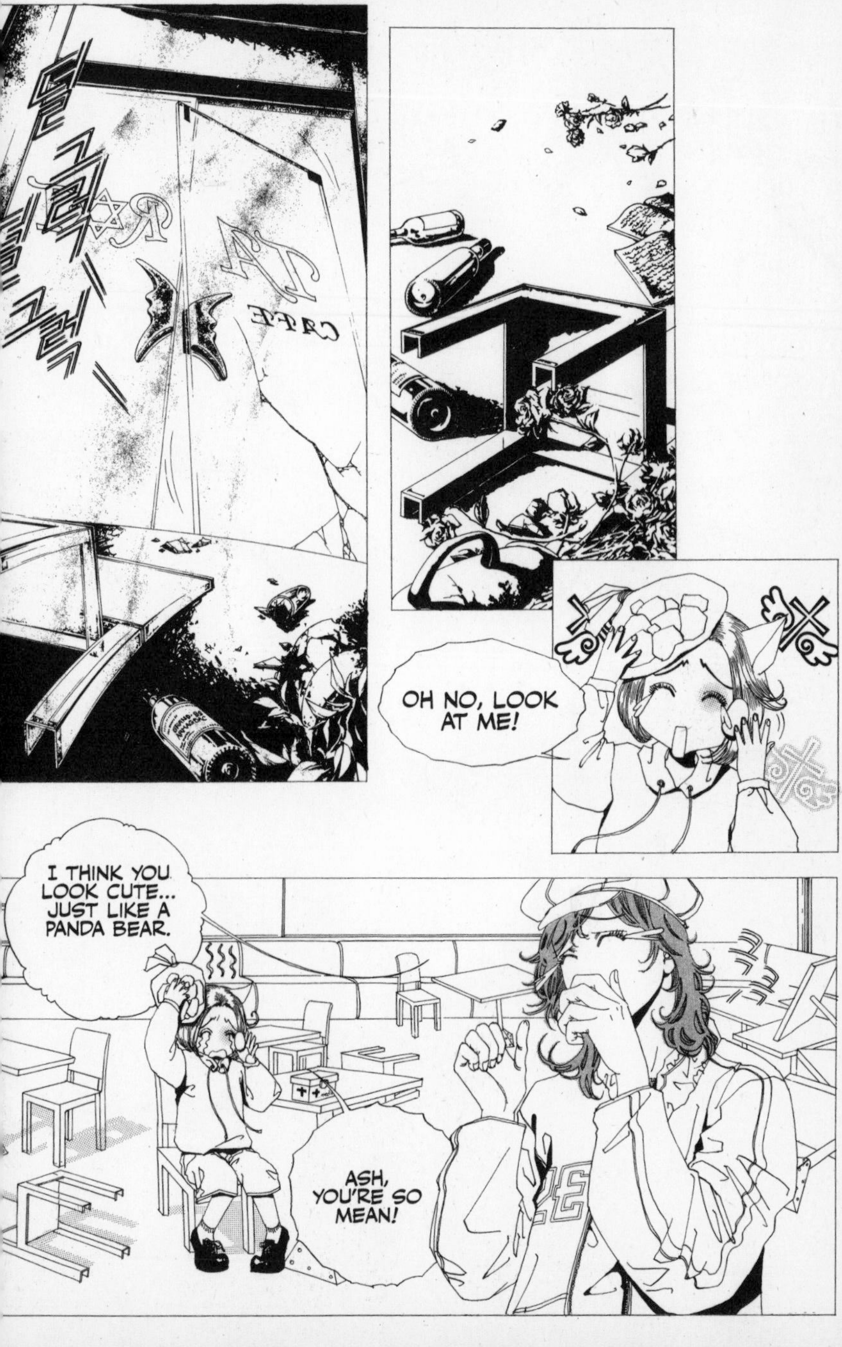
OH NO, LOOK AT ME!
I THINK YOU LOOK CUTE... JUST LIKE A PANDA BEAR.
ASH, YOU'RE SO MEAN!

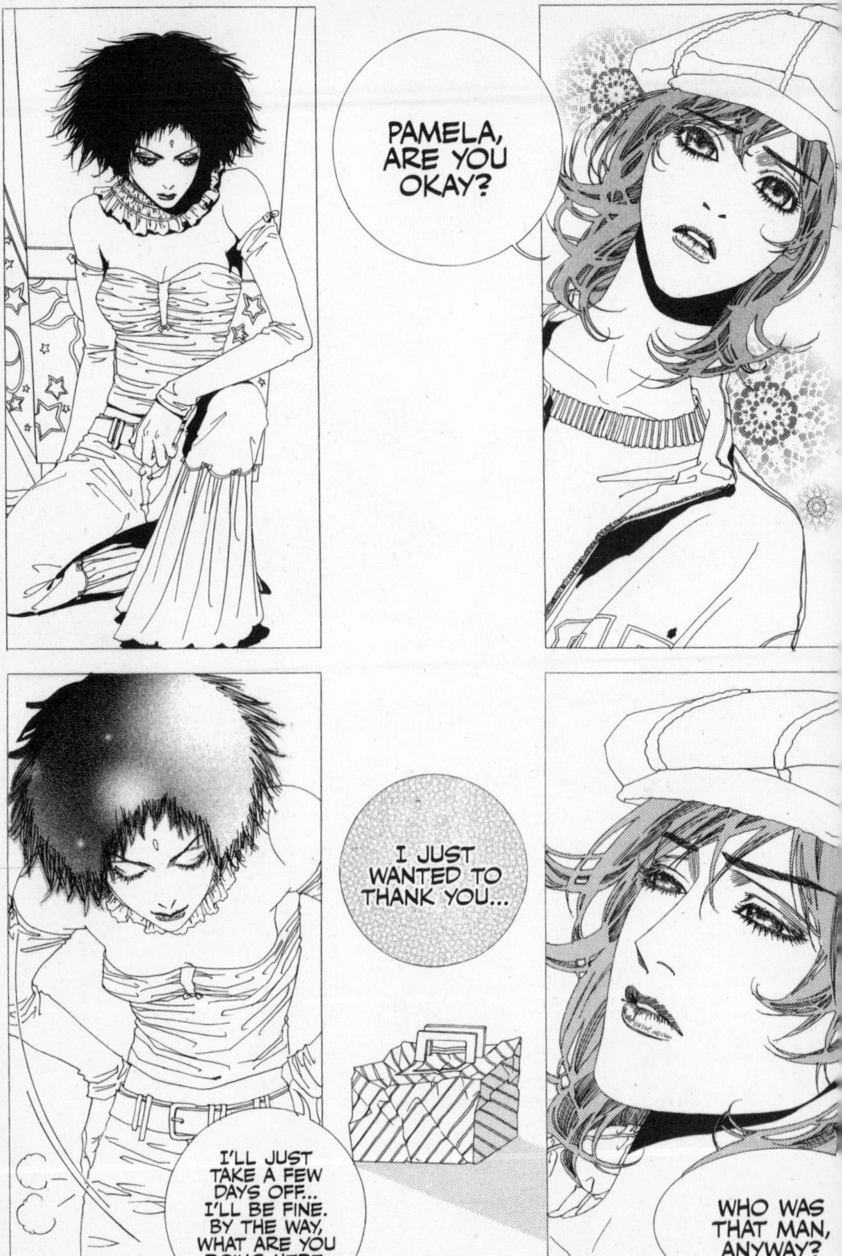
PAMELA, ARE YOU OKAY?
I'LL JUST TAKE A FEW DAYS OFF... I'LL BE FINE. BY THE WAY, WHAT ARE YOU DOING HERE, ASH?
I JUST WANTED TO THANK YOU...
WHO WAS THAT MAN, ANYWAY?

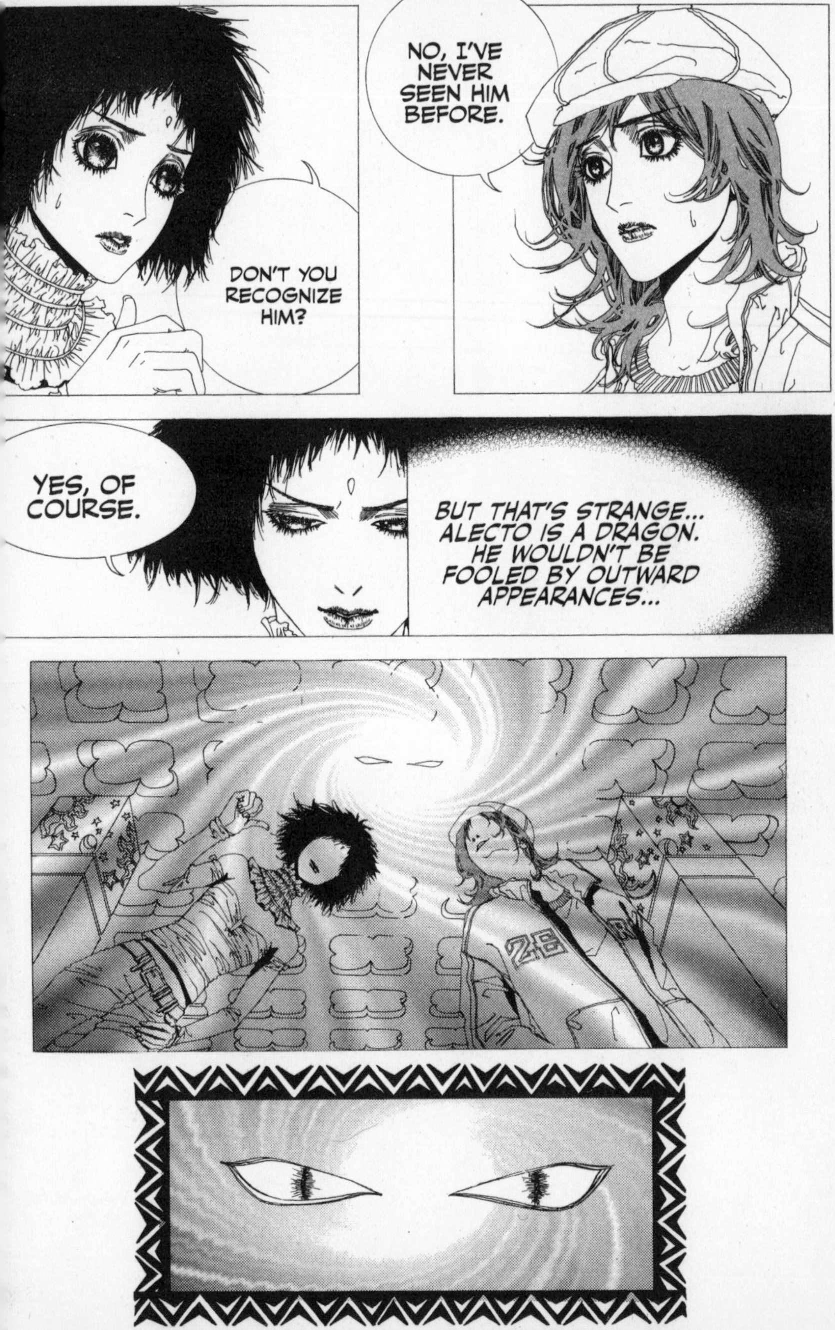
DON'T YOU RECOGNIZE HIM?
NO, I'VE NEVER SEEN HIM BEFORE.
YES, OF COURSE.
BUT THAT'S STRANGE... ALECTO IS A DRAGON. HE WOULDN'T BE FOOLED BY OUTWARD APPEARANCES...

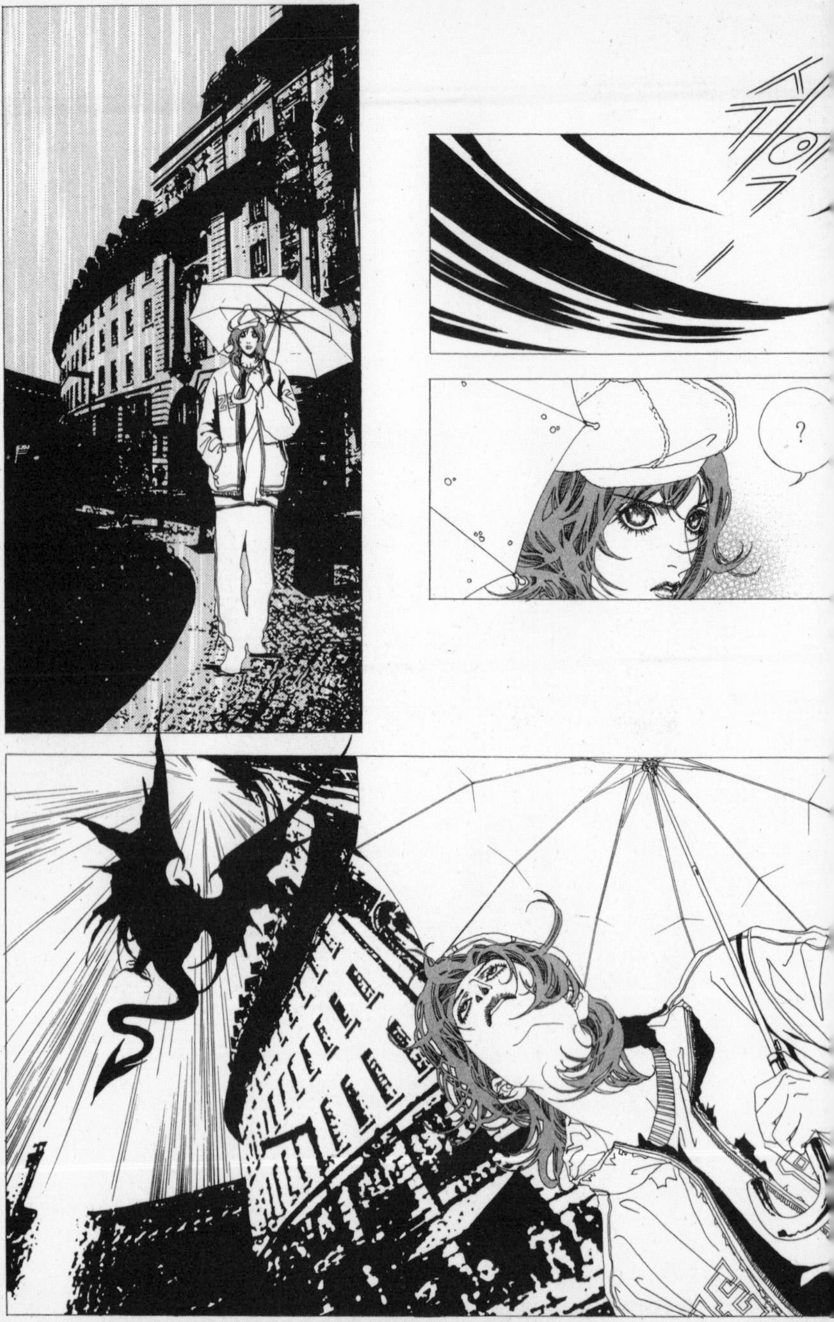

쉬익
?

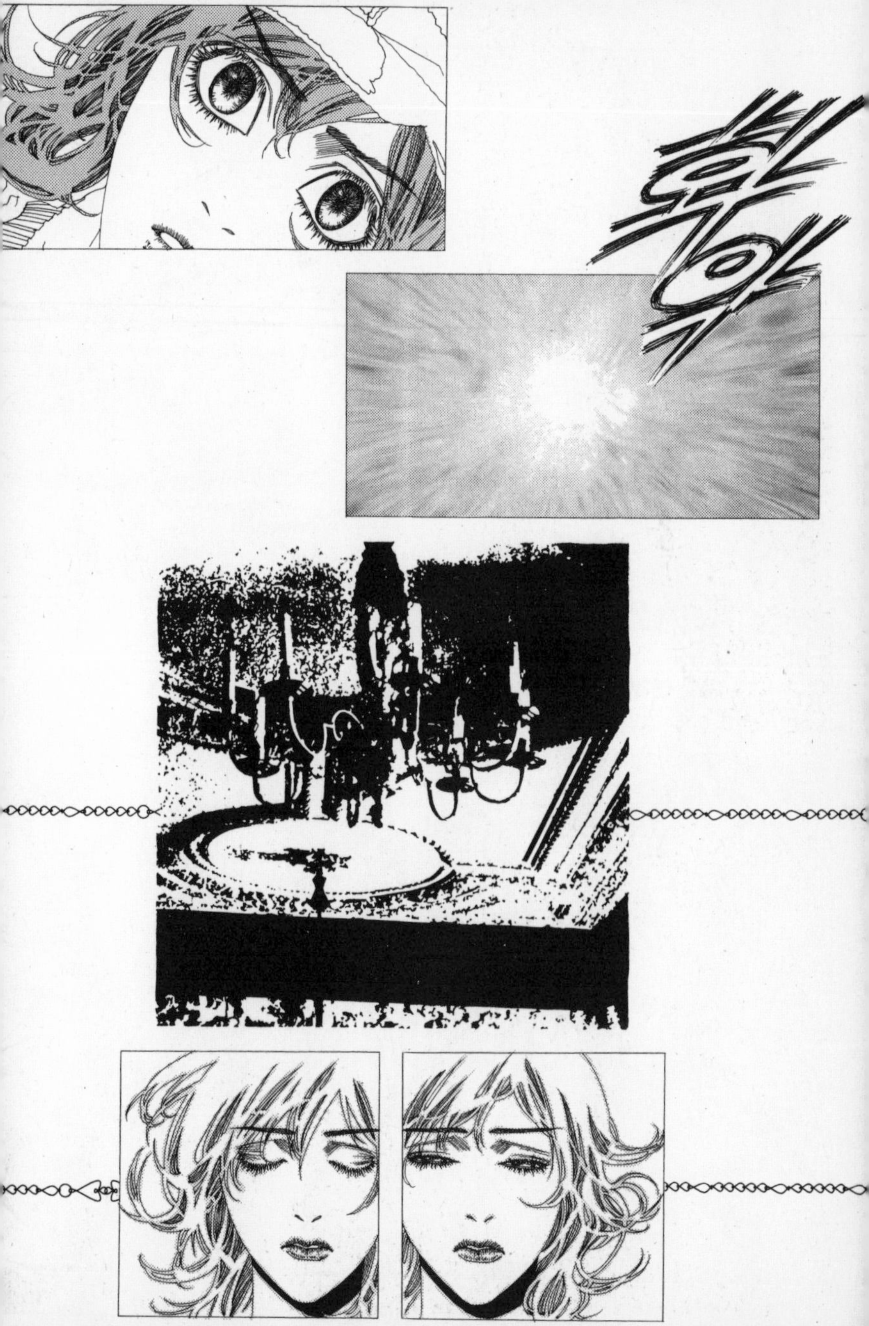

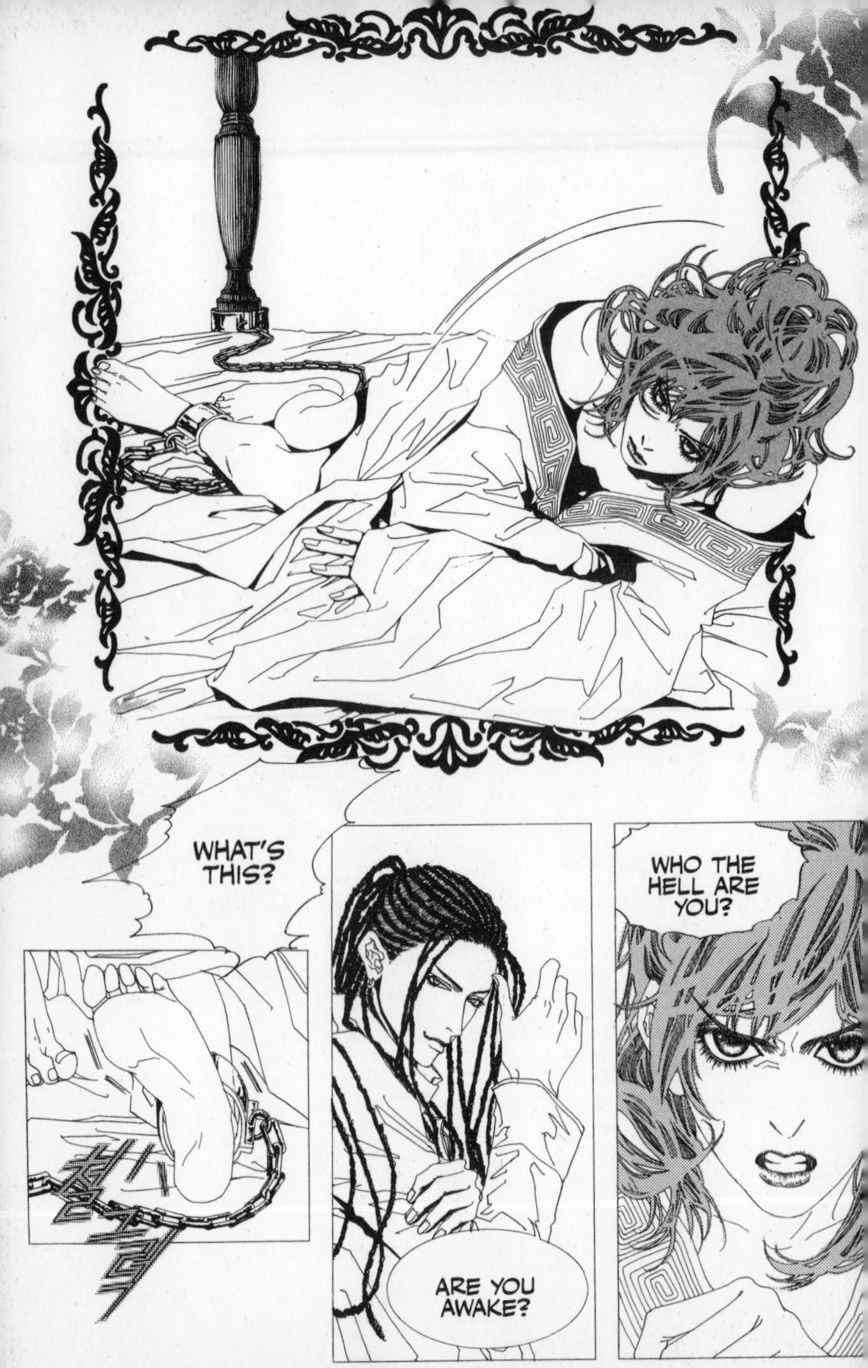
WHAT'S THIS?
ARE YOU AWAKE?
WHO THE HELL ARE YOU?

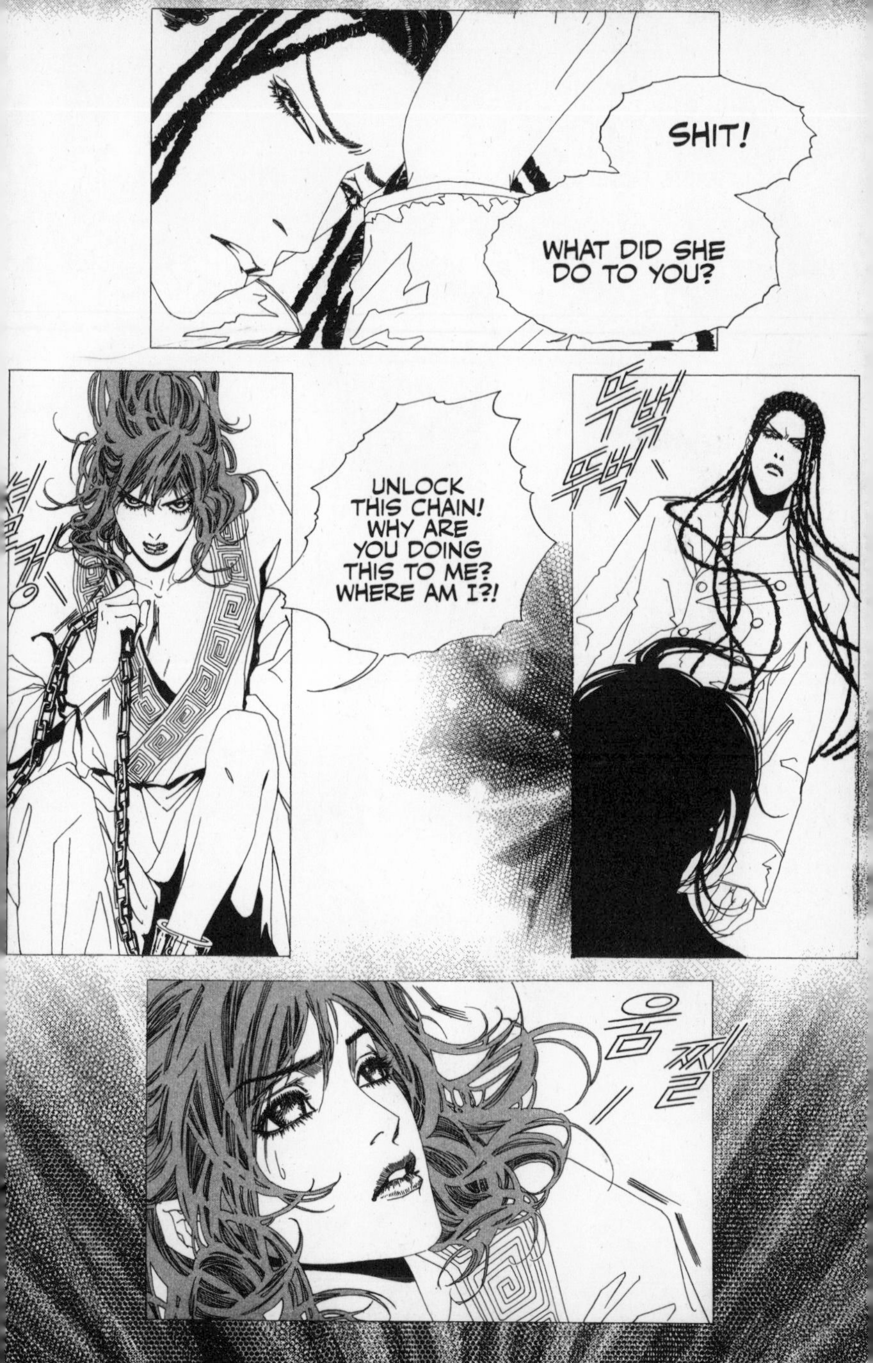
SHIT!
WHAT DID SHE DO TO YOU?
UNLOCK THIS CHAIN! WHY ARE YOU DOING THIS TO ME? WHERE AM I?!
뚜벅 뚜벅
움찔

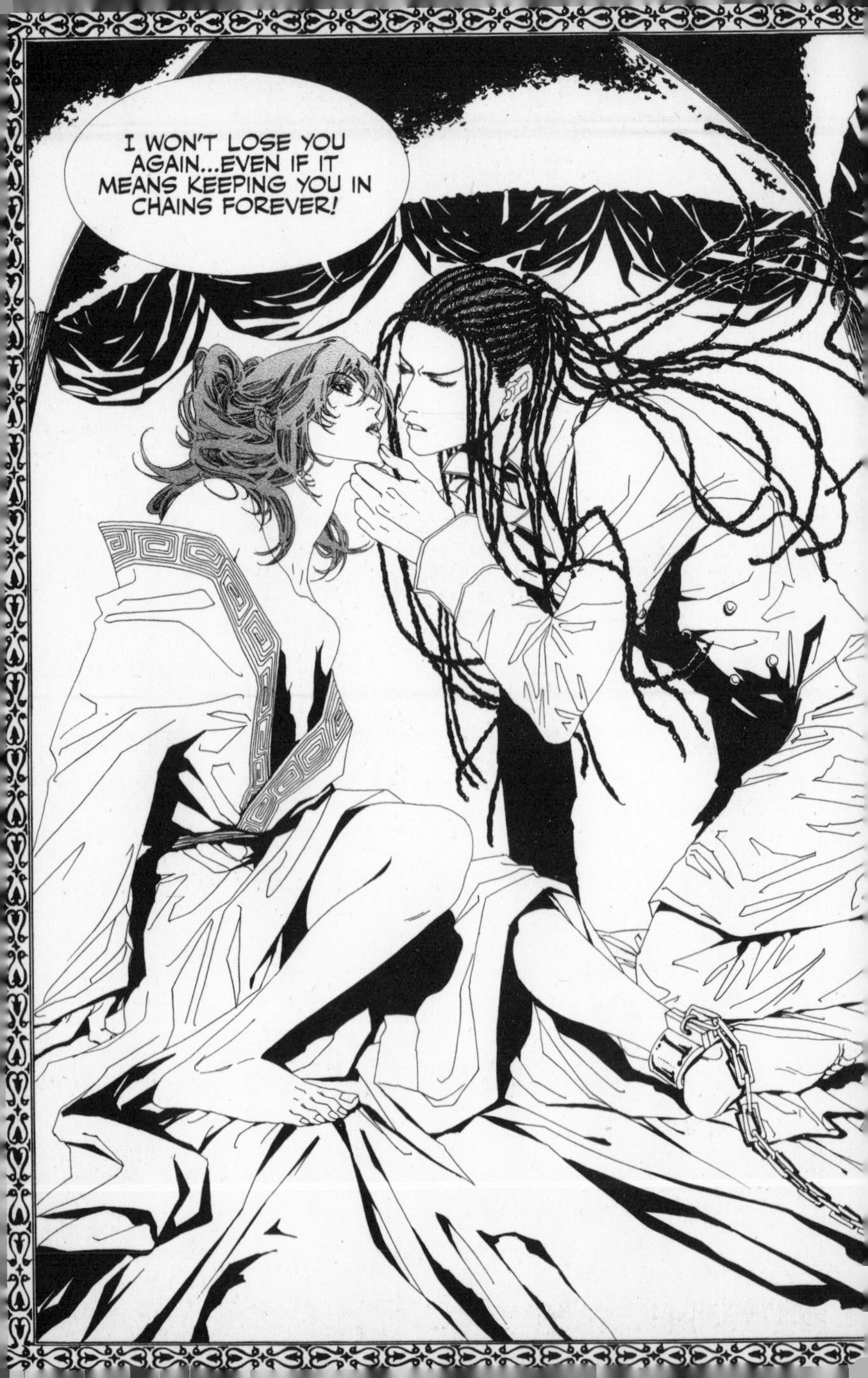
I WON'T LOSE YOU AGAIN...EVEN IF IT MEANS KEEPING YOU IN CHAINS FOREVER!

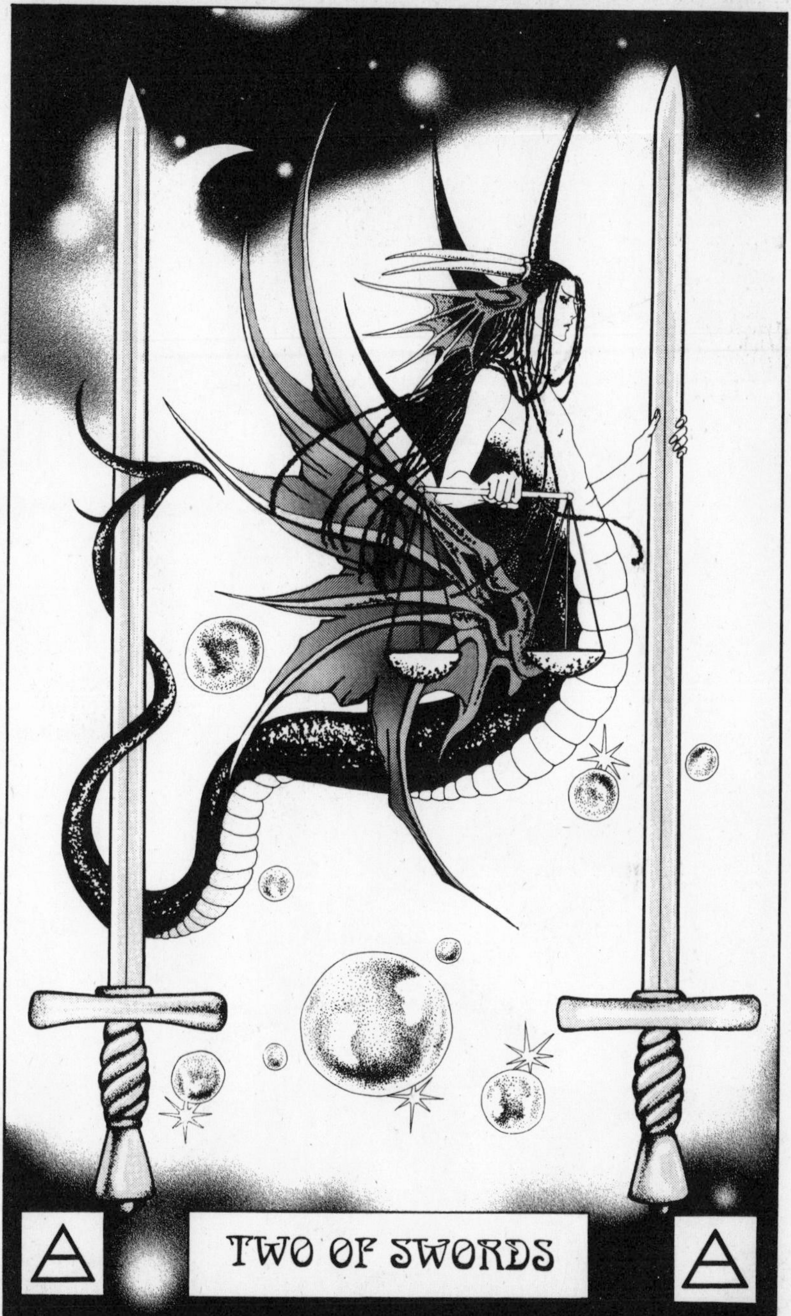
TWO OF SWORDS
*Two of Swords: This card signifies indecision, hesitation and avoiding the truth.

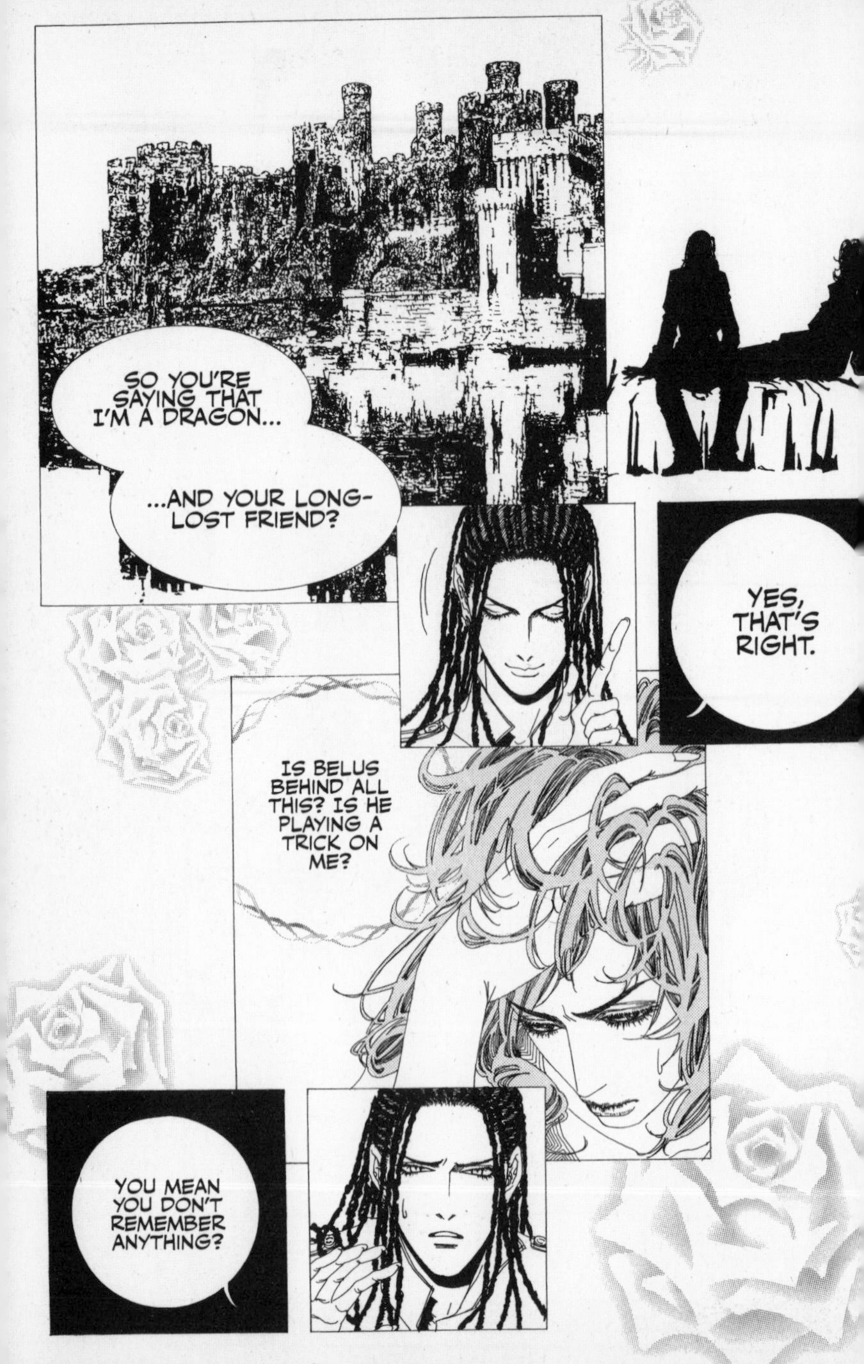
SO YOU'RE SAYING THAT I'M A DRAGON...
...AND YOUR LONG-LOST FRIEND?
YES, THAT'S RIGHT.
IS BELUS BEHIND ALL THIS? IS HE PLAYING A TRICK ON ME?
YOU MEAN YOU DON'T REMEMBER ANYTHING?

THERE'S NOTHING TO REMEMBER!

IF I REALLY WERE A DRAGON, I'D BREAK THIS CHAIN, BEAT YOU UP AND GET THE HELL OUT OF HERE.

I DON'T HAVE WINGS.

I CAN'T BREATHE FIRE.

THAT' BECAUSE YOU'VE LOST YOUR DRAGON HEART TO THAT WOMAN.

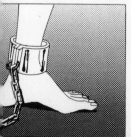

AND THAT CHAIN IS MADE OF ORIHALCON.* EVEN A DRAGON CAN'T BREAK IT EASILY.

*Orihalcon is mythical metal of extreme strength.

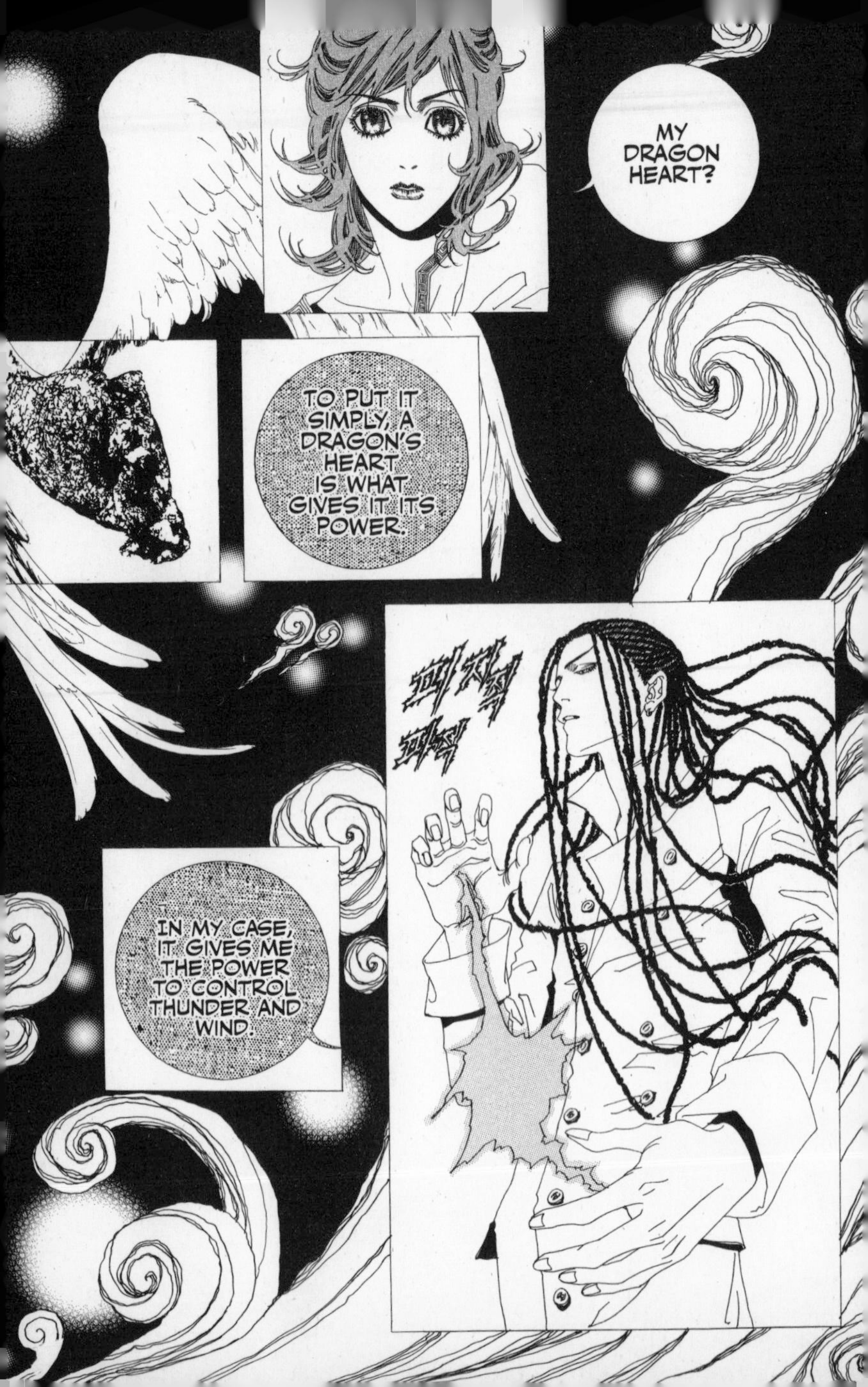
MY DRAGON HEART?
TO PUT IT SIMPLY, A DRAGON'S HEART IS WHAT GIVES IT ITS POWER.
IN MY CASE, IT GIVES ME THE POWER TO CONTROL THUNDER AND WIND.

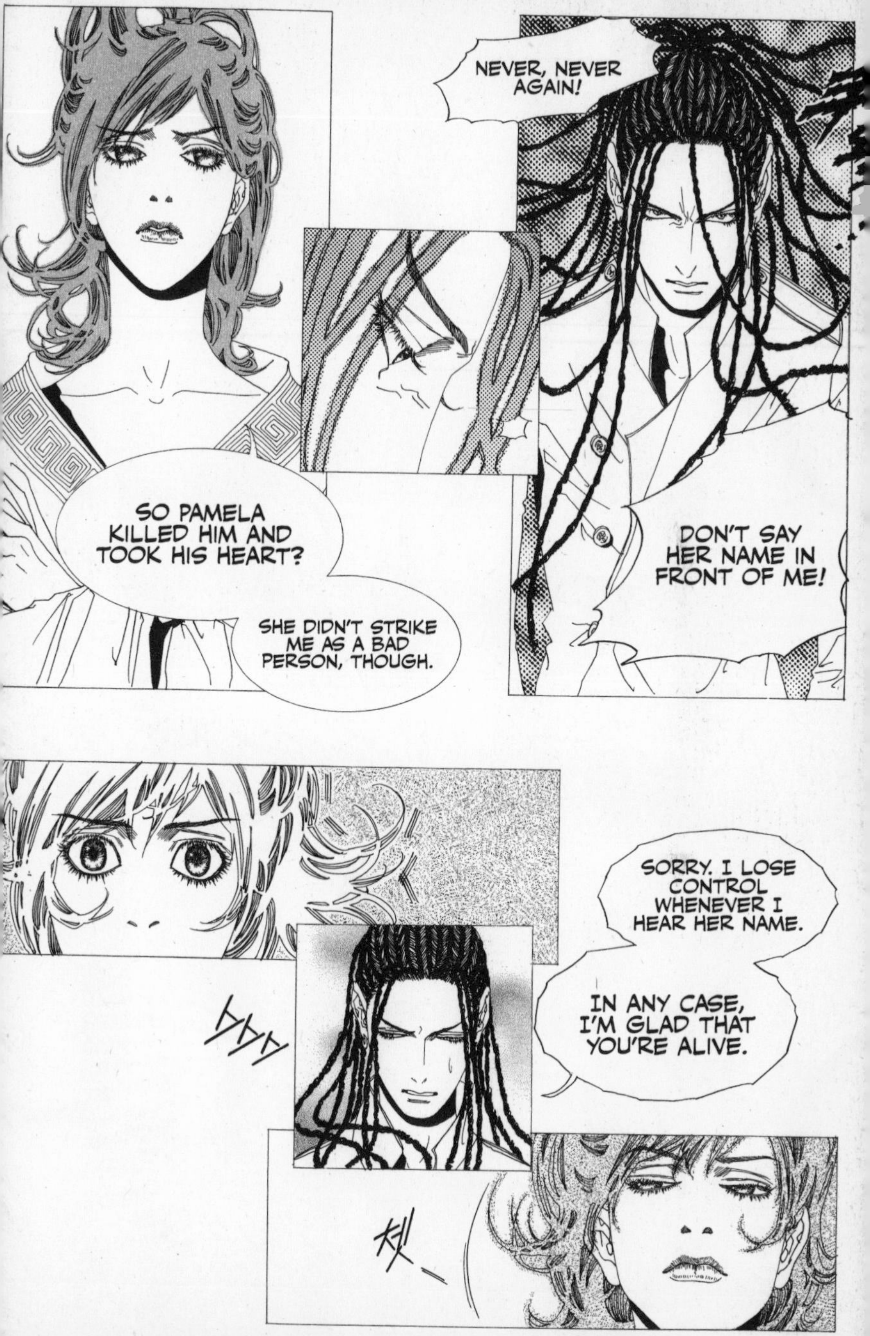
SO PAMELA KILLED HIM AND TOOK HIS HEART?
SHE DIDN'T STRIKE ME AS A BAD PERSON, THOUGH.
NEVER, NEVER AGAIN!
DON'T SAY HER NAME IN FRONT OF ME!
SORRY. I LOSE CONTROL WHENEVER I HEAR HER NAME.
IN ANY CASE, I'M GLAD THAT YOU'RE ALIVE.

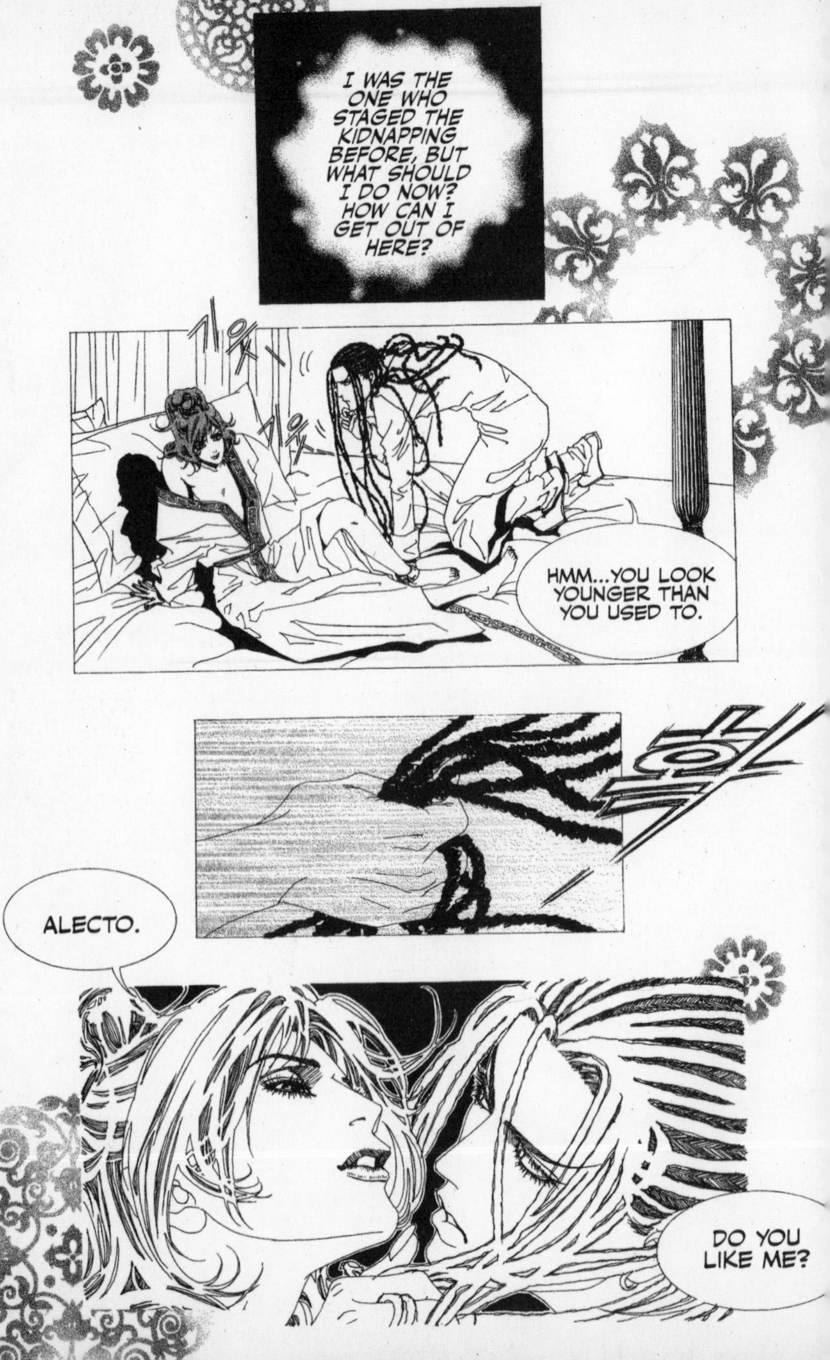
I WAS THE ONE WHO STAGED THE KIDNAPPING BEFORE, BUT WHAT SHOULD I DO NOW? HOW CAN I GET OUT OF HERE?
HMM...YOU LOOK YOUNGER THAN YOU USED TO.
ALECTO.
DO YOU LIKE ME?

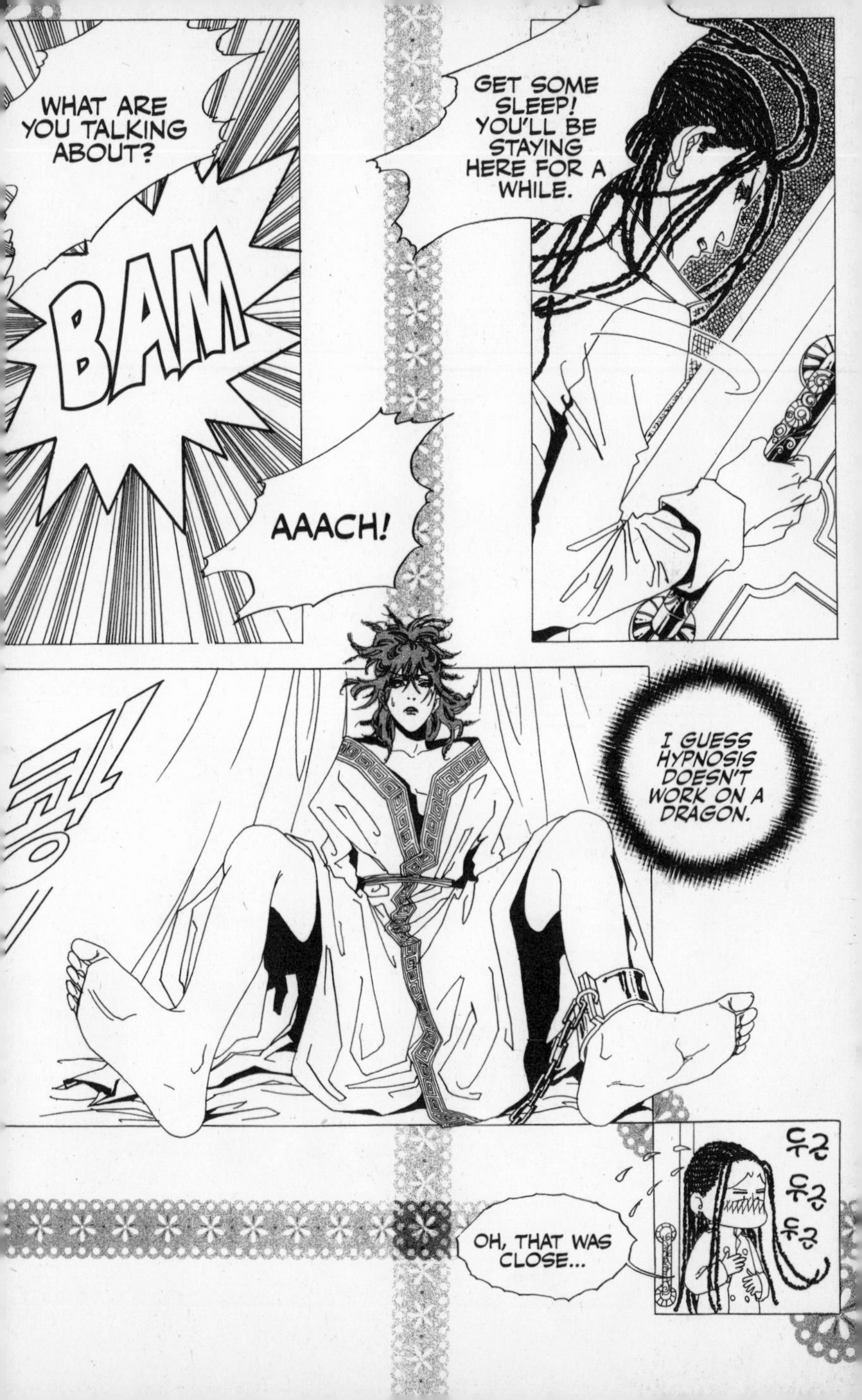
WHAT ARE YOU TALKING ABOUT?
BAM
AAACH!
GET SOME SLEEP! YOU'LL BE STAYING HERE FOR A WHILE.
I GUESS HYPNOSIS DOESN'T WORK ON A DRAGON.
OH, THAT WAS CLOSE...
두근 두근 두근

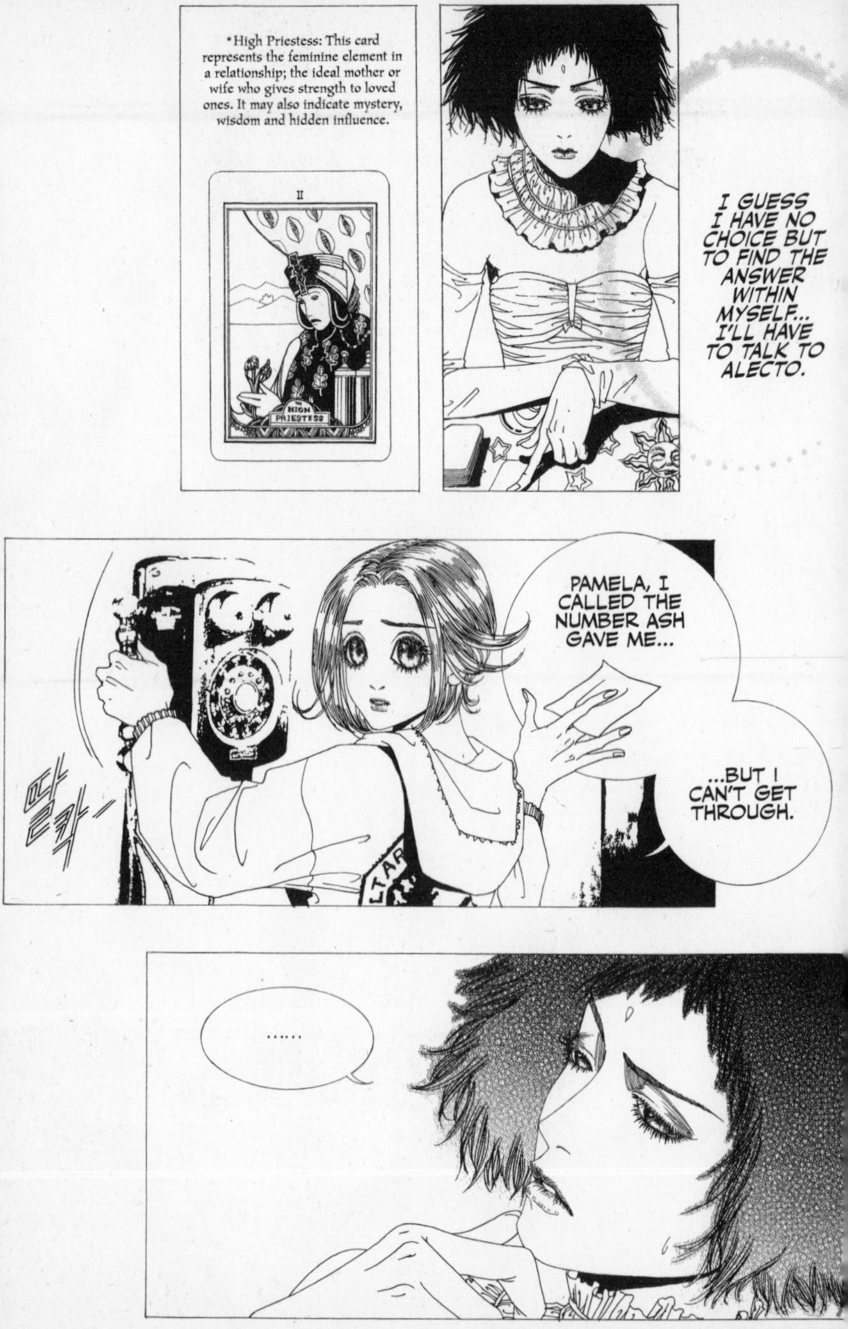
*High Priestess: This card represents the feminine element in a relationship; the ideal mother or wife who gives strength to loved ones. It may also indicate mystery, wisdom and hidden influence.
II
THE HIGH PRIESTESS
I GUESS I HAVE NO CHOICE BUT TO FIND THE ANSWER WITHIN MYSELF... I'LL HAVE TO TALK TO ALECTO.
딸칵
PAMELA, I CALLED THE NUMBER ASH GAVE ME...
...BUT I CAN'T GET THROUGH.
......

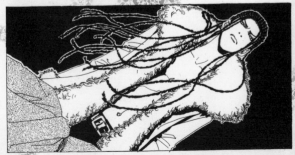

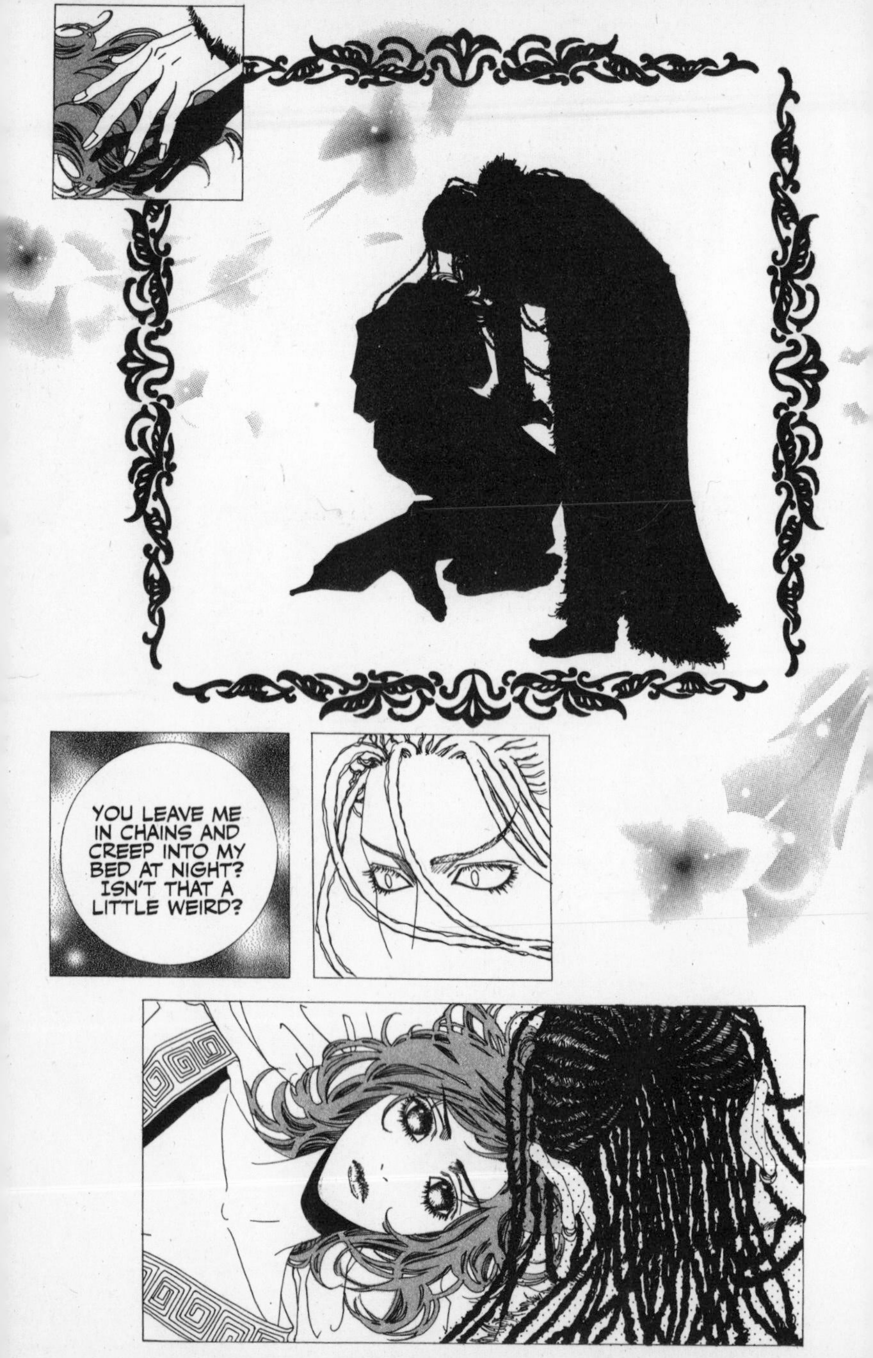
YOU LEAVE ME IN CHAINS AND CREEP INTO MY BED AT NIGHT? ISN'T THAT A LITTLE WEIRD?

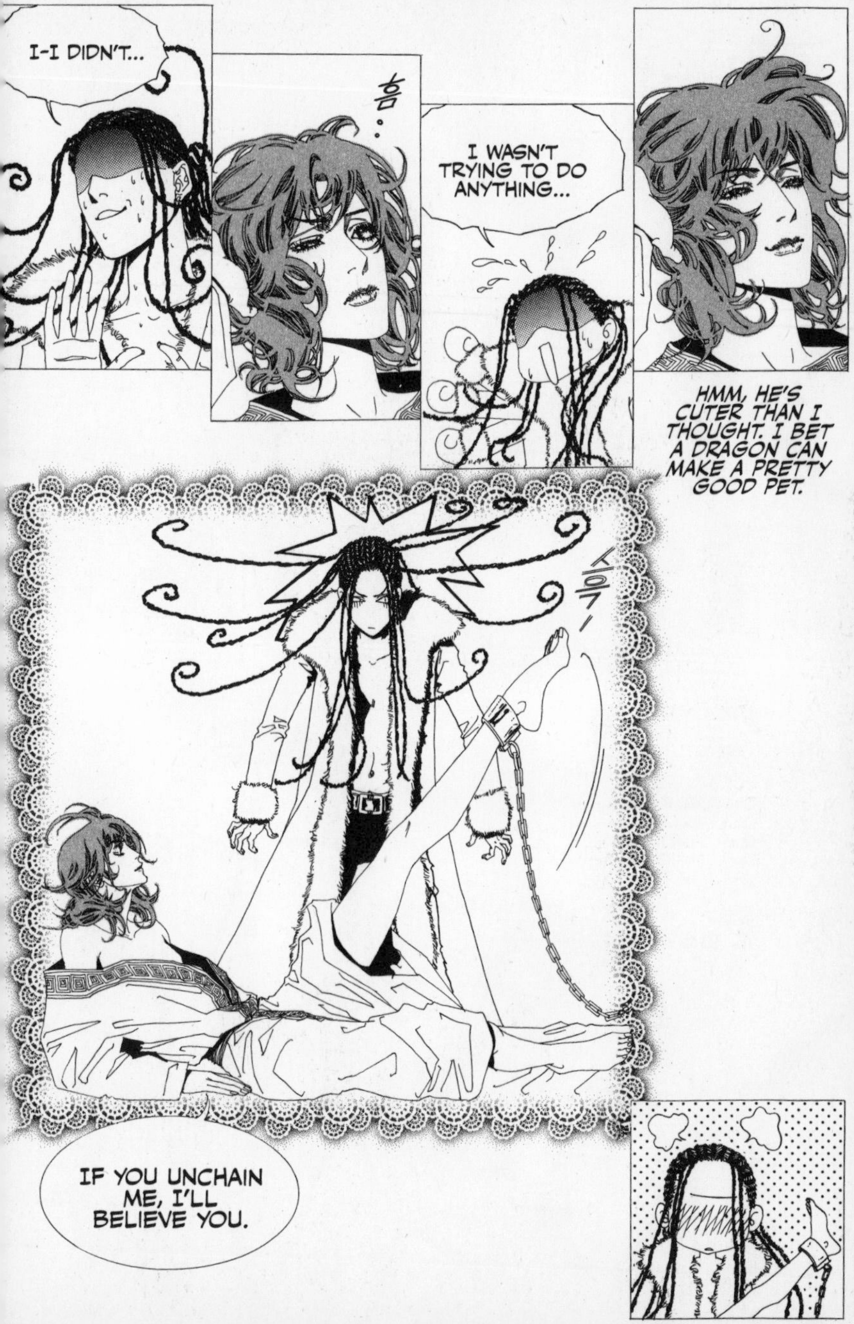
I-I DIDN'T...
흠
I WASN'T TRYING TO DO ANYTHING...
HMM, HE'S CUTER THAN I THOUGHT. I BET A DRAGON CAN MAKE A PRETTY GOOD PET.
IF YOU UNCHAIN ME, I'LL BELIEVE YOU.

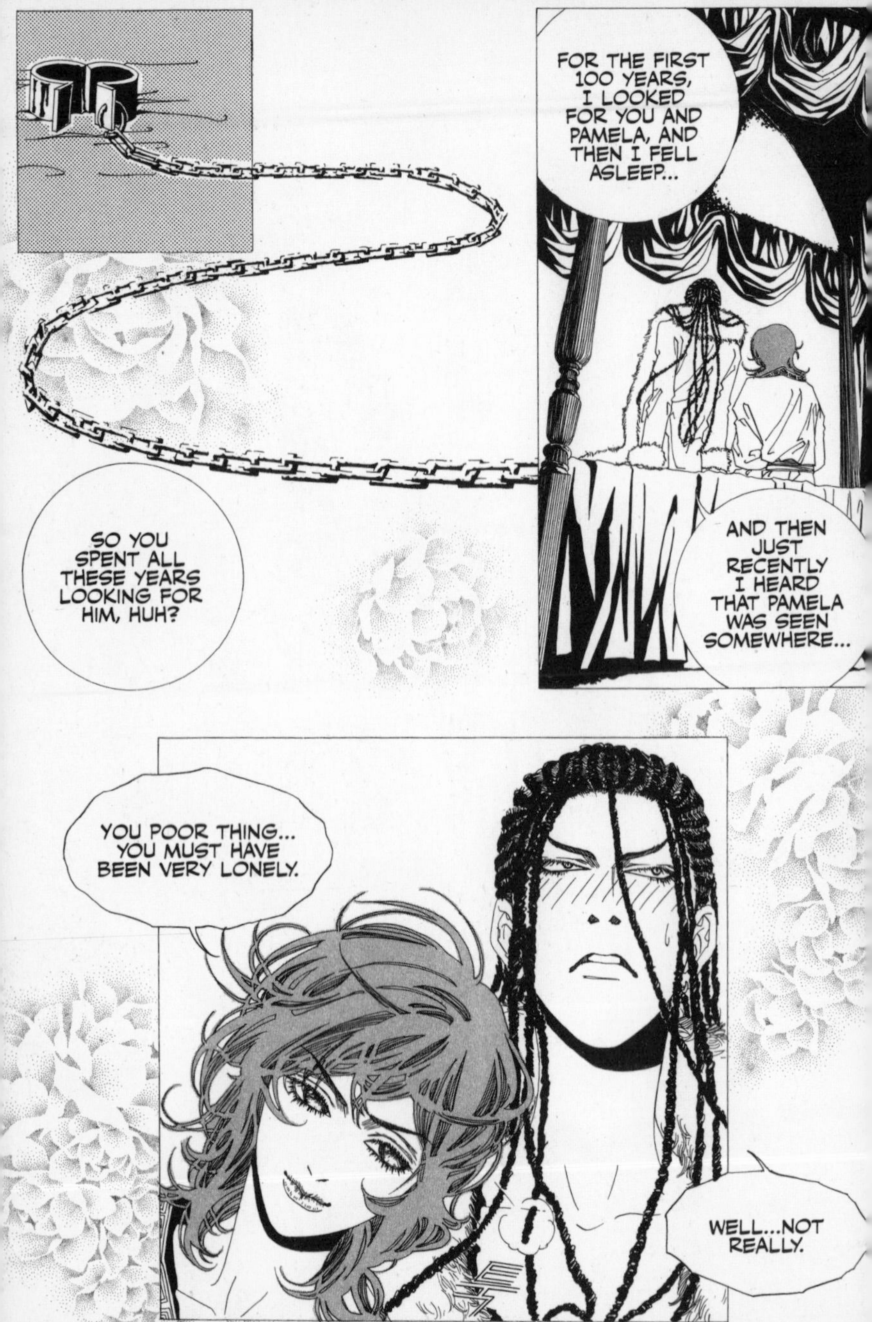
FOR THE FIRST 100 YEARS, I LOOKED FOR YOU AND PAMELA, AND THEN I FELL ASLEEP...
SO YOU SPENT ALL THESE YEARS LOOKING FOR HIM, HUH?
AND THEN JUST RECENTLY I HEARD THAT PAMELA WAS SEEN SOMEWHERE...
YOU POOR THING... YOU MUST HAVE BEEN VERY LONELY.
WELL...NOT REALLY.

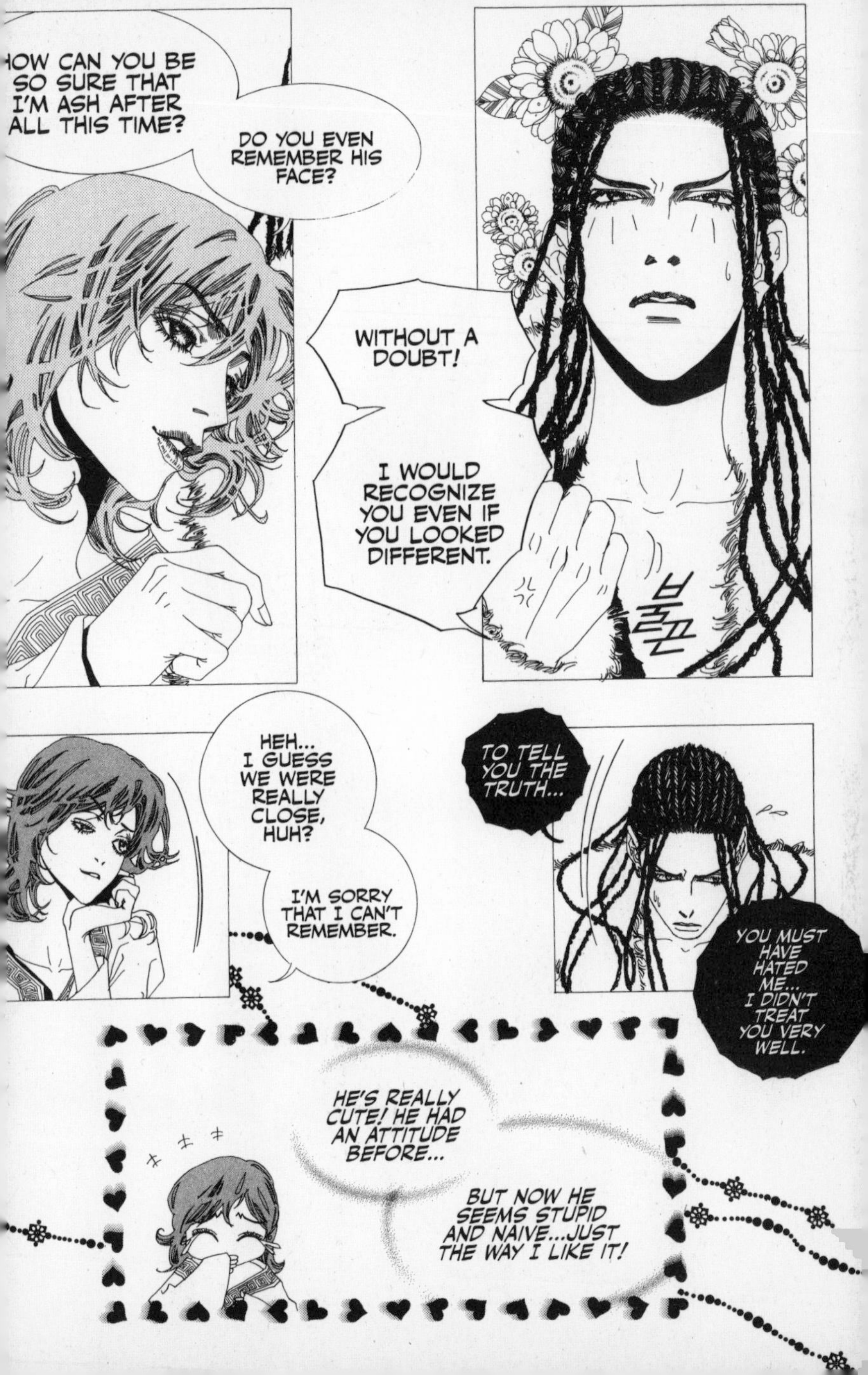
HOW CAN YOU BE SO SURE THAT I'M ASH AFTER ALL THIS TIME?
DO YOU EVEN REMEMBER HIS FACE?
WITHOUT A DOUBT!
I WOULD RECOGNIZE YOU EVEN IF YOU LOOKED DIFFERENT.
불끈
HEH... I GUESS WE WERE REALLY CLOSE, HUH?
I'M SORRY THAT I CAN'T REMEMBER.
TO TELL YOU THE TRUTH...
YOU MUST HAVE HATED ME... I DIDN'T TREAT YOU VERY WELL.
HE'S REALLY CUTE! HE HAD AN ATTITUDE BEFORE...
BUT NOW HE SEEMS STUPID AND NAIVE...JUST THE WAY I LIKE IT!

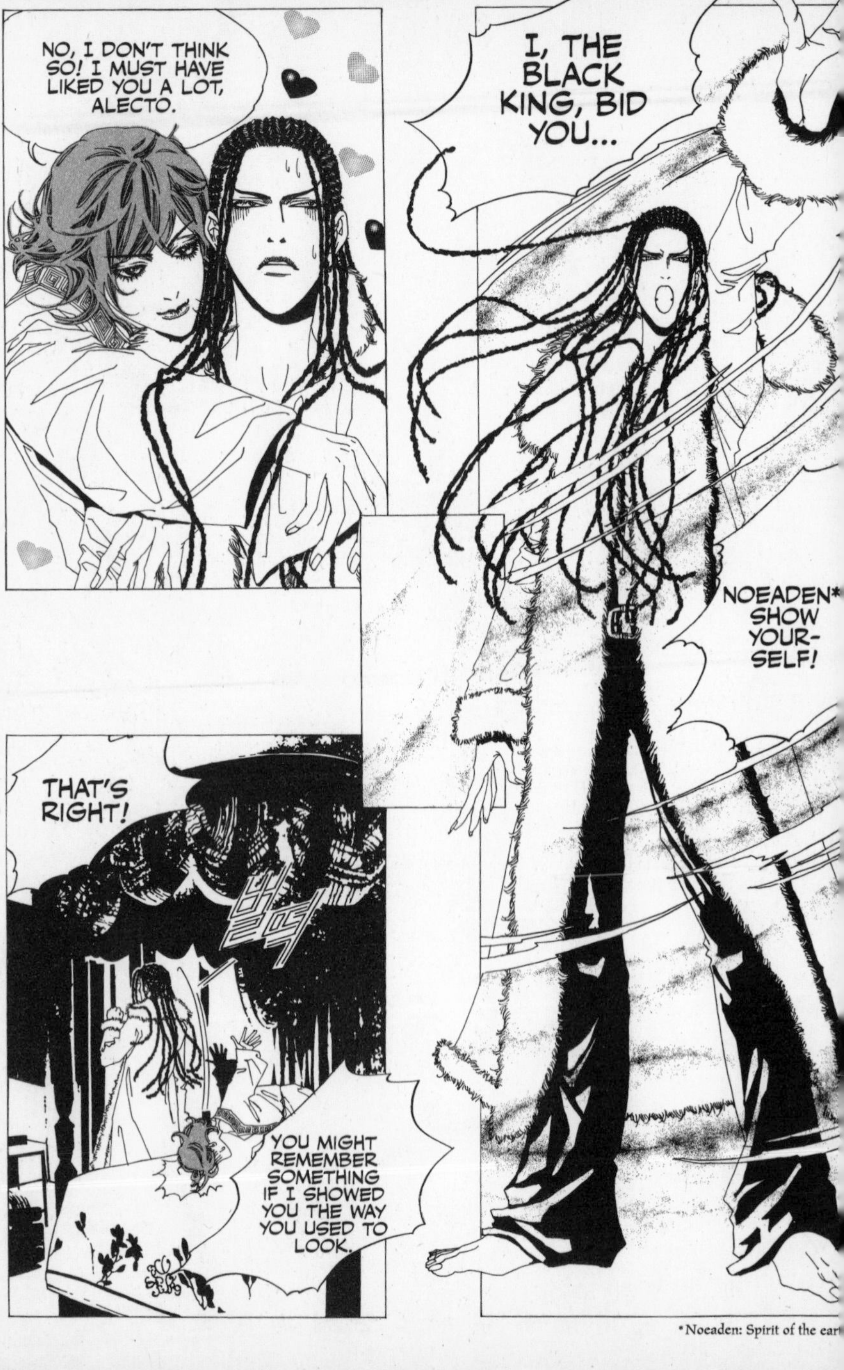
NO, I DON'T THINK SO! I MUST HAVE LIKED YOU A LOT, ALECTO.
THAT'S RIGHT!
YOU MIGHT REMEMBER SOMETHING IF I SHOWED YOU THE WAY YOU USED TO LOOK.
I, THE BLACK KING, BID YOU...
NOEADEN* SHOW YOUR-SELF!

*Noeaden: Spirit of the ear

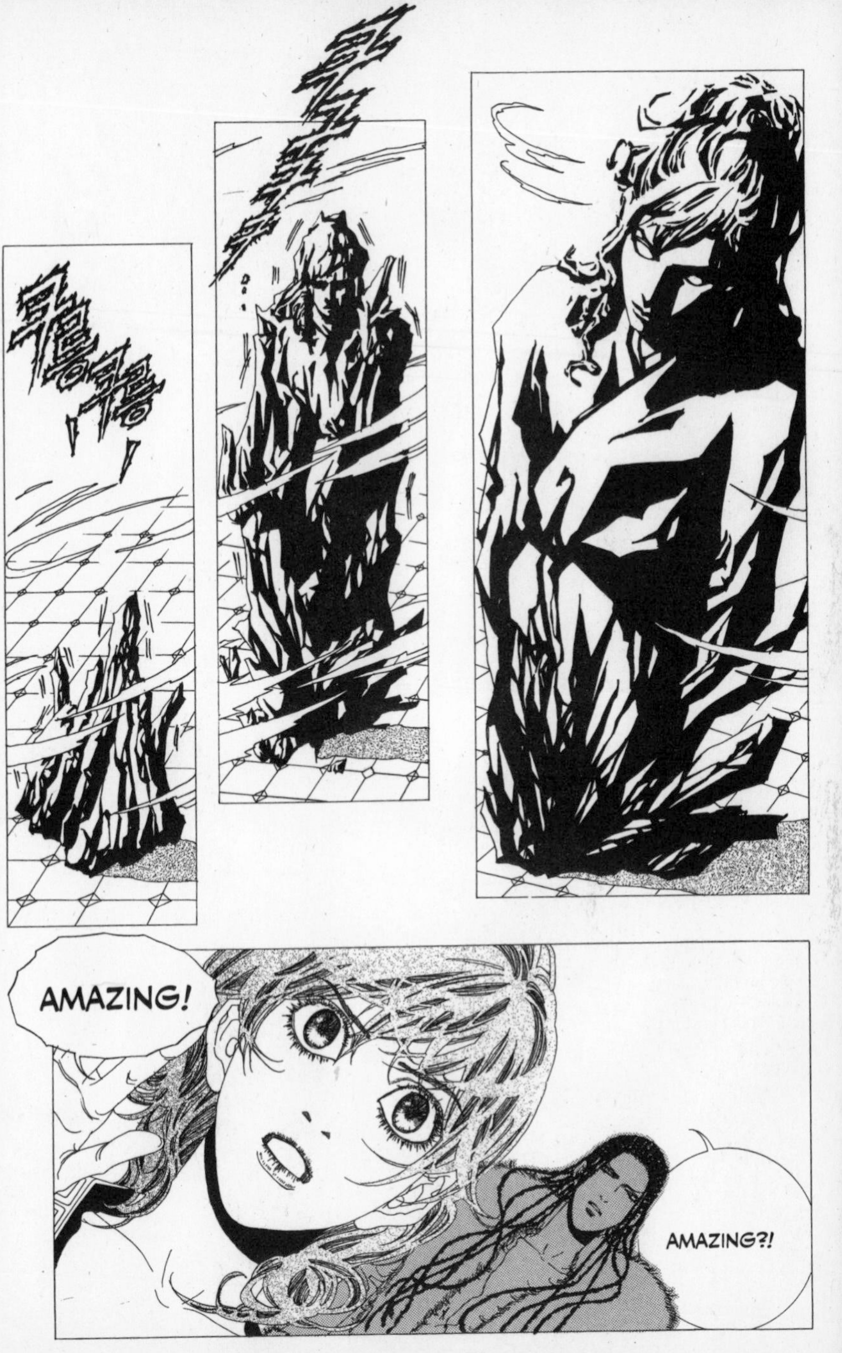
AMAZING!
AMAZING?!

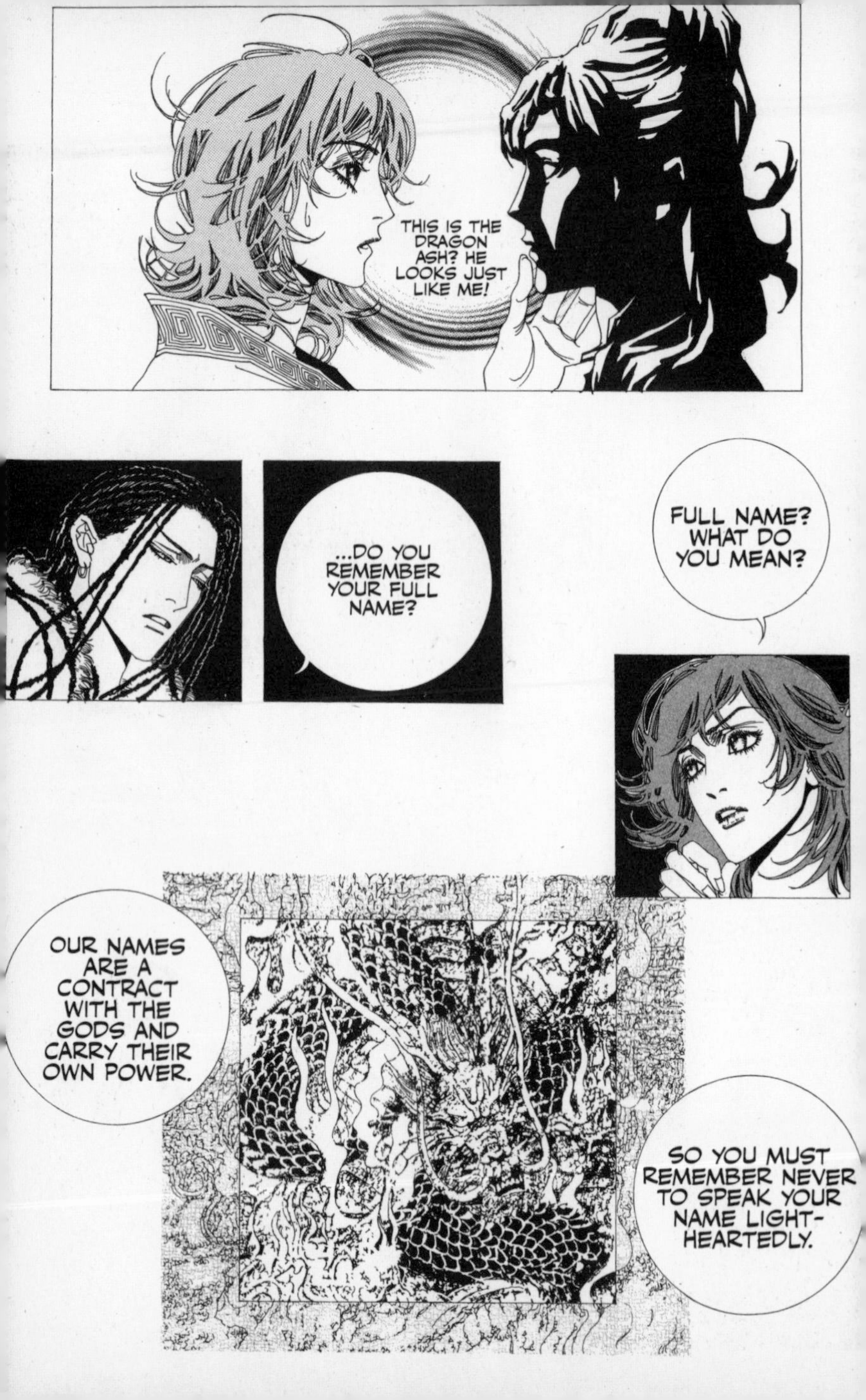
THIS IS THE DRAGON ASH? HE LOOKS JUST LIKE ME!
...DO YOU REMEMBER YOUR FULL NAME?
FULL NAME? WHAT DO YOU MEAN?
OUR NAMES ARE A CONTRACT WITH THE GODS AND CARRY THEIR OWN POWER.
SO YOU MUST REMEMBER NEVER TO SPEAK YOUR NAME LIGHT-HEARTEDLY.

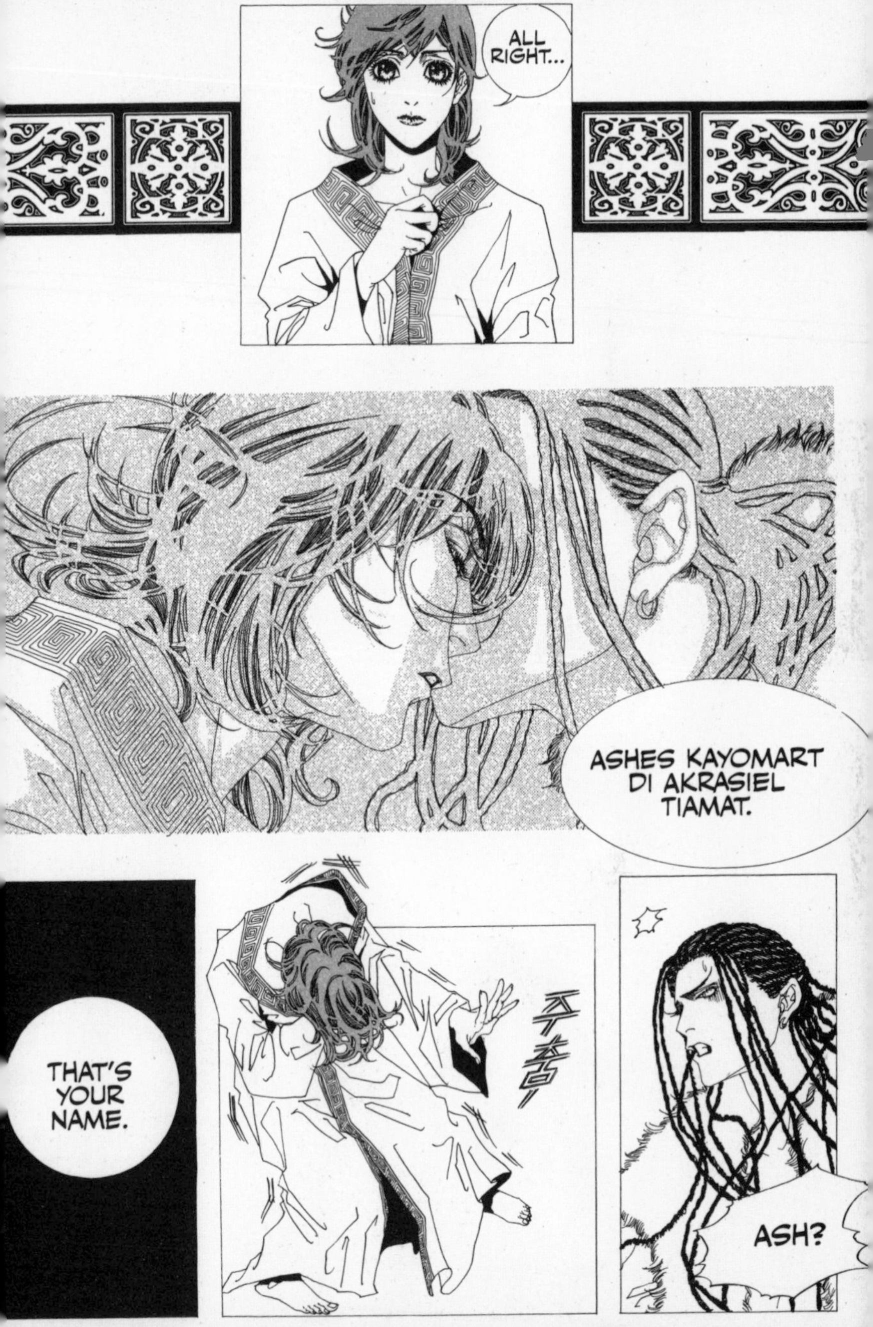
ALL RIGHT...
ASHES KAYOMART DI AKRASIEL TIAMAT.
THAT'S YOUR NAME.
ASH?

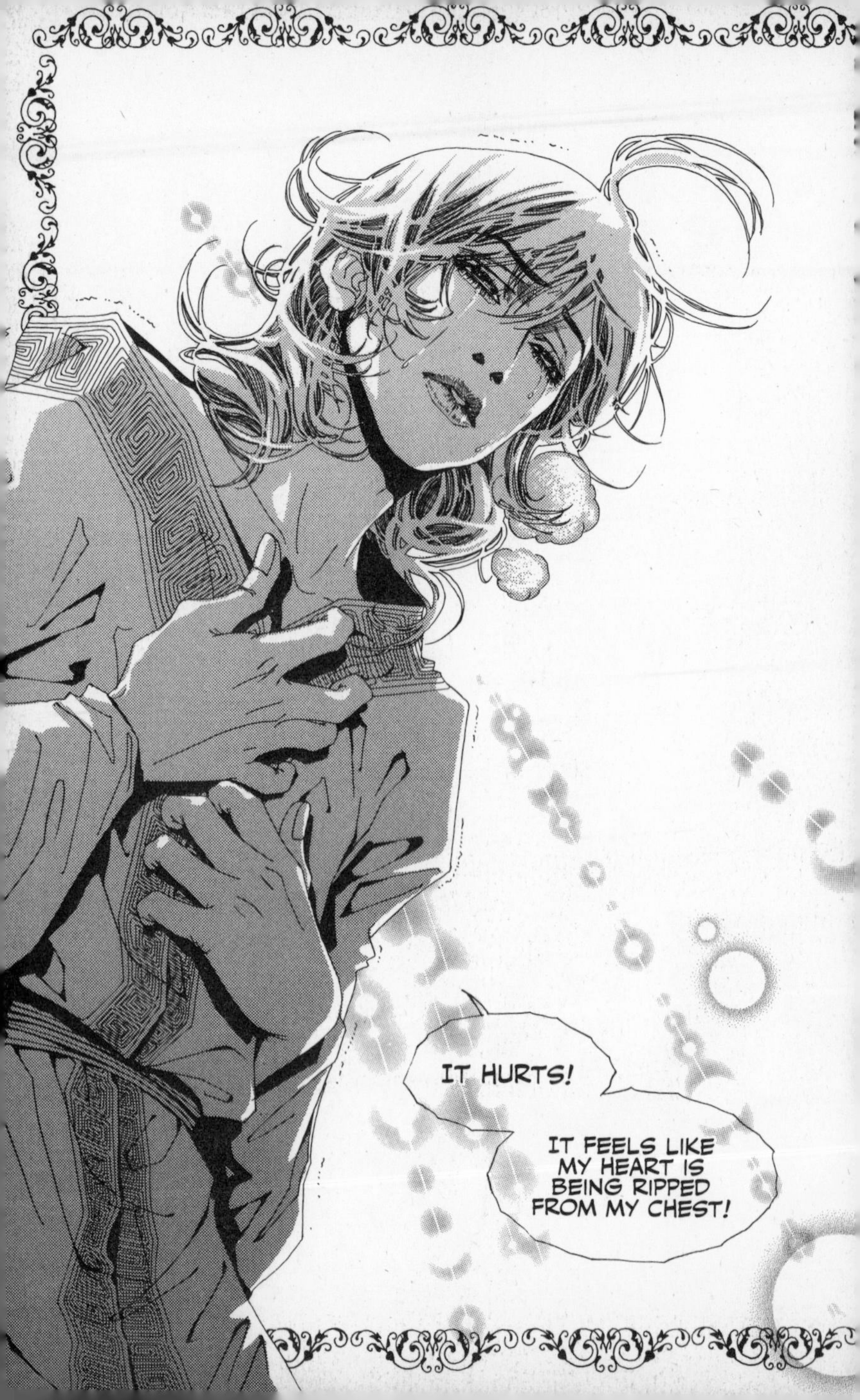
IT HURTS!
IT FEELS LIKE MY HEART IS BEING RIPPED FROM MY CHEST!

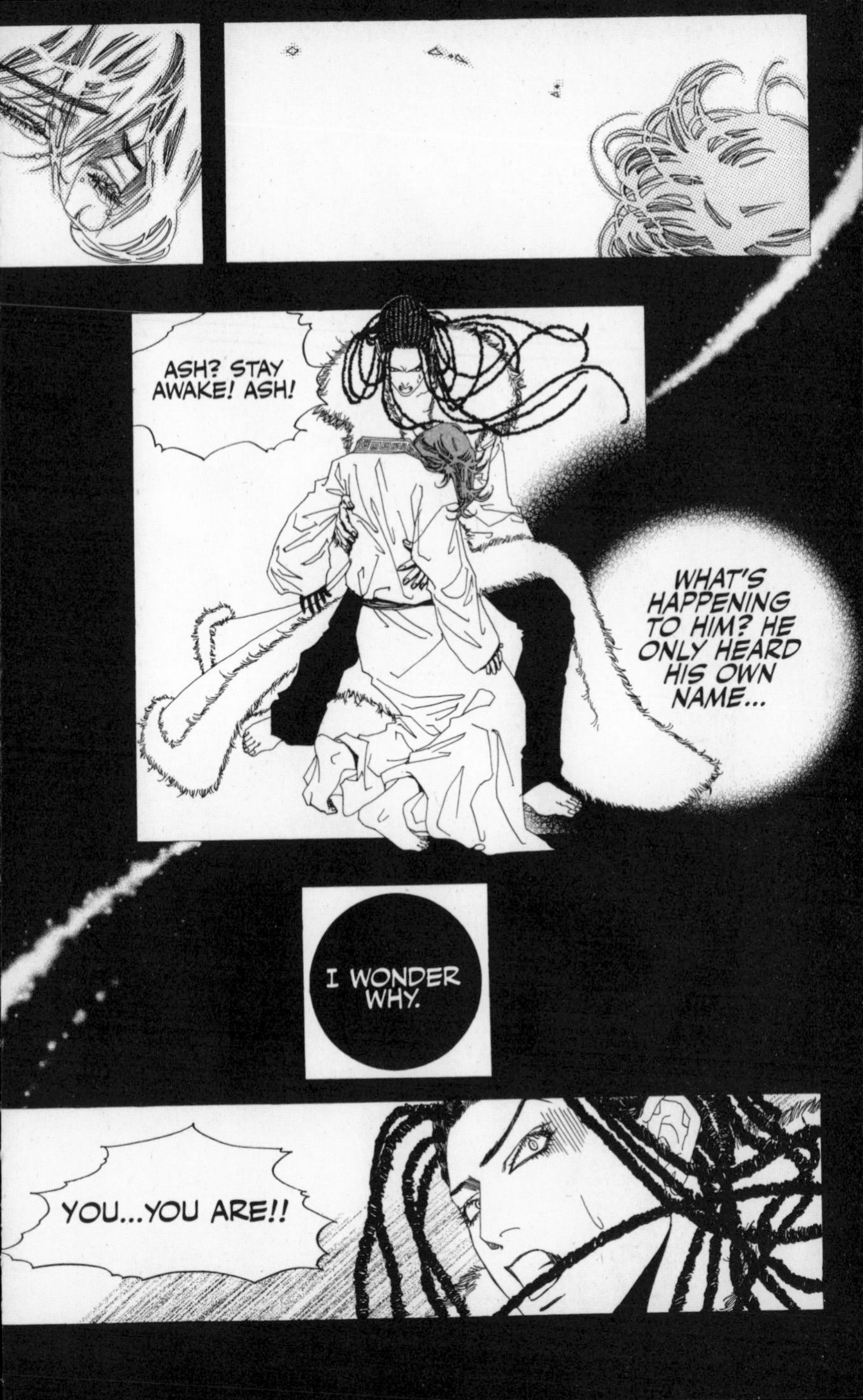
ASH? STAY AWAKE! ASH!
WHAT'S HAPPENING TO HIM? HE ONLY HEARD HIS OWN NAME...
I WONDER WHY.
YOU...YOU ARE!!

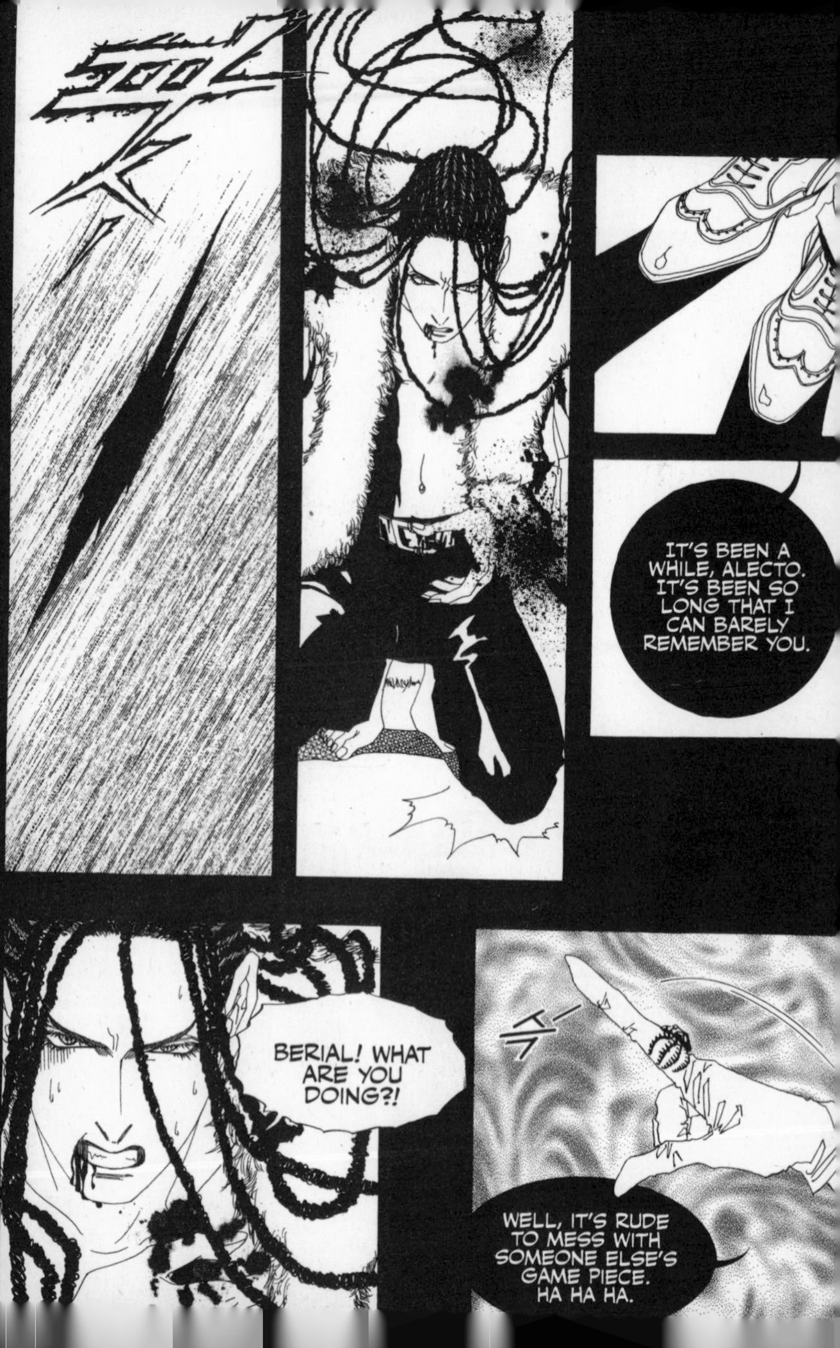
IT'S BEEN A WHILE, ALECTO. IT'S BEEN SO LONG THAT I CAN BARELY REMEMBER YOU.
BERIAL! WHAT ARE YOU DOING?!
WELL, IT'S RUDE TO MESS WITH SOMEONE ELSE'S GAME PIECE. HA HA HA.

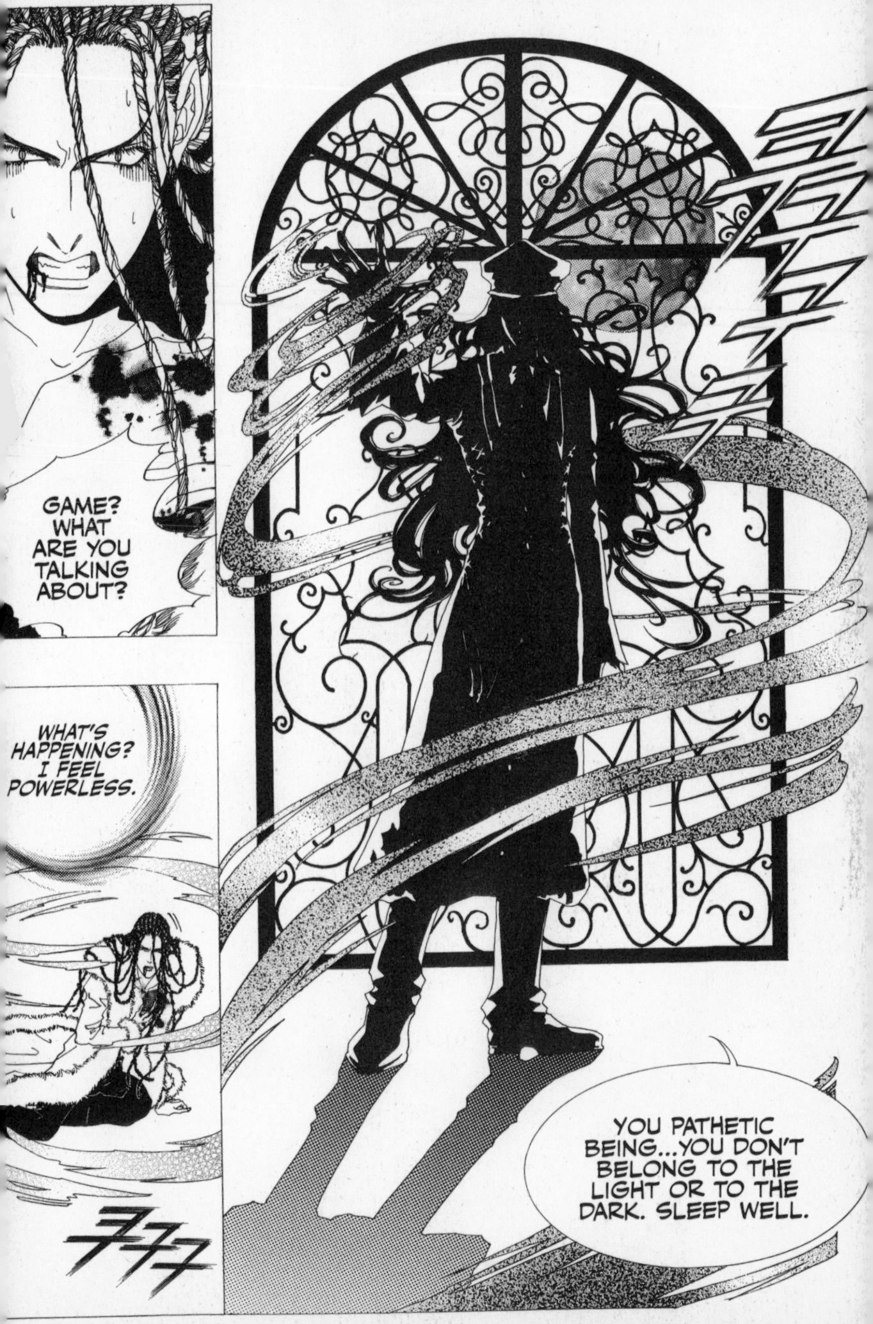
GAME? WHAT ARE YOU TALKING ABOUT?
WHAT'S HAPPENING? I FEEL POWERLESS.
YOU PATHETIC BEING...YOU DON'T BELONG TO THE LIGHT OR TO THE DARK. SLEEP WELL.

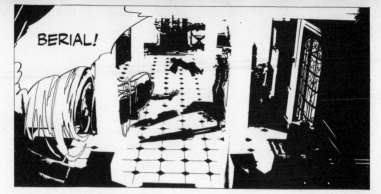

BERIAL!
?!!
XV
THE DEVIL
XVIII
THE MOON
DEVIL?!

*The Devil: This card represents submission, destruction, malice, flattery, bad influence, black magic and unexpected failure.

*The Moon: This card represents deception, uncertainty, disillusionment, danger and negative influences.

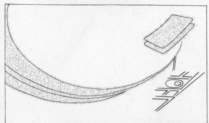

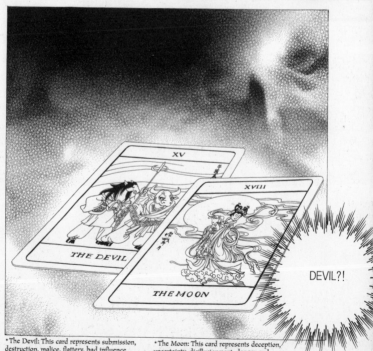

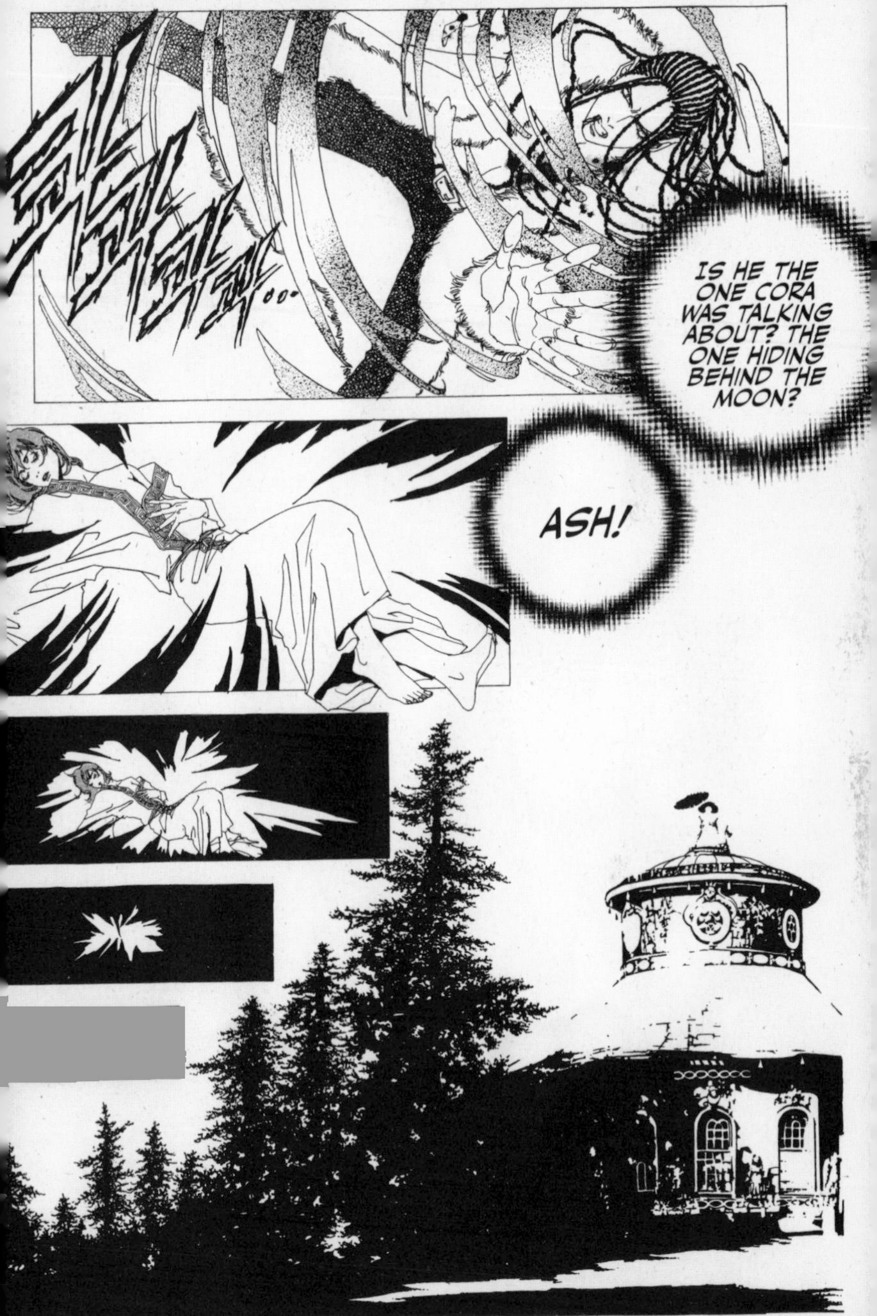
IS HE THE ONE CORA WAS TALKING ABOUT? THE ONE HIDING BEHIND THE MOON?
ASH!

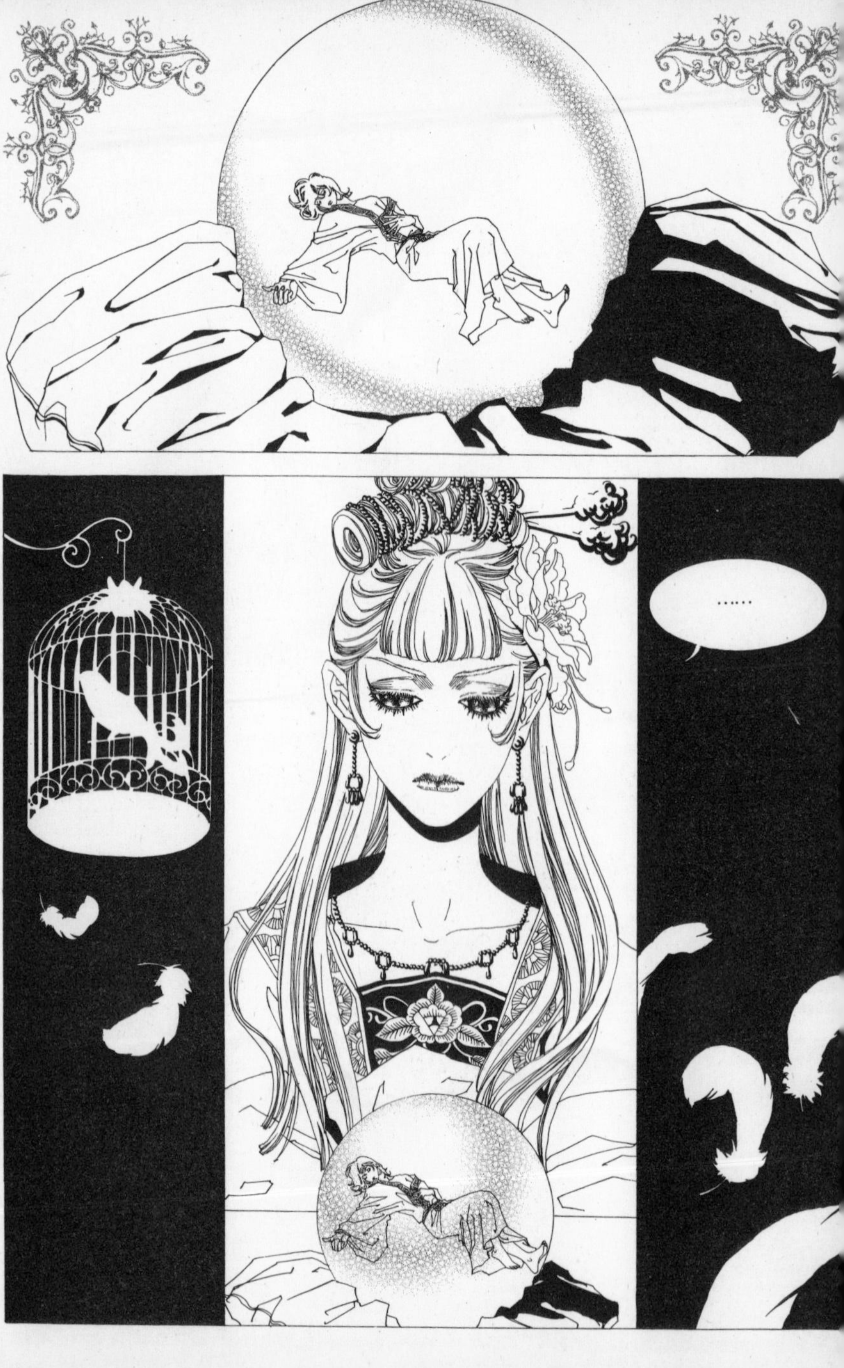
……

IN THE NEXT VOLUME OF

The Tarot Café

PAMELA ENCOUNTERS A SPIRIT
WHO WANTS TO RECONCILE
WITH THE PERSON WHO CAUSED
HIS UNEXPECTED DEATH. DOES
THIS DISEMBODIED ENTITY STAND
A GHOST OF A CHANCE OF
OVERCOMING A TRAGIC PAST OF
BETRAYAL AND CRUELTY?

MEANWHILE, AMONGST THE CRIES
OF LOST LOVE AND UNFINISHED
BUSINESS FROM VISITING SPIRITS,
THE POIGNANT PAST OF OUR
TAROT CAFÉ OWNER UNFOLDS. IN
A LIFE RICH WITH AIDING SPIRITS
CAUGHT IN THE HUMAN WORLD,
COULD PAMELA'S ONLY SOLACE
BE FOUND IN DEATH?

TOKYOPOP SHOP

WWW.TOKYOPOP.COM/SHOP

HOT NEWS!
Check out the
TOKYOPOP SHOP!
The world's best
collection of manga in
English is now available
online in one place!

GIRLS BRAVO

RIZELMINE

WAR ON FLESH

War on Flesh
and other hot
titles are
available at
the store that
never closes!

- **LOOK FOR SPECIAL OFFERS**
- **PRE-ORDER UPCOMING RELEASES**
- **COMPLETE YOUR COLLECTIONS**

I LUV HALLOWEEN™

Written by Keith Giffen, comic boo pro and English language adapter o *Battle Royale* and *Battle Vixens*.

Join the misadventures of a group of particularly disturbing trick-or-treaters as they go about their macabre business on Halloween night. Blaming the apples they got from the first house of the evening for the bad candy they've been receiving all night, the kids plot revenge on the old bag who handed out the funky fruit. Riotously funny and always wickedly shocking—who doesn't *love* Halloween?

OT
OLDER TEEN
AGE 16+

Preview the manga at:
www.TOKYOPOP.com/iluvhalloween

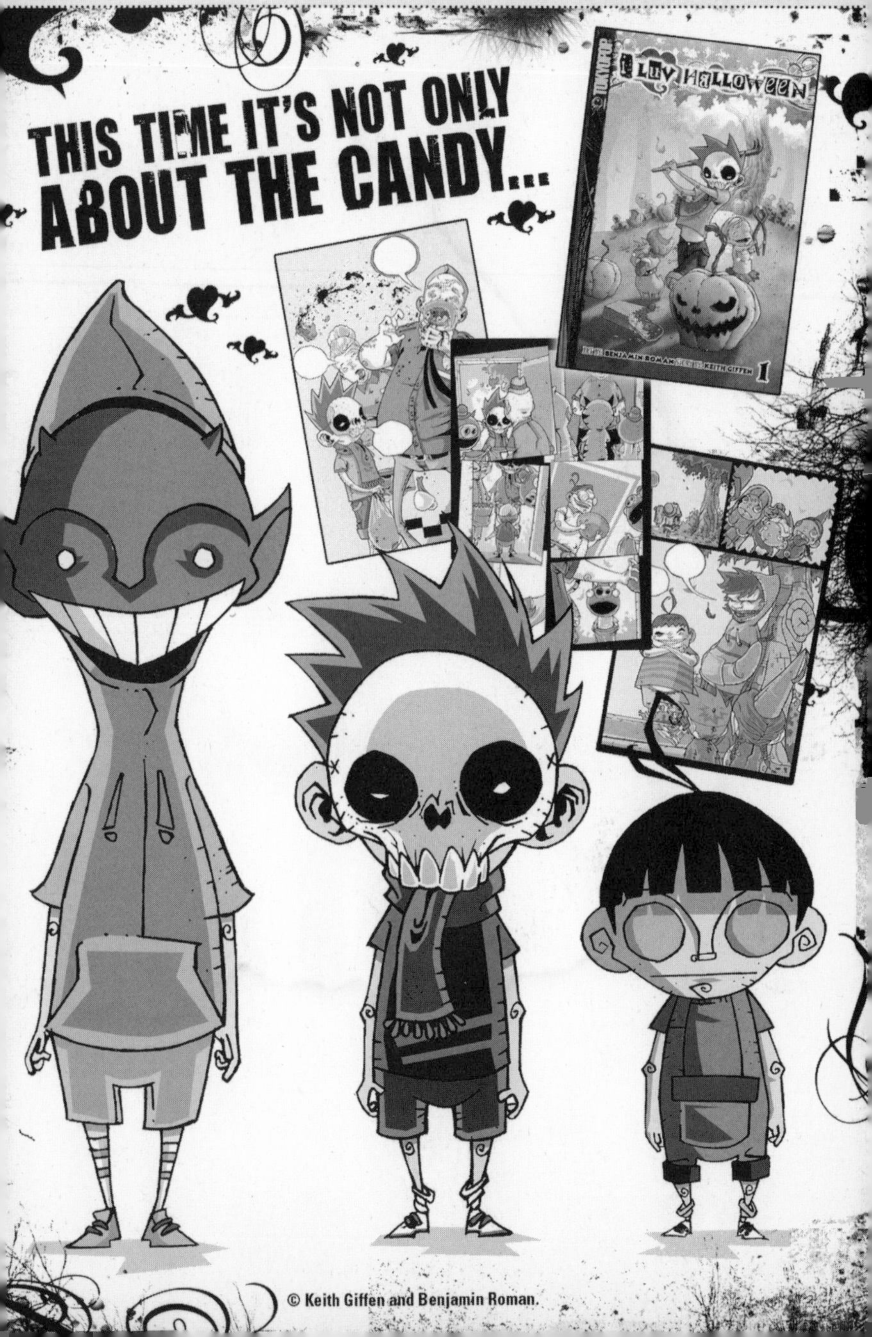
THIS TIME IT'S NOT ONLY ABOUT THE CANDY...
I LUV HALLOWEEN
BENJAMIN ROMAN
KEITH GIFFEN
1
© Keith Giffen and Benjamin Roman.

KAMICHAMA KARIN
BY KOGE-DONBO

Karin is an average girl...at best. She's not good at sports and gets terrible grades. On top of all that, her parents are dead and her beloved cat Shi-chan just died, too. She is miserable. But everything is about to change—little does Karin know that her mother's ring has the power to make her a goddess!

From the creator of *Pita-Ten* and *Digi-Charat!*

Y
YOUTH
AGE 10+

© Koge-Donbo.

KANPAI!
BY MAKI MURAKAMI

Yamada Shintaro is a monster guardian in training—his job is to protect the monsters from harm. But when he meets Nao, a girl from his middle school, he suddenly falls in love...with her neckline! Shintaro will go to any lengths to prevent disruption to her peaceful life—and preserve his choice view of her neck!

A wild and wonderful adventure from the creator of *Gravitation!*

T
TEEN
AGE 13+

© MAKI MURAKAMI.

MOBILE SUIT GUNDAM ÉCOLE DU CIEL
BY HARUHIKO MIKIMOTO

École du Ciel—where aspiring pilots train to become Top Gundam! Asuna, daughter of a brilliant professor, is a below-average student at École du Ciel. But the world is spiraling toward war, and Asuna is headed for a crash course in danger, battle, and most of all, love.

From the artist of the phenomenally successful *Macross* and *Baby Birth!*

T
TEEN
AGE 13+

© Haruhiko Mikimoto and Sostu Agency · Sunrise.

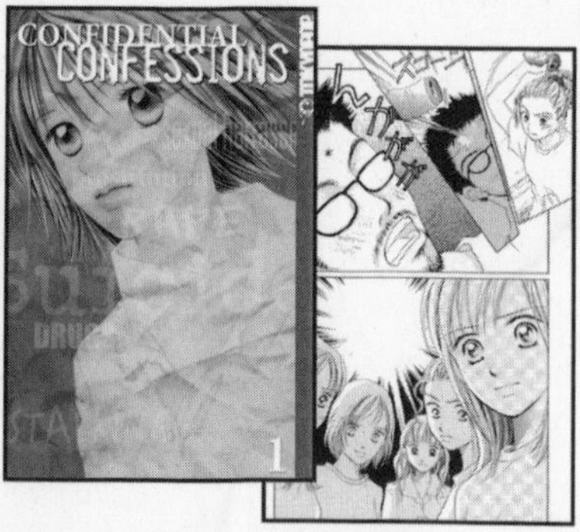
CONFIDENTIAL CONFESSIONS
1

BY REIKO MOMOCHI

CONFIDENTIAL CONFESSIONS

If you're looking for a happy, rosy, zit-free look at high school life, skip this manga. But if you're jonesing for a real-life view of what high school's truly like, *Confidential Confessions* offers a gritty, unflinching look at what really happens in those hallowed halls. Rape, sexual harassment, anorexia, cutting, suicide...no subject is too hardcore for *Confidential Confessions*. While you're at it, don't expect a happy ending.

~Julie Taylor, Sr. Editor

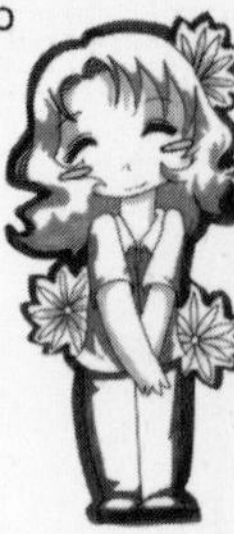

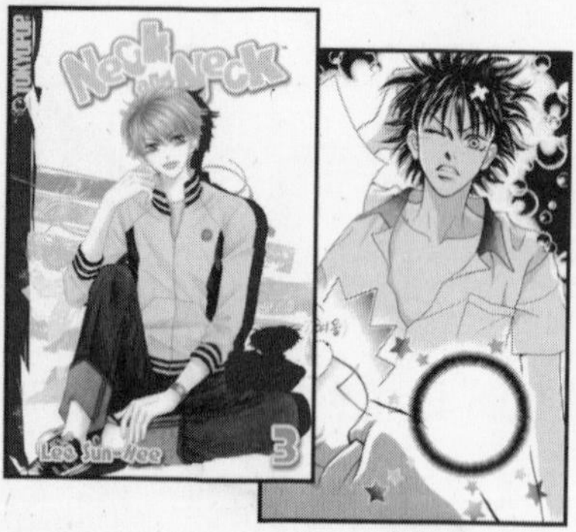
Neck and Neck
Lee Sun-Hee
3

BY LEE SUN-HEE

NECK AND NECK

Competition can bring out the best or the worst in people...but in *Neck and Neck*, it does both! Dabin Choi and Shihu Myoung are both high school students, both children of mob bosses, and each is out to totally humiliate the other. Dabin and Shihu are very creative in their mutual tortures and there's more than a hint of romantic tension behind their attacks. This book's art may look somewhat shojo, but I found the story to be very accessible and very entertaining!

~Rob Tokar, Sr. Editor

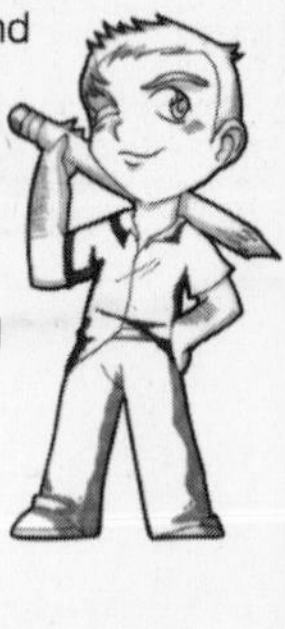

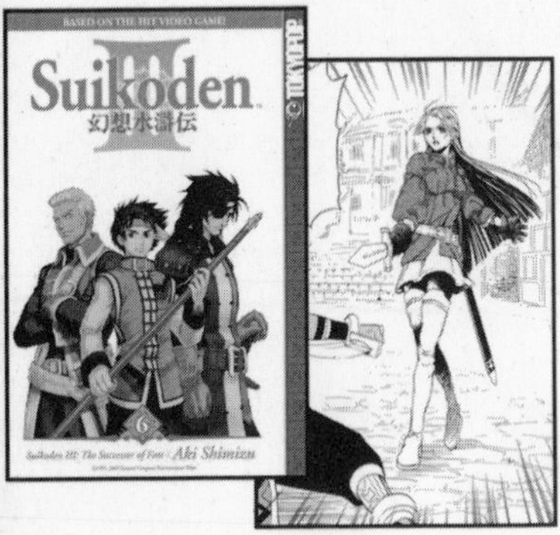
BASED ON THE HIT VIDEO GAME!
Suikoden
幻想水滸伝
TOKYOPOP
6
Aki Shimizu

BY AKI SHIMIZU

SUIKODEN III

I'm one of those people who likes to watch others play video games (I tend to run into walls and get stuck), so here comes the perfect manga for me! All the neat plot of a great RPG game, without any effort on my part! Aki Shimizu, creator of the delightful series *Qwan*, has done a lovely, lovely job of bringing the world of Suikoden to life. There are great creatures (Fighting ducks! Giant lizard people!), great character designs, and an engaging story full of conflict, drama and intrigue. I picked up one volume while I was eating lunch at my desk one day, and was totally hooked. I can't wait for the next one to come out!

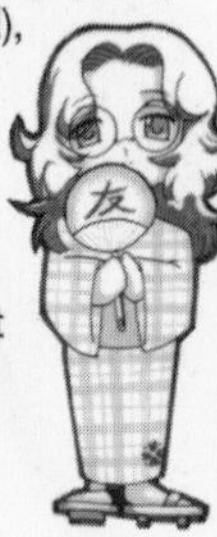

~Lillian Diaz-Przybyl, Editor

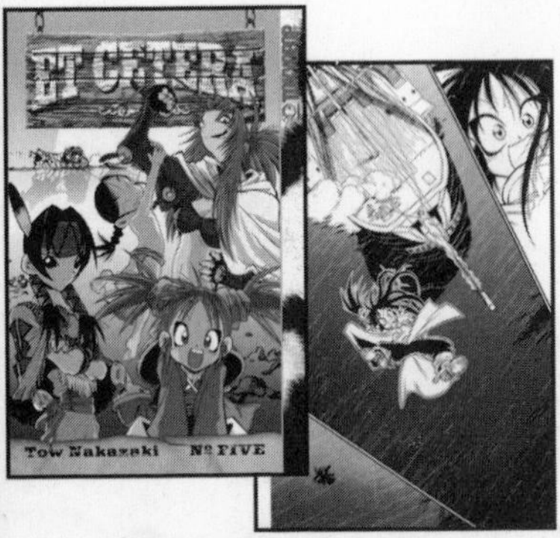
Tow Nakazaki
Nº FIVE

BY TOW NAKAZAKI

ET CETERA

Meet Mingchao, an energetic girl from China who now travels the deserts of the old west. She dreams of becoming a star in Hollywood, eager for fame and fortune. She was given the Eto Gun—a magical weapon that fires bullets with properties of the 12 zodiac signs—as a keepsake from her grandfather before he died. On her journey to Hollywood, she meets a number of zany characters...some who want to help, and others who are after the power of the Eto Gun. Chock full of gun fights, train hijackings, collapsing mineshafts...this East-meets-wild-West tale has it all!

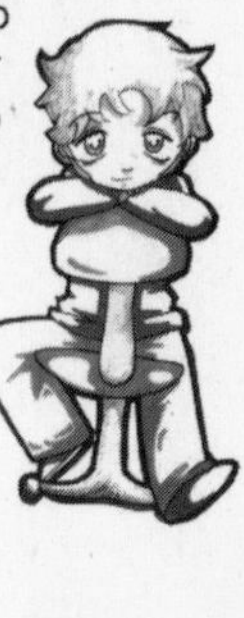

~Aaron Suhr, Sr. Editor

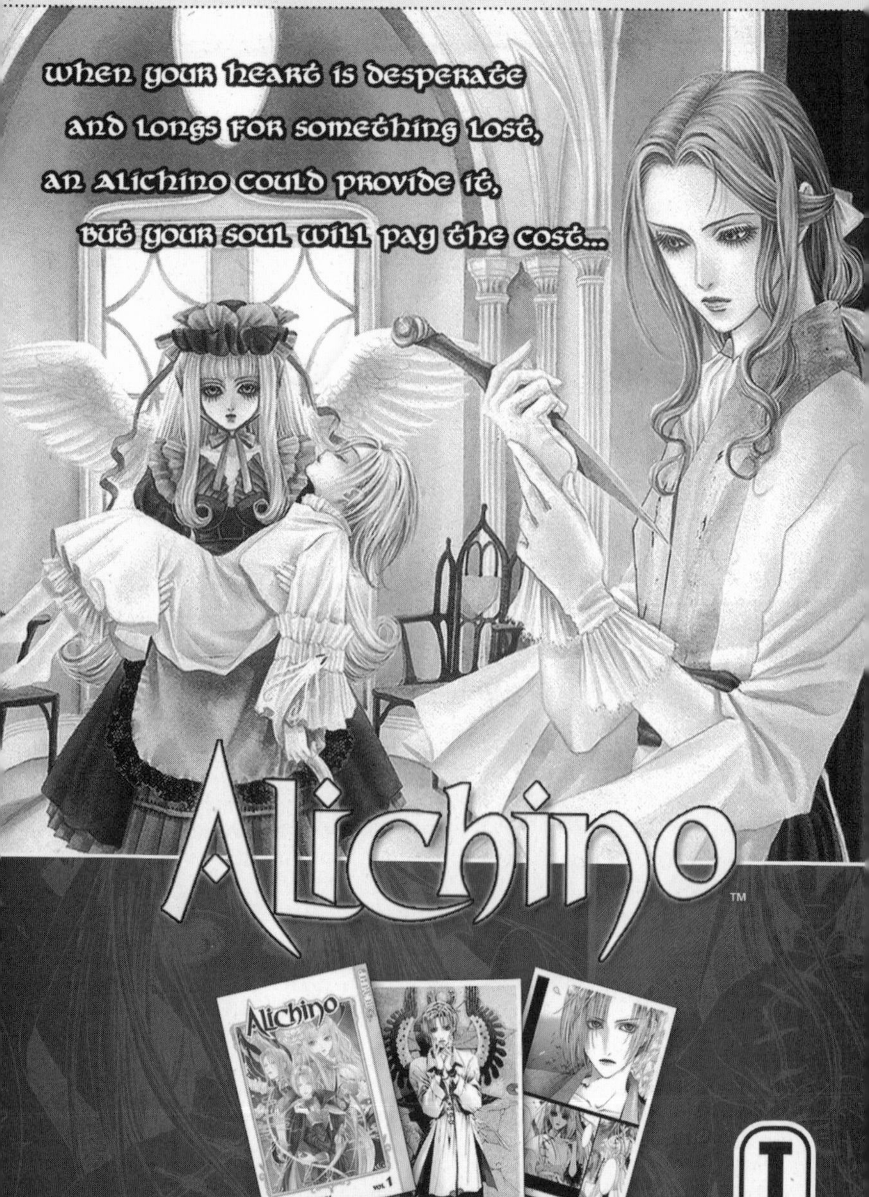
when your heart is desperate
and longs for something lost,
an Alichino could provide it,
but your soul will pay the cost...
Alichino™
Alichino
Kouyu Shurei
VOL 1
T
TEEN
AGE 13+

The breakout manga that put CLAMP on the map!

RG VEDA 聖伝

At the dawn of creation, the world was a beautiful and tranquil place. When a powerful warlord rebelled against the king, a violent, chaotic age began.... Three hundred years later, a group of noble warriors embarks on a quest to find the prophesied Six Stars before the land is torn apart!

© CLAMP

Princess Ai

A Diva torn
from Chaos...
A Savior doomed
⚔— to Love

Created by
Courtney Love
and D.J. Milky
♥

www.TOKYOPOP.com